BUILDIN[...]

BRITISH ATLANTIC WORLD

Delineated at Deerfield

Deerfield Meeting house

Nonbrd De

A Top

Dwelling houses

Convenient Convenb

BUILDING THE
BRITISH ATLANTIC WORLD

Spaces, Places, and Material Culture, 1600–1850

EDITED BY

DANIEL MAUDLIN & BERNARD L. HERMAN

THE UNIVERSITY OF NORTH CAROLINA PRESS

Chapel Hill

This book was published with the assistance of the
H. EUGENE AND LILLIAN YOUNGS LEHMAN FUND
of the University of North Carolina Press.
A complete list of books published in the Lehman Series appears at the end of the book.

Set in Monotype Bulmer by Tseng Information Systems, Inc.
Manufactured in the United States of America

The University of North Carolina Press has been a member of
the Green Press Initiative since 2003.

Jacket illustration: *A Mappe of the Somer Isles and Fortresses*,
from Captain John Smith's *The Generall Historie of Virginia, New-England,
and the Summer Isles*, London, 1624. Documenting the American South, University of
North Carolina at Chapel Hill Libraries. Background antique map: 123RF.com,
© Steve Estvanik. Background texture: depositphotos.com, photo © digieye.

Library of Congress Cataloging-in-Publication Data
Building the British Atlantic world : spaces, places, and material culture,
1600–1850 / edited by Daniel Maudlin and Bernard L. Herman.
pages cm — (H. Eugene and Lillian Youngs Lehman series)
Includes bibliographical references and index.
ISBN 978-1-4696-2682-6 (pbk : alk. paper) — ISBN 978-1-4696-2683-3 (ebook)
1. British—Material culture—Atlantic Ocean Region—History. 2. Atlantic Ocean
Region—History. 3. Architecture, British colonial—Atlantic Ocean Region—History.
4. Architecture, British—Atlantic Ocean Region—History. 5. Great Britain—Civilization.
6. Great Britain—Colonies—America—Civilization. 7. Great Britain—Colonies—Africa,
West—Civilization. I. Maudlin, Daniel, editor. II. Herman, Bernard L., 1951- editor.
III. Series: H. Eugene and Lillian Youngs Lehman series.
DA123.B85 2016
941'.009821—dc23
2015033880

CONTENTS

BUILDING THE
BRITISH ATLANTIC WORLD

INTRODUCTION

Daniel Maudlin and Bernard L. Herman

Building the British Atlantic World is an introduction to the ocean-going culture of the British Atlantic world as interpreted through its buildings, landscapes and settlements, exploring the extent, diversity, and sameness of the architecture built by the British overseas across their North Atlantic colonies. It explores the many meanings that buildings held for the colonists—and colonized—who built and occupied them and reflects on the profound architectural connections that were maintained between the colonies and Britain. As such, the book draws upon expertise from the fields of art and architectural history, archaeology, historical geography, folklore, environmental history, material culture and vernacular architecture studies, museum curation, cultural history, and economic history in order to present an overview of British Atlantic culture through its built spaces and places.

Driven by imperial expansion, religion, trade and migration from Canada to the Caribbean, from West Africa to the thirteen colonies, and the passage back to Britain, the cultural space of the British Atlantic world was mapped onto the landscapes of the northern Atlantic oceanic rim. Through periods of discovery and establishment in the seventeenth century, maintenance in the eighteenth century, and eventual dismantlement and decline in the nineteenth century, this world was made, seen, and experienced through its buildings: those built in distant, different lands and those built at "home." Today, across the vast expanse of this former Atlantic empire, buildings and towns remain as highly visible reminders of British colonial rule. Equally, throughout England, Scotland, Ireland, and Wales, other buildings stand today as monuments to the impact of the Atlantic colonies on Britain. Whether forts in Bermuda, churches in New England, plantation houses in South Carolina, or farms in Canada, historic buildings are markers of a historic British presence, artifacts of a coherent but complex Atlantic culture. While individual buildings and urban centers were fundamentally made in order to facilitate functions and activities—defense, prayer, shelter—they also served as important

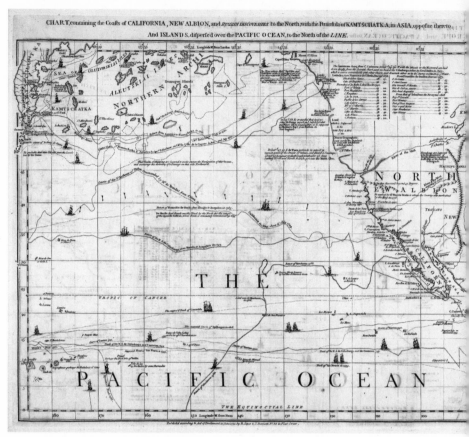

FIGURE 1.1. *Plate 2, Thomas Jefferys,* The American Atlas; or, A Geographical Description of the Whole Continent of America, *1776. Rare Book Collection, Wilson Special Collections Library, University of North Carolina at Chapel Hill.*

communicators of meaning and of the values and ideals held by that culture, which we can interpret in the attempt to understand that world better. Buildings were expressions of power, authority, dominion, oppression, resistance, and rebellion; of concepts such as religious faith; of *ethoi* such as modernity, progress, identity, and improvement; or expressions of social concerns such as self-fashioning, status, wealth, taste, social conformity, familiarity, belonging, and exclusion. For both colonists and the colonized, for good or ill, British-looking buildings were clear signs of a British presence across many different landscapes and climates. Abstracted from the local environment, carefully constructed, decorated, and furnished interior spaces provided the dressed stage for the repeated performance of British Atlantic society's rituals—from the extraordinary (such as court appearances) to the

DANIEL MAUDLIN & BERNARD L. HERMAN

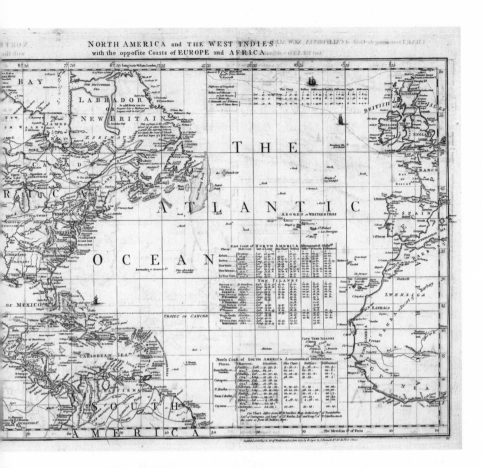

everyday (such as afternoon tea)—where consistency of design, dominated by neoclassicism, provided a consistent social space: whether the decorated parlor of a Canadian farmhouse, the dining room of Thomas Jefferson's villa, Monticello, the interior of a shop in downtown Falmouth, Jamaica, or even the new parlors of post-Fire London.

The British Atlantic world was driven by, and dependent upon, shipping and the various transatlantic trade networks between British ports, such as Southampton, Plymouth, Bristol, and Glasgow; North American ports, such as Boston, Charleston, Philadelphia, or Halifax in British Canada; and beyond to the Caribbean and West Africa: the transatlantic traffic in "goods, persons, books and ideas" (Fig. I.1).[1] It was this transatlantic trade that "disseminated a common culture" identified through furniture, paint, paintings, cloth, clothes, and books as well as people (from traders to emigrants and slaves).[2] In terms of buildings this meant building components such as house frames, tools, nails, window glass, books on building, and, of course, the knowledge held by migrant builders and house carpenters. The "conversational" pathways that maintained this British Atlantic culture and subverted and denied it were not straightforward. What emerges from *Building the British Atlantic World* is not only the history of direct exchange between Britain and her colonies but also exchanges between the so-called peripheries — the Atlantic regions and British provinces — either as part of trade networks with and within Britain, picking up and dropping off *en route*, or directly and exclusively between each other. This approach emphasizes that the colonized changed the colonizer as much as the colonizer changed the colonized and that cultural hybridity is more characteristic than a dichotomy of them and us. It also acknowledges that "colonization" was as much an import as an export. The origins of this model lie in postcolonial theory in cultural studies.[3] Postcolonial theory recognizes that Atlantic regions influence each other as much as they take their lead from the central "parent culture."[4] This "transnational" model of interrelated networks of exchange transcends the "nation" as the primary narrative and has largely replaced the "outward ripple" or center-periphery model in cultural studies. The application of postcolonial theory to the wider cultural history of early modern America has been assessed by Robert St. George in *Possible Pasts: Becoming Colonial in Early America* (2000).[5] *Building the British Atlantic World* interrogates these ideas through the shared experience of architecture; identifying buildings and settlement patterns that support a model of overlapping spheres of influence, such as the New England houses built by Scottish emigrants in Canada, and buildings that on close examination deny a transatlantic influence where one has been assumed, such as the plain churches of the English naval dockyard. Through this process of architectural analysis the Atlantic world emerges as a place rather than a series of wars and trades across the Atlantic map, where place is understood not as a fixed geographic site or locus but as an enlivening process of settlement and belonging between people with common values and a shared identity.[6]

But who were these people? The answer is that the Atlantic world was home, by birth or migration, to the full spectrum of British society as well as those indigenous peoples whose cultures were encountered and permanently altered by the British imperial project: men, women, and children from every social rank and every possible occupation, from "gentlemen" to government officials, soldiers, clerics, doctors, lawyers, merchants, farmers, skilled artisans (including builders), unskilled laborers, servants, indentured laborers, and slaves. In the early modern period most of these recorded occupations are attributed to men; however, women and their spaces and activities must also be accounted for even if they are hidden behind the name of a male "head of household." The subject of gender and material culture in the Atlantic World is more widely considered in John Styles and Amanda Vickery's *Gender, Taste, and Material Culture in Britain and North America, 1700–1830* (2007). Add to these dynamic cross-cultural interactions the experiences, contributions, and legacies of the American Indians and enslaved Africans.

The presence of a historic building, designed for a specific function—whether physical or symbolic—denotes the presence of its consumers—both intended and unintended—such as indicating their membership in a specific ethnic or social group, and can shed light on what they did, how they lived, and what they believed or valued—not infrequently through contradictory actions. For example, military forts indicate the mostly male presence of soldiers; farms the presence of farmers or farming families. The ordering and decoration of the spaces within a farmhouse provides information on the daily lives of its inhabitants including, importantly, women.[7] Nonresidential buildings such as stores, churches, and courthouses provide insight into public life, its exchanges, rituals, and ceremonies. These were often mixed gender spaces occupied or used by both men and women, though perhaps in different ways. Courthouses, for instance, indicate the presence of male government officials but also of a mixed and porous civil society of male and female would-be plaintiffs, witnesses, and criminals who passed through their chambers. Moreover, the presence of cognate buildings, the familiar spaces, throughout the Atlantic world suggests the common culture that made a single place, though constantly changing, out of multiple geographic sites. Buildings were an important cultural asset for Britain's Atlantic empire because they gave visual, experiential, and spatial coherence to a geographically diffused culture. While the weather and landscape were very different, things experientially felt reassuringly familiar coming into port in late eighteenth-century Jamaica, Bristol, or Charleston. Equally, you could be politely conversing in a well-furnished parlor, where communities of place yielded to communities of sensibility, and not know whether you were in the Caribbean, England, or the Carolinas without looking out the window. Architecture, therefore, accorded resonance to a divergent array of sites. That resonance emanated from a common spatial and decorative language—classicism—universally used by builders, carpenters, homeowners, and architects by the later eighteenth century. (Throughout the British Atlantic world regional vernacular forms that were commonplace in the seventeenth century were gradually straightened out, given symmetry, and codified through the eighteenth century).

Within an Atlantic colonial theatre shared with the French, Dutch, Portuguese, and Spanish, British classicism in building design in the early modern period was by no means unique. Nonetheless, it was a preeminent signifier of British Atlantic culture to those living within the dominions of the British Atlantic Empire, recognized and identified as British by soldiers, traders, and emigrants. What did this pervasive architectural style, this sameness, mean to the consumer of buildings within that British Atlantic world? Sameness, in any style or form of building, communicated familiarity, projected identity, and mapped the contours of belonging, but, more than this ready reassurance, in the early modern period classicism in particular also manifested a profound and widely understood symbolism. Of course, it was accepted as the best possible taste in fashionable design, driving consumer markets and maintaining social conventions, but more than that, to the early modern British mind, it was also a visual articulation of belonging to European civilization, of notions of morality and godliness as well as a range of other positive values drawn from Roman culture, such as learning or good imperial governance (although these associations are problematic in light of the transatlantic slave trade that paid for many expensive building programs on both sides of the Atlantic). On the ground, therefore, through this commonly understood architectural language, while implicitly if not consciously engaged on the British colonial project, a farmer in New England or a merchant in the Caribbean were both able to demonstrate directly and relatively easily through the material *lingua franca* of their social affiliations, their good taste, and their moral virtue. Although, while a common British transatlantic culture can be identified, it is important to note that most likely both the farmer and the merchant would have primarily acted and thought locally, responding first to their immediate circumstances. As such, while architectural coherence across the British Atlantic world was a manifestation of a common culture maintained through the circulation of goods, books, and design, a true overview of this transatlantic spatial and decorative *sensus communis* would only have been experienced in person by a small number of mobile groups such as migrants, merchant seamen, military personnel, and the wealthy traveler.

By the later eighteenth century, neoclassicism in European architecture was not just a tendency to bilateral symmetry and some applied classical ornament but involved the strict observation of established design principles. Classicism across the British Atlantic world was characterized by precise observation of codified spatial proportions that dictated the relationship between height and width in all elements of a building, from walls to windows, and the interrelationships between those elements. At the level of everyday craft production, the eighteenth-century shorthand for this precision was simply "neat" and "regular." Making classical buildings in the British Atlantic world was a preindustrial craft process practiced by highly skilled craftsmen and, therefore, was also dependent upon the migration of both skilled labor and knowledge. Consequently, the successful execution of a classical building—whether church, courthouse, merchant's dwelling, or colonist's farm—required the work of craftsmen familiar with bookish classical principles who were adept at modeling and manipulating classical ornament and who were familiar with building materials and the principles of construction. Stone masonry and house carpentry were well-established craft traditions in eighteenth-century Britain and British North America with interlinked international, national, and regional organizations and practices. While regional and subregional craft centers emerged throughout the British Atlantic world, craftsmen were also highly mobile, traveling between Atlantic regions in pursuit of changing demands for their skills (and were therefore not only the producers of Atlantic architecture but also among the few to experience it in more than one geographic site). Craftsmen were also highly responsive to the forward impulse of modernity and the consumer drive for fashionable good taste that was facilitated by the dissemination of ideas through migration (of craftsmen and connoisseurs), trade (the transatlantic shipping of books about buildings and supplies of building components), and through a high level of personal correspondence and visits between friends and family. In this way seemingly similar buildings were built contemporaneously throughout the British Atlantic.

And yet, as soon as this common culture is identified it is challenged and reinterpreted: from Atlantic region to region, climate to climate, social group to social group we see myriad adaptations and differences in building form, ornament, materials, and construction. The apparent sameness of buildings belied their many structural differences; and it demanded competence to inflect the international with a local accent and to adapt universal conventions to local circumstances. Whether timber, stone, brick, or coral block, building materials and construction methods varied regionally giving rise to localized craft subcultures, each with its own practitioners, trade bodies, customs, and educational traditions. Conversely, regional construction methods, often hidden behind a classical veneer by the later eighteenth century, also pointed to the persistence of historic craft practices associated with particular British regional traditions and the settlements of emigrants from those regions. If we look at housing design, for example, we can see that a universal ideal was constantly challenged by practical regional adaptations. White symmetrical boxes with pitched roofs and neatly arranged windows flanking a central doorway can be found in Scotland, the Caribbean, the Carolinas, and Canada. But this uniformity hides—often behind white surface finishes—a range of different building materials and construction as well as regional responses to climate, labor, sociability, and economics. In a wider geographic context, the British Atlantic world existed in parallel and geographic overlay with those of other European colonial Atlantic powers—including the Spanish and Portuguese to the south and the French in both Canada and Louisiana; Germans in Pennsylvania, Maryland, and Virginia; and Dutch in New York—and each home-nation exported its own architectural traditions, practices, and practitioners. At points of colonial intersection, as in Canada or West Africa, builders from one European nation rubbed shoulders with builders from another. Building contracts in British America consistently bear a polyglot of surnames representing British, Scandinavian, German, and other nationalities. And then there were the individuals wielding trowels, planes, hammers, and brushes. Atlantic architectures, therefore, are not defined by a monocultural process of imposition and reproduction but by hybridity, where different colonial cultures meet at the fringes and traditions intermingle or are overlaid, where one colonial power replaces another (such as the British replacing the French Acadians in Nova Scotia), or where peoples and architectures of noncolonial nations take root in the colonies of other nations (for instance, German settlers in North America or Scandinavians in the Caribbean).[8]

Complexities in building production were not only geographic. The top-down hierarchical model for the dissemination of knowledge and design from an aristocratic, architect-and-patron design culture down to the everyday builder has been repeatedly challenged and discredited as we find vernacular classicism coexisting alongside, and independent of, the small, elite transatlantic world of professional architects and their wealthy patrons, as discussed by Peter Guillery in the context of English churches. This social distinction itself has a regional character as everyday craft traditions were based, or took root, in specific geographic contexts while the "high culture" of professional design maintained a higher degree of exchange and mobility as wealthy patrons maintained cultural, social, and economic transatlantic links. As Elizabeth McKellar has observed of building in eighteenth-century Britain, "the reception and spread of classicism in the eighteenth century suggests not a top-down model but rather overlapping spheres of influence between the national and the provincial, the classical and the non-classical, the elite and the everyday."[9]

Sameness also obscured differences in the cultural reception of that universal architectural language — or what its users thought of a particular building — from one region to the next and from one social group to the next. Similar-looking buildings could mean different things in different places and to different people: national, social, and racial identities; political, cultural, and economic agendas; public, commercial, and private lives. A stone artillery fortress overlooking a bustling harbor in seventeenth-century Bermuda may have been a comforting symbol of authority and security for English merchants, but it was also a clear message of well-armed intent to other European colonial powers. A large house with classical columns may have represented the same image of money and social success to a gentleman landowner in England as it did to a plantation owner in South Carolina, but it meant something very different to the enslaved Africans on that plantation (though both may have been built on the profits of slavery). Or to look at differences over time, the pediments and columns of North America's early public buildings have represented both British imperial authority and American republicanism — and the politics of embrace and resistance to both. What emerges most clearly through the transatlantic architectural histories presented here is the tension between the apparent coherence of a historic transatlantic culture and the multiple and complex forces that continually interrogated and subverted that coherence.

Building the British Atlantic World aims to provide by example an overview of building activity across Britain's historic Atlantic empire with studies of as many British Atlantic colonies and types of buildings and as much chronological breadth as is possible in thirteen chapters — whether the northern Atlantic triangle of Britain, the United States, and Canada (Maudlin); the impact of the Atlantic on England (Guillery, Morgan); English religion in New England (Benes, Stanley); domesticity in the mid-Atlantic (Hague); the reinterpretation of English villa design in the South (Morrissey); British militarism in Bermuda (Mann); traders in the Caribbean (Nelson); the nature of British slave forts in West Africa (DeCorse); or the vernacular interiors of the London metropole itself (Herman). Inevitably, not all Atlantic regions or their buildings can be represented in a single volume, and it is hoped that, instead, a strong sense of the common ground and the complexities that characterize the architecture of the British Atlantic world is given. Notably absent, for reasons of space alone, are studies on the Gulf of Mexico and the interiors of the American Atlantic colonies such as the Mohawk, Ohio, and Hudson valleys, leaving much for future research. Similarly, while we have attempted to show examples of architecture from all Atlantic regions it has not been possible to discuss all building types in all regions. For example, southern plantation houses are discussed, but the distinct tradition of southern Anglican churches is not. Finally, the focus of the book is generally on relationships between Britain and Britain's overseas colonies in order to demonstrate the scale and spread of architecture across the Atlantic world. The book, with some regret, does not have the space to include studies on Britain's significant inner empire—colonial activities between the four nations of the British Isles, such as the Ulster plantations in Northern Ireland in the seventeenth century, the building of the Anglo-Irish monuments of Georgian Dublin, or the military architecture and planned settlements of the Scottish Highlands that followed the Jacobite rebellion. Here researchers should refer to the edited collection, *"The Mirror of Great Britain"* (2012), which considers the architecture of this inner empire in the seventeenth century.[10] *Building the British Atlantic World* is not a comprehensive encyclopedia of Atlantic architectures but an introduction to an emergent field and, hopefully, an encouragement to further research.

BUILDING ON ATLANTIC HISTORY
AND MATERIAL CULTURE

Architectural history in both Britain and North America has tended to focus upon national or regional studies (British, North American, Caribbean, and West African). Here, two edited collections should be mentioned, the aforementioned *"The Mirror of Great Britain"* and *Articulating British Classicism* (2004) edited by Barbara Arciszewska and Elizabeth McKellar, for their inclusion of the wider British Atlantic world in their analysis of British architecture in the seventeenth and eighteenth centuries respectively.[11] Similarly, David S. Shields's edited collection *Material Culture in Anglo-America* (2009) reaches beyond the United States to consider the Caribbean in the same cultural world as the Tidewater and Lowcountry regions of the South.[12] This volume builds upon these by drawing together case studies from across the Atlantic world and beginning to make transatlantic connections in light of thinking in other fields. The "British Atlantic world" is a well-established term in disciplines such as history and literary studies, with numerous monographs and edited collections published since the late 1980s. Within literary studies, Susan Manning and Andrew Taylor have defined the purpose of transatlanticism as drawing "attention to the ways in which ideas of crossing and connection have helped to rethink the ways that national identity has been formulated."[13] The wider field of Atlantic history encompasses Anglo-American, French, Spanish, and Latin cultures and their interlocking transatlantic exchanges across the vast geographic space of the northern and southern Atlantic oceans. Given such a large field, researchers have tended to focus on a specific cultural locus, axis, or network. The possibility of a specifically "British" Atlantic world was first explored by historians of early modern Britain and North America, such as Jack P. Green and J. R. Pole in *Colonial British America* (1984), Nicholas Canny and Anthony Pagden in *Colonial Identity in the Atlantic World* (1987), and Bernard Bailyn in *Strangers within the Realm* (1991).[14] Following the center-periphery model of exchange, these studies interpreted the principal cultural movement within this Atlantic world as an outward ripple from London and the English Home Counties—considered the center of eighteenth-century British politics, economics, and culture—to a federation of subnational groups spread throughout Britain and the British Atlantic. More recent studies and collections, such as *The British Atlantic World, 1500–1800* (2009), edited by David Armitage and Michael J. Braddick, have interpreted the cultural activity of the British Atlantic world not as an outward ripple, nor even a simple two-way exchange, but in terms of elaborate networks of exchange between Atlantic trading partners engaged with both Britain and each other.[15] The *Oxford Handbook of the Atlantic World 1450–1850* (2011) attempts to dissect these convoluted European trading networks across the northern and southern Atlantic.[16] Researchers can also look to the field of historical geography where the geographic parameters and cultural landscape approach of, for example, Stephen J. Hornsby's *British Atlantic, American Frontier: Spaces of Power in Early Modern British America* (2005) closely align with those of *Building the British Atlantic World*.[17] Historians of the Atlantic built environment can also draw upon a number of studies in urban history that deal with transatlanticism in terms of the history of the city, such as Emma Hart's *Building Charleston: Town and Society in the British Atlantic World* (2009), that precisely locates the socioeconomic history of Charleston within the wider context of the Carolinas, the South, and the British Atlantic world.[18]

One of the recent approaches in transamerican cultural studies is the relative importance of hemispheric focuses, northern and southern, and their relationship to studies of the Atlantic world.[19] Certainly, the history of transatlantic exchange between the northern and southern Atlantic and between Europe and South America is an important context for our understanding of the British Atlantic.[20] In focusing upon the northern hemisphere and the

British empire as a specific network of exchange, *Building the British Atlantic World* recognizes the importance of this distinction.[21] Moreover, in the same way that the British Atlantic world and the approaches of transatlanticism challenged the perceived nation-centricism of British and American studies, so transatlantic studies has itself been challenged by the concept of transnationalism and circum-Atlanticism, which celebrate the idea that texts, things, and other phenomena cross through, over, and beyond nation and empire and travel around global space, adding further nuances to the notion of a British Atlantic world.

A number of recent histories have also emphasized the specific transatlantic experiences of ethnic groups and social subcultures: the African diaspora (or so-called black Atlantic); the Scottish Atlantic; the Irish diaspora; the role of Native Americans; social class and the role of religious groups.[22] However, the primary focus of most studies is the white Atlantic, which in David Armitage's words "has become a self-conscious field of study rather than the defining model for all other Atlantic histories." Above all, these subcultural histories are concerned with identity and the delineation of cultural subgroups who identify with each other as a community through a shared experience (positive or negative), whether religion, class, or race. Within this expanding field there are a number of studies specifically concerned with the British Atlantic.[23] These themes are explored throughout *Building the British Atlantic World*: slavery is considered in Lee Morrissey's chapter on the Palladian villa ideal in South Carolina and, at source, in Chris DeCorse's chapter on the British slave forts of West Africa; the English, Scottish, Irish, and German emigration experience is considered in Daniel Maudlin's chapter on British Canada; the role of Native Americans in Alison Stanley's chapter on the praying Indian towns of New England; class distinctions are the focus of Stephen Hague's chapter on the gentleman's house and Peter Guillery's on dockyard churches; and, in addition to Guillery and Stanley's chapters, religion and nonconformist religious spaces are also the focus of Peter Benes's chapter on New England meetinghouses.

Building the British Atlantic World also looks to recent histories on the material culture of the British Atlantic world, namely Carole Shammas's *The Pre-industrial Consumer in England and America* (1990); Rebecca Ann Bach's *Colonial Transformations: The Cultural Production of the New Atlantic World, 1580–1640* (2000) and John Styles and Amanda Vickery's *Gender, Taste, and Material Culture in Britain and North America, 1700–1830* (2007).[24] *Material Life in America, 1600–1860*, edited by Robert Blair St. George (1988) remains an important forerunner to these transatlantic titles.[25]

The relationship between material culture studies, cultural history, and architectural history is explored in Carl R. Lounsbury's chapter in *The Oxford Handbook of Material Culture Studies* (2010).[26] More generally, useful works on material culture include *Everyday Objects: Medieval and Early Modern Material Culture and its Meanings* (2010) and *The Empire of Things: Regimes of Value and Material Culture* (1996).[27] Works such as Arjun Appadurai's *The Social Life of Things* (1988) or Daniel Miller's *The Comfort of Things* (2009) and, most notably, Pierre Bourdieu's *Distinction: A Social Critique on the Judgement of Taste* (1984) reflect the underlying influence of sociology and anthropology on the history of objects and the role of taste in maintaining group identities and patrolling social boundaries.[28] However, although these approaches inform many of the chapters, theory is not brought to the fore.

BUILDING THE BRITISH ATLANTIC WORLD

Whether plantations in the American South, forts in Bermuda, or English port cities, each of the thirteen chapters in this book presents an architectural intersection of time, place, and culture. By arranging chapters into four thematic parts according to different spheres or aspects of the British Atlantic experience — "Empire and Government"; "Religion and the Churches"; "Commerce, Traffic, and Trade"; and "Houses and the Home" — people, the producers and consumers of building design, are considered first and foremost. Thus this thematic approach shows architecture as a set of different responses, in different places and at different times, to common human concerns and activities. Most chapters present a case study of a specific region and the sense of a coherent wider British Atlantic world comes from the connections made in each study to a wider world as well as from the thematic grouping of chapters. There are, as in life, many overlaps between these spheres; these are illuminating in themselves with, for instance, imperial politics featuring in "Houses and the Home," where Maudlin considers farmhouses in British Canada, and the home also features in "Empire and Government" as Marley assesses the post-British political meaning of the interiors at Thomas Jefferson's Monticello, while the politics of race inevitably feature in Morrissey's study of the southern plantation house Drayton Hall.

The theme of part I, "Empire and Government," is explored through military, public, and private domestic buildings and across the chronological arc of early empire in the seventeenth century to its disintegration and reinvention in the late eighteenth century. Three chapters consider the design and use of buildings not just as the functional tools of imperial government but as symbolic representations of institutional authority, control, and ideology. Forts were the common architecture of the early British Empire. In the opening chapter, "To Build and Fortify," Emily Mann draws on surviving structures, archaeological studies, maps, surveys, and written records to investigate the physical, legal, and symbolic functions of the earliest Atlantic colonial fortifications. Over the course of the seventeenth century, the pre-Britain English established a series of settlements in quick succession across the Atlantic world, in America, Canada, Bermuda, and the West Indies. The buildings that physically and symbolically secured these sites were crucial to this expansion, and first among these buildings were fortified structures. Mann examines defensive architecture in Virginia, Bermuda, and Barbados, looking at the involvement of the Crown, companies, and individuals in the building process. The chapter raises questions about how varying conditions on the ground, physical and political, shaped the planning and construction of defensive structures in the early British Atlantic world.

As Britain's Atlantic colonies take root we move from forts to courthouses and from defense to administration. In chapter 2, "Seats of Government," Carl Lounsbury examines the public buildings erected by provincial and local governments in British America, examining how the combination of various functions influenced their design. Provincial statehouses accommodated legislative bodies, superior courts, and administrative offices, while city and county buildings often contained courtrooms, exchanges, markets, and spaces for social assemblies. As models of British governance, the inspiration for America's early public structures was intentionally derived from British precedents, but distinctive regional building practices shaped the interpretation of these forms. Balconies, arcades, colonnades, compass-headed apertures, cupolas, coats of arms, statuary, and other features long associated with British public buildings reappeared in American public buildings, but were sometimes used and arranged in novel ways to create distinctive regional forms. Small farm towns in rural New England, bustling seaports in the mid-Atlantic region, and slave-based staple-producing colonies in the South constructed public structures that responded to their own peculiar needs and aspirations. However, Thomas Jefferson's selection of an ancient Roman temple as the precedent for the new capitol of Virginia in the mid-1780s deliberately looked beyond traditional British sources and informed American public building design with the ideology of the new republic.

Anna Marley's chapter, "Landscapes of the New Republic at Thomas Jefferson's Monticello," follows the theme of a declining British Atlantic world in the late eighteenth century and the United States emerging out of the former thirteen British colonies as she assesses the westward-looking political allegory of Thomas Jefferson's picture-hanging scheme at his home in Monticello, Virginia. In 1786 future United States presidents John Adams and Thomas Jefferson embarked together upon a summer tour through the great estates and gardens of England. Though scholars have often noted the influence this tour had upon Jefferson's design for the gardens at Monticello, little attention has been paid to how this tour affected Monticello's interior. Jefferson and Adams visited the homes as well as the gardens of massive British estates such as Stowe and Blenheim. Though Adams praised the grandeur and beauty of these English country seats, he was critical of their cost and showiness and expressed the hope that it would be a long time before such artificial ornaments were established in America. No doubt Adams would have been dismayed to see Monticello, where some of this "greatness and luxury" was transported back to America. Jefferson's home was not only decorated with French furnishings brought back from his years spent abroad, but hung floor-to-ceiling with maps, mirrors, religious paintings, prints, still lifes, and landscapes. Jefferson's installation of paintings, particularly landscapes, at Monticello was directly influenced by the hang of paintings in the great estates of Britain that he visited in the 1780s, and yet in their subject matter these paintings looked westward to a new America beyond British rule.

Marley focuses on the landscape paintings Jefferson hung at Monticello upon his retirement from political office and in particular explores how Jefferson's 1786 tour of British gardens influenced his thinking about the function and fashion of both landscape and domestic interiors. However, in establishing a program of American landscapes, arranged around the western windows of his dining room with their views of the Blue Ridge Mountains and beyond, Jefferson was shifting his vantage point from the East to the West and crafting rooms with views of a new American empire. Unlike Washington, who had looked to an Arcadian Europe for his landscape and interior decoration, Jefferson's decoration of Monticello with American views highlights both the continued importance of landscape in American domestic interiors as well as a shift in the orientation of that view. While Washington's front parlor offered a kaleidoscope of transatlantic views, Jefferson's views stretched west, to the newly explored lands of the Louisiana Purchase. These landscapes, though indebted in their form to the British global landscape, in subject matter were a new expression of a specifically American imperial eye. Thus, Jefferson's arrangement of paintings represents both continuity with earlier "rooms with views" in eighteenth-century British Atlantic interiors, as well as a shift in landscape patronage from a transatlantic to a new western, American view.

Part II turns to the architecture of "Religion and the Churches," articulating an important distinction between religious belief and practices and the specific structures built by different Christian sects. Christianity was the dominant religion of the British Atlantic world; it was one of Britain's principal cultural exports and played a significant role in the entrenchment of white European culture in North America. However, not all Christians were the same. The term "church" covers the religious spaces of many different religious groups who lived in different parts of Britain and North America and who prayed in different types of buildings. "Religion and the Churches" provides a sense of the diversity of the Christian experience and Christian space within the British Atlantic. Starting in England, Peter Guillery's "English Artisans' Churches and North America" raises the notion of vernacular classicism as a form of building production distinct from Britain's architectural elites and takes as its starting point St. George in Portsea (Portsmouth), Hampshire, built in 1753–54. Guillery argues that the distinctive architecture of this church, both classical and vernacular, arose from a particular cultural milieu, that of the Calvinist shipwrights and other dockyard artisans who populated and developed eighteenth-century Portsea. Precedents for the building's centralized layout and simple brick classicism are to be found in churches that from the 1650s onwards were put up by and for largely self-sufficient, Nonconformist (Protestant Christian), culturally conservative, and politically radical artisan communities in southern English naval dockyard and maritime towns, from London's working-class Thames-side eastern suburbs and satellites such as Poplar, Bermondsey, Deptford, and Woolwich, to Chatham and Deal in Kent. The artisans' churches of the English maritime settlements are not formally analogous to American churches, but their architectural vocabularies, both material and spatial, are strikingly similar. It was from communities and social strata such as these that significant numbers of people emigrated to America, taking with them mentalities that were imaginative and opportunistic, as well as nostalgic, in search of simplicity and liberty. The common thread is that status in Nonconformist communities on both sides of the Atlantic was not primarily based on consumption habits or emulative behavior. These churches, plainly embellished auditory spaces, have much in common with each other, and they fit badly into narratives of high-style architecture. They represent a transatlantic tradition of vernacular-classical architecture.

Moving from Nonconformism in the English dockyard to Nonconformism in New England, in "The New England Meetinghouse," Peter Benes argues that the Great Migration of twenty thousand English Puritans to Massachusetts Bay and Connecticut between 1630 and 1640 put an immediate burden on the builders of communal structures in North America. The New England meetinghouse, a vernacular, multipurpose, and impermanent parish structure that served both religious and secular purposes, allowed for Calvinist services that focused on the sermon while also providing for judicial, administrative, and storage purposes. Unlike the British-based Anglican churches of the middle and southern colonies, however, these structures had a distinctly Reformist origin. A study of 205 Congregational, Presbyterian, Baptist, and Dutch Reformed meetinghouses still standing in New England and Long Island, supported by data from approximately two thousand additional examples known only from period documents and town histories, suggests that the first three generations of builders drew architectural ideas from French Huguenot, Scottish Reformed, and Dutch Reformed models, as well as from a few vernacular types (for example, long houses) known to have existed in England itself. Drawing on old-growth forests in North America, builders recreated these European forms in America with wood-frame barn-like structures, some heavily influenced by bridge-building traditions. Beginning in 1700, this reformed approach was gradually abandoned in favor of a more inclusive architectural model increasingly reflective of eighteenth-century British political and religious hegemony — but one that was still based on communally built wood-frame structures. However, by 1770 reformed congregations in Salem, Boston, and Providence were no longer raising meetinghouses but building churches that looked back across the Atlantic to London-based Anglican precedents.

The final chapter on the theme of religion turns our attention from Christian colonists to the indigenous non-Christian peoples they encountered and attempted to convert. Alison Stanley's chapter on "The Praying Indian Towns" investigates the ways religious and cultural identity were constructed in seventeenth-century New England through an analysis of a series of pamphlets written between 1643 and 1671 concerning Protestant missionary efforts to urbanize the Native Americans of the region and see them settled in formal grid-plan townships. These *Eliot Tracts* were published in London to entice English audiences to support the so-called "Praying Towns" across the Atlantic. However, they also depict efforts to persuade local colonists of the religious sincerity of Native American converts. Stanley argues that we can use these multiple audiences to examine the ways that the writers expected their audiences to understand place-making and town-planning as a means to convey religious identity. Through maps, plans, and written sources this chapter examines the nature of the Protestantism that English colonists brought to New England and attempted to manifest in prototowns. The *Eliot Tracts* provide evidence of how missionaries such as John Eliot attempted to mold Native American converts to fit classical European urban patterns, which English audiences correlated with religious salvation (highlighting what was perceived in the early modern European imagination as the implicit morality and godliness of neoclassicism). Eliot also began to adapt the ways he wrote about religious identity in response to the different cultural expectations of Native American converts. However, analysis of the *Tracts* reveals that the Indian residents of praying towns learned to recognize, exploit, and adapt these signs for their own benefit.

Part III, "Commerce, Traffic, and Trade," turns from the world of religion to the world of trade. In the context of the British Atlantic this meant ships, ports, and shipping, connecting an intercontinental network of wharves, harbors, cities, towns, villages, and farms. Following the slave trade from West Africa to the Caribbean to Britain, part III presents the dichotomy between the architecture of commerce in those Atlantic regions defined by the slave-based Atlantic trade and the architecture of urban sprawl that flourished in Britain on the back of the Atlantic trade and the slave trade in particular. The first chapter, "Tools of Empire," by Christopher DeCorse, examines how the British forts and trade posts of West Africa enabled England, and later Britain, to control access to resources, particularly gold and slaves, and laid the foundations for empire. Between the mid-seventeenth and early nineteenth centuries the British established dozens of outposts in West Africa, from the Senegambia to the Bight of Benin. The majority were established on the coast, with the notable exception of the Senegambia, where the Gambia River is navigable well into the interior. Often these outposts had small European staffs, for the most part men, who faced disease, high mortality rates, and poor supply. The function of the outposts was economic. They served as a base for trade, providing a place to store and gather trade goods. Some, such as Yamyamacunda founded on the Gambia River in the 1730s, were little more than small dwellings built of timber and clay in the style of local African buildings. Other outposts, such as the one at Cape Coast in modern Ghana, grew into substantial fortifications, well deserving of their popular appellation *castles*. These larger fortified trading depots provided protection, primarily from other European nations and their African allies. These forts varied substantially in size, form, and function. Their establishment, design, use, and ultimate disuse varied through time, indicating changes in both regional and global political alliances and economics. Often poorly built, vernacular in plan, and at times ill-suited for the tropics, these outposts collectively delineated an expanding British sphere of economic and cultural expansion, culminating with the imposition of colonial rule in the late nineteenth century.

Following the slave trade from West Africa to Jamaica, Louis P. Nelson's chapter on "The Falmouth House and Store" is not concerned, as might be expected, with the lavish plantation houses of the sugar planters but takes us down to the waterfront in order to examine the related growth of the urban shopping street and the merchant's house, focusing on the Barratt House in Falmouth, Jamaica built by British sugar-planter Edward Barratt. The Barratt house was a participant in the formation of a new urban space in the Caribbean, the shaded commercial street, a more socially and physically comfortable space than the warehouses that lined the city's wharves. Mixed-material merchant's houses with projecting upper stories that shade the pedestrian space below appear not only in Falmouth, but also in Kingston and other cities in Jamaica in these same years. And they can also be found in other British Caribbean contexts, for example St. John's, Antigua. Found almost exclusively in port towns, these mixed-use, commercial and residential buildings are consistently associated with merchants, suggesting that by this period the increasingly wealthy merchant class drew from a familiar vocabulary of parts as they sought to address multiple functions, increased consumption of household goods from shops along commercial streets, and shelter from the intense Caribbean climate. But these new merchant house/shops were more than participants in a newly genteel commercial space; they served also as counterpoints to a very different commercial landscape to which they are intimately connected: the wharves. Wharves did not disappear from the landscape; neither did their warehouses, nor their reputations. The new commercial street in the Caribbean was an alternative to the much less refined, less orderly, and far less reputable wharf warehouse, where earlier generations made most of their purchases, even of refined goods. Barratt's house was immediately across the street from his wharf, but that street was a gulf of separation between two very distinct social landscapes. Ranging across the Greater Caribbean—from South Carolina to Jamaica to the Leeward Islands to Barbados—Nelson explores the various dimensions of merchant house/ stores and examines their cultural position at the nexus of two very different landscapes of exchange.

Taking the eastward passage, in "Building British Atlantic Port Cities," Kenneth Morgan takes us back across the Atlantic to consider the expansion of British port cities in relation to the Americanization of British trade through the early modern period. Concentrating on the English cities of Bristol and Liverpool, outports on the western coast that grew demographically and commercially in a burgeoning Atlantic trading world, Morgan investigates the ways in which the built environment of these expanding port cities altered over time. Morgan focuses upon the promoters of urban development in British ports; the extent to which wharves, warehouses, shipping, and harbor facilities were transformed; the construction of industrial buildings near the waterfront that helped to sustain trade; the provision of new urban squares, streets, neighborhoods, and suburbs that reflected the residential patterns of merchants; the contribution of mercantile houses to the urban renaissance of the eighteenth century; and the wealth, social aspirations, and desire for upward mobility of the merchants closely involved in these developments. Through the analysis of the historic spatial distribution of buildings we gain an understanding of how the commercial and political ethos of port cities was reflected in their expansion, connecting the built environment of British port cities to wider patterns of urban civic development.

Building the British Atlantic World concludes with four chapters on the theme of "Houses and the Home." The distinction between house and home is significant. A house or dwelling is the artifact, a building or structure used for habitation. Home imbues the artifact of the house with lived experience. In essence, the house is the thing; the home is the thing enlivened. While all four chapters are concerned with what can be broadly categorized as domestic architecture, they encompass a range of buildings and spaces: from the modest English country house, to the parlor of the transatlantic city, and from the modest Canadian farmhouse to the scale and luxury of the South Carolina plantation house. Interpretations of these dwellings vary not just according to the relative wealth of their occupants but according to their occupants' self-image and the values their homes were built to project. We also return to the notion of overlapping spheres of production discussed earlier, where ordinary everyday houses are designed and made in regional classical craft traditions that engaged with a wider Atlantic consumer culture, while in a parallel self-contained cultural sphere, the intellectual architectural discourse of a wealthy transatlantic cultural elite is exercised in the design and production of country houses, villas, and complex interior design schemes. As the home reflects the concerns and preoccupations of the residents, cross-references can also be made to other parts of this book. For instance, chapter 3 on Monticello is as much a study of domestic display as it is an account of Jefferson's political vision of a post-British America.

In the first chapter, "Building Status in the British Atlantic World," Stephen Hague discusses two contemporaneous "gentry houses" and their owners on opposite sides of the Atlantic: one in the English West Country and one in Pennsylvania. Beginning in about 1680, classical gentleman's houses or gentry houses began to develop as an important architectural type distinct from larger country houses. Such houses drew upon a classical design vocabulary, were usually five bays wide, and had double-pile floor plans. This flexible housing form, built in both urban and rural settings throughout Britain and its colonies, offered the lesser gentry and rising middling sorts of the British Atlantic world a relatively affordable opportunity to materially define their status. The histories of John Elbridge of Cote near Bristol, England, and James Logan of Stenton near Philadelphia, Pennsylvania, examined as case studies, illustrate many of the common characteristics of life in the eighteenth-century British Atlantic world. Both men had strong colonial connections, hailed from modest origins, rose to prominence as a result of positions in public life, and accumulated fortunes through a range of investments. Such endeavors introduced a series of tactical maneuvers and strategic approaches that record multilayered campaigns to win favor and secure position. More to the point, at about the same time in their lives, both acquired classical houses as important markers of their and their families' status. Logan and Elbridge are representatives of an important segment of British Atlantic society that provided the civil and imperial administration, commercial control, and social direction in Britain and its colonies. They typified the collaboration between the gentry and the upper elements of bourgeois society. In the aspiration to and adoption of social tastes, here the top-down model holds sway. But, far from being simply a ubiquitous form, these gentlemen's houses represented a specific and tangible approach for staking claims to gentility. Hague evaluates the gentleman's house as one among a range of strategies that families employed to navigate the complex relationships between commerce, land, and social status. By assessing figures like Elbridge and Logan in relation to their houses, Hague examines how gentlemen grappled with rising status, accumulated wealth, increased power, and what to do with the resulting material outcomes in the British Atlantic world.

Moving from the countryside and the gentleman's house into the city, Bernard L. Herman considers the "Parlor and Kitchen in the Borderlands of the Urban British-American Atlantic World, 1670–1720" and the cultural borderland these rooms occupied in London and the emerging cities of colonial North America. In London, "parlor" (in various spellings) appears in the proceedings of the Old Bailey court a dozen times between 1674 and 1695 and in forty-two cases from 1696 to 1720. Significantly, no mention of parlors occurs prior to 1687. By the early 1730s, the term "parlour" had been codified as "a fair lower Room design'd principally for the Entertainment of Company."[29] Parlors, it seems, were a relatively late development in the formalization of urban domestic spaces in London. Outside of London, at the various outports of the British Atlantic world, parlors appeared at the same time as, soon after, or much later than London, depending on the specific trade links, building industry connections, and social interactions of each with London and with each other. However, what is clear is that the emergence of the parlor through the eighteenth century connects changes and innovations in domestic space with the changing social activities and values demanded of those spaces; but what was the nature of the understanding and the social practices that lent parlors significance? From house to house and owner to owner, Herman argues that, in the aggregate, parlors were understood as rooms that housed and displayed valued objects like plate and textiles. Evidence in housebreaking and theft trials often places parlors at the front on the ground floor in a manner where their contents could be seen from the street. Parlors also appear on contemporary plans in a variety of locations within the house, suggesting that in the socially aware urban world of the transatlantic city, the parlor became viewed as an essential room, but one of variable location. Parlors, therefore, were designated social spaces intended for both public exterior display and to impress friends and invited guests: dressed stages for the performances of eighteenth-century domestic life.

Returning to the rural landscape and the country house in a study of the eighteenth-century plantation house Drayton Hall in "Palladianism and the Villa Ideal in South Carolina," Lee Morrissey questions the morality and godliness of eighteenth-century intellectual discourse surrounding neoclassicism and English Palladianism, in particular, when placed in the transatlantic context of slave ownership — an eighteenth-century European worldview that can also be challenged in the context of British country houses built on the profits of slavery. Drayton Hall, outside Charleston, South Carolina, was built between 1738 and 1742. The owners of Drayton Hall were an English family that moved to Carolina from a slave-worked plantation in Barbados. The Draytons designed the house themselves from the Anglo-Palladian architectural publications and pattern books that circulated within the British Atlantic world alongside other shipped goods, imitating British architectural standards for the appropriate home of the wealthy. However, unlike country houses on the eastern side of the Atlantic, Drayton Hall was built on the back of enslaved African labor, on the edge of a swampy tidal marsh, in an area given to malaria outbreaks. For the slave population of the Drayton plantation it was a visually dominating building in a physically appalling location, a symbol of violent oppression—not virtue, morality, and godliness. As such, Drayton raises questions about the transatlantic politics of seemingly abstract forms and architectural discourses on morality.

In the final chapter, "Politics and Place-Making on the Edge of Empire," we move north to Nova Scotia where Daniel Maudlin considers the house as a site for settler families to express their social aspirations and cultural identities within a colonial theater otherwise defined by conflict and political unrest. In Nova Scotia, the Atlantic edge of British Canada, migration, settlement, and place-making took place against a backdrop of war and political turmoil. In 1783, after eight years of war between Britain and her North American colonists, the sovereignty of the United States of America was ratified by the Treaty of Paris. The thirteen Atlantic-seaboard colonies of British America were no longer British colonies but American. However, to the south, the British islands of the Caribbean remained British, and to the north, only twenty years earlier, Canada had become a new British colony— briefly the fourteenth colony—following victory in the Seven Years' War with France. The political seascape of the British Atlantic world had shifted, and due to its geographically strategic position in the North Atlantic, Nova Scotia briefly became the focus of these political changes. Yet within this politically charged environment ordinary people made ordinary homes, as national and subnational settler groups—loyalist British American, Scots, Irish, English, German, and French Acadian—established their own geographic territories according to ethnic identity, each with its own farming communities and regional urban centers. Moreover, these settlers from different countries and ethnic groups built and occupied the same type of home. However, this universal British Canadian farmhouse was in fact the archetypal New England "saltbox" brought to Canada by loyalist refugees from New England: a British American invention taken out of the United States and reestablished in British Canada. Through the late eighteenth and early nineteenth centuries the saltbox became the home of the new British frontline. Yet, to the south, in New England, the same house also continued to be built and identified as the archetypal American home. In Nova Scotia, the sameness of this universal farmhouse veneered over many political complexities and provided settlers a refuge from politics where architectural meaning lay in material comfort and social cohesion.

Building the British Atlantic World is an introduction to transatlantic architectural history. It is a beginning—an incomplete history of the buildings, environments, and building processes that made the British Atlantic world of the seventeenth to nineteenth centuries—and a starting point for future research. Buildings, periods, and the cultural contexts of politics, religion, commerce, and social identity are examined through chapters that explore: early Atlantic fortifications; public buildings; Thomas Jefferson's Monticello; Calvinist churches in both England and New England; the Puritans' promotion of praying Indian towns; slave forts and trade posts in British West Africa; the merchant houses and wharves of the Caribbean; the growth of port cities in eighteenth-century Britain; the gentleman's house in England and Pennsylvania; the parlor in London and Philadelphia; plantations in South Carolina; and farmhouses in Canada. From these studies we find that the British Atlantic world was made and experienced through buildings and built spaces that appeared similar: the products of a common culture. Yet, underneath a surface of apparent stylistic and spatial sameness, building the British Atlantic world emerges as a complicated process of design, construction, and occupation defined by ambiguity, experimentation, adaptation, change, and transformation as much as conformity—the call and response of design and experience.

NOTES

1. John Clive and Bernard Bailyn, "England's Cultural Provinces: Scotland and America," *William and Mary Quarterly* 11, no. 2 (1954): 207.

2. Fiona A. Black, "Advent'rous Merchants and Atlantic Waves: A Preliminary Study of the Scottish Contribution to Book Availability in Halifax, 1752–1810," in *Myth, Migration and the Making of Memory: Scotia and Nova Scotia, c.1700–1990*, ed. Marjory Harper and Michael E. Vance (Edinburgh: John Donald Publishers, 2000), 157–89.

3. See Homi K. Bhabha, "DissemiNation: Time, Narrative, and the Margins of the Modern Nation" in *Nation and Narration*, ed. H. K. Bhabha (Oxford: Routledge, 1990), 291–332.

4. Elizabeth McKellar, "Preface," in *Articulating British Classicism: New Approaches to Eighteenth-Century Architecture (Reinterpreting Classicism: Culture, Reaction and Appropriation)*, ed. Elizabeth McKellar and Barbara Arciszewska (Oxford: Ashgate, 2004), ix–xxv.

5. Robert St. George, *Possible Pasts: Becoming Colonial in Early America* (Ithaca: Cornell University Press, 2000).

6. This view of place, as tied to the relativity of people rather than the fixed geography of site, stems from human geography and writers such as Edward Relph, *Place and Placelessness* (London: Pion Press, 1976) and, more recently, Doreen Massey, *For Space* (London: SAGE, 2005).

7. Bernard L. Herman, "Tabletop Conversations: Material Culture and Everyday Life in the Eighteenth-Century Atlantic World," in *Gender, Taste, and Material Culture in Britain and North America, 1700–1830*, ed. John Styles and Amanda Vickery (New Haven: The Yale Center for British Art, 2007), 44.

8. See, for example, William Chapman, "Irreconcilable Differences: Urban Residences in the Danish West Indies, 1700–1900," *Winterthur Portfolio* 30 (Summer–Autumn 1995): 129–172.

9. Elizabeth McKellar, "Preface," ix–xxv.

10. Olivia Horsfall Turner, ed., *"The Mirror of Great Britain": National Identity in Seventeenth-Century British Architecture* (Reading: Spire Books, 2012).

11. Ibid.; McKellar and Arciszewska, *Articulating British Classicism*.

12. David S. Shields, ed., *Material Culture in Anglo-America: Regional Identity and Urbanity in the Tidewater, Lowcountry, and Caribbean (Carolina Lowcountry & the Atlantic World)* (Columbia: University of South Carolina Press, 2009). For other regional studies, see also Bernard Herman, "Tabletop Conversations," in *Gender, Taste, and Material Culture in Britain and North America*, ed. John Styles and Amanda Vickery; Carl Lounsbury, *Essays in Early American Architectural History: A View from the Chesapeake* (Charlottesville: University of Virginia Press, 2011); and Daniel Maudlin, *The Highland House Transformed: Architecture and Identity on the Edge of Empire, 1700–1850* (Dundee: Dundee University Press, 2009).

13. Susan Manning and Andrew Taylor, eds., *Transatlantic Literary Studies: A Reader* (Edinburgh: Edinburgh University Press, 2007), 4.

14. Bernard Bailyn and P. D. Morgan, eds., *Strangers within the Realm; Cultural Margins of the First British Empire* (Chapel Hill: University of North Carolina Press, 1991); Nicholas Canny and Anthony Pagden, eds., *Colonial Identity in the Atlantic World, 1500–1800* (Princeton, N.J.: Princeton University Press, 1987); Jack P. Greene, & J. R. Pole, eds., *Colonial British America: Essays in the New History of the Early Modern Era* (Baltimore: Johns Hopkins University Press, 1984).

15. Bernard Bailyn, *Atlantic History: Concepts and Contours* (Cambridge, Mass., and London: Harvard University Press, 2005); David Armitage and Michael J. Braddick, eds., *The British Atlantic World, 1500–1800*, 2nd ed. (Basingstoke: Palgrave Macmillan, 2009); Manuela Albertone and Antonino De Francesco, eds., *Rethinking the Atlantic World: Europe and American in the Age of Democratic Revolutions* (Basingstoke: Palgrave Macmillan, 2009); Thomas Benjamin, *The Atlantic World: Europeans, Africans, Indians and Their Shared History* (Cambridge: Cambridge University Press, 2009); Elizabeth Mancke and Carole Shammas, eds., *The Creation of the British Atlantic World* (Baltimore: Johns Hopkins University Press, 2005). Also see Bernard Bailyn and Patricia L. Denault, eds., *Soundings in Atlantic History: Latent Structures and Intellectual Currents, 1500–1830* (Cambridge, Mass. and London: Harvard University Press, 2009); David Hancock, *Citizens of the World: London Merchants and the Integration of the British Atlantic Community, 1735–1785* (Cambridge: Cambridge University Press 1995); Stephen J. Hornsby, *British Atlantic, American Frontier: Spaces of Power in Early Mod-*

ern British America (Lebanon: University Press of New England, 2005); Ken MacMillan, *The Atlantic Imperial Constitution: Center and Periphery in the English Atlantic World* (New York: Palgrave Macmillan, 2011).

16. Nicholas Canny and Philip Morgan, eds., *The Oxford Handbook of the Atlantic World, 1450–1850* (Oxford: Oxford University Press, 2011).

17. Stephen J. Hornsby, *British Atlantic, American Frontier: Spaces of Power in Early Modern British America* (Lebanon: University Press of New England, 2005).

18. David Hancock, *Citizens of the World: London Merchants and the Integration of the British Atlantic Community, 1735–1785* (Cambridge: Cambridge University Press, 1995); Adrian Green and Roger Leech, eds., *Cities in the World, 1500–2000* (Leeds: Maney Publishing, 2006); Franklin W. Knight and Peggy K. Liss, eds., *Atlantic Port Cities: Economy, Culture, and Society in the Atlantic World, 1650–1850* (Knoxville: University of Tennessee Press, 1991); and Emma Hart, *Building Charleston: Town and Society in the Eighteenth-Century British Atlantic World* (Charlottesville: University of Virginia Press, 2009).

19. Ralph Bauer, *The Cultural Geography of Colonial American Literatures: Empire, Travel, Modernity* (Cambridge: Cambridge University Press, 2003).

20. On the Hispanic Atlantic, see Edmundo O'Gorman, *The Invention of America. An Inquiry into the Historical Nature of the New World and the Meaning of its History* (Indiana: Indiana University Press, 1961); William Roseberry, Lowell Gudmundson, and Mario Samper Kutschbach, eds., *Coffee, Society, and Power in Latin America*, Johns Hopkins Studies in Atlantic History and Culture (Baltimore: Johns Hopkins University Press, 1995); Edwin Williamson, *The Penguin History of Latin America*, revised edition (London: Penguin, 2009); Liam Matthew Brockey, *Portuguese Colonial Cities in the Early Modern World*, Empires and the Making of the Modern World, 1650–2000 (London: Ashgate, 2008); Jay Dearborn Edwards and Nicolas Kariouk Pecquet du Bellay de Verton, *A Creole Lexicon: Architecture, Landscape, People* (Baton Rouge: Louisiana State University Press, 2004); Richard Kagan, *Urban Images of the Hispanic World, 1493–1793* (New Haven: Yale University Press, 2000).

21. Caroline F. Levander and Robert S. Levine, eds., *Hemispheric American Studies* (New Jersey: Rutgers University Press, 2007).

22. Paul Gilroy, *The Black Atlantic: Modernity and Double Consciousness* (Cambridge, Mass.: Harvard University Press, 1993); Patrick Griffin, *The People with No Name: Ireland's Ulster Scots, America's Scots Irish, and the Creation of a British Atlantic World, 1689–1764* (Princeton, N.J.: Princeton University Press, 2001); Paul Lovejoy, *Transformations in Slavery: A History of Slavery in Africa* (Cambridge: Cambridge University Press, 2012); Patrick Manning, *Slavery and African Life: Occidental, Oriental, and African Slave Trades* (Cambridge: Cambridge University Press, 1990); Kenneth Morgan, *Slavery, Atlantic Trade and the British Economy, 1660–1800* (Cambridge: Cambridge University Press, 2000); Carla Gardina Pestana, *Protestant Empire: Religion and the Making of the British Atlantic World* (Philadelphia: University of Pennsylvania Press, 2009); S. D. Smith, *Slavery, Family and Gentry Capitalism in the British Atlantic: The*

World of the Lascelles, 1648–1834, Cambridge Studies in Economic History — Second Series (Cambridge: Cambridge University Press, 2010).

23. David Armitage, in Armitage and Braddick, eds., *The British Atlantic World*, 16. Robert Olwell and Alan Tully, *Cultures and Identities in Colonial British America* (Baltimore: Johns Hopkins University Press, 2006); Iain Chambers, *Migrancy, Culture, Identity* (London: Routledge, 1994); Ned Landsman, *From Colonials to Provincials: American Thought and Culture, 1680–1760* (Ithaca: Cornell University Press, 1997); Dror Wahrman, *The Making of the Modern Self: Identity and Culture in Eighteenth-Century England* (New Haven: Yale University Press, 2004).

24. Rebecca Ann Bach, *Colonial Transformations: The Cultural Production of the New Atlantic World, 1580–1640* (Basingstoke: Palgrave Macmillan 2000); Robert Blair St. George, ed., *Material Life in America, 1600–1860* (Seattle: Northeastern University Press, 1988); John Brewer and Roy Porter, eds., *Consumption and the World of Goods* (London: Taylor and Francis, 1993); John Styles and Amanda Vickery, eds., *Gender, Taste, and Material Culture in Britain and North America, 1700–1830* (New Haven: The Yale Center for British Art, 2007); Carole Shammas, *The Pre-Industrial Consumer in England and America* (Oxford: Oxford University Press, 1990); Lorna Weatherill, *Consumer Behavior and Material Culture, 1660–1760*, 2nd edition (London: Routledge, 1996).

25. Robert Blair St George, ed., *Material Life in America, 1600–1860* (Boston: Northeastern University Press, 1988).

26. Carl R. Lounsbury, "Architecture and Cultural History," in *The Oxford Handbook of Material Culture Studies*, ed. Dan Hicks and Mary C. Beaudry (Oxford: Oxford University Press, 2010), 484–502.

27. Tara Hamling and Catherine Richardson, eds., *Everyday Objects: Medieval and Early Modern Material Culture and its Meanings* (Farnham; Ashgate, 2010); Fred R. Myers, ed., *The Empire of Things: Regimes of Value and Material Culture* (Santa Fe: School of American Research Press, 1997).

28. Pierre Bourdieu, *Distinction: A Social Critique of the Judgement of Taste* (Cambridge Mass.: Harvard University Press, 1984); Arjun Appadurai, *The Social Life of Things* (Cambridge: Cambridge University Press, 1988); Daniel Miller, *The Comfort of Things* (London: Polity, 2009).

29. W. H. Toms, *The Builder's Dictionary: or, Gentleman and Architect's Companion* (London: A. Bettersworth, C. Hitch and S. Austen, 1734), n.p.

PART I
Empire and Government

1

TO BUILD AND FORTIFY

DEFENSIVE ARCHITECTURE IN THE
EARLY ATLANTIC COLONIES

Emily Mann

Royal charters that gave English adventurers sanction to settle in the Atlantic world from the late 1500s through the seventeenth century made provisions for defense a priority. To "inhabit and remain," in the words of the Virginia Company's charter of 1606, the colonists were authorized to "build and for-tify." The Avalon and Maryland charters of 1623 and 1632 encouraged settlers to construct "castles, forts, and other places of strength" for "the public and their own defence." A century later, in 1732, the new colonists of Georgia were expected to "erect forts, and fortify any place or places within our said colony" and to furnish them "with all necessary ammunition, provisions and stores of war."[1] Drawing on Roman law, according to which possession of territory required the physical presence and effective control necessary to resist an attack, these founding documents suggested that military prepared-ness was a responsibility as much as a right.[2] The license to fortify and to transport all necessary "habiliments of war, both for defence and offence" implicitly warned the far-flung colonists that their future security lay princi-pally in their own hands, yet at the same time expressed the crown's interest in each colony's strength and growth. The imperative to build a strong de-fense was in effect an offensive measure on the metropole's part to claim and maintain sovereignty over contested territories: a targeted preemptive strike aimed not simply at discouraging the resistance of indigenous peoples and opposition of European enemies, but at encouraging new bands of English colonists to settle and stay.

So much for words. To what extent were they matched by deeds? What priority did colonists on the ground give to constructing defenses, and what forms did their defenses take? To explore the meaning and materiality of building and fortifying in the process of English colonization, this chapter concentrates on the beginnings of permanent settlement in Virginia and Bermuda from 1607 and 1609 respectively, followed by the development of Barbados from 1627. Comparing settlements on islands in the Atlantic and the Caribbean, and on the North American mainland, reveals how the built defenses varied depending on the conditions of the territory and type of colony. It also invites consideration of their interconnections and interaction. Men, methods, and materials not only flowed from mother country to colony, but migrated between colonies too. Moreover, while the successive committees and councils established in London to oversee trade and foreign plantations were vested with responsibility for the colonies' "flourishing condition" and protection (ensuring the inhabitants were adhering to the conditions of the charters), the English authorities also became concerned with how the colonies could be "serviceable" to one another as constituent parts in a system of "mutual sustenance and defence."[3]

TO GAIN A FOOTHOLD

England's pursuit of territory for settlement in the late sixteenth and early seventeenth centuries was spurred on and shaped by the schemes and successes of its principal European rivals. Spanish and Portuguese claims that dominion rested on discovery, albeit marked by some ceremony of possession such as a solemn speech and the setting up of colors or a cross, presented both a challenge and an opportunity to other European colonists.[4] The challenge was that Spain and Portugal claimed to have discovered a vast amount of territory; the opportunity was that, by fortifying only parts of it, they left ground open for others. In the eyes of the English authorities, even if Spaniards had "touched here and there upon the coasts, built cottages, and given names to a river or a cape," these things did not entitle them to ownership. This was but "imaginary propriety."[5] By building forts, Richard Hakluyt the younger urged Queen Elizabeth I and her closest advisors in his "Discourse of Western Planting" of 1584, the English would be able to "hold fast our first footing" on overseas territory.[6]

Hakluyt accompanied his discourse with a practical note on how best to equip a colonizing voyage. Top on his list of "provisions tending to force" were "men expert in the art of fortification," followed by prefabricated platforms and all manner of artisans, from the makers of spades and shovels to carpenters, brick-makers and bricklayers, lime-makers and masons, and even makers of baskets for carrying earth to the ramparts.[7] His lawyer-cousin, Richard Hakluyt the elder, added that these men who were "cunning" in the

EMILY MANN

art of fortification should be able to "choose out places strong by nature to be fortified" and "plot out and direct workmen."[8]

The colonists on board the first ships sent by the Virginia Company of London (the younger Hakluyt was one of the eight men named in the 1606 charter) included four carpenters, two bricklayers, and a mason. Their instructions from the company were to settle in a safe harbor as far as possible up a navigable river, out of reach of passing Spanish or French ships and leaving no land between the settlement and the water that might be used against them by native peoples.[9] In May 1607, they began building on an island located on what they called the James River. Captain Christopher Newport, in seeking out the "most apt and securest place," was also keen that the settlement should cause the least "offence and distaste" to the local inhabitants, but the settlers nonetheless raised a fortress "with the ablest and speediest means they could."[10] The craftsmen were instructed to work "first for the company and then for private men"—"public and necessary use" came before private comfort.[11] The colonists sent by the Virginia Company of Plymouth, granted land to the north of the territory allotted to its London-based sister company, took a similar approach in founding their settlement the same summer: the first days and weeks after they disembarked near the mouth of the river Kennebec (then called Sagadahoc) were spent laboring "hard in the trenches" and "about the fort."[12]

Each colony took the form of a military outpost; fort and town were one. "The fort is called [. . .] James Town," reported William Strachey, the London company's secretary in 1610.[13] Strachey described how the dwellings, storehouses, and a church were enclosed within three timber palisades joined by a bulwark at each corner, the triangular form following the contours of an elevated piece of ground, and archaeological investigations have confirmed that this was the design.[14] The Plymouth company's settlement, called Fort St. George, was built in a modified star shape and likewise molded to the land. That sketches of both forts very quickly fell into Spanish hands is evidence of the external threat; Spain was watching.[15] As with Jamestown, archaeological excavations have verified the layout shown on the map of Fort St. George, but the progress which this image suggests had been made in a matter of months was almost certainly exaggerated—for promotional purposes, or perhaps even in the awareness that it might reach enemy eyes. The local people were harder to fool. The reason why Fort St. George was abandoned in 1608 is not certain, but uneasy relations with the local people are likely to have contributed to the English colonists' swift departure.

It is known that local tribes repeatedly attacked Jamestown, where the colonists stayed on but struggled to survive. Living in fear and facing famine, they were soon desperate for resources and reinforcements, and neither of the two supply voyages in 1608 provided adequate relief. Jamestown's council president Captain John Smith blamed the delay in "laying a foundation" in Virginia on a lack of skilled settlers and entreated the company to send thirty carpenters and other craftsmen rather than a thousand more settlers "such as we have" (by which he meant unskilled gentlemen who were not disposed to doing much for themselves).[16] When the bigger and better-equipped third supply fleet of 1609 sailed into a storm and the flagship was wrecked on the uninhabited islands of Bermuda, around five hundred miles east of the mainland, it might have been the final blow to the Virginia colony, but the disaster was transformed into a providential "discovery." Recognizing the islands' potential as a supply base for strengthening the mainland settlement and English trade routes, the Virginia Company in 1612 attained a new charter to colonize Bermuda. That the islands were initially referred to as Virginiola signals the supporting role they were understood to play from the start.

Spanish sailors had landed on the remote Atlantic islands in the early sixteenth century (the commander Juan de Bermudez apparently giving them the name Bermuda), and again in 1603, but left them unoccupied. In 1611, after reports of the English shipwreck spread, King Philip III claimed Bermuda for Spain, but he soon received intelligence that the Virginia Company (which had renamed the territory the Somers Isles after its own admiral) was preparing to send a ship equipped with "whatever is necessary to erect a fort," intending to "secure a better footing and continue more conveniently in their design."[17] The Spanish authorities, regarding the combined English colonies of Virginia and Bermuda to be a "danger to their West Indies," determined to act swiftly to prevent their growth.[18] It was with this threat and the troubled experience of building Jamestown in mind (not to mention the failure of the Plymouth venture and the earlier loss of the Roanoke colony) that the Virginia Company's investors took Hakluyt's advice more seriously and in 1612 appointed a master carpenter of the City of London, Richard Moore, as the islands' first governor. Moore was the likely author of *The Carpenter's Rule* (1602), a manual that instructed masons, joiners, and shipbuilders how to avoid the "common errors" that led to material waste and thus loss of profits for company and city.[19] His commission from the Virginia Company, echoing its earlier instructions to settlers on the mainland, stated that his priority after landing "must be to look out some convenient place wherein to set yourselves fortifying in places convenient as your means will afford."[20]

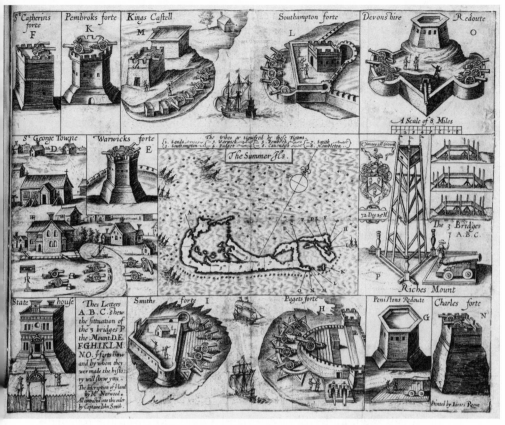

FIGURE 1.1. A Mappe of the Somer Isles and Fortresses, *from Captain John Smith's* The Generall Historie of Virginia, New-England, and the Summer Isles, *London, 1624. Documenting the American South, University of North Carolina at Chapel Hill Libraries.*

Captain John Smith, in his *Generall Historie of Virginia, New-England, and the Summer Isles* (1624), described Moore's "industry in fortifying" and illustrated it with a map (Fig. 1.1).[21] One of the earliest surviving images of Bermuda, Smith's print is dominated by views of ten stone fortifications, eight or nine of which were completed or begun under Moore's governorship between 1612 and 1615.[22] The views surround a map of Bermuda as though the forts formed a solid ring around the islands, reinforcing the reef of rocks represented by crosses along the coastline. Yet such was the danger of the reef to outsiders, dramatized by the masts of wrecked ships jutting above the waves, that forts were needed only where the land was not protected by this natural barrier, to the east. As the key letters on the map show, this is where

Defensive Architecture in the Early Atlantic Colonies

Moore set about fortifying. The rocks made the country "very strong," Smith explained, to which the adventurers "added by art."[23]

Smith's schematic representations of the forts might be read as pure propaganda, a visual manifestation of his promotional tract, but archaeological investigations of the structural remains have found that the essential forms shown are reasonably accurate.[24] They mark a departure from the timber and earth defenses built at Jamestown and Fort St. George, and Roanoke before them, which were in the European tradition of bastioned structures enclosing settlements. With no internal threat to deal with (apart from unruly settlers), Bermuda's forts were directed against enemy ships and designed both to counter and to launch an attack. The low, thick-walled masonry towers and gun platforms bear comparison with the chain of "device forts" and blockhouses developed along the south coast of England under Henry VIII, in the face of the French and Spanish threat.[25]

Bermuda's defenses also incorporated elements that reflect the influence of Continental theories and practices on English military architecture. According to an account by Nathaniel Butler, the colony's governor from 1619 to 1622, who added to the works begun by Moore, ravelins were built at Southampton Fort.[26] These triangular bastions or outworks had been recommended for rapid defense by Paul Ive in *The Practise of Fortification* (1589), one of the earliest treatises on the subject printed in English, and similar upgrades were made to Henry VIII's south coast forts, such as Pendennis Castle in Cornwall, under Elizabeth I and after.[27] Moreover, the rectangular and hexagonal towers shown in Smith's map are likely to have been conceived as an improvement on the Henrician rounded bastions, which were hard to protect from enemy fire.[28] Nonetheless, the English builders in Bermuda seem for the most part to have adapted familiar coastal-defense types to new conditions. The low height of most of the structures meant they were less exposed to attack from ships out at sea, but it is also possible that the designers had hurricanes in mind.[29] The walls were not only made from the local limestone, but in part hewn directly out of the bedrock. Smith's depictions of Charles Fort and Devonshire Redoubt emphasize the relationship he praised between nature and art — the former forged out of a mass of rock, the latter seeming almost to erupt from the mounds of earth below — and remains of the early forts reveal the extent, considerable in some cases, to which they were fused with their natural setting.[30] Governor Butler remarked that his work at Southampton Fort was designed so that the adjoining natural rock would add to the appearance of strength.[31]

To build on strong natural foundations not only maximized defensive

EMILY MANN

capabilities while minimizing demands on labor and materials—a crucial consideration for settlers with limited resources or hope of military assistance from England—but also gave the occupation and coercion of colonization an appearance of legitimacy. Edmund Spenser, a neighbor of Walter Raleigh's in the Munster plantation in Ireland, wrote in a poem dated 1596 that a new colony "from earth's base groundwork should begin," while Hakluyt recommended "planting forts" as if it were an act of nature rather than military control.[32] The seamless collaboration between man and nature was a common theme in the promotion, or justification, literature that celebrated England's "providential" settlement of Bermuda and other lands. Contemporary authors would have been familiar with Thomas More's *Utopia*, first published in 1516, which itself drew on Amerigo Vespucci's descriptions of his voyages to the New World printed a decade before. Of Utopia's defenses, More wrote that "the landing is so surely fenced, what by nature, and what by workmanship of men's hands, that a few defenders may drive back many armies."[33] Bermuda's rocky reefs were likewise conceived as a fence or curtain wall around the fortifications (the poet Edmund Waller described the islands as "wall'd with rocks"), and the sea as their moat.[34] Nature and art are one in Smith's definition of the islands' natural defenses in architectural terms, conjuring up a picture of Bermuda itself as a castle or fort: "no place known," he said, "has better walls, nor a broader ditch."[35] The conception of the colony as a defensible edifice drew additional strength from the implicit comparison to the mother country. England is described in Shakespeare's *Richard II* (c.1595) as a "fortress built by nature," set in a sea "which serves it in the office of a wall, or as a moat defensive to a house"; and the poet George Wither, in a work published the year before Smith's *Generall Historie*, wrote that God "hath (as it were) moated this island with the sea" and "walled it with natural bulwarks."[36]

Harder to defend, in literary as well as literal terms, was the colony on the American mainland. In the 1630s, a six-mile-long "strong palisade" wall was built across the Virginian peninsula between the James and York Rivers, turning a 300,000-acre tract of the peninsula in effect into an island.[37] The lack of any such defined and therefore more defensible frontier had helped lose the Virginia Company its charter in 1624. It is no coincidence that Smith's promotional *Generall Historie* was rushed into print amid the crisis that led to the crown taking control of the American colony that year. In a single day in 1622, according to the English accounts, the Powhatan people launched an attack that killed one-third of the settlers. At the end of his governorship of Bermuda in early 1623, Butler visited Virginia and helped lead attacks against Native Americans. On his return to England he delivered an indictment entitled "The Unmasked Face of Our Colony in Virginia."[38] The colony's governor, council, and assembly responded to Butler's scorn for Virginia's weakness by arguing that while there may be "no fortifications against a foreign enemy," the colonists' houses were "strongly fortified against the Indians." James City, Flowerdieu Hundred, Newport News, Elizabeth City, Charles City, Henrico, and "diverse private plantations" were "mounted with great ordnance."[39] The Virginia Company thus stressed that the principal threat to its control of the territory, namely the resistant indigenous population and the geographical spread of settlement, required an architectural strategy different from that which Butler had put into action as governor in Bermuda. Conditions on the mainland, and the fortification of dispersed individual plantations, had more in common with the colonization of Ireland, which was likewise under scrutiny at this time.[40] To its cost, the Virginia Company had failed to build a visibly strong defense of the interests of its investors back in England.

The problem of image-making for the Virginia colony is suggested by Smith's reuse in 1624 of his 1612 map of the territory, on which the anglicization of Native American place names fails to overcome the sheer scale of the land. A line of crosses demarcates the "discovered" and the vaster unknown, thus exposing the limits of colonial knowledge and control. By contrast the map at the center of his image of Bermuda, based on a survey completed by Richard Norwood in 1616–17, affirms the comprehensive occupation and ownership of the islands. The familiar forms of the built fortifications (drawings of which Smith may have acquired from Butler) offered reassurance of their protection. With company men's names imprinted both on the land and in the names of the forts, the image declared the company's investment in administering and defending the island, and therefore the company itself as a safe investment. The stark difference between the two maps illuminates why the crown revoked the Virginia Company's charter and allowed the Bermuda Company to carry on.

A 1626 engraving based on Norwood's map (Fig. 1.2) expresses Bermuda's pivotal importance for English interests in the Atlantic world, distorting geography and scale to show the islands in relation to Virginia and New England (top left and right) and Hispaniola (bottom left).[41] In his written description of the islands, Norwood, who like Butler was also employed in Virginia, emphasized their value "for the easy and commodious planting of other parts of this new world."[42] Bermuda's security strengthened the fledgling colonies on the American mainland and encouraged the settlement of a series of islands in the Caribbean—St. Kitts in 1624, Barbados in 1627, Nevis in 1628,

EMILY MANN

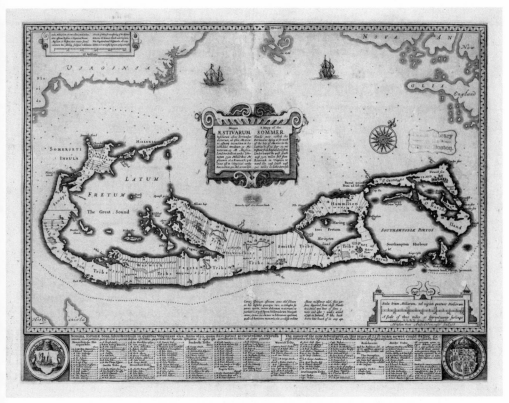

FIGURE 1.2. A Mapp of the Sommer Ilands, *engraved by Abraham Goos*
after Richard Norwood's survey, Amsterdam, 1626. Courtesy of the
Norman B. Leventhal Map Center at the Boston Public Library.

Providence Island in 1629, and Antigua and Montserrat in 1632—and the
men who had demonstrated their "cunning" in Bermuda's fortification found
their skills in demand elsewhere.

ENTRENCHMENT AND EXPANSION

When in 1638 the Providence Island Company's investors (most of them veterans of the Virginia, Bermuda, and New England companies) were seeking
"a man of ability in regard of the danger from the Spaniard," they appointed
Butler governor and made overseeing the fortifications and military training
his "principal care."[43] He was one of many men who played a cross-colonial
role in the early years of development. Providence Island's first governor,
Philip Bell, was poached directly from Bermuda, where he was governor
from 1627 to 1629, and among the men Bell brought with him was the for-

tifications expert Samuel Axe. The commission Bell was sent from England in 1631 contained the stern edict that "None to be allowed to leave the island until it is fully fortified and peopled."[44] As in Bermuda, the natural strengths of Providence Island were exploited so that Spanish invaders (twice repelled) found it "naturally fortified and more so by art."[45]

Building on his experience in Bermuda and Providence Island, Bell took up the governorship of Barbados in 1641. His appointment and relatively long employment, until 1650, suggests that his experience under two companies was considered to be useful even for a different kind of proprietary colony. Founded in 1627, the English settlement of Barbados was not carried out under one company. In the early years two proprietors claimed and fought over the island: Sir William Courteen and the Earl of Carlisle, who eventually wrested control.[46] The divisions and disgruntlements caused by this conflict, and by Carlisle's uncompromisingly commercial approach to his proprietorship, hindered the development of forts. Henry Colt, who wrote an account of visiting Barbados in 1631, demanded of the settlers: "What places have you of defence?"[47] Two decades later, Richard Ligon, in his *True and Exact History of the Island of Barbados* (1657), recounted how fortifications in Carlisle Bay were in the process of being pulled down and rebuilt, having been found "pernicious."[48] So neglected had the defenses been by the proprietor, Ligon wrote, that the planters refused to call Carlisle by that name.[49] While Thomas Loftfield has called this the "period of local responsibility" for fortifications on the island, Ligon's text suggests that the locals, themselves at odds, placed responsibility firmly with the absent proprietor.[50]

Colt raised the specter of the Spanish routing of the English and French from the island of St. Christopher (St. Kitts) in 1629, when the French fort was "sacked, burnt and the men slain in less than one night."[51] Yet what that invasion was more likely to have suggested to the Barbados planters was that one or two isolated forts were of limited use to an island of individual property holdings.[52] Over the decades that followed Colt's visit, the colonists in Barbados developed a complex system of defense that combined public and private projects and incorporated the militarization of people as well as land.

In conjunction with forts in the main towns of Oistin's, Bridgetown, Holetown, and Speightstown, the governors oversaw the creation of a chain of batteries or sconces along the twenty-four-mile exposed western shore, a linear system of defense similar to that developed on Nevis and which Bell had overseen in Providence Island.[53] Bell's muster master general, William Rudyerd, had in 1634 returned to London and advised the Providence Island Company that their possession could easily be fortified by adding to the existing structures with a series of small timber and sand forts along the shoreline.[54] The company directed the colonists to use Rudyerd's ideas, and there is evidence that Bell drew on them in Barbados too, creating a line of defenses that incorporated (as Ligon described it) a combination of "trenches, and rampiers, with pallisadoes, horn-works, curtains, and counter-scarps."[55] Timber and sand defenses were bolstered by stone where extra strength was required. The trenches, once dug, were planted with cacti and thorns—perhaps the ultimate collaboration between nature and art.

That a fairly strong line of defense was in place by the time Cromwell's fleet arrived to confront the royalist settlers in 1651, after a decade of Bell's governorship, is suggested by the reports of surveillance swimmers that the fleet's general sent out at night. These led the general to conclude that, if the island resisted, his forces could subdue it only by preventing trade ships from arriving—in effect, besieging the whole island without attempting to invade.[56] As it was, the general could order little more than quick, surprise raids, which helped give Parliament's supporters on the island an upper hand in bringing about negotiations. The island's strength, and the independence it could potentially thereby assert, encouraged the restored crown to take control of the colony in 1663.

From then on, funds for public works including fortifications were supposed to come out of the duties imposed by Charles II, but islanders complained that they never saw this money again. Requests from England for information about the forts were frequent in this period, and tension over their condition and cost is palpable. In 1680, Governor Jonathan Atkins reported that artillery was mounted at fifteen stone fortifications along the coast, the construction of which had cost the island "a great deal of money"; by 1695, Governor Francis Russell could record twenty-two different structures.[57] Russell bemoaned the lack of ditches and palisades around the forts, but plans received by the Board of Trade in 1696 are striking for the variety of defensive forms they show had been adopted. They display an inventive approach to the physical environment of each site that is comparable to the adaptation seen in Bermuda.[58] Despite the variety, though, many of these structures took the essential form, as in Bermuda, of a gun platform defined by a rampart or parapet pierced with embrasures for guns, ranged at different angles to cover the bay; and they were likewise low-lying and constructed of the local stone. Bermuda's forts typically had a keep or a redoubt to the rear of the gun platform, and the Barbados plans contain examples of a similar layout—for example, at Holetown Fort (Fig. 1.3), excavation of which revealed a guardhouse built to the rear and, generally, that the remains con-

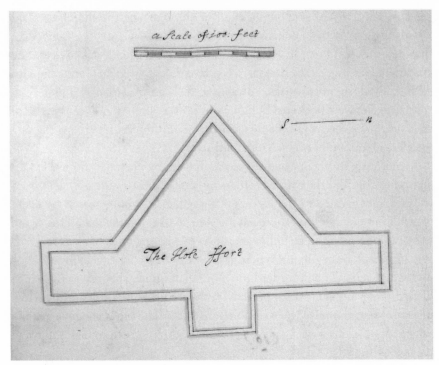

a Scale of 100: feet

The Hole ffort

FIGURE 1.3. *Plan of Holetown Fort, from "Ground Plats of all the Forts, Batteries and Magazines in Barbadoes, with their Names and number of Guns. Rec. from thence in September 1696," British Library Add. MS 14034, 18v. Detail, author.*

formed well to the plan.[59] In Bermuda, the man-made fortifications took advantage of the natural defense of a rocky shoreline; in Barbados, they had to work with flatter, lower-level conditions. Most sit on or very near to the beach, as can be observed today at Maycock's Bay (Fig. 1.4), designed to confront directly the risk of enemy landings as Rudyerd had intended in Providence Island, and able to communicate with ships acting as floating forts.[60]

Meanwhile, planters' houses were "built in the manner of fortifications" with the aim of controlling servants and slaves.[61] In Barbados, fortifications and plantation houses can thus be seen to have worked together as part of a composite system of defense that addressed internal and external threats. Their dual and interdependent role, forming a kind of collective type, is embedded in the name of the first plantation in Barbados—Fort Plantation or Plantation Fort. The trace of similar seventeenth-century architectural forms still visible in the entrances to Holetown Fort (Fig. 1.5) and St. James's Church close by (Fig. 1.6) hints at the fluid, hybrid nature of types more generally.[62] In a kind of privatization of defense that reflected the individualistic

EMILY MANN

FIGURE 1.4. *Maycock's Fort, St. Lucy, Barbados, April 2011. Author.*

FIGURE 1.5. *Entrance to Holetown Fort (now Holetown Police Station), St. James, Barbados, April 2011. Author.*

FIGURE 1.6. *South entrance to St. James's Church, Barbados, April 2011. Author.*

enterprise of the island, the plantations each made provisions for their own protection; a survey of Fort Plantation dating from around 1650 shows it had its own powder mill and saltpeter house. Yet they also worked in conjunction. Ligon wrote, "If any tumult or disorder be in the island, the next neighbor to it, discharges a musket, which gives the alarm to the whole island."[63] Bell can be assumed to have adapted this system from that employed in Providence Island, where the colonists were given elaborate instructions for sending signals from one part of the island to the next on the approach of any suspect ship.[64] Sounding the alarm was eventually outlawed in Barbados, after too many false alarms.

Governor Butler's exhortation to the settlers in Bermuda "to be soldiers," with its echo of Niccolo Machiavelli's argument for the value of local militias in *The Prince*, anticipated and summed up what was to be a widespread and persistent demand in the Atlantic world.[65] In 1631, Colt praised the English settlers of St. Christopher for living like soldiers, and Bell made reorganizing the militia in Barbados a priority so that by the late 1640s it was believed to consist of "10,000 foot, as good men and as resolute as any in the world."[66] Barbados's western line of defense allowed for alarms to be sent quickly (once the firing of guns had been prohibited) and militia to move easily along it.

EMILY MANN

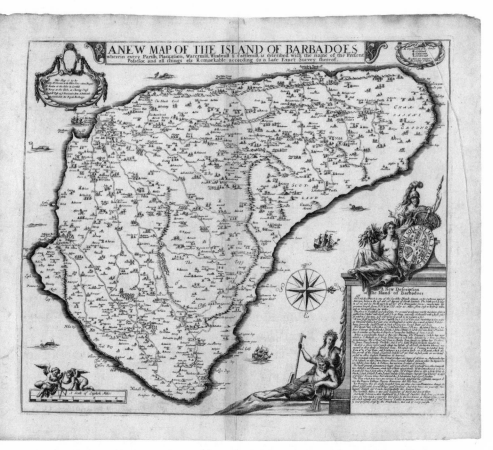

FIGURE 1.7. A New Map of the Island of Barbadoes, *after a survey by Richard Ford,*
London, ca. 1675–76. Courtesy of the John Carter Brown Library at Brown University.

One contemporary account even records militia lining up between batteries,
forming a human wall. People and plantations were together organized for
the maximum defensive effect. In the first known survey map of Barbados,
published in Ligon's *True and Exact History*, the plantations appear to be
lined up almost like troops along the coast. Richard Ford's map, produced
around 1675, shows the entire territory studded with English names (Fig.
1.7). This can be interpreted as a visual testimony to Henry Whistler's description of the island in 1655 as "fully inhabited" and evocative of More's
line in *Utopia*: "They have in the country in all parts of the shire, houses or
farms builded."[67] In Smith's print of Bermuda (Fig. 1.1), the map shows the
division of land and inhabitants into tracts called "tribes," evoking the tribes
and tributes paid in ancient Rome. These were separated and further divided

Defensive Architecture in the Early Atlantic Colonies   45 by public pathways (around thirty of these tribe roads still exist) and laid out with towns near the shoreline, each town eventually having its own church. To be "fully fortified and peopled," as the Providence Island edict put it, was considered mutually reinforcing.

From offshore, the visual effect of this construction and organization could be powerful. The French traveler Guillaume Coppier, who had been an indentured servant in St. Christopher during the Spanish invasion in 1629 and published an account of his voyages and experiences in the colonies in 1645, was struck by what he saw of Bermuda. The impression he gained from his ship, which strong winds had blown toward the shoreline, was that it was being "divinely used" by the English, who had built fortified houses or castles and continued to build fortresses that looked "almost impregnable."[68] Governor Butler had earlier noted that his work at Southampton Fort was designed to make "a very fair show out at sea," though he warned the Bermuda Company that without sufficient munitions even the colony's best forts "are little better than scare-crows."[69] Asked by some of Bermuda's settlers to cease or postpone the work on the fortifications in order to devote more labor and resources to improving general living conditions, Butler had replied, "In vain we build houses and churches, if we do not provide for the preservation of them when we have done so. There is no other way to do this except by providing adequate fortification at the mouths of the harbours."[70] Yet he perhaps underestimated the more encompassing power of appearances. As Hugo Grotius summed up in *The Free Sea*, published in 1609 (the year of the Bermuda shipwreck) and translated by Hakluyt soon after, "And he which hath built shall become lord of the soil."[71] Butler paid special attention to the development of the town of St. George. As well as designing the fashionable yet defensible State House, he completed the construction of a solid timber church on a rise in the town (where the rebuilt church still stands), requesting from the company in London bells for which they would build a steeple.[72] These buildings, expressing civic and religious power, dominated the townscape as well as the view from the harbor, and the representation of this view alongside the forts in Smith's image (Fig. 1.1) suggests the established town's participation in the colony's defense.[73]

An account of Barbados dating from 1666–67 describes the appearance of military might and magnificence seen at a small distance from the coast: "Their buildings, very fair and beautiful . . . present themselves like castles," the eyewitness observed, adding that the sugar works, slave huts, and other buildings were "like so many small towns, each defended by its castle."[74] The impression gained was that a well-managed invasion of the island would be "too great a task for any Prince in Europe."[75] It was a strong endorsement of Leon Battista Alberti's suggestion that victories could be won "by the art and skill of architects" as much as by "the conduct or fortune of generals."[76]

The importance of being seen to fortify is apparent in Governor Russell's comprehensive report on the defenses of Barbados sent to the Board of Trade in Whitehall in 1695: "Had not the French known of my reinforcing" of the forts, he wrote, "I dare swear that we should have had them here."[77] That these signals were picked up and interpreted as intended is suggested by a French map produced in 1702, and printed in the account of the priest and suspected spy Jean-Baptiste Labat in 1722, which defines the island purely in terms of its defenses.[78] Another French plan from 1719 even includes two forts that were never completed, as if its author had been duped into believing the country's defenses to be stronger than they were.[79] An ordnance office engineer sent from England to survey the forts in 1696 scoffed that they "would serve only to deceive the island but not to defend it" — not such a worry, if their enemies were deceived too.[80] The engineer inadvertently pointed to the great psychological value of the fortifications.

It was important to Russell that the metropole, as much as the French, should see him building and fortifying. In his report, Russell gave evidence that he was fulfilling his duty, as colonial governor, to attend to the island's defense capabilities. Shortly afterwards, a dispatch from the Barbados Council made explicit that those capabilities relied on intercolonial connections and collaboration. It stressed to the English authorities the "great importance of Bermuda to the colonies in America," and warned that if these islands (by then under crown control following the company's loss of its charter in 1684) should fall into the wrong hands, their enemies could "with eight or ten small vessels easily stop or destroy the trade of the West Indies and make themselves masters thereof."[81] Likewise, the lines of defense developed in Barbados also served St. Kitts, Nevis, Antigua, Barbuda, and Montserrat lying to the west — Barbados had been, as the assembly put it in 1699, a "bulwark and defence to our neighbouring islands."[82] In England's emerging empire, no island was an island, and the frontiers to be fortified were fluid.

NOTES

1. Many of the charters and related documents relevant to North America are available online at *The Avalon Project*, http://avalon.law.yale.edu (May 20, 2015). The same or similar wordings were used in successive charters.

2. For a detailed discussion of the charters and directives dealing with defense, see Ken MacMillan, *Sovereignty and Possession in the English New World: The Legal Foun-*

dations of Empire, 1576–1640 (Cambridge: Cambridge University Press, 2006), particularly 79–147.

3. Quotations from the instructions for the Council for Foreign Plantations, 1670–72, and the Council of Trade and Foreign Plantations, 1672–74, in Charles McLean Andrews, *British Committees, Commissions and Councils of Trade and Plantations, 1622–1675* (Baltimore: Johns Hopkins Press, 1908), 117 and 130.

4. For the "symbolically significant gestures" by which Europeans claimed possession, see Patricia Seed, *Ceremonies of Possession in Europe's Conquest of the New World 1492–1640* (Cambridge: Cambridge University Press, 1995).

5. Elizabeth I to the Spanish ambassador, Don Bernardino de Mendoza, in William Camden, *The History of the Most Renowned and Victorious Princess Elizabeth* (London: R. Bentley, 1688), 255.

6. Richard Hakluyt, *Discourse of Western Planting, 1584*, ed. David B. Quinn and Alison M. Quinn (London: Hakluyt Society, Extra Series 45, 1993), chapter 15.

7. Ibid., chapter 21.

8. Richard Hakluyt (the elder), "Inducements to the liking of the voyage intended towards Virginia" (1585), in John Brereton, *A Briefe and True Relation of the Discoverie of the North Part of Virginia* (London, 1602), 25–36 (34–35).

9. "Instructions Given by Way of Advice," in *The Jamestown Voyages under the First Charter, 1606–1609*, 2 vols., ed. Philip L. Barbour (Cambridge: Cambridge University Press for the Hakluyt Society, Second Series 136, 1969), 1:49–54.

10. William Strachey, "A True Repertory of the Wracke, and Redemption of Sir Thomas Gates Knight; upon, and from the Ilands of the Bermudas: his Comming to Virginia, and the Estate of that Colonie then, and after, under the Government of the Lord La Warrre, July 15, 1610," in *Hakluytus Posthumus; or, Purchas His Pilgrimes*, ed. Samuel Purchas, 4 vols. (London: Henrie Fetherstone, 1625), 4:1734–58 (1752).

11. Barbour, *Jamestown Voyages*, 53.

12. See "The Davies Journal of the 1607 North Virginia Voyage," in *The English New England Voyages, 1602–1608*, ed. David B. Quinn and Alison M. Quinn (London: Hakluyt Society, 1983), 397–441 (432–33).

13. Strachey, "True Repertory," 1753.

14. Ibid., 1752–53. For a firsthand account of the excavations by the head archaeologist, see William M. Kelso, *Jamestown: The Buried Truth* (Charlottesville and London: University of Virginia Press, 2006).

15. For the sketch of Jamestown, see Barbour, *Jamestown Voyages*, 238–40; for Fort St. George, see Quinn and Quinn, *New England Voyages*, 441–43, and Jeffrey P. Brain, "The John Hunt Map of the First English Colony in New England," *Northeast Historical Archaeology* 37 (2008): 69–74.

16. See Smith's letter to the Virginia Company of 1608, in John Smith, *The Generall Historie of Virginia, New-England, and the Summer Isles* (London: Michael Sparkes, 1624), 70–72.

17. Letter from the Spanish ambassador in London, Don Alonso de Velasco, to King Philip III, June 18, 1612, in Alexander Brown, *The Genesis of the United States* (Boston and New York: Houghton Mifflin, 1891), 560.

18. Letter from the English ambassador in Madrid, Lord Digby, to Lord Salisbury, March 9, 1612 (1613?), in ibid., 539.

19. Allen Mardis Jr., "Richard Moore, Carpenter," *Virginia Magazine of History and Biography* 92, no. 4 (1984): 416–73 (419).

20. Moore's commission, granted April 27, 1612, is cited in J. H. Lefroy, *Memorials of the Bermudas*, 2 vols. (London: Spottiswoode, 1876; repr. Bermuda: Bermuda Historical Society and Bermuda National Trust, 1981), 1:59.

21. Smith, *Generall Historie*, 178.

22. Ibid., 178. For a fuller discussion of the image, see Emily Mann, "First Lines of Defence: The Fortification of Bermuda in the Seventeenth Century," in *"The Mirror of Great Britain": National Identity in Seventeenth-Century British Architecture*, ed. Olivia Horsfall Turner (Reading: Spire, 2012), 51–71. See also Neil Kennedy, "William Crashaw's Bridge: Bermuda and the Origins of the English Atlantic, 1609–1624," in *English Atlantics Revisited*, ed. Nancy L. Rhoden (Montreal and Kingston: McGill-Queen's University Press, 2007), 107–35 (122–23).

23. Smith, *Generall Historie*, 169 and 172.

24. Edward Harris provides a comprehensive assessment of the forts, principally from an archaeological perspective, in Edward Harris, *Bermuda Forts, 1612–1957* (Bermuda: Bermuda Maritime Press, 1997). See also Harris's "Bermuda's First Forts, 1612–22," in *First Forts: Essays on the Archaeology of Proto-Colonial Fortifications*, ed. Eric Klingelhofer (Leiden and Boston: Brill, 2010), 105–25. More than half of the ten forts survive in some form, and in 2000 were designated a UNESCO World Heritage Site along with the town of St. George.

25. Harris, *Bermuda Forts*, 35 and 81. On the device forts, see D. Donnelly, "A study of Coastal Forts built by Henry VIII," *Fort* 10 (1982): 105–26. On their development in a colonial context, see Eric Klingelhofer, "Tudor Overseas Fortifications: A Review and Typology," in *First Forts*, ed. Klingelhofer, 65–83.

26. Butler cited by Harris, *Bermuda Forts*, 73.

27. Paul Ive, *The Practise of Fortification* (London: Thomas Man and Toby Cooke, 1589).

28. Harris, *Bermuda Forts*, 73.

29. Harris has pointed out that at least one of the towers with two stories in Smith's image can be seen from the surviving structure to have had only one (ibid., 70). Destruction by hurricane was the fate of many of Bermuda's early buildings, and continues to be. The standing remains of Southampton Fort were hit in 2004.

30. Harris, *Bermuda Forts*, 67, 69, and 70.

31. C. F. E. Hollis Hallett, ed., *Butler's History of the Bermudas* (Bermuda: Bermuda Maritime Museum, 2007), 223.

32. Edmund Spenser's line from "An Hymne to Heavenly Love" is cited by Eric Klingelhofer at the beginning of *Castles and Colonists: An Archaeology of Elizabethan Ireland* (Manchester and New York: Manchester University Press, 2010).

33. Raphe Robinson, trans., *Sir Thomas Moore's Utopia* (London: Bernard Alsop, 1624), bk 2, p. 46. This "newly corrected" edition, based on the first English translation published in 1551, appeared in the same year Smith published his *Generall Historie*. See Alfred A. Cave, "Thomas More and the New World," *Albion* 23, no. 2 (1991): 209–29.

34. Edmund Waller, "Battel of the Summer Islands," in *Poems &c* (London: Humphrey Moseley, 1645), 52.

35. Smith, *Generall Historie*, 175.

36. John of Gaunt in William Shakespeare, *Richard II*, act II, scene 1. George Wither, *The Hymnes and Songs of the Church* (London: George Wither, 1623), song 81 (a song for St. George's day), 55.

37. Philip Levy, "A New Look at an Old Wall: Indians, Englishmen, Landscape, and the 1634 Palisade at Middle Plantation," *Virginia Magazine of History and Biography* 112, no. 3 (2004): 226–65.

38. Susan Myra Kingsbury, ed., *Records of the Virginia Company of London, 1622–24*, 4 vols. (Washington, D.C.: Government Printing Office, 1906–35), 2:374–76.

39. The Governor, Council, and Assembly of Virginia to the King, February 1623, in W. Noel Sainsbury, ed., *Calendar of State Papers Colonial, Volume 1: 1574–1660* (henceforth abbreviated as *CSPC 1*), British History Online, http://www.british-history.ac.uk/report.aspx?compid=68994 (May 20, 2015).

40. For discussions of the connections between mainland America and Ireland, see Klingelhofer, *Castles and Colonists*; Robert Blair St. George, "Bawns and Beliefs: Architecture, Commerce, and Conversion in Early New England," *Winterthur Portfolio* 25, no. 4 (1990): 241–87; and Audrey Horning, *Ireland in the Virginian Sea: Colonialism in the British Atlantic* (Chapel Hill: University of North Carolina Press, 2013).

41. An engraved version of Norwood's map was registered at Stationers' Hall in 1622. The printed map shown, a proof without imprint, was made for John Speed's *Prospect of the Most Famous Parts of the World* (London: George Humble, 1627).

42. Vernon A. Ives, ed., *The Rich Papers: Letters from Bermuda, 1615–1646* (Toronto: University of Toronto Press, 1984), 380.

43. Karen Kupperman, *Providence Island, 1630–1641: The Other Puritan Colony* (Cambridge: Cambridge University Press, 1993), 275.

44. Company of Adventurers of Providence Island to Governor Bell, February 7, 1631, Sainsbury, ed., *CSPC 1*, British History Online, http://www.british-history.ac.uk/report.aspx?compid=69076 (May 20, 2015).

45. Kupperman, *Providence Island*, 289.

46. The governors appointed by each side, William Deane and Charles Wolverstone, both had previous experience in Bermuda.

47. J. Edward Hutson, ed., *The Voyage of Sir Henry Colt to the Islands of Barbados and St. Christopher: May–August 1631* (Bridgetown: Barbados National Trust, 2002), 18.

EMILY MANN

48. Richard Ligon, *True and Exact History of the Island of Barbados* (London: Humphrey Moseley, 1657), 100.

49. Ligon, *True and Exact History*, 100.

50. Thomas C. Loftfield, "Creolization in Seventeenth-Century Barbados: Two Case Studies," in *Island Lives: Historical Archaeologies of the Caribbean*, ed. Paul Farnsworth (Tuscaloosa and London: University of Alabama Press, 2001), 207–33 (208).

51. Hutson, *Voyage of Sir Henry Colt*, 18.

52. See Richard Pares, *War and Trade in the West Indies, 1739–1763* (Oxford: Clarendon Press, 1936), 227.

53. For the forts of Nevis, see Roger Leech, "'Within Musquett Shott of Black Rock': Johnson's Fort and the Early Defenses of Nevis," in *First Forts*, ed. Klingelhofer, 127–38 (136), and Tessa C. S. Machling, *The Fortifications of Nevis, West Indies, from the 17th Century to the Present Day: Protected Interests?* (Oxford: Archaeopress, 2012).

54. Kupperman, *Providence Island*, 197. Rudyerd, like many men employed in designing and building English fortifications in the Atlantic world, was a veteran of the Low Countries.

55. Ligon, *True and Exact History*, 100.

56. Larry Gragg, *Englishmen Transplanted: The English Colonization of Barbados, 1627–1660* (Oxford: Oxford University Press, 2003), 50.

57. Governor Atkins to William Blathwayt, April 1, 1680, in W. Noel Sainsbury and J. W. Fortescue, eds., *Calendar of State Papers Colonial, Volume 10: 1677–1680*, British History Online, http://www.british-history.ac.uk/report.aspx?compid=70001 (May 20, 2015). Governor Russell to the Lords of Trade and Plantations, August 25, 1695, in J. W. Fortescue, ed., *Calendar of State Papers Colonial, Volume 14: 1693–1696* (henceforth abbreviated as *CSPC 14*), British History Online, http://www.british-history.ac.uk/report .aspx?compid=70823 (May 20, 2015).

58. The plans are in British Library Add. MS 14034, 1–29. For local adaptations in Barbados, see Thomas Loftfield, "Creolization in Seventeenth-Century Barbados."

59. Maureen Bennell, "An Archaeological Survey of the Holetown Fort, Barbados," *Journal of the Barbados Museum and Historical Society* 48 (2002): 12–28.

60. Archaeological research at Maycock's Bay is ongoing as part of the Speightstown Archaeological Research Project.

61. Ligon, *True and Exact History*, 29.

62. Consider also Montserrat's Fort House Plantation. For Holetown Fort and St. James's Church, see Bennell, "Archaeological Survey of Holetown Fort," 27.

63. Ligon, *True and Exact History*, 29.

64. Kupperman, *Providence Island*, 31.

65. Hollis Hallett, *Butler's History*, 157. For the use of servants and slaves in militias, see Pares, *War and Trade*, 252–57.

66. Hutson, *Voyage of Sir Henry Colt*, 18. Ligon, *True and Exact History*, 100. For the division of land for defense purposes see Roger H. Leech, "'In What Manner Did They Devide the Land': The Early Colonial Estate Landscape of Nevis and St. Kitts," in

Estate Landscapes: Design, Improvement and Power in the Post-Medieval Landscape, ed. Jonathan Finch and Kate Giles (Woodbridge: Boydell Press, 2007), 191–204.

67. Henry Whistler in C. H. Firth, ed., *The Narrative of General Venables* (London: Longmans, 1900), 145. Robinson, *Sir Thomas Moore's Utopia*, bk 2, p. 47.

68. Guillaume Coppier, *Histoire et voyage des Indes Occidentales, et de plusieurs autres regions maritimes, & esloignées, divisé en deux livres* (Lyon: Jean Huguetan, 1645), 136.

69. Hollis Hallett, *Butler's History*, 223. Ives, ed., *The Rich Papers*, 229.

70. Hollis Hallett, *Butler's History*, 136.

71. Hugo Grotius, trans. Richard Hakluyt and ed. David Armitage, *The Free Sea* (Indianapolis: Liberty Fund, 2004), 27.

72. Hollis Hallett, *Butler's History*, 173.

73. On the development of the town, see Brent Russell Fortenberry, "Church, State, and the Space In Between: An Archaeological and Architectural Study of St. George's, Bermuda" (Ph.D. diss., Boston University Graduate School of Arts and Sciences, 2013).

74. Jerome S. Handler and Lon Shelby, eds., "A Seventeenth Century Commentary on Labor and Military Problems in Barbados," *Journal of the Barbados Museum and Historical Society* 34 (1973): 117–21 (118).

75. Campbell, *Some Early Barbadian History*, 246.

76. Leon Battista Alberti, *De Re Aedificatoria* (ca. 1445–50), excerpted in *Emergence of Modern Architecture: A Documentary History, from 1000 to 1800*, ed. Liane Lefaivre and Alexander Tzonis (London: Routledge, 2004), 55.

77. Governor Russell to the Lords of Trade and Plantations, August 25, 1695, in Fortescue, ed., *CSPC 14*, British History Online, http://www.british-history.ac.uk/report .aspx?compid=70823 (May 20, 2015).

78. The 1702 manuscript map is in British Library Maps K.Top.123.116. For the printed version, see Jean-Baptiste Labat, *Nouveau voyage aux isles de l'Amérique*, 6 vols (Paris: G. Cavelier and P.-F. Giffard, 1722), 4:387. For Labat's account of visiting Barbados, see John Eaden, trans. and abridg., with an introduction by Philip Gosse, *The Memoirs of Père Labat, 1693–1705* (London: Constable, 1931), 124.

79. Newberry Library, Ayer MS map 30, sheet 65.

80. Report of Talbot Edwards to the Board of Ordnance, following his return from Barbados in June 1698, in Cecil Headlam, ed., *Calendar of State Papers Colonial, Volume 18: 1700*, British History Online, http://www.british-history.ac.uk/report .aspx?compid=71376 (May 20, 2015).

81. The President and Council of Barbados to the Council of Trade and Plantations, September 8, 1696, in J. W. Fortescue, ed., *Calendar of State Papers Colonial, Volume 15: 1696–1697*, British History Online, http://www.british-history.ac.uk/report .aspx?compid=70867 (May 20, 2015).

82. Barbados General Assembly to Captain Talbot Edwards, November 10, 1699, in Cecil Headlam, ed., *Calendar of State Papers Colonial, Volume 17: 1699 and Addenda 1621–1698*, British History Online, http://www.british-history.ac.uk/report.aspx ?compid=71064 (May 20, 2015).

2

SEATS OF GOVERNMENT

THE PUBLIC BUILDINGS OF BRITISH AMERICA

Carl Lounsbury

Memory shaped the conceptual models of America's early public build-ings and the ceremonies associated with their functions. Many immigrant governors and mayors, magistrates and merchants, masons and carpenters could well recall the physical characteristics of English town halls, market houses, and shire halls with their arcades and colonnades, balconies, cupo-las with bells and clock faces, and walls prominently festooned with civic, manorial, and royal arms. Trimmed out in classical details, these prototypes had compass-headed openings, pilasters, cornices, pediments, parapets, and low hip roofs punctuated by cupolas, dormers, and balustraded roof walks. Prominently placed along broad thoroughfares and in open market squares, they were the unmistakable face of corporate authority. This was the civic design kit well understood by British subjects in North America in the late seventeenth and eighteenth centuries. Yet, there was a strong provincial filter that altered and sometimes rejected elements of that inheritance as local con-ditions reshaped English building types and construction practices. Minor public buildings such as town halls and courthouses were as often influenced by the form of provincial meetinghouses as by English civic architecture. In some places, the absence of towns forced local authorities to reconsider the plans and attributes of public buildings when set in rural locations. Provincial and local governments developed in ways that diverged distinctly from one region to another and from those in the mother country, which had a tremen-dous impact on the kinds of public buildings erected in the various colonies. Some places, especially seaports and large cities felt drawn to metropolitan ideas and tastes, whereas other localities with a well-established cohort of leaders were sometimes more reluctant to accept fashion as readily, having developed strong local building practices that were perceived as suitable to their needs and aspirations.

The construction of public buildings was usually a long process and sometimes a very contentious one. Opinions in communities and corporations often differed over the necessity and the costs of erecting a new town hall or courthouse. A reluctance to burden freeholders with a spike in taxes over a two- or three-year period to pay for new structures restrained authorities in some jurisdictions, while in other places disagreements over where to build sometimes retarded projects for years. Despite these impediments, the growth in the expenditure on public buildings in the American colonies increased significantly in the eighteenth century. However, that progress was uneven, straining the resources in sparsely populated backwater communities or those on the frontiers of settlement, which had to make do with rudimentary court buildings, while in wealthier and more established towns and counties the replacement of older structures often lead to the construction of larger and more pretentious buildings in the decades before the American Revolution.

ENGLISH PRECEDENTS

Eighteenth-century public buildings in the American colonies and the ceremonial rituals associated with them reflected the shared sensibilities of colonial subjects who were loyal to the crown and placed great stock in being part of an imperial order that protected civil liberties and nourished the rule of law. These structures were also emblematic of changing economic and social circumstances in England and her colonies. The refined Palladian Mansion House in York (1726–33) and the more protean City Hall in New York (1699–1701, enlarged 1763–64) were part of a rising tide of investment in public buildings erected in English and American cities and towns in the long century bracketed by the restoration of the monarchy in 1660 and the outbreak of the American Revolution in 1775. English public buildings provided many of the symbols and design precedents for America's town halls, courthouses, and statehouses that emerged at the beginning of the eighteenth century when the rapid growth in the population and wealth of a number of cities made it possible to construct corporate structures that sometimes matched the scale and ambitions of those in the mother country (Fig. 2.1).

Public buildings erected in English towns during this period were symbols of rising prosperity after a long period of urban stagnation throughout much of the country. Many English towns initiated programs of rebuilding and refining their architectural fabric, transforming many irregular streetscapes of wooden buildings with jettied gables into uniform brick rows and squares embellished in classical details.[1] Nowhere was this architectural renaissance more evident than in the construction of new civic halls, judges'

CARL LOUNSBURY

FIGURE 2.1. *Front of New York City Hall after it had been raised to three stories in 1763–64. Sketch by Pierre Du Simitière, ca. 1769. Library Company of Philadelphia.*

lodgings, and gaols. As many as 110 new county halls were erected across England during this long century.[2] The buildings grew larger in size, more complex in plan and function, and more ornate in design. Town halls, market houses, guildhalls, and shire halls, to list but a few of the many names given these civic structures, contained a variety of public functions from courtrooms to lockups, which sometimes produced odd juxtapositions of spaces such as grand assembly rooms located next to dungeons or fire engines stored in rooms with gunpowder. The ad hoc quality of the City Hall in New York, where down-on-their luck merchants were confined to debtors' quarters in the garret above the assembly chamber where their more solvent brethren debated economic issues, derives from this tradition of housing all sorts of corporate activities under one roof.

Two distinctive types of English public buildings — the market house and the county hall — influenced American forms.[3] The market house was the oldest and most basic type, which developed in the late medieval period in response to one of the primary functions of towns as centers of exchange. From small towns to great regional cities, economic life centered on specialized trades and the exchange and distribution of goods, in particular agricultural produce and foodstuffs necessary to feed urban populations. Markets were held in large open spaces in or near the center of town where country people and local tradesmen set up moveable wooden stalls and other flexible trading stands. In most thriving market towns, corporate officials or lords of the manor erected one- and two-story market houses where sheltered stalls could be rented to certain groups such as butchers.

More ambitious structures contained a second story above the open arcade where one or more rooms provided space for courts and corporate gatherings. Most town governments had two distinct bodies though of overlapping membership. As the executive arm, the mayor and aldermen convened meetings in an upstairs room in the market house where they discussed the administrative affairs of the corporation, including the regulation of the market. As magistrates of the borough or manorial court, many of the same officials met in a conspicuously public place to preside over judicial matters. Sometimes this meant that these local courts sat in taverns, while others were housed in a room in the market house. Through much of the seventeenth century there was little to distinguish these courtrooms as magistrates conducted the court's business around a long table on benches or in armchairs at the same level as the rest of the courtroom in a manner similar to the arrangement of early fittings in the Town Hall in Fordwich, Kent. A moveable railing at one end was the bar that separated those who had business from bystanders. However by the end of the century, certain new perceptions about the nature of the law helped transform the physical arrangement of these courtrooms. Out went the old, haphazard arrangement of magistrates' table and other portable fittings to be replaced by permanent and more ornate ones, which featured a raised and balustraded curved bench, ceremonial chief magistrate's chair with the royal arms overhead that conveyed an image of the hierarchy of authority emanating from the crown and vested in corporate magistrates. One of the grandest of these market houses with courtrooms in the upper story is the Abingdon Town or County Hall, Oxfordshire (formerly Berkshire), erected at a cost of nearly £3,000 in 1678–82 by Christopher Kempster, one of Christopher Wren's principal masons. Well designed for the diverse function of court, corporation, and market, the arcaded or colonnaded market house or town hall standing in the market place provided one of the models for American public buildings (Fig. 2.2).

FIGURE 2.2. *Town Hall, Abingdon, Oxfordshire, 1678–82.*
Early eighteenth-century engraving. Author.

The second influential building type was the county hall, the venue for quarter session and assize courts and the locus of ceremonial and social events that attracted the gentry to the leading shire towns. These structures were far larger than market houses since they had to accommodate much more than civic business. County government was vested in justices of the peace, men appointed by the crown to keep the peace and preside over the quarter session courts and the assizes in concert with professional crown judges who traveled different circuits twice a year. An array of ceremonies marked the occasion beginning with the sheriff and gentlemen of the region who often met the crown judges outside the city and accompanied them in a great procession into town. Special religious services were held before the opening of the assizes. The crown judges, the local gentlemen justices, lawyers, and civic officials marched through the street to the shire hall for the formal opening of the sessions. These judicial ceremonies reappeared in prominent American cities where the general courts of the provinces met. Divine service preceded the opening day of the courts, and judges and lawyers paraded through the streets of Boston to the courthouse on King Street. A similar procession of men in judicial gowns and wigs in Charleston accompanied the chief justice of South Carolina from his home to the statehouse at the corner of Broad and Meeting Streets.[4]

Investing in civic structures promised handsome dividends for county towns in an age when the business of the law courts was integrally bound with the social pursuits of a rising genteel society. To compete with rival towns, cities constructed costly buildings that not only enhanced the dignity of the law with imposing courtrooms but included large public spaces to accommodate gatherings of polite society which flocked to town during court season. Most buildings had no association with the market and were therefore enclosed on the ground floor and were located to one side of the marketplace or central square. Because of their orientation, they featured prominent columned and pedimented front façades with grand frontispieces such as those of the Northampton Sessions House (1675–78) and the Worcester Guildhall (1721–24), which marked entrances into courtrooms for criminal and civil cases or into spacious ceremonial halls. The public entrances to these courtrooms, which featured decorative symbols of judicial and corporate authority, were often through a screen or colonnade, emblematic of the openness of the judicial system. In addition, some county buildings contained assembly rooms given over to dancing and concerts, while one or two smaller rooms opened off them and served as card rooms and places for retirement and refreshments. Polite society, gathered for the county assizes, filled these entertaining rooms in the public buildings in Worcester, Doncaster, Hertford, Newark, and a host of other provincial towns.

TOWN HALLS AND COURTHOUSES IN BRITISH AMERICA
For most of the seventeenth century, public building scarcely existed in colonial America. Conditions worked against the construction of permanent market houses and court buildings. It took some years for initial settlements to coalesce into self-sustaining and self-governing counties and towns with well-established borders and the financial wherewithal to invest in civic architec-

CARL LOUNSBURY

ture. Some regions saw little need for such structures. When New Englanders needed to discuss public business, they filled the pews and benches of their Congregational meetinghouses since their Puritan beliefs did not ascribe numinous qualities to their places of worship. As discussed by Peter Benes in chapter 5, they thought of them as conveniently located public halls, suitable for town meetings, court sessions, or religious services. The idea that a place of worship could serve public functions was not unusual. Although at odds with their prelatic authority, Puritans simply followed the precedent of ecclesiastical courts that were held in some English churches. In lieu of the meetinghouse, some towns shifted their legal venues to a local tavern, another English tradition that still flourished in many places.[5]

It was not until the first decades of the eighteenth century that some New England town meetings and other public business began to vacate the meetinghouse for purpose-built town houses or town halls, especially in larger Massachusetts and Connecticut county towns with more heterogeneous populations of Baptists or Anglicans and subdivided parishes of Congregationalists.[6] Many of these structures contained courtrooms and served as county, as well as town, offices. There was little about them to distinguish them on the outside from their meetinghouse progenitors. A few had cupolas, but all were fully enclosed and lit with domestic-scale windows. The two-story framed town houses built in Marblehead, Massachusetts (1727–28), and Plymouth, Massachusetts (1749–50), exemplify the type. Each contains five bays along the long walls and is three bays wide and enclosed on the ground floor (Fig. 2.3). The Marblehead town house measures fifty by thirty feet with entrances on the short walls (as was the case in Plymouth originally). It now stands on granite piers installed in 1836 to accommodate a fire engine and market. Buildings such as these featured a large hall for municipal meetings and occasionally spaces for commercial activities. The second floor of town houses in larger shire towns, such as Salem, Marblehead, Cambridge, and Plymouth contained a courtroom and offices for local and county courts.

As in New England, the courthouses in the middle Atlantic colonies exhibited few distinctive characteristics that marked them out as specific building types. After early peripatetic lodgings in farmhouses and rural taverns, county courts found permanent homes in towns, but the earliest buildings were modest log and frame structures. These were later replaced by the middle of the eighteenth century by larger masonry structures. In 1724 the Chester County magistrates constructed a two-story rubble stone courthouse in Chester, the county town located on the Delaware River south of Philadelphia. Its short gable end faces the street with an eight-foot-deep polygo-

FIGURE 2.3. *Town House, Marblehead, Massachusetts, 1727–28.*
The building was raised on granite piers in 1836 to accommodate a
fire engine and public market. Arthur Haskell, HABS, 1934.

nal apse for the magistrates' bench opposite the two entrance doors on the
longer sidewall, which is perpendicular to the street. Unlike the New England
court buildings, the courtroom in the Chester courthouse is on the ground
floor with three jury rooms located above the stairs.[7] Other county towns in
Pennsylvania followed the lead of the Chester magistrates and erected two-
story masonry buildings, though none replicated the awkwardly sited apsi-
dal Chester courthouse. As in the northern colonies, the squarish rectangular proportions and central long-wall entrances of these public buildings
resembled the form of the churches and meetinghouses erected by Anglican,
Presbyterian, Lutheran, Reformed, and other congregations in the province.
Only the central cupolas and their location set them apart from their ecclesiastical neighbors. Following the precedent established by William Penn's
plan for Philadelphia, the magistrates in Lancaster, York County, placed their
county courthouses on a central square in the shire towns. The Lancaster
courthouse (mid-1730s) was brick and measured fifty by forty-eight feet; the

CARL LOUNSBURY

York courthouse (1756) was also brick and slightly larger at fifty-five by forty-five feet. This and other well-built but unpretentious courthouses suited the demands of these growing counties through the colonial period but were replaced by larger and more elaborate structures following the Revolution.

In the Chesapeake with its dispersed settlement of tobacco planters thinly spread along hundreds of miles of navigable waterways, the failure to establish towns had a profound impact on public building. In the absence of towns, this rural society had few commonly accepted venues of economic or political activity. Early courts were peripatetic, moving from one tavern or magistrate's plantation to another on a regular circuit. Gradually, Chesapeake society had to develop an alternative to the English tradition of situating public buildings in towns. Eventually, planters in the region began to accept the concept of geographic centrality as the most equitable means of determining where to locate county courthouses in a landscape nearly devoid of clustered settlements. County magistrates decided to build their buildings at isolated rural crossroads, which clearly had a profound effect on the form of these public structures. Deep in the countryside, there was little need for towers, dials, and bells, or two-story buildings with market arcades and balconies.[8] Although buildings specifically erected to house the county courts had appeared in Virginia, Maryland, and northeastern North Carolina by the third quarter of the seventeenth century, these early courthouses were no more than impermanent hole-set buildings, scarcely distinguishable from neighboring farmhouses.

With the growing wealth, stability, and power of the gentry who came to dominate Chesapeake society in the late seventeenth century, attitudes toward public building began to change. The professionalization of the law, the increased bureaucratic routine of the county court, and the identification of local government with gentry leadership led to greater spending on public buildings. In the long-established Tidewater region, brick replaced wood in the construction of new courthouses, which began to develop special attributes that set them apart. Some courthouses had compass-headed windows enlarged to fit the taller proportions of the building. Arcades also became an integral part of some of these structures. An English visitor to the small port of Yorktown in 1732 observed the construction of a "Court house or Town hall of Brick with a Piazza before it [which is] very handsome and Convenient."[9] The arcade clearly indicated in his mind the market house prototype. Here, and in other Virginia county seats such as King William, Hanover, and Isle of Wight, the building was not a two-story structure with

FIGURE 2.4. *Hanover County Courthouse, Virginia, ca. 1740. Author.*

an open ground floor (Fig. 2.4). Rather, the arcade was integrated into the hipped-roof design of a single-story structure where it stretched across the front façade with the entrance to the courtroom opening off the back of the piazza, as it was commonly known in Virginia. The English reference was secondhand, as the immediate precedent for the arcade in the region was the capitol in Williamsburg (1701–5), where an open arcade linked two wings of the provincial statehouse.[10]

Inside, the courtroom developed the same type of specialized fittings for magistrates and court officials that had emerged in English courts, though there were marked differences. Commonly understood English symbols, such as balustraded railings and elevated platforms, were incorporated into courtroom designs to express concepts of restricted access and places of deferential honor. Magistrates sat on a raised platform like their English brethren with the royal arms squarely placed above the pedimented, armed chair of the chief magistrate. However, below the curved railing of the bar was another curved bench occupied by jurymen instead of a large table where clerks and barristers sat in many English courtrooms. There was a small table for the county clerk just in front of the jury bench, and a few paces beyond it were two or three benches enclosed with a railing known as the lawyers' bar, a particular regional arrangement. Small, cramped seats set apart from the magistrates indicated that those who occupied them were by no means the social equals of the amateur gentlemen justices loftily perched on the magistrates' bench.[11]

MARKET HOUSES

If social and economic circumstances in rural New England and isolated courthouse grounds of the Chesapeake worked against the wholesale adaptation of English public building forms, a more receptive place for the transplanting of such elements were the major ports, provincial capitals, and large county towns stretching from New Hampshire to South Carolina. In the half-century between 1690 and 1740, Boston, New York, Philadelphia, and Charleston blossomed into entrepôts that rivaled such British ports as Hull, Bristol, and Glasgow. Population density was much greater in such places, with many inhabitants engaged in specialized trades and services. To feed this urban population, corporations in large cities as well as smaller towns, such as Providence, Perth Amboy, Lancaster, New Castle, Williamsburg, Norfolk, Fredericksburg, and New Bern, established public markets where produce and other items were sold several times a week. As in English market towns, city officials carefully regulated market hours and the quality and prices of basic foodstuffs. They erected imposing, two-story arcaded market houses and more modest one-story wooden structures set on paved masonry floors with stout posts supporting low-gabled roofs with deeply projecting jetties. Some functioned solely as places to vend meat and produce, but others had rooms overhead and were used as meeting places for courts and other public assemblies.

At the hub of this activity in Philadelphia was a two-story brick market house or courthouse erected in 1710–11 in the middle of High or Market Street at the intersection with Second Street. From its central location, with a cupola crowning the central apex of the roof, the building would not have looked out of place in an English market town. Queen Anne's arms hung over the frontispiece on the second-floor entrance on the front gable end that led to the public rooms shared by provincial, county, and municipal authorities. The arcaded market beneath the courthouse soon filled to capacity and in 1720 the city erected forty-eight additional stalls in a covered wing that was built at the west end of the building, and, when these too were fully occupied, another addition was made so that the market ran the full length of the block of High Street between Second and Third Streets where it was terminated at its west end by the jail (Fig. 2.5).[12]

In New York and Charleston the city markets were scattered across neighborhoods. New York had five markets by the time of the Revolution. One

FIGURE 2.5. Old Courthouse, *High Street, Philadelphia, Pennsylvania, 1710–11.*
Watercolor by William Breton, 1830. Philadelphia Athenaeum.

stood in the middle of Broadway on the west side of town a few blocks above
Trinity Anglican Church, and the others were spaced several blocks apart
along the East River close to the wharves.[13] Charleston's market houses were
also located near the wharves along the Cooper River where there were separate markets for fish and produce. The beef market stood prominently on the
northeast corner of Meeting and Broad Streets several blocks west of the river
in an area which formed one of the most impressive clusters of public build-

CARL LOUNSBURY

ings in colonial America. The market house shared this intersection with the Palladian-inspired South Carolina Statehouse (1753–56), St. Michael's Anglican Church (1752–61) with its colossal west portico, tower and steeple, which recalled St. Martin-in-the-Fields in London, and the smaller Treasury building.

While the market houses in these and other towns were modest workaday structures, a few such as Faneuil Hall, Boston (1742), the Fredericksburg Market House (ca. 1763), and the Brick Market in Newport (1772), were architecturally ambitious and illustrate the many purposes that corporations made of their upper stories. In 1740 merchant Peter Faneuil offered to build an elegant market house in Dock Square next to the town docks in Boston. Its citizens nearly turned this gift down because of the regulatory strings attached to a city-run market. Boston had a history of higglers sabotaging efforts to regulate markets even going so far as to pull down an earlier wooden market house in the same location.[14] However, with the support of provincial leaders and the principal merchants, the obstructionists were outvoted and a two-story brick market house was completed in 1742. Surrounded by open space around Dock Square where market activities spilled out from the building, Faneuil Hall must have made an impressive landmark for ships landing at the nearby docks. It measured one hundred by forty feet with an arcaded ground floor set off by Tuscan pilasters. Town meetings, which had formerly been held at the town house or courthouse on King Street, shifted to the second-story meeting room, which was capable of holding a thousand people and became the principal venue for grand public entertainments (Fig. 2.6).[15]

Further south, the diversions of urban life also attracted the gentry who lived in the countryside surrounding Fredericksburg, a small market and court town on the Rappahannock River in Virginia. In the late colonial period, the city erected a two-story, cruciform-shaped brick market house (approximately sixty by forty-two feet) that was trimmed with local sandstone. The partially arcaded ground floor flourished as a market, but it was the second story that drew the attention of the tobacco planters, for it functioned as an assembly room and was used on occasion as a venue for theatrical performances. A New England traveler described it as being "opened entirely for dissipation. It . . . contains a room for dancing and two for retirement and cards."[16] Damaged during the War for Independence, the building was thoroughly repaired through donations made by the local gentry who believed it to be a vital part of their community because it "rendered accommodation to polite and numerous assemblies by which youth were greatly

FIGURE 2.6. Faneuil Hall, *Boston, Massachusetts, 1742. Engraving by S. Hill after W. Pierpoint,1789. Courtesy of the Massachusetts Historical Society.*

benefitted" as well as provided a venue for "all sorts of ancient and modern societies of Fellowship."[17]

STATEHOUSES

At the apex of public building in British America were the colonial state-houses. They had no direct English pedigree but were hybrid forms, combining the functions and architectural attributes of English market houses and county halls. Although they were given various names—courthouse, town hall, and statehouse—what linked them together and set them apart from municipal or county buildings was the fact that they were the meeting places of provincial legislatures (Table 1). Most of the deliberative bodies that met in them were fully cognizant of the rituals associated with the House of Commons in London and appropriated many of the ceremonies and symbols of that body in the use of maces, speaker's chairs, seating arrangements, balustraded gates, and liveried doorkeepers. Along with these large legislative chambers, most statehouses also contained the highest provincial courts and the governor's advisory council housed in either one or two additional rooms (Table 2). Filled with the royal arms and portraits of monarchs, fine paneled woodwork, and upholstered furnishings, the council chambers in royal colonies matched and often surpassed in decorative sumptuousness the meeting halls of the legislatures. The richness of the interiors in these statehouses was

TABLE 1 Eighteenth-Century Colonial Statehouses

Colony	City	Building Name(s)	Date of Construction	Materials	Number of Stories	Size in Feet: Length × Width
New Hampshire	Portsmouth	Statehouse; city hall; courthouse	1758–60	Wood	2	80 × 30
Massachusetts	Boston	Town house; courthouse; statehouse	1712–13; rebuilt 1747	Brick	2	110 × 36
Rhode Island	Providence*	Courthouse; statehouse	1729–31 1761–62	? Brick	2 2	? 60 × 38
Rhode Island	Newport*	Colony house	1739–40	Brick	2	80 × 40
Connecticut	Hartford*	Courthouse, statehouse	1719–20	Wood	2	70 × 30
Connecticut	New Haven*	Statehouse, town house; courthouse	1st 1719–20 2nd 1763–64	1st Wood 2nd Brick	2 2	1st 45 × 22 2nd 7 bays × 4 bays
New York	New York	City Hall	1699–1701; Enlarged 1763–64	Brick	2 3	H-shaped; 92 × 52
New Jersey	Burlington*	Courthouse	Late 1680s	Brick	2	?
New Jersey	Perth Amboy*	Courthouse, city hall; town house	1st 1713 2nd 1745 3rd 1767	Brick Brick Brick	2 2 2	? ? 5 bays
Pennsylvania	Philadelphia	Courthouse,+ statehouse	1710–11 1732–35	Brick Brick	2 2	? 107 × 44 with wings, tower
Delaware	New Castle	Courthouse	1732	Brick	2	37 × 36
Maryland	Annapolis	Stadthouse; statehouse	1st 1698 2nd 1707 3rd 1772	Brick Brick Brick	2 2 2	1st 52 × 28 2nd 52 × 28 3rd 136 × 92
Virginia	Williamsburg	Capitol	1701–5; rebuilt 1752–53	Brick	2	Two wings 83 × 31; arcade 30 × 30
North Carolina	New Bern	Courthouse	1764	Brick	2	60 × 40
South Carolina	Charleston	Statehouse	1753–56	Brick	2	103 × 52
Georgia	Savannah	Courthouse	ca. 1765	Wood	?	?

* Legislature alternated sessions between cities

+ The legislature moved out of the courthouse to the statehouse in the mid-1730s

TABLE 2 Room Functions in Colonial Statehouses (Size in Feet: Length by Width)

Building, City	Legislative Chamber	Council Chamber	Courtroom	Exchange/ Public Hall	Prison	Other Rooms
Statehouse, Portsmouth, N.H.	2nd	2nd 19 × 26	2nd	1st	–	
Town House, Boston, Mass.	2nd 57½ × 32	2nd 32 × 32	2nd *	1st	–	
Courthouse, Providence, R.I.	2nd 38 × 34	2nd 23 × 23	2nd +	1st	–	2nd: Library in council chamber
Colony House, Newport, R.I.	2nd 23 × 34	2nd 23 × 25	2nd +	1st	–	C: storage
Courthouse, Hartford, Conn.	2nd 30 × 30	2nd 30 × 30	2nd +	1st	–	
Statehouse, Town House, New Haven, Conn.	2nd Same size as council	2nd Same size as legislative	1st	1st	–	
City Hall, New York, N.Y.	2nd 21 × 28	2nd 21 × 20	2nd 45 × 25	–	C: Dungeon G: Debtors rooms	1st: fire engines; 1st: gaoler's apt.; 2nd: library; 2nd: arms
Courthouse, Burlington, N.J.	2nd	2nd	2nd +	–	1st	
Courthouse, Perth Amboy, N.J.	2nd	2nd	2nd	–	–	
Statehouse, Philadelphia, Pa.	1st 40 × 40	2nd 38 × 20	1st 40 × 40	–	–	2nd: long gallery for entertainment, 100 × 20; 2nd: storage room for small arms; wing: keeper's apt.; library
Courthouse, New Castle, Del.	2nd	–	1st	–	–	
2nd Statehouse, Annapolis, Md.	1st	–	1st ^	–	–	2nd: offices
Capitol, Williamsburg, Va.	1st 35 × 25	2nd ca. 35 × 25	1st 50 × 25	–	–	2nd: Library in council chamber; 2nd committee rooms used for entertainment; G: offices
Courthouse, New Bern, N.C.	2nd	–	2nd ^	–	–	2nd: long room for entertainment

Statehouse,	2nd	2nd	1st	-	-	1st: secretary's office;
Charleston, S.C.	32 × 32	32 × 32	32 × 32			1st: housekeeper's
						apt.; G: armory
Courthouse,	1st	-	1st	-	-	
Savannah, Ga.		^				

Location in the building: C = cellar; 1st = first floor; 2nd = second floor; G = garret

* Council chamber used as courtroom

^ Legislative chamber used as courtroom

+ Location of courtroom unknown

replicated on the exterior with symbols and architectural ornamentation that expressed the power of the institutions that met in them.

In smaller, less wealthy, or more fractious colonies, the statehouse was scarcely distinguishable from county and municipal structures and sometimes shared the same space with local jurisdictions. Some colonies were simply too poor or politically divisive to invest in grand provincial structures. Authorities in New Jersey could never overcome their earlier history when the colony had been divided into two separate jurisdictions, each with its own capital city — Burlington in the west and Perth Amboy in the east. When joined together at the beginning of the eighteenth century, vested interests in the two former divisions thwarted efforts to select a more central capital so that the colony fell into the pattern of alternating provincial meetings of the legislature between one town and the other. In small New England colonies such as Rhode Island and Connecticut, dual capitals posed little hardship, but New Jersey was far larger with poor roads running from Burlington on the Delaware River and Perth Amboy on Raritan Bay just below New York. Governor Lewis Morris criticized the inefficiency of the arrangement in towns that were "both inconsiderable places and likely to remain so; neither of them fit for the seat of Government, not so conveniently situated for that purpose as some others."[18] As a result, the provincial government suffered to meet in a series of inconsequential buildings in each place, which it shared with local jurisdictions until after the Revolution.

Provincial government in the large and sparsely populated colony of North Carolina had even more difficulty establishing a permanent home. For most of the colonial period, it was peripatetic, meeting primarily in Edenton in the northeast from the 1710s through the 1730s before moving south to newer settlements in the Neuse and Cape Fear Valleys where it had no fixed abode but met on various occasions in Bath, Brunswick, New Bern, and Wilmington. Officials in Edenton managed to build a thirty- by twenty-foot brick Council House for the governor and his councilors by the early 1730s, but this did not prevent the migration of the government southward.[19] In the mid-1760s, Governor William Tryon and the General Assembly finally agreed that New Bern at the confluence of the Trent and Neuse Rivers would be the permanent capital. The legislature met in a large arcaded market house, while Tryon oversaw the construction of a substantial governor's residence designed in the English Palladian style by émigré architect John Hawks. However, the governor badly misread the political implications of public money spent on such opulence as angry "Regulators" in the backcountry rose in open revolt in the early 1770s when they were forced to pay for the "palace" as it was derisively known. The two-story, seven-bay brick house, with the king's arms prominently displayed in the tympanum of the front pediment, had a council chamber, which measured thirty-six by twenty feet, and walls covered in "modern" wainscoting. The room contained enriched architraves, a surbase, and an Ionic entablature.[20] The imported marble chimneypiece featured a bas-relief bust of King George III on one side and Queen Charlotte on the other, which probably cost more than what most backwoods protestors would have earned in a lifetime. Out of place in poor North Carolina, the palace provoked the ire of the people rather than their awe.

The impact of regional building practices is evident in the statehouses erected in the New England colonies. The form of the buildings in these colonies derived from the town house/market house model. Those in New Hampshire, Massachusetts, Rhode Island, and Connecticut were of a similar type; the main differences were in their orientation and degree of elaboration. Most were two-story, elongated rectangles located in the center of prominent squares or main thoroughfares. In Boston and Newport, they stood on axis with the main wharves. Located at the head of King Street as it rose from the Long Wharf, Boston's brick town house replaced the 1658 wooden market house built on the same site that was destroyed in a fire in 1711. Three times as long as it was wide (110 by 36 feet) with doors on the two short walls and in the center of the two long ones, the town house was enclosed on the ground floor, which served as a meeting space or walk for merchants. Two staircases led to the second floor chambers occupied by the House of Representatives and the governor's council.[21]

The statehouses built in Portsmouth, Providence, Newport, Hartford, and

FIGURE 2.7. *Colony House, Newport, Rhode Island, 1739. Author.*

New Haven followed the pattern of the Boston town house. The ground floor in these buildings was an enclosed exchange with rows of posts supporting the second floor, which contained council chamber, legislative assembly room, and sometimes a separate courtroom as in Portsmouth. The elongated wooden statehouse erected in the New Hampshire capital in 1758 had only entrances in each of the shorter ends of the building. Above one of these was the ceremonial balcony, which opened from the council chamber.[22] The Colony House in Newport, built twenty years earlier, reoriented the principal façade of this regional type to give the building a more monumental presence. In 1739 the Rhode Island General Assembly laid out the specifications for a new brick statehouse, which called for its long side to front the Parade, the town's principal civic square, so that it "would look more commodious."[23] With its contrasting stone quoins, string course, rusticated window jambs, clipped central pediment, and two-story wooden Corinthian frontispiece and balcony, the Colony House is a vigorous local interpretation of English public building features, made all the more rich by the carved woodwork in the council chamber (Fig. 2.7).[24]

In wealthier colonies with strong stable governments, such as Virginia, South Carolina, Pennsylvania, and New York, provincial officials erected large and ambitious statehouses. When Francis Nicholson moved the seat of government from Jamestown to Williamsburg in 1699, he laid out a walled precinct in the center of the main street where he erected a two-story statehouse, which was self-consciously named the Capitol in reference to its classical forebear in ancient Rome. It was a deliberate attempt on the part of Nicholson to establish its prestige since the old statehouse in Jamestown (1663) had few architectural attributes that distinguished it from the collection of neighboring taverns and dwellings. The plan of the H-shaped Capitol consisted of a pair of two-story wings connected by an open arcade or piazza and provided a logical and equitable division of space for the various functions. The front west building contained the general courtroom and secretary of the colony's office on the ground floor with the governor's council chamber above, while the House of Burgesses convened in the east wing. For the first time, all branches of the provincial government were housed under one roof. With nearly five thousand square feet of space for offices, the general courtroom with its marbleized woodwork, the paneled council chamber with its royal portraits, and the House of Burgesses with its ceremonial speaker's chair, a grand semicircular west porch with a balcony above it, Queen Anne's arms engraved on the exterior along with those of the governor, and a cupola projecting high above the roofline, the Capitol set the precedent for other colonies.[25]

The Pennsylvania Statehouse (1732–35) and the South Carolina Statehouse (1753–56) rivaled the Virginia Capitol in terms of scale and elaboration. The Philadelphia building started as a rather pedestrian design composed of a large two-story brick rectangle surmounted by a squat cupola. Stone dressings used for the quoins, panels, string courses, and keystones enlivened the Chestnut Street façade, but were entirely absent on the rear elevation. Unlike the Williamsburg Capitol or even the earlier courthouse on Market Street that it replaced, the location of the Pennsylvania Statehouse was an afterthought in a rapidly growing city. It was not centrally situated, but sited on a secondary street several blocks from the river outside the most densely built part of the city.[26] Advantageously sited on one corner of the centrally planned public square in Charleston, the South Carolina Statehouse was a more architecturally ambitious regional interpretation of English Palladian design, a fashion that had taken root in the colony by the 1740s. The statehouse had an engaged two-story pedimented portico on its front façade with the royal coat of arms prominently affixed within the tympanum. The building was made more imposing in the late 1760s when the Flemish bond brickwork was covered in

FIGURE 2.8. Pennsylvania Statehouse, *Philadelphia, Pennsylvania, 1732–35.*
Watercolor by William Breton, 1828 after C. W. Peale, 1778. Philadelphia Athenaeum.

stucco in imitation ashlar with quoins at the corners. Both buildings followed
the English county hall custom of having an open accessible courtroom. In
Charleston, an outside door opened directly into the main courtroom on the
west side of the statehouse, and in Philadelphia, entrance into the Supreme
Court was through the arcaded central corridor (Figs. 2.8 and 2.9).

The best rooms in most statehouses were the council chambers, for it was
in these spaces that royal governors and members of His Majesty's Council convened. In Charleston, the council chamber on the second floor of
the statehouse was thirty-two feet square, the same dimensions as the room
in which the Commons House of Assembly met. It was located in the corner room overlooking the public square and had a state gallery centered in
the middle of the narrower Meeting Street façade. The fully paneled room
was ringed with sixteen wooden Corinthian pilasters fashioned from white
pine imported from New England and contained the king's arms carved by a
Philadelphia craftsman. On one wall, a portrait of George III was ceremoni-

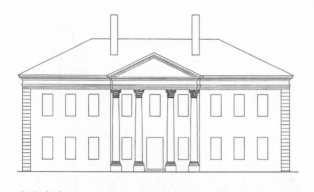

FIGURE 2.9. *Reconstructed south and east elevations of the South Carolina Statehouse, Charleston, South Carolina, 1753–56. Author.*

ously draped with a curtain. The fireplace contained an expensive stove grate. Furniture included a large armchair for the governor and a set of chairs for the councilors carved by the leading Charleston cabinetmakers.[27]

After the town house in Boston burned in 1747, it was rebuilt within its original walls. The plan remained the same, but the upper rooms were more elaborately decorated. Besides the arms of the colony, the legislative chamber was filled with maps of the province, John Rocque's large map of London (1746), and Henry Popple's "Map of the British Empire in America" (1742). Representatives were well informed of their place in the empire and the world. To remind them of the source of the colony's wealth, a carved and gilded codfish hung from a line above them. The council chamber in the Boston town house matched the lavishness of the one in Charleston. It, too, measured approximately thirty-two square feet, was trimmed with paneling, gilded royal arms, a fine stone mantelpiece, pedimented doorways, and was filled with elegant furniture, including velvet-covered chairs, and contained an array of royal and gubernatorial portraits.[28] It also served as the General Court of the colony.

The similarities of public buildings in the ports, capitals, and market towns of colonial America and their counterparts in the provincial towns of eighteenth-century Britain are testaments in brick, stone, and wood to a shared social, economic, and political culture. In the abstract, public architecture projected the ideals of a British empire united under a Protestant monarchy, which valued liberty, the rule of law, and civic order. Despite great regional differences in Britain and in her American colonies, a gentleman planter from Virginia or an English merchant from Bristol would not have felt too disoriented in the Georgian structures that housed the markets,

CARL LOUNSBURY

law courts, and assembly rooms in places like Blandford Forum and Boston, Charleston and Chelmsford. Local circumstances tempered their appearances, giving them distinctive variations within commonly accepted forms, like a musical fugue. Materials and building practices certainly distinguished structures in one region from another, but so too did the melding of functions, which created variations or even new types, such as the town meeting and courtroom in New England's otherwise domesticated town houses or the single-story arcaded courthouse in rural Virginia.

Provincial filters were stronger in some places than others. If our English merchant and Virginia planter had traveled away from coastal cities into the American backcountry, they would have discovered different and less recognizable public buildings, whether a meetinghouse or a courthouse, that were no less important to members of rural society. The appearance and function of these structures might have struck our visitors momentarily as odd, but gradually, whether by noticing a cupola or series of arched apertures or by observing the fittings and listening to words in the opening rituals in the courtroom of a log building, they would have begun to see certain familiar monarchical and corporate symbols, which would have alerted them as to their use and meaning. Listening, they might have even caught familiar accents among the cacophony of voices that swore their oaths of allegiance as loyal subjects of George III. Yet, as the arguments stirred by the American Revolution proved, the abstract ideals embodied in the rituals in those places could be and were interpreted quite differently. That too was part of the inheritance.

NOTES

1. Peter Borsay, *The English Urban Renaissance: Culture and Society in the Provincial Town, 1660–1770* (Oxford: Oxford University Press, 1990), 39–113.

2. Christopher Chalkin, *English Counties and Public Building 1650–1830* (London: The Hambledon Press, 1998). For new court buildings during this period, see Clare Graham, *Ordering Law: The Architectural and Social History of the English Law Court to 1914* (Aldershot: Ashgate, 2003), 337–453.

3. Mark Girouard, *The English Town: A History of Urban Life* (New Haven: Yale University Press, 1990), 9–30, 45–56.

4. Martha J. McNamara, *From Tavern to Courthouse: Architecture and Ritual in American Law, 1658–1860* (Baltimore: Johns Hopkins Press, 2004), 58; Carl Lounsbury, *From Statehouse to Courthouse: An Architectural History of South Carolina's Colonial Capitol and Charleston County Courthouse* (Columbia: University of South Carolina Press, 2001), 19.

5. McNamara, *From Tavern to Courthouse*, 20–22.

6. Kevin M. Sweeney, "Meetinghouses, Town Houses, and Churches: Changing Perceptions of Sacred and Secular Space in Southern New England, 1720-1850," *Winterthur Portfolio* 28 (1993): 59-93.

7. Clarence Wilson Bazer, "The Colonial Courthouse, Chester, Pennsylvania," *Architectural Record* 60 (1926): 527-32.

8. Carl Lounsbury, *The Courthouse of Early Virginia: An Architectural History* (Charlottesville: University of Virginia Press, 2005), 49-60.

9. "Virginia in 1732: The Travel Journal of William Hugh Grove," eds. Gregory Stiverson and Patrick H. Butler III, *Virginia Magazine of History and Biography* 85 (1977): 22.

10. Lounsbury, *The Courthouse of Early Virginia*, 109-24.

11. Ibid., 137-64.

12. *Minutes of the Common Council of the City of Philadelphia, 1704-1776* (Philadelphia: Cressy & Markley, Printers, 1847), 136-37, 177-78, August 9, 1717, July 4, 1720.

13. Thomas De Voe, *The Market Book: Contains a Historical Account of the Public Markets in the Cities of New York, Boston, Philadelphia, and Brooklyn* (New York: Printed for the author, 1862).

14. *Boston News-Letter*, April 1, 1737.

15. *Re-Dedication of the Old State House, Boston, July 11, 1882* (Boston: City Council, 1883), 149-51; *New York Mercury*, October 16, 1760; *New York Gazette and Weekly Mercury*, June 12, 1769; and *Norwich Packet*, May 9, 1774. Faneuil Hall was thoroughly gutted by fire in 1761 and restored and opened two years later. In 1805 the building was doubled in width and had a third story added to it.

16. Fred Shelley, ed., "The Journal of Ebenezer Hazard in Virginia, 1777," *Virginia Magazine of History and Biography* 62 (1954): 403.

17. The building was replaced by a much larger town hall in 1814. Fredericksburg City Council Minute Book 1782-1801, 34-35.

18. Quoted in Peter Wacker, *Land and People: A Cultural Geography of Preindustrial New Jersey; Origins of Settlement Patterns* (New Brunswick: Rutgers University Press, 1975), 333.

19. The foundations of the Council House were discovered beneath the 1767 Chowan County Courthouse at the top of the town green.

20. Letter from John Hawks to Francis de Miranda, July 12, 1783. Archivo de Franciso de Miranda, Tomo 5, folios 95-97, Academia Nacional de la Historia, Caracas, Venezuela.

21. Sara B. Chase, "A Brief Survey of the Architectural History of the Old State House, Boston, Massachusetts," *Old-Time New England* 68 (Winter-Spring 1978): 31-33.

22. James L. Garvin, "The Old New Hampshire State House," *Historical New Hampshire* 46 (1991): 202-29.

23. John Russell Bartlett, ed., *Records of the Colony of Rhode Island and Providence Plantations in New England, vol. IV, 1707-1740* (Providence: F. Knowles, Anthony & Co., 1859), 557-58.

24. Richard Munday's design inspired the builders of the Providence courthouse

CARL LOUNSBURY

some twenty years later.; Norman Isham, "The Colony House at Newport, Rhode Island," *Bulletin of the Society for the Preservation of New England Antiquities*, 8 (1917): 3–22.

25. Marcus Whiffen, *The Public Buildings of Williamsburg* (Williamsburg, Va.: Colonial Williamsburg, 1958), 34–50.

26. Edward M. Riley, "The Independence Hall Group," in *Historic Philadelphia: From the Founding until the Early Nineteenth Century* (Philadelphia: American Philosophical Society, 1953), 7–8.

27. Lounsbury, *From Statehouse to Courthouse*, 39–41.

28. T. W. Parker, "Notes on the Furnishings in the Town House, 1748–1776," Bostonian Society.

3

LANDSCAPES OF THE NEW REPUBLIC AT THOMAS JEFFERSON'S MONTICELLO

Anna O. Marley

In 1786 future United States presidents John Adams and Thomas Jefferson embarked together upon a summer tour through the great estates and gardens of England. John Adams recalled: "The gentlemen's seats were the highest entertainment we met with. Stowe, Hagley, and Blenheim, are superb; Woburn, Caversham, and the Leasowes are beautiful. Wotton is both great and elegant, though neglected. Architecture, painting, statuary, poetry, are all employed in the embellishment of these residences of greatness and luxury" (Fig. 3.1).[1] Scholars have noted the influence this tour had upon Jefferson's design for the gardens at Monticello, his home in Virginia, yet little attention has been paid to how this tour affected the interior decoration of Monticello.[2] The above quote makes clear that Jefferson and Adams visited the interiors as well as the gardens of the houses. While Adams offered praise for the estates he and Jefferson visited, he also critiqued their cost and showiness and expressed hope that it would be a long time before such artificial ornaments were established in America.[3] What would have been his surprise, then, to see that Jefferson had transported back to America and installed some of this "greatness and luxury" at his own Monticello? Jefferson not only decorated with the French furnishings he acquired during the five years he spent abroad, but he hung the walls floor to ceiling with maps, mirrors, religious paintings, prints, still lifes, and landscapes. Jefferson's installation of paintings at Monticello, in particular landscapes, is directly indebted to the hang of paintings in the grand English estates he visited in the 1780s.

This essay relates the landscape paintings Jefferson hung at Monticello upon his retirement from political office to the larger history of landscape paintings hung in American interiors. I examine how Jefferson's 1786 tour of British gardens influenced his thinking about the function and fashion of landscape paintings in domestic interiors and how he adapted British traditions to his American home. I contend that despite the political break with

FIGURE 3.1. *Crimson dining room, Hagley Hall, West Midlands, 1754–1760. Author.*

Britain as a result of the American Revolution, transatlantic artistic taste remained a constant for early national Americans.[4] The garden tour was to have a profound effect both on how Jefferson decorated his house and how he conceived of the purpose of American landscape painting. Yet, despite the shared taste for landscape paintings in domestic interiors in the British Atlantic world, Jefferson's choice of landscape subject matter reveals a newly American politics at work in his domestic display. Specifically, in establishing a program of American landscapes that he deemed "worth a voiage across the Atlantic," arranged around the western windows of his dining room with their views of the Blue Ridge and beyond, Jefferson was shifting his political vantage point from the East to the West and crafting rooms with views of a new American, rather than British Atlantic, empire.[5]

BRITISH LANDSCAPE TRADITIONS IN THE AMERICAN COLONIAL DOMESTIC INTERIOR

Jefferson was undoubtedly influenced by British practices and worked within a British tradition in how he hung landscape paintings at Monticello, yet his landscape commissions for his home in the early nineteenth century performed a different ideological and aesthetic function than those landscape paintings commissioned by colonial British Americans fifty years earlier. In the following section, I examine landscape painting in the home of Jefferson's presidential predecessor George Washington in order to illustrate the changing nature of landscape consumption from the colonial to early national period. The eighteenth-century house was a place of business, entertainment, and reception, and since landscape paintings hung not in private rooms such as back parlors or bed chambers, but rather in the most visible places in domestic interiors—parlors and dining rooms—they must be read in terms of these public functions. When a young George Washington commissioned a landscape for his front parlor at Mount Vernon during the French and Indian War he was emulating British decorative practices in an attempt to secure his position within the plantocracy of the Chesapeake region of Virginia.[6] Fellow future presidents Washington and Jefferson spent many years planning the aesthetic construction of their plantation homes from afar—be it from a battlefield in North America or on a tour of the English countryside. It is thus instructive to frame Jefferson's decorative use of landscape paintings at Monticello between 1809 and 1815 with a discussion of Washington's earlier domestic interior.[7]

At the same time that he was fighting at Fort Loudon during the French and Indian War, George Washington was thinking about decorating his house. In April of 1757 he wrote to the London merchant Richard Washington, "Whatever goods you may send me where the prices are not absolutely limited you will let them be fashionable—neat—and good in their several kinds."[8] When the young general ordered "A Neat Landskip" from England for his front parlor at Mount Vernon, he was not alone in his request for a landscape, described at the time as "after Claude Lorrain," to decorate the "best room" at his estate.[9] He directed Richard Washington to send him "a marble Chimney piece of the dimensions inclosed (given by the workmen) the cost not to exceed 15 guineas. N.B. let it be carefully packd." Also "1 neat landskip 3 feet by 21½ inches = 1 inch margin for a chimy."[10] In November of that year Washington's goods came. They included a chimneypiece of "fine new veined marble," with accessories for mounting it; two mahogany tables, and "best gothick chairs, wt. Pincushion seats, stufft in ye best manner and covered with horse hair."[11] The landscape, "after Claude Lorrain," cost 3.15.6 pounds (Fig. 3.2). The front parlor, where the painting hung, also known as the west or blue parlor, was constructed in 1757–59. Following prevailing fashions, Washington used rococo woodwork and stuccowork designs and patterns in both the front parlor and the small dining room, and included a carving of his own crest on the front parlor overmantel that he had also

ANNA O. MARLEY

FIGURE 3.2. *West parlor at Mount Vernon, Mount Vernon, ca. 1758.*
Courtesy of Mount Vernon Ladies' Association.

ordered from London in the 1750s. The crest, like the chimneypiece ornaments, alluded to landed status, creating an image of stable family patrimony
and nobility tied to landownership.[12]

In the 1780s Washington added neoclassical, Adamesque ceiling decoration to the front parlor.[13] The original paint scheme from the 1750s to 1780s
consisted of trompe l'oeil grained mahogany and stone-colored details. It
was painted Prussian blue in 1785, which is how the room is currently interpreted. In a letter to his dear friend the Marquis de Lafayette, to thank him
for a gift of a portrait of the marquis and his family, Washington referred to his
front parlor as "the best place in my house."[14] This "best place" was a highly
constructed and decorated front parlor filled with performative objects, as
well as a space for social, political, and mercantile performance on the part
of its owners and visitors.[15] In this room the Washingtons served tea and
coffee in their export porcelain service of "fine image china" in the famille
rose style, with Chinese genre scenes upon it. Washington's front room is
a virtual British colonial world unto itself, with landscapes of Asia on his
china, an Arcadian Italianate Europe represented on his overmantel, and
views from his front window of the grounds of his plantation. Washington
was only twenty-three when he was designing this highly calculated interior,
and one has to ask what he was trying to achieve by ordering a "neat" British
landscape. It seems that in ordering a "neat" landscape he wanted something
elegant and simple that would harmonize with the Georgian architecture of
his plantation house.[16] The young planter was also associating himself with
British aristocratic collecting practices and with a taste for landscape popular with British gentlemen knowledgeable of the Grand Tour. The ownership
of Claudian landscapes was *de rigueur* in British country house collections
such as Houghton, the country house of Britain's first prime minister, Sir
Robert Walpole, and home to one of the best known painting collections
in Europe.[17] It is stimulating to think about the future first president of the
United States decorating his house in the taste of the first prime minister of
the United Kingdom, and that despite being an ocean and eventually an empire apart, both landowners and tastemakers wanted the same sort of paintings to hang on their walls.

Shortly after Washington designed his parlor and installed his landscapes,
Americans began to think differently about landscape. Orders for Claudian-
style European landscapes such as Washington's, commissioned in the late
1750s during a period of imperial wars, reflect a desire on the part of wealthy
Americans to connect with the tastes and landscapes of the British imperial
center. However, in the early 1770s, on the eve of the American Revolution,

ANNA O. MARLEY

eminent American gentlemen began to shift their artistic patronage away from Great Britain.[18] Charles Carroll of Carrollton, for example, demonstrated a new trend when he chose to hang what he described as "rough" but local paintings in his important spaces of entertainment and sociability, rather than the imported British paintings his countrymen had preferred a few years previously.[19] The stories of Washington, Carroll, and their parlors frame a history of British American landscape practices through which one can trace interconnections between European landscape aesthetics, popular British architectural pattern books, and colonial landscape painting commissions. Of particular importance are the landscape paintings that were ordered for parlors and dining rooms, the most public rooms of eighteenth-century British homes. Influenced by travel, the international exchange of pattern books, and the desire to establish gentlemanly status in the Americas, British American colonists engaged in sociopolitical acts through the transatlantic trade in landscape overmantels. The prominent place afforded to landscape in the British American interior continued in early national America, though changing architectural tastes rendered the overmantel form obsolete.

Jefferson's decoration of Monticello with American views highlights both the continued importance of landscape in American domestic interiors as well as a shift away from the focus on the European, classical past epitomized by Washington's commissions. While Washington's front parlor offered a kaleidoscope of transatlantic British imperial vistas of China, Europe, and America, Jefferson's views stretched west, to the newly explored lands of the Louisiana Purchase and the American landscape that was to become associated with the country's manifest destiny. The subject matter of these landscapes, though indebted in their form to the British global landscape, was a new expression of a specifically American imperial eye.[20] Thus Jefferson's arrangement of paintings reveals both a continuity with earlier American rooms with views as well as a shift in landscape patronage from a transatlantic to a western continental horizon.

A COMMUNITY OF TASTE:
JEFFERSON AND ADAMS'S COUNTRY HOUSE TOUR

Jefferson's western views and landscapes represent an adaptation and transformation of British Georgian-style landscape aesthetics to the conditions of a budding American republic. His approach to collecting and arranging landscapes in the first decades of the nineteenth century paved the way for the popular reception in the decades to come of the artists of the Hudson River school of American landscape painting. This school of nineteenth-century painting, founded by the artist Thomas Cole, is often identified as the first national school of American art. However, though Jefferson was to choose—with only one exception—to hang American views in Monticello, his *taste* for views was cemented by his typically British elite experience of touring British country houses in the 1780s.[21] Jefferson's experience viewing domestic picture collections in the great houses of Britain exposed him to the practices and taste of the British gentry and the importance they placed on the structure of their domestic space as a place of display and projection of identity.[22] The arrangement of paintings in these domestic interiors was not haphazard, but part of a system of elite self-fashioning, and the understanding and recreation of such systems of pictorial arrangement in an American domestic interior embodied Jefferson's continued engagement with this system even as he adapted it for an American context. [23]

The homes that Jefferson and Adams visited on their British tour were Jefferson's primary reference when he constructed his own home in Virginia. These houses included: Chiswick, Lord Burlington's Palladian villa outside London, owned by the Duke of Devonshire when Jefferson and Adams visited; Hampton Court, the historic royal palace; Twickenham, site of the poet Alexander Pope's famed grotto; Painshill, with its influential landscape garden by Hamilton; Wotton House, belonging to the Dukes of Buckingham, a grand baroque house and "natural" garden; Stowe, the country house of the Dukes of Buckingham, with its famous gardens and superlative paintings in its state rooms in the eighteenth century that are now dispersed about Britain and America; The Leasowes, Shenstone's famous ferme ornée, one of the most visited gardens of the late eighteenth century; Hagley Hall, a grand Palladian hall with impressive gardens, elaborate baroque interiors, and a dining room display that may have influenced the hang in Monticello's dining room; and Blenheim Palace, home of the Dukes of Marlborough, which was surrounded by large picturesque and formal gardens and had grand state rooms filled with a tour de force art collection.

In compiling a catalog of paintings at Monticello, Jefferson was echoing the practice of many British country estate owners who wrote catalogs of their collections that visitors could use to explore their public rooms.[24] In his memorandum book, Jefferson notes that he bought a guidebook at either Wotton or Stowe, although he does not note having purchased a guide at any of the other houses that he and Adams visited.[25] This purchase was almost certainly Seely's *Description of Stowe* (1783) as Jefferson later included it in his 1783 *Catalog of Books*. Seely's *Description* includes a "Plan of the House" and a "Description of the Inside of the House," as well as a description of the gardens and thirty-eight engraved illustrations. The practice of displaying and cataloging paintings was indeed popular at many of the estates Jefferson and Adams visited. Also included in Jefferson's 1783 catalog are *Heely on the gardens of Hagley etc.* (1777) and Horace Walpole's *Aedes Walpoliana* (1752). Jefferson purchased the *Aedes* from the Reverend Samuel Henley in 1785, and it contained a detailed description of the hang of the pictures in Sir Robert Walpole's Houghton Hall in Norfolk. Jefferson's visits to Stowe, Blenheim, and Hagley, as well as his purchase of such books as the *Aedes*, influenced his taste for how paintings should be hung. [26]

At the same time that he was viewing interiors such as those at Hagley, and learning about ways to showcase paintings, Jefferson was also buying art that would eventually be displayed in his own public rooms. Partway though his tour, presumably at a stopover in London, Jefferson bought "plates of iron bridge," the print identified today as depicting the Coalbrookdale Bridge. Jefferson would later hang this print amid a series of landscapes in his dining room.[27] This was the only non-American view included in his dining room hang, and this marvel of the Industrial Revolution in England, the world's first cast-iron bridge, complemented the natural wonders of America such as Virginia's Natural Arch and New York's Niagara Falls. Undoubtedly seeing England's grand houses inspired Jefferson to think about Monticello and how he would display art in his own interior. Though he did not draft house notes the way he did garden notes on his tour, his letters allow us a window into his thoughts on the landscape paintings he saw on this journey.

SHIFTING THE VIEW:
FROM THE BRITISH ATLANTIC WORLD
TO THE AMERICAN IMPERIAL EYE

In his famous "Head and Heart" letter to the Anglo-Italian artist Maria Cosway, written five months after his tour, Jefferson directly conjoins Monticello and the future of American landscape painting in an effort to encourage his friend Maria to visit America. In October of 1786 he wrote to Maria from Paris that artists should make America's remarkable landscapes "known to all ages," describing the "Cascade of Niagara," "the Natural bridge" in Virginia, and the "Passage of the Potowmac thro the Blue mountains" at Harpers Ferry, West Virginia, as among the natural wonders "worth a voiage across the Atlantic to see."[28] All of these subjects would eventually hang in his dining room.[29] This suggests that seeing the art and landscapes of the great houses of England provoked thoughts in his mind about how the American landscape might be treated by artists and deployed in a similar way to those Italianate Grand Tour landscapes that were in British domestic interiors. Jefferson goes on to say in his letter, "And our own dear Monticello, where nature has spread so rich a mantle under the eye? Mountains, forests, rocks, rivers. With what majesty do we there ride above the storms!"[30] In this letter he relates the most sublime landscapes of the United States to his own views from Monticello. The "compass rose" of Jefferson's world, Monticello was where he assembled his universe.[31]

As with the Lewis and Clark artifacts displayed in his front hall, the landscapes hung in Jefferson's dining room created an overarching and panoptic view of the American landscape, reinforced by Monticello's location on a mountaintop looking west to sublime views.[32] The dining room installation at Monticello incorporates landscapes that, as early as 1786, Jefferson had determined were representative of America. More than merely representative, the choices of the landscapes were strategic — in that they visually embodied Jefferson's process of nation building and territorial expansion. The "lower tier" — as noted in the c. 1809–15 *Catalog of Paintings &c. at Monticello* — of the dining room includes a comprehensive program of landscape and city views, including:

77. Vandernoot. A print
78. Washington. A print from a drawing by Made de Brehan.
79. New Orleans a print.
80. Colebrook-dale bridge. A print.
81. The Natural bridge of Virginia on Canvas by Mr. Roberts.
82. The passage of the Patomak through the Blue ridge. do.
83. A distant view of the falls of Niagara from the Indian ladder.
84. A view of the falls of Niagara from the table rock. Both of these are prints from designs of Vanderlin.
85. The President's house at Washington, in water colours by King.
86. Mount Vernon. A print from a design of Birch
87. An elevation of the house at Monticello. By Mills.
88. The Diocletian Portico, a print [vice the Environs of N. Orleans].[33]

This program of views encompassed an ever-expanding American territory — from the newly acquired city of New Orleans at the juncture of the Mississippi and the Atlantic Ocean, to the sublime Niagara Falls that divided the United States from British Canada. On the upper tier of the dining room hang are classical history paintings and religious scenes, copies after artists such as Van Dyke and Rubens, themselves omnipresent in the collections of the great British estates that Jefferson had visited. Jefferson also notes the presence in the upper tier of a still life "76. A marketpiece on canvas, to wit, fruit, vegetables, game &c."[34] Like landscapes, still lifes, with their illustrations of the productivity and bounty of the land, were very popular items to hang in eighteenth-century dining rooms.

Jefferson was adapting older models of Adamesque country house design in England when he installed his dining room landscapes within a complementary arrangement of floor-to-ceiling framed window views of his property. In 1762 the owner of Kedleston Hall, Nathaniel Curzon, had worked with designer Robert Adam to ensure that each of his public "state rooms," such as the dining room, would coincide with the elevation drawings that factored in a fixed hanging position of Curzon's collection of paintings, as well as a symbiotic relationship with the views from the rooms.[35] The dining room at Kedleston, for example, incorporates a program that to this day has a lower tier of landscape paintings and an upper tier of religious and still life scenes similar to Jefferson's "marketpiece" (Fig. 3.3). In the dining room at Kedleston, fixed uniform picture frames were set in the walls displaying a program of landscape paintings by Francesco Zuccarelli surmounted by still lifes representing agricultural bounty. The paintings and still lifes reflected the Arcadian vistas seen out the front windows of the hall. Kedleston was, and still is, a popular site of British country house tourism and had a published guidebook in circulation by 1770. [36] Jefferson's program of landscapes in his dining room is an adaptation of this tradition. Rather than installing Italianate landscapes in fixed overmantel frames, he instituted a program of mainly American landscapes, crafting a different message of rural retirement than did Curzon and the subsequent owners of Kedleston.

Instead of looking back to Arcadia, Jefferson looks west across America. Landscapes were a part of the larger didactic decorative program Jefferson established at Monticello. As Elizabeth Chew has discussed in her work on the installation of the entrance hall, Jefferson hung his double story "Indian Hall" with an assortment of natural history objects brought back from the Lewis and Clark expedition, along with objects of European fine and decorative arts.[37] This mélange of objects crafted a very public, museum-type space and displayed a particular kind of Jeffersonian knowledge to all who visited Monticello's public rooms. The hall acted as a cabinet of curiosity, equally mixing Old and New World cultures, and served as a visual manifestation of Jefferson's worldview. Jefferson similarly constructed very particular, and multiple, messages with his hanging of objects in the dining room. In the progression from the entrance hall, through the parlor, to the dining room, Jefferson completed a comprehensive didactic message through the paintings

FIGURE 3.3. *The dining room at Kedleston Hall, Derbyshire, looking toward the domed apse, painting hang ca. 1760s. © National Trust Images/Nadia Mackenzie.*

and prints he installed, ending with a view from the windows of the dining room (Fig. 3.4) and tea room to Charlottesville and the Blue Ridge (Fig. 3.5), and via William Roberts's paintings southwest to the Natural Bridge and northwest to Harpers Ferry.[38]

Both the subject matter and the placement of paintings in a room constructed meaning in Jefferson's home. It is difficult to establish from Jefferson's catalog of paintings at Monticello exactly where in the dining room Roberts's two paintings of the Natural Bridge and Harpers Ferry would have hung, but it is important to try to unravel where these might have been. The artist presented Jefferson with the paintings by 1808, a gift that was perhaps inspired by a meeting they had in 1786.[39] Though the paintings were lost sometime soon after Jefferson's death with the auctioning of Monticello's furnishings, a print made after one painting, which now hangs at Monticello, and a watercolor study for the other painting, allow us to recreate the the-

ANNA O. MARLEY

FIGURE 3.4. *West wall of the dining room, Monticello, Virginia.*
© *Thomas Jefferson Foundation at Monticello.*

matic feel, if not the scale and tactility, of the placement of the original oil paintings. The J. C. Stadler colored aquatint of the *Natural Bridge* made in 1808 (Fig. 3.6) is a large vertical view of Jefferson's favorite natural Virginian "antiquity." Two small figures stand on a rock, gesturing in amazement at the sublime soaring natural arch towering above them. Roberts's *Junction of the Potomac and Shenandoah Rivers* (Fig. 3.7) represents another famous mid-Atlantic spot on which not only Jefferson, but many of his contemporaries, waxed poetical. It would have been natural for the Roberts paintings to hang

FIGURE 3.5. *View into tea room, Monticello, Virginia.*
© *Thomas Jefferson Foundation at Monticello.*

as overdoor paintings, like those found at Kedleston, but this is not likely given the fact that Jefferson includes all the landscapes on the lower tier of his catalog. Another logical place for grand landscapes, such as the view of the Natural Bridge and the Potomac, was over the mantel, but, again, their inclusion in the lower tier of hangs seems to preclude this possibility. They could not have been hung next to the fireplace, as they were in the dining room at Hagley Hall, since at Monticello there are doors flanking the fireplace.

This leaves the most probable place for the paintings to hang as on either side of the floor-to-ceiling windows facing west. Large printed views of Niagara Falls by Vanderlyn and views of the Natural Bridge and the Potomac by Roberts served as pendant pairs, hung on this wall. If these paintings and prints were all hung on the same wall surrounding the west window, then Jefferson created a wall of views.[40] Perhaps then it is best to think of these views in discourse with each other and with the windows they surrounded. After all, it was these sublime views, along with the mysterious "Falling Spring," that Jefferson noted in 1786 were worth a voyage across the Atlantic. It would make sense that he grouped them together on either side of

ANNA O. MARLEY

FIGURE 3.6. *J. C. Stadler print of* Natural Bridge, *ca. 1808, copied after William Roberts.* © *Thomas Jefferson Foundation at Monticello.*

FIGURE 3.7. *William Roberts,* Junction of the Potomac and Shenandoah Rivers, *1808, Harpers Ferry, Virginia. Watercolor, pencil, and ink on paper. Collection of the Museum of Early Southern Decorative Arts (MESDA).*

the window: arranged at eye level—just above the chair rail when diners were sitting around the table—the pictures presented Jefferson's dinner guests with a sublime tour of America's "enchanting objects," surely a nice complement to a long, afternoon meal as they made polite conversation and enjoyed Monticello's famed French cuisine.[41] While it might seem disjointed to hang a print of the Coalbrookdale Bridge amongst such natural beauties, this juxtaposition of the natural and industrial sublime would have been second nature to Jefferson and his dining companions, and, no doubt, inspired conversations about the merits and wonders of the American landscape and how Virginia wonders such as the Natural Bridge surpassed even the most sublime examples of British industrial ingenuity.

Other objects that decorated Monticello's walls were the French mirrors across from the windows in the parlor, and the maps in the front hall.[42] All of these objects, the windows, the mirrors and the maps, could be said to act as windows to the West, greatly expanded by Jefferson's Louisiana Purchase. Maps hung in the front hall introduced Monticello visitors to territories added to the country during Jefferson's presidency. By placing the large imported mirror in the dining alcove directly across from the western wall

ANNA O. MARLEY

where he hung his American landscapes alongside his floor-to-ceiling windows, Jefferson created a panoramic enclosure of views. While Jefferson was working within established European notions of landscape patronage, he was very consciously crafting an American identity, and directing his gaze westward seems to have been his way of doing it. The amazing visual program of the dining room—namely views of Washington, the nation's capital; a print dedicated to Jefferson of the western city of New Orleans, newly under the country's dominion; the sublime landscape of Virginia; views of Jefferson's and George Washington's houses; and the iconic and sublime Niagara Falls—create a refracted kaleidoscope of the new American empire. From the objects of American natural history, maps, and Native American objects that lined the walls in his front hall to the landscape views in his dining room Jefferson constructed a virtual visualization of an empire that stretched from the Canadian border to the Gulf of Mexico.

CONCLUSION

Let us return now for a brief moment to Washington's Mount Vernon, where in the 1780s and 1790s a dining room similar to that at Monticello was constructed alongside Washington's old-fashioned Georgian parlor. Unlike Washington's 1756 parlor with its painted view east across the ocean to European Claudian traditions, Mount Vernon's large dining room was a space contemporary to the dining room at Monticello. Upon their retirements both men chose to decorate their dining spaces with native landscape paintings. George Beck's painting for Washington's new dining room included local scenes that reached westward—sublime views of the Potomac River and Great Falls, whose canals were bringing trade to the west.[43] Likewise, in his dining room, Jefferson hung landscapes with personal associations. Roberts's paintings of Harpers Ferry and the Natural Bridge were landscapes Jefferson had written about in *Notes on the State of Virginia*. Washington and Jefferson were both literally invested in these landscapes—Washington with his project for building a canal on the Potomac past Great Falls, and Jefferson who actually owned the property on which stood the Natural Bridge. In these dining rooms, Jefferson and Washington adapted British decorative traditions to their own advantage, crafting rooms with views not of a European Arcadia, but of the seemingly boundless American West.

With the decoration of their homes at Mount Vernon and Monticello, Washington and Jefferson were consummate men of their time. Their display of landscape paintings from the 1750s through the turn of the nineteenth century reveals them to be participants in an exchange of aesthetics that began in the 1750s as a process of transatlantic emulation of British identity and developed in the early 1800s into a burgeoning American imperialism. Rather than expressing a cohesive national identity, landscapes hung in the domestic interiors of the early national American elite offer a window through which might be glimpsed the complicated and multifaceted development of the American landscape genre within the context of a contested imperial Atlantic world. Presidents Washington in the Chesapeake and Jefferson in the Piedmont were participants in a network of personal and trade relationships, along with the houses and landscapes that contained and embodied them, which stretched up the eastern seaboard from the Carolina Lowcountry, up the Chesapeake Bay to the mid-Atlantic, and to New England and across the Atlantic World. Connected by mercantile relationships, political concerns, and artistic interests, the rooms with views constructed by late colonial and early national Americans were part of a larger commercial and aesthetic web in the transatlantic world, including the British colonies of the Greater Caribbean and Atlantic Canada. The landscapes in the front parlor at Mount Vernon and the dining room at Monticello are but two of the most prominent American flashpoints that embody this highly connected aesthetic, commercial, and political world, and signify continued links across the British Atlantic in these worlds, despite the ruptures of the American Revolution.

NOTES

The author would like to thank Amy H. Henderson for her close editorial reading of this essay. Acknowledgments are also due to the kind staff members at the Museum of Early Southern Decorative Arts (MESDA), Monticello, Mount Vernon, and the National Trust for help securing images. A Robert H. Smith International Center for Jefferson Studies Fellowship at Monticello and a Madelyn Moeller Research Fellowship in Southern Material Culture at MESDA helped make possible this research.

1. Thomas Jefferson, *The Papers of Thomas Jefferson*, ed. Julian P. Boyd, 41 vols. (Princeton, N.J.: Princeton University Press, 1954), 9:374.

2. For this scholarly focus on gardens, see, for example, Robert P. Maccubbin, Peter Martin, and Colonial Williamsburg Foundation, *British and American Gardens in the Eighteenth Century: Eighteen Illustrated Essays on Garden History* (Williamsburg, Va.: Colonial Williamsburg Foundation, 1984).

3. The Adams quote is cited in the notes on "Jefferson's Tour of English Gardens," *Jefferson Papers*, vol. 9, taken from John Adams, *The Works of John Adams*, ed. C.F. Adams III (Boston: Little, Brown and Company, 1850–56), 394–96.

4. Thinking about American landscape in a British Atlantic or transatlantic context marks a shift away from traditional American landscape historiography in which scholars emphasized American identity and exceptionalism, the latter of which is perhaps best

ANNA O. MARLEY

exemplified by Barbara Novak's *Nature and Culture: American Landscape and Painting 1825–1875* (New York: Oxford University Press, 1980).

For other case studies of shared tastes and communal identities in British Atlantic domestic interiors in the years after the American Revolution, see, for example, Amy H. Henderson, "A Family Affair: The Design and Decoration of 321 South Fourth Street, Philadelphia," in *Gender, Taste, and Material Culture in Britain and North America, 1700–1830*, ed. John Styles and Amanda Vickery (New Haven: Yale Center for British Art, 2007), 267–91; and J. Thomas Savage and Robert A. Leath, "Buying British: Merchants, Taste, and Charleston Consumerism," in *In Pursuit of Refinement: Charlestonians Abroad, 1750–1800*, ed. Maurie McInnis and Angela Mack (Charleston: University of South Carolina Press for the Gibbes Museum of Art, 1999), 55–64.

This trend in art history follows an earlier trajectory in American historiography in which scholars traced persistent imperial ideals and shared British cultural values in post-Revolutionary America. See John Murrin, "A Roof without Walls: The Dilemma of American National Identity," in *Beyond Confederation: Origins of the Constitution and American National Identity*, ed. Richard Beeman, Stephan Botein, and Edward Carter (Chapel Hill: University of North Carolina Press, 1987), 333–48; and T. H. Breen, "Ideology and Nationalism on the Eve of the American Revolution," *Journal of American History* 84 (June 1997): 13–39. More recently Kariann Akemi Yokota has examined this shift away from seeing the United States as culturally and politically independent from Great Britain in her study *Unbecoming British: How Revolutionary America became a Postcolonial Nation* (New York: Oxford University Press, 2011).

5. The quote is from Thomas Jefferson, "To Maria Cosway, Paris Octob. 12, 1786," *The Papers of Thomas Jefferson*, 10:447. For studies of the westward thrust of Jefferson's empire, see Donald Jackson, *Thomas Jefferson and the Stony Mountains: Exploring the West from Monticello* (Norman: University of Oklahoma Press, 1993); James P. Ronda, *Thomas Jefferson and the Changing West: From Conquest to Conservation* (Albuquerque: University of New Mexico Press, 1997); and Carolyn Gilman, *Lewis and Clark: Across the Divide* (Washington, D.C., and London: Smithsonian Books, in association with the Missouri Historical Society, St. Louis, 2003).

For more on landscape in the British Atlantic world, see John E. Crowley, "A Visual Empire: Seeing the British Atlantic World from a Global British Perspective," in *The Creation of the British Atlantic World*, ed. Elizabeth Mancke and Carole Shammas (Baltimore and London: Johns Hopkins University Press, 2005), 283–303; Jill H. Casid, *Sowing Empire: Landscape and Colonization* (Minneapolis and London: University of Minnesota Press, 2005); and Beth Fowkes Tobin, *Colonizing Nature: The Tropics in British Arts and Letters, 1760–1820* (Philadelphia: University of Pennsylvania Press, 2005).

6. Carol Borchert Cadou discusses George Washington's rise as a planter and argues that Washington was very aware of the need to advance himself in polite society and how material culture could be used to that end. He copied out notes from the conduct manual *Rules of Civility and Decent Behavior in Company and Conversation* and ordered the finest objects he could afford from overseas. Carol Borchert Cadou, *The George Wash-*

ington Collection: Fine and Decorative Arts at Mount Vernon (Manchester, Vt.: Hudson Hills Press, 2006), 24.

7. These dates are derived from Jefferson's Catalogue of Paintings at Monticello, Thomas Jefferson Papers (#2958-b), Special Collections Department, University of Virginia Library.

Yokota has likewise examined the consumption and display of material culture of Jefferson and Washington's homes and their mediation of American and British identities, though not their displays of landscape painting, in *Unbecoming British*, 3–18, 86–95.

8. George Washington to Richard Washington, Fort Loudon, 15 April 1757, in George Washington, *The Papers of George Washington: Colonial Series*, ed. W.W. Abbot, vol. 4 of *The Papers of George Washington: Colonial Series* (Charlottesville: University of Virginia Press, 1983), 133.

9. For a history of American colonial landscape overmantel patronage, see Anna O. Marley, chapter 1, "'. . . the most eminent thing . . .' Landscape Overmantels in British-Atlantic Interiors 1756–1780," in "Rooms with a View: Landscape Representation in the Early National and Late Colonial Domestic Interior" (Ph.D. diss., University of Delaware, 2009), 26–65.

10. Worthington Chauncey Ford, *Inventory of the Contents of Mount Vernon, 1810* (Cambridge: University Press, 1909), xii.

11. Ford, *Inventory*, xii.

12. The mantelpiece in the large dining room is also a performative piece, elaborately carved with an agricultural scene highlighting Washington's mythical role as Cincinnatus. This is from the 1790s however.

13. The so-called Adam style is named for the Scottish architects and interior designers Robert and James Adam (1728–92 and 1732–94, respectively). The Adam brothers introduced ornaments derived from classical antiquity into eighteenth-century British homes, and their neoclassical style was widely imitated abroad.

14. Wendell Garrett, *George Washington's Mount Vernon* (New York: The Monacelli Press, 1998), 169.

15. Theories of space in vernacular architecture and landscape provide a foundation from which to examine the geography of the house as its own kind of landscape fraught with positions of privilege, access, and power. Central to the interpretive framework of this study is the work of Bernard Herman and Dell Upton, who argue that dynamics and relationships of power between objects and people can be read in such artifacts as the architectural finish surrounding an overmantel or the location of landscapes in certain rooms. See, for example, Bernard Herman, *Town House: Architecture and Material Life in the Early American City, 1780–1830* (Chapel Hill: Published for the Omohundro Institute of Early American History and Culture, Williamsburg, Virginia by the University of North Carolina Press, 2005); Dell Upton, *Holy Things and Profane: Anglican Parish Churches in Colonial Virginia* (New Haven: Yale University Press, 1997); and Dell

Upton, "White and Black Landscapes in Eighteenth-Century Virginia," *Places* 2, no. 2 (November 1984): 59–72.

16. Amanda Vickery defines "neat" in the mid- to late eighteenth century as the opposite of showy excess. "Neatness was an utterly positive quality. . . . Indeed, 'neat' emerges as a Georgian key word of unexpectedly wide social purchase, which could be applied to towns, houses, objects, personal appearance, and even events. . . . 'Neat' conveyed a simple elegance of form. . . . Neatness often connoted a spare elegance in keeping with Palladian or neoclassical architectural ideals. . . . Neat things were well contrived, cleverly put together and smoothly finished." See Amanda Vickery, " 'Neat and Not Too Showey': Words and Wallpaper in Regency England," in *Gender, Taste, and Material Culture*, ed. Styles and Vickery, 216.

17. Until it was sold to the empress of Russia to form the base of the collection of the Hermitage, Robert Walpole's collection of paintings, in particular his collection of paintings by Poussin and Claude, was one of the preeminent collections of Old Master paintings in England. Walpole's collection of paintings is cataloged by his son: see Horace Walpole, *Aedes Walpolianae, or, A Description of the Collection at Houghton-Hall in Norfolk*, 2nd ed. (London: Private printing, 1767).

18. Indeed, Washington ordered the landscape painting for his dining room in a period of heightened imperial patriotism. John E. Crowley examines this shift in landscape taste from the Seven Years' War to the early American republic in his essay "The American Republic Joins the British Global Landscape" in *Shaping the Body Politic: Art and Political Formation in Early America*, ed. Maurie D. McInnis and Louis P. Nelson (Charlottesville: University of Virginia Press, 2011), 92.

19. For a narrative of the negotiation of a commission for a British landscape overmantel—Carroll's London contact had suggested topographical and marine painter William Marlow (1740–1813) who specialized in scenes of Italian and British gardens as well as oil and watercolor views of London—and the decision to substitute it with a "rough" American version (probably commissioned of Charles Willson Peale), see Charles Carroll, "A Lost Copy-Book of Charles Carroll of Carrollton," *Maryland Historical Magazine* 33, no. 3 (September 1937): 217.

20. For a formulation of the British global landscape, see John E. Crowley, "A Visual Empire: Seeing the British Atlantic World from a Global British Perspective," in *The Creation of the British Atlantic World*, ed. Elizabeth Mancke and Carole Shammas (Baltimore and London: Johns Hopkins University Press, 2005), 283–303.

On nineteenth-century conceptions of American imperial landscape vision see Albert Boime, *The Magisterial Gaze: Manifest Destiny and the American Landscape, c. 1830–1865* (Washington: Smithsonian Institution Press, 1991); and Angela L. Miller, *The Empire of the Eye: Landscape Representation and American Cultural Politics, 1825–1875* (Ithaca: Cornell University Press, 1993).

21. As Gordon Wood has argued, "The Revolutionary leaders never intended to create an original and peculiar indigenous culture. Despite all their talk of American excep-

tionalism and American virtue in contrast with European corruption, they were seeking not to cut themselves off from Europe's cultural heritage but to embrace it and in fact fulfill it." Gordon Wood, *Empire of Liberty: A History of the Early Republic, 1789–1815* (New York: Oxford University Press, 2009), 544.

22. For more on taste and the crafting of the domestic environment in Georgian England, see "Setting up Home" and "Wallpaper and Taste" in Amanda Vickery, *Behind Closed Doors: At Home in Georgian England* (New Haven and London: Yale University Press, 2009), 83–105, 166–83.

23. For a persuasive model of scholarship on how sets of paintings enact elite self-fashioning in domestic space, see Mimi Hellman, "The Joy of Sets: The Uses of Seriality in the French Interior," in *Furnishing the Eighteenth Century: What Furniture Can Tell Us about the European and American Past*, ed. Dena Goodman and Kathryn Norberg (New York and London: Routledge, 2007): 147.

24. See, for example, Nathaniel Curzon Scarsdale, *Catalogue of the Pictures, Statues, &C. At Kedleston, with Some Account of the Architecture* (S.l.: s.n., 1769).

25. Thomas Jefferson, James Adam Bear, and Lucia C. Stanton, *Jefferson's Memorandum Books: Accounts, with Legal Records and Miscellany, 1767–1826* (Princeton, N.J.: Princeton University Press, 1997), 1:618.

26. E. Millicent Sowerby, *Catalogue of the Library of Thomas Jefferson, The Thomas Jefferson Memorial Foundation Edition* (Charlottesville: University of Virginia Press, 1983), 4:388. In response to those who might question why I do not attribute the hang of Jefferson's paintings to his time in Paris and the influence of French interior design I point to the fact that though Jefferson owned catalogs of private painting collections in England, he had no such books on France. His 1783 catalog of books did include catalogs and descriptions of French public collections, particularly those French collections that included antiquities. Jefferson was definitely interested in French art, but the painting hang at Monticello, unlike its furnishings, is most definitely based on the hanging practices that Jefferson saw and read about in England.

27. Jefferson, Bear, and Stanton, *Jefferson's Memorandum Books: Accounts, with Legal Records and Miscellany, 1767–1826*, 1:620.

28. Ann M. Lucas, "Jefferson's Print Collection," *Antiques* 144, no. 1 (July 1993): 89. She cites 10:447 of Jefferson's papers.

29. He also mentions the "Falling Spring" in the letter, which on page 21 in his *Notes on the State of Virginia* he describes as a spring near Warm Springs in Augusta, Virginia. But by the time he hangs his paintings at Monticello the "Falling Spring" is the only scenic wonder he mentioned to Cosway that is not illustrated. Perhaps after the discoveries of Lewis and Clark, the Falling Spring was not quite so awe-inspiring.

30. Thomas Jefferson, "To Maria Cosway, Paris Octob. 12, 1786," *The Papers of Thomas Jefferson*, 10:447.

31. Ann M. Lucas, "Sublime Views above Utility: Monticello's Offices," *Architectural History Symposium* (paper presented at the annual Architectural History Symposium, University of Virginia, Charlottesville, 1993).

ANNA O. MARLEY

32. For more on the Lewis and Clark artifacts see Elizabeth V. Chew, "Authority and Privilege in Thomas Jefferson's 'Indian Hall,'" in *Faces and Places in Early America* (Philadelphia: McNeil Center, forthcoming).

For more on the panoptic landscape see Allan Wallach, "Making a Picture of the View from Mount Holyoke," in *American Iconology: New Approaches to Nineteenth-Century Art and Literature*, ed. David Miller (New Haven and London: Yale University Press, 1993), 80–91.

33. See Thomas Jefferson, "Catalogue of Paintings at Monticello," c. 1809–15, Thomas Jefferson Papers (#2958-b), Special Collections Department, University of Virginia Library, printed as Appendix II in Susan Stein and Thomas Jefferson Memorial Foundation, Inc., *The Worlds of Thomas Jefferson at Monticello* (New York: H. N. Abrams, in association with the Thomas Jefferson Memorial Foundation, 1993), 434–436.

34. Stein and Thomas, *The Worlds of Thomas Jefferson at Monticello*, 435.

35. Francis Russell, "The Hanging and Display of Pictures, 1700–1850" (paper presented at *The Fashioning and Functioning of the British Country House*, Center for Advanced Study in the Visual Arts, National Gallery of Art, Washington, D.C., 1986), 143.

36. Scarsdale, *Catalogue of the Pictures, Statues, &C. At Kedleston, with Some Account of the Architecture*.

37. Chew, "Authority and Privilege in Thomas Jefferson's 'Indian Hall.'"

38. Both Washington and Jefferson hung prints along with paintings in their public rooms. This was not the practice in elite British public spaces like Kedleston and Hagley, where dining rooms were hung exclusively with paintings.

39. Stein and Thomas, *The Worlds of Thomas Jefferson at Monticello*, 190.

40. Indeed, in 2010, two years after my presentation of this research as a 2008 Robert H. Smith International Center for Jefferson Studies Fellow at Monticello, the Dining Room at Monticello was reinstalled to reflect this painting hang.

41. Paraphrased from letter to Cosway asking of landscape painters, "Where could they find such objects as in America for the exercise of their enchanting art?"

42. Conversations with Diane Ehrenpreis, curatorial art historian at Monticello, in October of 2008, have informed my references to Monticello's mirrors.

43. For more comparisons between the two presidents' painting hang see Roger Stein, "Mr. Jefferson as Museum Maker," in *Shaping the Body Politic*, ed. Maurie D. McInnis and Louis P. Nelson, 194–230; and Stein and Thomas, *The Worlds of Thomas Jefferson at Monticello*.

PART II

Religion and the Churches

4

ENGLISH ARTISANS' CHURCHES
AND NORTH AMERICA

TRADITIONS OF VERNACULAR CLASSICISM

IN THE EIGHTEENTH CENTURY

Peter Guillery

The church of St. George, Portsea (Fig. 4.1), was built in 1753–54 by and for shipwrights and other artisans who worked in, and lived just outside, Portsmouth's great naval dockyard, the single most important working hub of British sea power. Of this church, Nikolaus Pevsner, the German architectural historian who founded the *Buildings of England* series, wrote, "It must strike American visitors as a greeting from New England."[1] The direction of travel was in fact, if unsurprisingly, the other way around. But if the church has been understood as looking American yet is not, why is that so, and what does it mean?[2] When Pevsner wrote those words about the church of St. George, Portsea, it was a commonplace that the transmission of polite or high-status architectural ideas and styles across the Atlantic in the eighteenth century was a straightforward flow from east to west. John Summerson summed up that period's perceptions of this relationship, arguing that American architectural standards were "English standards pure and simple. Up to the revolution of 1775–83 it is not possible to discern any autonomous vitality in American architecture. A remote provincial outcrop of the English school, there was no local leadership of any consequence and a total dependence on contacts with England through the immigration of craftsmen and the circulation of books."[3] That perspective on architectural history was one that was essentially about major buildings, those conceived by and produced for the highest strata of society, such as steepled churches: Christ (Old North) Church, Boston (1723), or Christ Church, Philadelphia (1727–54), for example, which bear comparison in these terms to London churches like St. James, Piccadilly (1676–84), or St. Martin in the Fields (1721–26).[4] But scholarship has for the most part moved on, and much architectural-historical writing of the last

FIGURE 4.1. *The church of St. George, Portsea, Hampshire, England,*
built in 1753–54 by and for artisans of Portsmouth Naval Dockyard.
© *Colin Cromwell; source: Historic England.*

few decades has delved deeper. In America, particularly, Henry Glassie, Dell
Upton, Bernard Herman, Carl Lounsbury, Louis Nelson, and others, have
shown that what Summerson asserted cannot be said for vernacular building traditions.[5] There was no comparably inevitable flow of architectural for-
mulae, and relationships with English precedent were much more complex.
There are significant aspects of building practice and specific local instances
where humbler buildings in North America did follow British precedents, as
recent research has explored in novel ways, as by Laurie Smith in the context of geometrical design, Daniel Maudlin in relation to Nova Scotia, Roger
Leech on Bristol, or Peter Benes on meeting houses.[6] But a Vernacular Architecture Group conference titled "Diffusion and Invention: Vernacular Building in England and the New World" (2005) produced strong emphases on
divergences in building traditions during the seventeenth century, the speed
of the separation laying bare the crucial roles of humble agency and local conditions, especially climate and available building materials.[7]

What has perhaps not been sufficiently considered is that polite culture,
or, in an architectural context, classicism, was not the only source from
which English emigrants to North America who set about building might

PETER GUILLERY

have drawn. Those emigrants who were inclined to build did not necessarily arrive with architectural sensibilities that were primarily or even significantly derived from polite precedents. The purpose of addressing here a part of the English end of this relationship is not to provide, or even to suggest, precise vernacular prototypes or models. It would, after all, be paradoxical to speak of the spread of any vernacular, if the word is to retain its meaning as an indicator of the local and indigenous. Instead, the intention is to consider and illustrate a certain English cultural environment, based in towns and among artisans who had their own cohesive vernacular building traditions and distinctive outlooks. This part of English society would, through emigration, have contributed substantially to the formation of a sound base for inventive architectural development in America, independent of a top-down model and definitely not mimetic in nature, generating something that was both new and derivative. The result, in a new country, can also, but separately, be termed vernacular or indigenous.

It would be possible to divert at length on the question of definitions of the term artisan, but suffice it to say that for present purposes the word is used here as from the context of urban England in the late seventeenth and eighteenth centuries, and that in economic terms it refers to roughly the second quartile of the urban English population in the eighteenth century, the bottom half of the top half, broadly, tradespeople—those who were neither poor nor rich. More importantly and specifically, in cultural terms the label artisan refers here to a long urbanized social stratum that defined itself in almost exclusively masculine and retrospective terms (and this exclusivity was deliberate and self-protective). For this group respectability and, increasingly, economic survival, derived from what was perceived as ancient or at least long-standing custom or tradition, rooted in trade skills and economic independence. Status was not primarily based in consumption habits or emulative behavior.[8]

In the culturally conservative environment inhabited by eighteenth-century English urban artisans there was great continuity of vernacular building practices. This was true in and around London, by far England's biggest concentration of artisans, as well as in other towns with concentrations of skilled workers, among which ports, especially those with naval dockyards, were important. Church building is a field that American scholars, led by some of those already named, have had no difficulty in embracing as vernacular, but one which in England, for ecclesiological and many other reasons, is generally considered only as high-style architecture, and wholly separated from discussions of things vernacular. There, perhaps, in part at least, is the rub, as well as something of what lies behind Pevsner's peculiar and seemingly unhistorical observation about St. George, Portsea.

English emigrants to America, many of whom were artisans or of artisan descent, in the sense adumbrated here, would have taken with them vernacular customs and cultures and a good deal of nostalgia, that is, a yearning for a past perceived as better but lost. This was manifest, not insignificantly, in a search for liberty and simplicity. Emulative politeness may have been in the ascendant in eighteenth-century England, but its roots were in a dominant section of society, the established and prospering members of which would not, as a rule, have been inclined to leave for the hardships of a new country. For many, of course, emigration offered an open road to gentility where other routes were obstructed. The American path to politeness, which Richard Bushman has called the acquisition of vernacular gentility, may have been relatively open, but for most it was a long haul from a humble starting point, and many of the travelers on this path will have carried within themselves ambivalence about fashion and emulative behavior in relation to respectability rooted in custom.[9] There were other important differences. Where many English artisans, notably in London and the dockyard towns, might have perceived themselves as a rearguard attached to an old culture, artisans in America were seeking a better life in a new place, with fewer barriers to mobility. The New World lacked the coercive and oppositional social countercurrents of seventeenth- and eighteenth-century England. The mentalities of emigrants might, therefore, have been more imaginative and opportunistic, as well as nostalgic.

These generalizations need to be tied down to some particulars. England's dockyard and other maritime towns are key places in terms of the subject matter of this volume. There are, no doubt, many ways in which it would be germane to consider aspects of their building culture. In just one of these the focus hereafter is on three naval towns: Deptford, Deal, and Portsmouth. These were settlements that mixed determined cultural conservatism with oppositional political radicalism. In the dockyards there was great and cultivated continuity of practice; skilled workers could not be easily replaced. From at least the 1720s onward difficult labor relations were endemic. Communication between the workforces in the naval dockyards was good enough as to enable effective combined strike action on numerous occasions, perhaps most seriously in 1775 when, it has been argued, a strike may have compromised the effectiveness of the British response to the American rebellion.[10] In the working practices of these dockyard towns there was strong adherence to

PETER GUILLERY

customary practice, and an outlook that was anything but uncritically emulative in relation to polite culture. Yet, population growth, comparative affluence, and the absence of the social hierarchies that were usual elsewhere fostered entrepreneurial endeavor and innovation.

Deptford, now an inner-city suburb, was at this time just outside London, but a good-sized town in its own right, one that had grown enormously since the 1660s to become a significant maritime-industrial satellite of the metropolis, centered on its naval dockyard.[11] Artisan identity in Deptford was nicely captured by the German tourist Sophie von la Roche when she visited in 1786. She was struck by the sight of the dockyard men, reporting:

> Seeing the carpenters go out through the gate for lunch, each carrying his ration of wood on his shoulder, while a number carried a large net full of shavings. A nice sight indeed, this crowd of family fathers with their domestic provision of tinder going to their midday soup, weary from their labours and honest toil. God! How small a portion of these six million guineas they help to earn, falls to their lot! They were mostly fine-looking fellows; many of them with the eye of a mathematician, still making calculations. In them I saw embodied the fine English schools, where the citizen's son, like the son of the aristocrat, is taught all kinds of mathematics and really good Latin. I am sure many of them will be reading the papers this evening and talking of the common welfare. . . . The respect with which our coachman had to treat these working-people, not being allowed to turn in the narrow street until they had passed, gave me time to consider and contemplate them.[12]

Similar scenes might have been seen on England's south coast in Portsmouth, on similar streets. Portsmouth was the naval town par excellence, its dockyard the nation's biggest, with a workforce ranging from fifteen hundred to three thousand through the eighteenth century. The "suburb" of Portsea was built alongside the great naval dockyard to house its workers and associated tradespeople, growing from nothing at the beginning of the eighteenth century to a population of more than four thousand in its own right by 1801.[13] In both Deptford and Portsea there was wealth and literacy, and polite commodities like tea and silver were widely available. In both places eighteenth-century housing development was led by speculating dockyard workers, who, with their independent and self-sufficient traditions, also built their own churches. Movement between these and other dockyard towns, especially Woolwich and Chatham, was common. Against any perception that architectural conservatism was a product of isolation, it should be remembered that through the eighteenth century, as has already been mentioned, naval dockyard workers were able effectively to organize strikes on a national basis.

In southeast England, on Kent's east coast, just around the corner from Chatham, is Deal, an eighteenth-century maritime town, where virtually all ships traveling between London and points overseas stopped for servicing and to await fair winds. Deal was a chartered port from 1699 with a naval provisioning yard from 1703. It was also a flourishing center of boatbuilding, less formal marine provisioning, corruption, and smuggling: an "impious and remorseless town" of "fraud, oppression, theft and rapine."[14] There was money, wherever it came from. Along and around Middle Street in Deal there is still an astonishingly large and varied group of modest eighteenth-century urban houses, built for habitation by sea pilots, mariners, traders, and victualers.[15]

Buildings of a similar nature, if regionally somewhat various, could be shown from many other coastal places, but the purpose here in sticking with London and these few southern dockyard or navy towns is to home in on some churches to look more exactingly at a particular building tradition, that, as indicated at the outset, was not directly diffused across the Atlantic, but which illustrates the existence of and scope for independent architectural development among artisans, and demonstrates that, through people of comparable backgrounds, this kind of improvisation occurred in England as well as in America, where it is perhaps more familiar.

To show this it is necessary to track the transmission of a particular type of building from one group of English urban, and largely maritime, artisans to another, from the 1630s through to the 1730s. Deptford's medieval parish church of St. Nicholas was rebuilt, all save its tower, in 1696–97. Money for this rebuilding was raised locally through a voluntary subscription and a hefty rate. There was, as has been stressed, wealth in the newly expanded and largely artisan town. The inhabitants of Deptford were, unusually, able to provide themselves with an essentially new church without external involvement or support. Prominent among those behind this project was Isaac Loader, an anchorsmith. The latterly famous diarist, and high Anglican, John Evelyn, who lived grandly nearby at Sayes Court, described Loader, with distaste, as being of Anabaptist descent.[16] But this was the parish (that is Anglican) church, not a Dissenter's chapel. The rebuilding was carried out to designs by Charley Stanton, a carpenter from Southwark, on the south side of London Bridge, a place densely populated with artisans and laborers. Stanton provided a centralized auditory interior (for sermons not processions), employing an architectural formula that he had previously tried out in 1675–79 for the church of St. Mary Magdalene, Bermondsey, the riverside district that lies between

FIGURE 4.2. *The church of St. Mary Magdalene, Bermondsey, Surrey (now London), England, built in 1675–79, showing the interior from the east. Photographed for the Royal Commission on the Historical Monuments of England in 1929.© Historic England.*

Southwark and Deptford (Fig. 4.2).[17] The combination in late seventeenth-century London of such purely classical interiors with plain brick exteriors is usually associated with Christopher Wren's post-Fire churches. But none of Wren's comparable buildings antedate the Bermondsey church. Every part of Stanton's buildings, from the chaste almost Palladian Tuscan interiors, to the scrolled gables over the transeptal bays on plain brick exteriors, to the overall dimensions, and, most significantly, the plan form, in fact derives from even earlier churches that had been built by and for largely artisan populations in other working suburbs of seventeenth-century London, at Westminster Broadway in 1635–42, and at Poplar in 1642–54 (Figs 4.3 & 4.4). This last chapel also served the adjoining east London hamlet of Blackwall, where the East India Company built its ships, and from where, most pertinently in the context of this volume, the Virginia settlers embarked in December 1606. The prime mover in the completion of the Poplar Chapel in the 1650s was Maurice

FIGURE 4.3. *The Poplar Chapel (latterly the church of St. Matthias, Poplar), Middlesex (now London), England, built in 1642–54, showing the interior from the west. Photographed by Derek Kendall in 2004. © Historic England.*

Thompson, an eminent Puritan merchant who had made his fortune in Virginia and become a close associate of Oliver Cromwell's.[18]

In all these eastern suburbs of London there was strong commitment to Cromwell's side of England's great seventeenth-century political and liturgical divides. These places were characterized by a Calvinist consensus at the beginning of the seventeenth century, which led to the rejection of Arminian or Laudian religious reforms in the 1630s, and thence to widespread Dissent or Nonconformity after the Restoration. These are not Puritan churches, but they are demonstrably anti-Laudian in their chancel-less centralization and simple and undecorated Protestant functionality. The perpetuation of this originally moderate Calvinist church type in places like Bermondsey and Deptford in the late seventeenth century is a rejection of the more ceremonial or re-Laudianizing alternatives that Wren and others introduced after the Fire. The tacking on of small chancels may simply be a concession to the post-Restoration settlement. That some of Wren's churches are similar needs

PETER GUILLERY

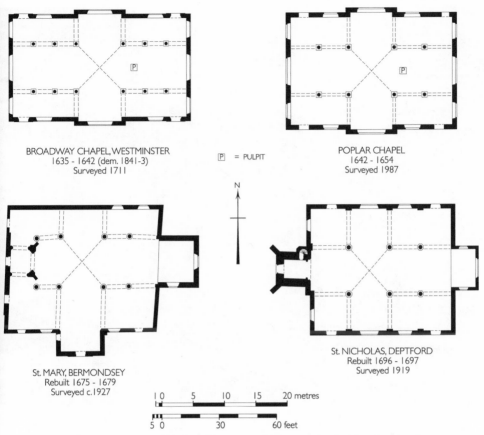

BROADWAY CHAPEL, WESTMINSTER
1635 - 1642 (dem. 1841-3)
Surveyed 1711

$\boxed{P}$ = PULPIT

POPLAR CHAPEL
1642 - 1654
Surveyed 1987

N

St. MARY, BERMONDSEY
Rebuilt 1675 - 1679
Surveyed c.1927

St. NICHOLAS, DEPTFORD
Rebuilt 1696 - 1697
Surveyed 1919

1 0   5   10   15   20 metres

5 0   30   60 feet

FIGURE 4.4. *Reconstructed plans of seventeenth-century suburban London churches.*
Drawing by Andrew Donald, reproduced by permission of Historic England.

to be understood as the result of inventive compromises with an existing vernacular approach on Wren's part. In the past this aspect of Wren's architecture has been ascribed to the influence of Dutch architecture, something in
which he is not known to have shown any interest. The Dutch influence is
there, but at a remove, mediated by earlier seventeenth-century Londoners
who were more broadly sympathetic to the Dutch approach to religion and
religious architecture in the first place.

This strongly centralized auditory church type found further echoes in
other places with maritime links and artisan populations. There was a working and mercantile Danish population in London's eastern maritime suburbs, in Wapping, principally because of the Scandinavian timber trade. The
Danish or so-called mariners' church in Wellclose Square of 1694-96, de-

FIGURE 4.5. *The church of St. George in the East, Wapping, Middlesex (now London), England, built in 1714–29, Nicholas Hawksmoor, architect, showing the interior from the west. Photographed by Bedford Lemere for the National Buildings Record in April 1941, a few months before the church was gutted by incendiary bombs. Reproduced by permission of Historic England.*

signed by Caius Gabriel Cibber, himself a Danish immigrant, had a strongly centralized cross-axial interior. In the same decade, it might be noted, Scandinavian, Dutch, and English people combined to build the differently centralized church of Holy Trinity in Wilmington, Delaware.

The cross-axial kind of interior was even adopted and scaled up by Nicholas Hawksmoor in some of the great east London churches that were initiated by the high Anglican Tory government following the Fifty New Churches Act of 1711 which showered munificence, and awe-inspiring buildings, on what were thought to be dangerously godless suburbs, as at St. George in the East of 1714–29, also in Wapping (Fig. 4.5). Despite, or maybe even because of, this high-level appropriation, this sort of centralized church interior fell outside the mainstream of church building in later eighteenth-century England.

But it can be picked up in Deal and Portsea. The church of St. George the Martyr in Deal was built in 1706–16. It is a rectangular brick box with slight cross-axial transeptal projections, its overall plan proportions close to those of St. Nicholas Deptford and its predecessors. It was intended principally for use by those engaged with the sea for what was in effect then a new town, and was probably designed by a local builder, Samuel Simmons, following a fundraising campaign chiefly promoted by the mayor, Thomas Powell, a ships' victualer. Outside help had to be garnered to complete the building, but this would not significantly have influenced its form. Inside, much has been altered, but early plans show that the seating and fittings were originally oriented north–south, the pews facing a three-decker pulpit on the south side, the altar off to the east side in a mere gesture of a chancel that is, unexpectedly perhaps, under a cupola at the front. This layout is a departure from that of the forerunners that have been described, but the functionality of the auditory intent is perhaps even more explicit.[19]

And so, finally, attention must return to the church of St. George Portsea (Fig. 4.1). The leaflet historical guide to this church produced by the local parish tells us, echoing Pevsner in being illuminatingly misleading, that "its style is known as American Colonial."[20] It was built in 1753–54 by dockyard artisans to serve their own community and to assert Portsea's independence of Portsmouth. Its designer was probably Nicholas Vass, a house carpenter who had worked in the dockyard since 1734.[21] The builders working under him were fifteen shipwrights, three gentlemen, a carpenter, a tallow chandler, and a grocer. There is no known evidence that any of them had crossed the Atlantic. Here, it is the exterior that departs from the London forerunners. There are no obvious models for this strangely blockish assemblage. It is a pragmatically devised and simple functional shell for another auditory interior (Figs. 4.6 and 4.7). This does very much hark back to the seventeenth-century London type. There is a cross-in-square plan and Tuscan columns. Originally a centralized triple-decker pulpit was located in front of the altar, an arrangement that seems to follow on from the seventeenth-century forerunners, but which was unusual in the mid-eighteenth century. It did become more common in late Georgian urban churches, and was, in fact, adopted in a reseating of St. George's, Deal, in 1822.[22]

It is well documented that the artisans of Deptford, Deal, and Portsea had extensive contacts with each other through the eighteenth century. So it is

hardly surprising that their churches should have certain common qualities. The crucial point is not just that there were these links, but that architectural initiatives were taken and seen through without significant high-style influence or interference. There is a kind of cultural cocoon around these buildings. The metaphor of a cocoon has protective and closed connotations, but it also speaks of inner transformation. The organism within has existed without protection, and will so exist again, in a new form, but in the meantime interaction with an external environment has shut down. In all these places and times there was receptivity to new forms, that is to the polite, but there is also an evident unwillingness to be overwhelmed or determined by it.

These English artisans' churches, it must be acknowledged, have little in common with eighteenth-century American churches. The argument here is not that in narrow formal terms there are transatlantic analogs. These English churches were apparently not closely imitated across the Atlantic. Transatlantic differences of landscape and climate did mean that vernacular build-

PETER GUILLERY

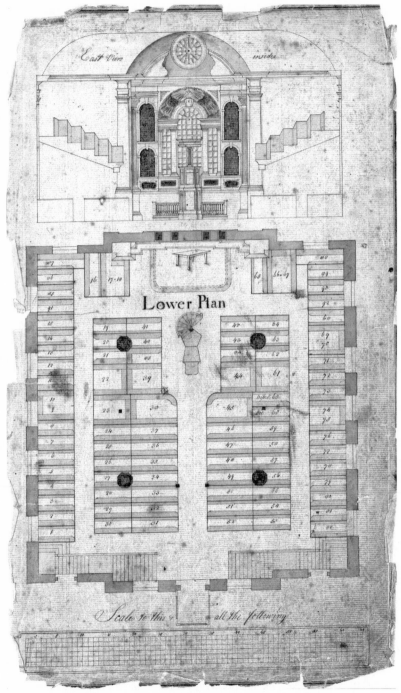

FIGURE 4.7. *The church of St. George, Portsea, plan and section drawn in 1753. Portsmouth Museums and Records Service.*

ing practices quickly diverged. Yet there is a kind of kinship. The architectural vocabulary, in both its material and spatial aspects, is broadly similar to that of many early American churches, suggesting something in the way of common cultural frameworks and experiences. Virginia's chancel-less room churches, even those larger examples of cruciform plan, developed differently and separately, and, if formal similarities are sought in England, perhaps they are more to be found in early Nonconformist chapels.[23] But, to return to the opening quotation, Pevsner's perception of American-ness in St. George, Portsea, was a recognition, if unwitting, that the inventive vernacular approaches to building on which English emigrants to America and their descendants drew, continued to find expression in eighteenth-century England as well.

NOTES

1. Nikolaus Pevsner and David Lloyd, *The Buildings of England: Hampshire and the Isle of Wight* (Harmondsworth: Penguin, 1967), 439.

2. This essay presents material published elsewhere, reworked to arrive at new conclusions. See Peter Guillery, *The Small House in Eighteenth-Century London: A Social and Architectural History* (New Haven and London: Yale University Press, 2004); Peter Guillery, "Suburban Models, or Calvinism and Continuity in London's Seventeenth-Century Church Architecture," *Architectural History* 48 (2005): 69–106.

3. John Summerson, *Architecture in Britain: 1530 to 1830*, 5th ed. (Harmondsworth: Penguin, 1970), 539.

4. Stephen P. Dorsey, *Early English Churches in America, 1607–1807* (New York and Oxford: Oxford University Press, 1952). This perspective has been perpetuated in Terry Friedman, *The Eighteenth-Century Church in Britain* (New Haven and London: Yale University Press, 2011), 608–14.

5. Henry Glassie, *Folk Housing in Middle Virginia* (Knoxville: University of Tennessee Press, 1975); Henry Glassie, *Vernacular Architecture* (Bloomington: Indiana University Press, 2000); Dell Upton, *Holy Things and Profane: Anglican Parish Churches in Colonial Virginia* (New Haven and London: Yale University Press, 1997); Gabrielle M. Lanier and Bernard L. Herman, *Everyday Architecture of the Mid-Atlantic: Looking at Buildings and Landscapes* (Baltimore: Johns Hopkins University Press, 1997); Bernard L. Herman, *Town House: Architecture and Material Life in the Early American City, 1780–1830* (Chapel Hill: University of North Carolina Press, 2005); Carl Lounsbury, "Anglican Church Design in the Chesapeake: English Inheritances and Regional Interpretations," in *Constructing Image, Identity, and Place: Perspectives in Vernacular Architecture IX*, ed. Alison K. Hoagland and Kenneth A. Breisch (Knoxville: University of Tennessee Press, 2003), 22–38; Louis P. Nelson, *The Beauty of Holiness: Anglicanism and Architecture in Colonial South Carolina* (Chapel Hill: University of North Carolina Press, 2009).

6. Laurie Smith, "Following the Geometrical Design Path: From Ely to Jamestown,

Virginia," in *Built from Below: British Architecture and the Vernacular*, ed. Peter Guillery (Abingdon: Routledge, 2011), 11–32; Daniel Maudlin, "Architecture and Identity on the Edge of Empire: The Early Domestic Architecture of Scottish Settlers in Nova Scotia, Canada, 1800–1850," *Architectural History* 50 (2007): 95–123; Roger H. Leech, *The Town House in Medieval and Early Modern Bristol* (Swindon: English Heritage, 2014), chapter 12, "Bristol and the Atlantic World," 357–68; Peter Benes, *Meeting Houses of Early New England* (Amherst, Mass: University of Massachusetts Press, 2012).

7. A first version of the present essay was presented at this conference.

8. See, among much else on this subject, Edward P. Thompson, *The Making of the English Working Class* (Harmondsworth: Penguin, 1968); Geoffrey Crossick, ed., *The Artisan and the European Town, 1500–1900* (Aldershot: Scolar Press, 1997); David R. Green, *From Artisans to Paupers: Economic Change and Poverty in London, 1790–1870* (Aldershot: Scolar Press, 1995); Guillery, *The Small House in Eighteenth-Century London*.

9. Richard L. Bushman, *The Refinement of America: Persons, Houses, Cities* (New York: Vintage, 1992).

10. Roger Knight, "From Impressment to Task Work: Strikes and Disruption in the Royal Dockyards, 1688–1788," and Roger Morriss, "Government and Community: The Changing Context of Labour Relations, 1770–1830," both in *History of Work and Labour Relations in the Royal Dockyards*, ed. Kenneth Lunn and Ann Day (London: Routledge, 1999), 1–20 and 21–40.

11. Bernard L. Herman and Peter Guillery, "Negotiating Classicism in Eighteenth-Century Deptford and Philadelphia," in *Articulating Classicism: New Approaches to Eighteenth-Century Architecture*, ed. Barbara Arciszewska and Elizabeth McKellar (Aldershot: Ashgate, 2004), 187–225.

12. Sophie von la Roche, *Sophie in London, 1786: Being the Diary of Sophie von la Roche*, trans. Clare Williams (London: Jonathan Cape, 1933), 253.

13. For links to North America, see Roger Leech, "Portsmouth—A Window on the World?," in *Cities in the World, 1500–2000*, ed. Adrian Green and Roger Leech (Leeds: Maney, 2006), 299–306. For Portsea more generally, see Christopher William Chalklin, *The Provincial Towns of Georgian England: A study of the building process, 1740–1820* (London: McGill-Queen's University Press, 1974), 122–29; Ann Veronica Coats, "The œconomy of the Navy and Portsmouth: A Discourse between the Civilian Naval Administration of Portsmouth Dockyard and the Surrounding Communities, 1650–1800" (Ph.D. diss., University of Sussex, 2000).

14. Anonymous, *Deal in an Uproar*, 1709, as quoted in Friedman, *The Eighteenth-Century Church in Britain*, 77, 131.

15. John Newman, *The Buildings of England: North East and East Kent*, 3rd ed. (Harmondsworth: Penguin, 1983), 281; Gregory Holyoake, *Deal and Walmer: A Celebration* (Wimborne Minster: Dovecote Press, 2009).

16. British Library, Add. MS 78629A, Evelyn Papers, map of Deptford in 1623, copied and annotated by John Evelyn, ca. 1703; B. R. Leftwich, "The Parish of St Nicholas, Deptford," *Ecclesiological Society Transactions* 1/4 (1941): 41.

17. Royal Commission on Historical Monuments (England), *London, v: East London* (London: Her Majesty's Stationery Office, 1930), 1–3, 15–16, with supporting inventory cards in Historic England Archives, of 1919 for St. Nicholas and ca. 1927 for St. Mary Magdalene, both by A. W. Clapham; Bridget Cherry and Nikolaus Pevsner, *The Buildings of England; London 2: South* (Harmondsworth: Penguin, 1983), 402, 599; Howard Colvin, *A Biographical Dictionary of British Architects, 1600–1840* 4th ed. (New Haven and London: Yale University Press, 2008), 976.

18. Guillery, "Suburban Models."

19. Newman, *The Buildings of England*, 282; Barbara Collins, *A Short History of the Civic Church of St. George-the-Martyr, Deal, Kent* (Deal: Mercury Printing Service, 1966); "St. George's Church, Deal, 1716–1799: A Commemorative Booklet" (1999). The architectural design has recently been attributed to John James; see Friedman, *The Eighteenth-Century Church in Britain*, 474–75. In 1712 James was brought in to oversee completion of the church, but it is not evident that he had any earlier involvement, and the building, its cupola apart, does not look like something James would have designed.

20. "A Brief History of St. George's Portsea, by the congregation and others," n.d.; Coats, "The œconomy of the navy and Portsmouth."

21. Nigel Yates, *Buildings, Faith and Worship: The Liturgical Arrangement of Anglican Churches 1600–1900* (Oxford: Oxford University Press, revised 2000), 87, 89.

22. Upton, *Holy Things and Profane*; Lounsbury, "Anglican Church Design in the Chesapeake."

23. Benes, *Meeting Houses of Early New England*.

5

THE NEW ENGLAND MEETINGHOUSE

AN ATLANTIC PERSPECTIVE

Peter Benes

The "Great Migration" of twenty thousand English Puritans to Massachusetts Bay, Connecticut, and New Haven between 1630 and 1640 put an immediate burden on builders of religious and civic structures in North America. The New England meetinghouse, an impermanent and multipurpose wood-framed structure that lay at the heart of immigrants' transition from the Old World to the New, allowed space for Calvinist services that focused on the sermon and Communion while also providing areas for civil and defensive use. Unlike British-based churches of the middle and southern colonies, however, these buildings had a distinctly Reformist origin that distinguished them from the Anglican structures that sprang up in the Chesapeake region and Virginia, which conformed to types already well known in England. A study of 205 seventeenth- and eighteenth-century Congregational, Presbyterian, Baptist, and Dutch Reformed meetinghouses still standing in New England and Long Island, supported by data from approximately two thousand additional examples known only from documents — primarily taken from town histories, parish histories, and town records — suggests that the first two generations of builders derived architectural ideas from French Huguenot, Scottish Reformed, and Dutch Reformed models, as well as from vernacular, agricultural, or domestic structures known to have existed in England itself. Drawing on old-growth forests in North America, builders recreated Protestant European forms in America with wood-framed, barn-like structures, some examples heavily influenced by mill-building and bridge-building traditions.[1]

The Reformed approach was gradually abandoned in favor of a more inclusive architectural model increasingly reflective of eighteenth-century British political and religious hegemony — but one that was still based on communally built wood-framed structures. The "flat" or "English" gabled roof replaced the Puritan "four-square" roof; standing bell towers replaced central turrets; and private pews replaced uncomfortable benches. This eventually allowed men and women to sit together as families. By 1790 most Reformed congregations in New England were no longer raising "meetinghouses" but building "churches," many ultimately modeled on London-based Anglican precedents. Some congregations were even employing masons and looking for architectural permanence.

Most scholars agree on how to interpret these early structures.[2] With one or two exceptions they were built as "meetinghouses," meaning they were raised by towns or parishes at public expense and were primarily intended for religious meetings and occasional lectures held by Congregational denominations. (The exceptions were communities in Rhode Island, which often were Baptist, Anglican, or Quaker.) Virtually all served important secular or defensive purposes that provided a place for town meetings, for convening trials, or holding political conventions; many were surrounded by a palisade or stone enclosure to help secure them from attacks by armed men. These same structures also served as hospitals, powder houses, and singing schools, and in some cases loft and gallery spaces were reserved for civic purposes. Architecturally, they all were part of a long-term process that transformed the early multipurpose meetinghouse into a church as Reformed or formerly Puritan congregations gradually became reconciled to the more inclusive and formalized Anglicanism they had left behind in England. This transformation was usually accompanied by the disestablishment of the Congregational/Presbyterian taxing system and changes to a number of liturgical practices.

What historians have failed to agree on is the origin of their architectural style. Opinions fall into three basic schools of thought. One group believes that both the term *meetinghouse* and its architecture were exclusively American.[3] A second group believes that they came from known English precedents (hip-roofed East Anglian market halls, London churches designed by Christopher Wren, vernacular designs from farmyard barns and stables).[4] A third group has suggested that joiners were influenced by an Atlantic conglomerate made up of Huguenot, Dutch Reformed, and Scottish church building traditions of the sixteenth and seventeenth centuries.[5] I generally subscribe to the last of these positions while also acknowledging the former two make valid points.

This chapter attempts to sort out and identify the Atlantic conglomerate that influenced New England meetinghouses. It begins by examining four seventeenth-century meetinghouses raised by towns and parishes in New England between 1639 and 1699: the "four-square" meetinghouse built in the New Haven Colony in 1639; a "long house" raised in Plymouth, Massachusetts, in 1683; the octagonal meetinghouse built in Fairfield, Connecticut, in 1698; and the large meetinghouse built at Brattle Square in Boston in 1699. While we have contemporary images only of the last example, we do have period descriptions and a few specifications of all four. In each case we will trace their possible source to earlier models in Europe and Great Britain.

We begin with the "four-square" meetinghouse raised in New Haven in November of 1639.[6] The New Haven colony was founded by Reverend John Davenport, formerly of Oxford and London, who had also spent time as a preacher in Amsterdam. Davenport had earlier declined the opportunity to stay in the Boston area and determined instead to settle a new colony in Connecticut with his followers. Accordingly, he and Theophilus Eaton explored the country along the seacoast west of the Connecticut River and finally fixed on Quinnipiac as the place for their settlement. To meet the long-range religious and municipal requirements of the new colony, its founders set aside £500 to build the first large meetinghouse in New England whose dimensions are known from town records. The meetinghouse was framed by William Andrews, a joiner of some wealth, who became a proprietor of the new colony. At "fifty foot square," it may have been the largest such structure in New England at the time and one apparently provided with most key components of the four-square, wood-framed, meetinghouse: a hip roof, gallery seats for about sixty persons, and a "tower and turret" in the center of its roof, with the turret surmounted by a railed platform. "Halfe pillars" tied with a crossbeam were added in 1648, presumably to help support the galleries, and despite recurring problems with rotting timbers, this house was used by the town for thirty years.[7] In its outward appearance, the structure may have resembled all or part of two hypothetical meetinghouses pictured in the diary of young Dudley Woodbridge, who visited Deerfield, Massachusetts, in 1728. On the same page as his illustration of the Deerfield thirty-by-thirty-foot meetinghouse he drew two views of larger meetinghouses with double towers and what appear to be two tiers of galleries (Fig. 5.1). Dormers project from each roof. Neither structure is identified, but this may have been Woodbridge's way of recalling what larger versions of Deerfield might have looked like. Mounted over the uppermost turret was a dated iron weathervane much like the one removed from the Hartford meetinghouse when it was taken down in 1737.

These descriptions suggest that builder William Andrews not only had an intimate knowledge of vernacular English bridge-making, barn-building, and fort-building traditions, but a familiarity with one or several contemporary European Protestant houses of worship. About 1566 the artist Jean Perrissin

FIGURE 5.1. Delineated at Deerfield, Deerfield Meeting houses [and] Dwelling houses. *Pen and ink and watercolor drawings in a journal kept by Dudley Woodbridge (1705–1790) during his trip to the Connecticut Valley. Page 5, Dudley Woodbridge journal, October 1–10, 1728. Dimensions: 14.2 cm x 8.8 cm. Collection of the Massachusetts Historical Society.*

FIGURE 5.2. Temple de Lyon, Nommé Paradis. *Interior painting of a marriage
ceremony in the Huguenot temple at Paradis, Lyon, France, ca. 1566, showing
benches, raised pulpit, and galleries. Attributed to Jean Perrissin (ca. 1536–1611).
Paint on wood. Bibliothèque de Genève, Centre d'iconographie genèvoise.*

painted a wedding scene in a recently constructed Huguenot house of worship in Lyon, France. According to early Huguenot practice, this *temple* appears to be round, with exterior railed stairways leading to the second-floor
gallery. One of scores of such Protestant houses of worship built in France
after Henry IV issued the Edict of Nantes in 1598, the Temple de Lyon,
Nommé Paradis embodies the full range of Reformist ideals (Fig. 5.2). The

preacher is at the center. The pulpit is raised so that everyone can hear him, including those in the gallery. Benches and crude seating surround him on all sides.

Andrews may also have been familiar with the four-square design at Burntisland, Scotland. A sixty-foot-square masonry structure raised in 1592, the Burntisland kirk supported its roof and central tower on four massive stone pillars, one of which held the pulpit. The structure was remodeled at least three times in the eighteenth, nineteenth, and early twentieth centuries, but enough remains to indicate it had a centrally located pulpit, a second-floor "loft" (or gallery) on four sides, a "squat" central turret topped by a wooden spire, and a hip roof. The builder was probably John Roche, a mason, who is also credited with being the architect. Described locally and by past historians as a copy of an Amsterdam church, the kirk is now thought to have antedated this by many years. The English architectural historian Andrew Spicer writes that the building was a "sturdy home product" or a "home-spun solution to the demands of Reformed worship."[8]

Could William Andrews have drawn on these sources? We have no proof, but he likely did. The Quinnipiac planters came from a tightly knit and relatively sophisticated group of professional Puritans that emigrated from London, England. The group is also known to have adopted other aspects of classical or European town planning in designing their fledgling colony. John Brockett (or another unknown surveyor), who laid out the original bounds for New Haven, followed a concept introduced by the Roman engineer and architect Marcus Vitruvius Pollio, whose writings encouraged planners to divide new towns into nine equal squares diagonally oriented away from prevailing winds.[9] Without specific evidence, we can only say that William Andrews and other early New England meetinghouse joiners were probably familiar with Huguenot temples and Scottish kirks and that they found similar "Protestant" solutions. That they chose four-square meetinghouses rather than hexagonal or octagonal ones and designed wood frames rather than masonry or brick walls may have been less important than that they were following a well-established European formula for Reformed ecclesiastic architecture whose bell towers were mounted centrally and whose interior pews and benches were arranged *"en manière de théâtre"* — in short, a Protestant house of worship grounded on Calvinist principles and articulated through vernacular English barn-building and bridge-building traditions.[10]

The new "four-square" style resonated widely with New Englanders. In 1668 William Andrews's son, Nathan Andrews, built New Haven's second meetinghouse, a square structure on the same site as the old one, and it may have virtually duplicated the first. A plan of the second drawn by Reverend Ezra Stiles shows the pulpit in the center, men and women sitting in separate benches, with wealthy individuals occupying separate pews. It was apparently followed by other large congregations in the early 1640s, among them Hartford and Boston, and it became the leading period-one meetinghouse type in the region. Out of 176 Reformed first-period structures built between 1622 and 1715 whose dimensions are known, sixty-eight followed an exactly square shape—most commonly thirty by thirty or forty by forty feet. But approximately half that number came fairly close to this ratio, such as the one built in 1700 at Newbury, Massachusetts, whose dimensions were sixty by fifty feet, posts twenty-four feet, with four large gable windows—an almost square design whose length exceeded its width by only a few feet. Dimensions are unknown for approximately 172 meetinghouses during this same period.

Our second example is a "long house" erected in Plymouth, Massachusetts, in 1683 whose dimensions were forty-five feet long and twenty-two feet wide; it was presumably covered in cedar shingles and its sixteen-foot posts suggest it was provided with a tier of galleries (Fig. 5.3). "Long houses" are named after a vote taken in 1699 in Branford, Connecticut, which considered erecting a "long brick [meeting] house" in that town.[11] Small congregations may have preferred them, because of the ease of building the frame. Approximately twenty-three are known from descriptions or dimensions given in town records between 1638 and 1710, but the actual number may have been higher. A classic one-story long house was built in Edgartown, Martha's Vineyard, in 1655. Its dimensions were thirty-three by nineteen feet with a plate height of eight feet, an elevation that made it difficult to install galleries. Many long houses were topped with turrets for bells or lookouts. In 1645 a "tower" was placed at each end of the forty-five-by-twenty-five-foot long house in Springfield, Massachusetts, one of which was designed as a "watch house." The known proportions of other long houses suggest that the short dimension was usually a little more than one-half its length, but their sizes varied considerably. The largest long house in the New England region was built in 1640 in Windsor, Connecticut; it was calculated by one church historian to have been seventy feet long and thirty-six feet wide, possibly the result of later additions.

A European source for the design is neither known nor suspected. Long houses appear to be adaptations of domestic homes and/or animal sheds, a possibility suggested by two instances in New England when meetinghouse builders were directed to follow domestic or agricultural specifications. In

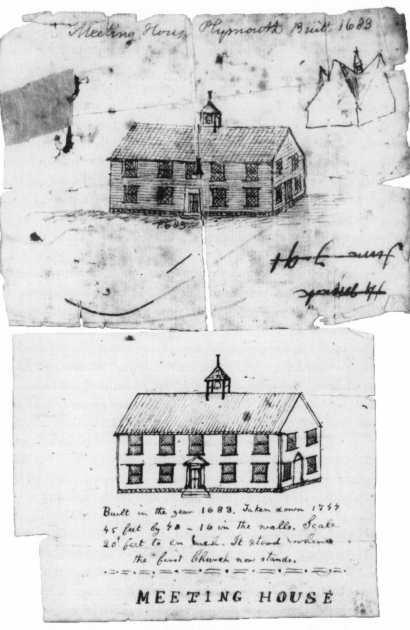

Meeting House, Plymouth, Built 1683

1683

Built in the year 1683. Taken down 1744
45 feet by 40 – 16 in the walls. Scale
20 feet to an inch. It stood where
the first Church now stands.

MEETING HOUSE

FIGURE 5.3. Meeting House. *Late-eighteenth-century memory drawings of the second meetinghouse in Plymouth, Massachusetts, built 1683 in the form of a "long house." The caption identifies its dimensions as 45 by 40 feet, but the structure shown here may represent the original appearance of the meetinghouse before it was expanded 18 feet by lean-tos in 1712. Drawing possibly by Samuel Davis (1765–1829). Courtesy of the Pilgrim Hall Museum, Plymouth, Massachusetts.*

1651 New London, Connecticut, voted that its meetinghouse was to be "the same dimension of Mr. Parke his barn."[12] And in 1659 when Rehoboth, Massachusetts, was enlarging its 1646 meetinghouse, the town specified that it be "shingled as well as Goodman Payne's house."[13] Perhaps these congregations had previously gathered in barns or houses for their religious services, which may help explain why so many nineteenth-century parish historians colloquially refer to their meetinghouse as "the Lord's Barn."[14] There was a European connection, however, even if it was remote. Recent evidence has revealed that English Dissenters and Nonconformists had developed a long-form meetinghouse well before the arrival of Puritans in New England. Christopher Stell reports that thatched and wood-framed cottages were turned into houses of worship by dissenting sects in western and eastern England, possibly as early as the late sixteenth century. Some were long houses in the sense defined here. Bramhope Chapel in Yorkshire, a one-story structure of stone built in 1649, was sixty feet long and seventeen feet wide, similar to an animal shed. Bramhope had two entrances on the south or long side, but the Communion table (and possibly the pulpit) was located on one of the narrow ends. Other long forms include the meetinghouse in Guyhirn, Cambridgeshire, a brick and stone structure forty-four by twenty-four feet. The form persisted in England well into the early eighteenth century.[15]

Our third example is a so-called Dutch-style meetinghouse raised in Fairfield, Connecticut, in 1698. Here the information is relatively incomplete, and there is some question whether the main source of evidence (a 1744 diary entry) is accurate. But it is included here because the available data demonstrate that European architectural concepts reemerged almost intact in British North America. The principal citation consists of a comment made by Alexander Hamilton, a Maryland physician, who left a journal of his trip from Baltimore to New England in 1744. On his way north from Baltimore he wrote of reaching the Connecticut Colony, entering "Fairfield, which is another town in which is an octagonal church or meeting built of wood like that of Jamaica upon Long Island, upon the cupola of which is a public clock."[16] When compiling *New England Meeting Houses of the Seventeenth Century*, the architectural historian Marian Card Donnelly assumed the octagonal structure mentioned by Hamilton was the 1698 meetinghouse in that town. But neither Elizabeth Schenck's 1889 *History of Fairfield* nor Frank S. Child's 1909 *Fairfield, Ancient and Modern* (whose authors had access to original parish documents) notes that it was octagonal, and neither offers any information about its roof structure or whether it had a gallery. Child in fact calls it a "45 feet square" frame building.[17] We do have partial confirmation that this octagonal type existed, however, because in July 1749, another diarist—Joshua Hempstead of New London, Connecticut—entered into his diary the same reference to octagonal structures on Long Island. "I soon came to Jamaica. . . . Here is first westward a Dutch 8 Squar[e] meeting-house or Church & then a Ch of England & then a Stone meetinghouse for the Presbyterians & Courthouse all near together, a well Compact Town."[18]

If Fairfield's "octagonal church or meeting" was as Hamilton described it, the structure may be the only one of its kind built for a Congregational society in Connecticut. But the type may have been fairly common among Dutch Reformed congregations and Quakers in Long Island, New York, and New Jersey. Bushwick, Long Island (now part of Brooklyn), raised an octagonal stone meetinghouse in 1711; it was used until 1840. The "8 Squar[e]" Dutch Reformed church raised in 1715 in Jamaica, Long Island, also was stone and had a diameter of thirty-four feet. According to the nineteenth-century Long Island historian Nathaniel S. Prime, the stone meetinghouse in New Utrecht, New York, was erected in 1700 "in the usual octagonal form."[19] One of the first in New Jersey was the 1681 octagonal meetinghouse in Bergen, constructed in stone by a congregation that had ties to Dutch communi-ties in Long Island. The anonymously written "Brief History of Old Bergen Church" provides a memory picture and informs us the "archways over the door and windows were ornamented with small bricks imported from Hol-land."[20] Even if we did not have Hempstead's "Dutch 8 Squar[e] meeting-house," the origin of this style in France and the Netherlands is spelled out by several recent studies of European Protestant architecture, including Per Gustaf Hamberg's classic 1955 work, *Protestant Temples*, as well as Andrew Spicer's *Calvinist Churches in Early Modern Europe*, published 2007. Hex-agonal and octagonal plans with turreted roofs and one or two tiers of gal-leries became the Protestant standard in both countries. A typical example is the Willemstad Reformed Church (built in 1596) pictured in Hamberg's work; it provided benches for men and women on the ground floor and stairs on either side of the pulpit leading to "three tiers of pews against the walls *en manière de théâtre*."[21] Another example is at La Rochelle, France, pictured on Martin Zeiller's 1620 map as Figure 14.[22] In some instances, the circular concept was dramatically expanded. The Huguenot temple built at Rouen, France, in 1600 was a half-timbered dodecahedron approximately eighty to ninety feet in diameter, with posts approximately twenty to twenty-five feet high (Fig. 5.4). It possessed at least one gallery. A central bell tower sur-mounted the roof with each section relieved by a dormer. An accompanying plan reveals that most of the benches faced the pulpit.

PETER BENES

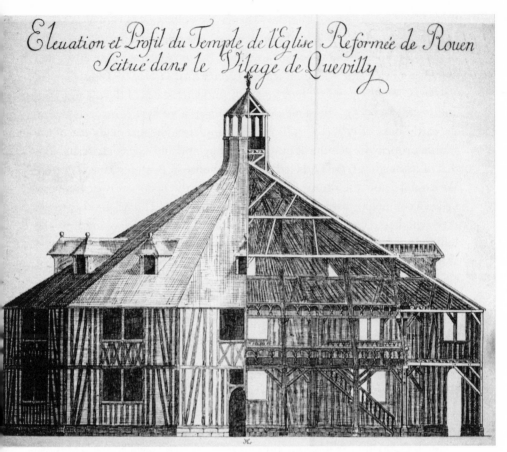

Elevation et Profil du Temple de l'Eglise Reformée de Rouen Scitué dans le Vilage de Quevilly

FIGURE 5.4. Elevation et Profil du Temple de L'Eglise Reformée de Rouen Scitué dans le Vilage de Quevilly. *Engraving of the twelve-sided Huguenot temple at Le Petit-Quevilly, near Rouen, France, built 1600–01. Combined exterior view and interior section showing timber construction, galleries, and turret. From Philippe LeGendre,* Histoire de la persécution faite à l'église de Rouën sur la fin du dernier siècle *(Rotterdam, 1704). Facsimile engraving by Jules Adeline (1874). Harvard Library, Fr 7082.70.4.11.*

Our final example brings us to the beginning of the eighteenth century. The Brattle Square meetinghouse in Boston was raised in 1699 by a newly formed religious society whose principals included some of the wealthiest merchant families in that town who favored a more Anglican-oriented Congregationalism—described by twentieth-century historians like Perry Miller as "moderate Puritans."[23] Their meetinghouse was a seventy-two-by-fifty-two-foot structure that in part resembled a Greek temple. Its pitched or "flat" roof rising at a twenty- or twenty-five-degree angle of pitch was about half that of four-square meetinghouses—hence the colloquial period term "flat." In addition, the builders added a prominent balustrade or rail along the edges of the roof, a feature not seen on any other Boston meetinghouse illustrated in William Price and William Burgis's *A South East View of the Great Town of Boston in New England in America* (1725, and later states of the plate in 1736 and 1743) (Fig. 5.5). The same detail is seen in a view of Boston depicting the earthquake of 1755 (Fig. 5.6). When completed, the meetinghouse of the Brattle proprietors was the largest in New England and exceeded by one foot that of its neighbor, the Old Cedar meetinghouse of Boston's Third Church. We do not know the source for the design, but the historian Rick Kennedy makes a compelling case that its architect was probably Thomas Brattle (1658–1713) who had recently visited England with Samuel Sewall looking at public buildings.[24] The matching castellation on the roof and tower in fact was an architectural characteristic of London churches of the seventeenth century. Claes Van Vissher's *View of London* of 1616 reveals that St. Laurence Poultney was one of about ten Anglican churches that had comparable castellation on its bell tower and eaves.[25] Another bird's eye view, *Civitas Londinum* from 1663, shows two more examples. The Brattle Square meetinghouse inaugurated what architectural historians now call the second-period or Georgian style. Terms like "flattish roof," "long roof," "straight roof or barn fashion" began to enter into town votes, suggesting that a region-wide exchange was taking place—spreading by word of mouth, through chains of imitations, from reports by traveling merchants, justices, and militia officers, and even through clergymen exchanging pulpits with their colleagues. Many of these structures used at least some classical orders in their doorways, cornices, and window surrounds, but for the most part they still resembled large barns with lots of windows. Basically replacing the four-square design, this became the most common meetinghouse type in New England in the eighteenth century.

The first towns in rural Massachusetts documented to have built in this style were Concord and Chelmsford, two Middlesex County communities that almost simultaneously accepted this design when they were replacing meetinghouses in the years 1709 to 1711. Concord may have started the process a few months before Chelmsford. After agreeing in 1709 that its existing forty-two-year-old structure was in "decayed condition," Concord appointed a committee of six men to research the issue and to present several models from which to choose. When the committee reported on January 20, 1710, they offered two designs. One was a mostly square structure, fifty-five by sixty feet, with two galleries, and the usual "bevel Roof," that is, a larger version of Concord's existing period-one structure. The alternative was

FIGURE 5.5. *Detail of William Price and William Burgis's view of the 1699 Brattle Square meetinghouse, Boston, Massachusetts, showing its "flat" roof—the first to appear on an important urban congregation in New England. The bell tower (with its matching balustrade) was probably added in 1717. From* A South East View of the Great Town of Boston in New England in America, *1743. Courtesy of the American Antiquarian Society.*

FIGURE 5.6. Earthquakes Improved: or Solemn warning to the World: by the
tremendous earthquake which happen'd on Tuesday morning the 18th of November 1755,
between four and five o'clock. *View of the Boston townscape during the 1755 earthquake.*
While the meetinghouse on the right is unidentified, the bell opening and matching roof
and tower balustrades are similar to those on the Price-Burgis view seen in figure 5.5.
Woodcut, 1755. John Green, Boston. Courtesy of the American Antiquarian Society.

what the planners called an "English Built" roof with end-to-end gables on
a slightly more rectangular dimension of sixty by fifty-two feet. The decision
was marked by considerable controversy. To resolve it, the inhabitants voted
"by papers," writing "E" for English or "B" for bevel. The count was sixty-
six in favor of the "English moad" and twenty-seven for the old style. The
resulting meetinghouse, completed by Charles Underhill in the fall of 1711,
was sixty feet long and fifty feet wide, with a plate height of twenty-eight
feet and two tiers of galleries. Its pitched roof was unbroken by the customary dormers or lucarnes.[26] As usual, towns copied their nearest neighbors,
among them Lexington (1714), Lynnfield (1715), and Natick (1721). Lexington, for example, voted to build a new meetinghouse "on the plan of the one
at Concord."[27]

Towns in central and southern New England followed the same trend.
In 1712, only one year after Concord had raised its "English" roof, Guilford,
Connecticut, more than 120 miles southwest of Concord, built a three-tier
sixty-eight-by-forty-six-foot structure with a pitched roof. Hadley, Massa-
chusetts, voted for a "flattish roof" in 1713; both parishes in Middletown,
Connecticut, selected identical pitched-roof structures in 1714; Stratfield

(now Bridgeport), Connecticut, chose a "long roof" in 1716; East Haven, Connecticut, voted for a "straight roof or barn fashion" in 1714 and again in 1717; Wallingford voted to imitate Guilford in 1717; Westfield, Massachusetts, stipulated a roof built in "barn fashion with a bell Coney upon the middle" in 1719. Within a decade, gathered or four-square roofs, presumably derived from seventeenth-century Atlantic sources, had become a stylistic liability. Towns with first-period roofs that did not want to bear the cost of replacement chose to modify them—in other words to make them more acceptable to current "English" taste. Votes were taken to remove dormers and lucarnes or to change the roof design from gathered to pitched.

In the meantime, new questions were being asked about the role of bell towers. Turret-mounted belfries in Boston (such as the one on the Old Cedar meetinghouse of the Third Church) may have been considerably higher than the one Anglicans raised on King's Chapel, but they were still mounted centrally on roofs—the critical indicator of their congregation's dissenting Protestant persuasion. While these belfries and bell towers played no part in the Congregational liturgy, they did provide a civic and architectural rivalry with Anglican parishes—particularly after St. Michael's Church in Marblehead raised a spire 103 feet high in 1714. Perhaps in response to this, three Congregational religious societies in Boston almost simultaneously erected meetinghouses with standing bell towers or added standing bell towers to existing structures. The first may have been the New North. According to the permission given them by the town in 1713, they were allowed to erect "a timber Meeting House 65 × 48 × 35 [with a] flat roof and battlements [possibly meaning a castellated cornice or bell tower]" on Hanover Street.[28] The structure was raised the following year and enlarged in 1719 with an eighteen-foot lean-to containing additional ground-floor pews and two tiers of galleries. That same year John Frizell, a Boston merchant, gave a bell to the congregation. A second bell tower in Boston was raised by the New South in 1716 that was "finished after the Ionic order."[29] A third bell tower was raised by the Brattle proprietors, the same affluent but controversial congregation that built the first "flat" roof in New England. The Brattle's spire can be dated from an entry in Samuel Sewall's diary on June 24, 1717: "Mr. [Benjamin] Colman's New Steeple is raised."[30] It is the same one seen in both the 1725 and 1755 images.

Standing bell towers soon spread to other colonies. When initially raised in 1712, the flat-roof meetinghouse in Guilford, Connecticut, lacked a bell tower. Twelve years after it was raised, however, the parish was given surplus money from a mill operation to provide a bell. They first turned to Boston. An initial vote, made by the town meeting in 1724, was to purchase a bell "like that in Mr. Coleman's meeting house in Boston."[31] It is fair to presume that the town expected a bell tower similar to the one attached to Colman's meetinghouse. In December 1725 the building committee set aside "Timber and Materials for building a Steeple to the Meeting House at the west end thereof with a suitable Belfry and Spire."[32] But the following January, not long after Trinity Church had erected an ostentatious new Anglican house of worship in Newport, Rhode Island, Guilford changed its mind and voted that, instead, "the belfry and spire of the meeting house in this Society shall be built in the Fashion and proportion of the Belfry and Spire at Rhode Island."[33] Then, two months later, the January 17 vote was "repealed," and the society proceeded with another design that was raised the following year.[34] While no description of it survives, the new bell tower must have been impressive. The tip of the spire was 120 feet off the ground, an indication that the bell itself may have been as high as ninety feet from the ground.

It was during the mid-eighteenth century, too, that New England meetinghouses began to acquire flamboyant exterior colors—a new American innovation that changed their character. Early meetinghouses were normally left unpainted (or simply oiled or tarred). But after the mid-eighteenth century when Mendon, Massachusetts, voted "to color the Meeting-House doors, window frames, weather boards, corner boards, eve troughs, and the two bottom boards"—meaning they applied paint to exterior surfaces—colors became more widespread.[35] Altogether 229 sources of evidence have been uncovered from town and church records, diaries, and town histories, but also from school art, landscape paintings, surveying maps, and meetinghouse names. Yellow was the most common color. By 1800 Kensington, New Hampshire, had painted its 1771 meetinghouse bright yellow with orange doors and a brown roof. Keene, New Hampshire, painted its house light yellow with green doors in 1790. Chelmsford, Massachusetts, chose a dark yellow in 1793. (It is still possible to find evidence of that color on fragments taken from surviving buildings.) At least ten meetinghouses were painted "red" or "red ochre" or "peach-blossom color."[36] In 1762 Pomfret, Connecticut, voted to paint its meetinghouse "orange color—the doors and bottom boards of a chocolate color—the windows, jets, corner boards, and weather boards, colored white."[37] Scituate, Massachusetts, painted its Old Sloop "Dark Stone Color, the roof red and Doors a Chocolate Colour, with white trim."[38] An old mourning picture shows that the 1747 meetinghouse in Cohasset, Massachusetts, was given a coat of green paint picked out in white sometime before 1812.[39]

Colors sometimes had a geographic range. Yellows were concentrated primarily in southern New Hampshire and eastern Massachusetts—possibly because there was considerable yellow ochre found in New Hampshire. Blues and lead colors dominated the Connecticut coastline. Some nineteenth-century historians have suggested that "sky colors"—including the blue paint on the meetinghouse of the 1742 White Haven Society in New Haven—may have signified a belief in religious "enthusiasm." But this interpretation has yet to be proved.[40] Orange colors clustered around towns in northeastern Connecticut, each trying to outdo its neighbors. Orange meetinghouses were so ingrained in this area that when families moved elsewhere they brought their colors with them. Gilsum, New Hampshire, which was settled by a group of eastern Connecticut proprietors, voted to paint their meetinghouse a "Bright Orring" in 1792.[41]

Toward the end of the eighteenth century, meetinghouses began to resemble churches. This final transformation took place after 1790 and involved a new church-like form that changed the manner in which parishioners entered the building. The congregation responsible for this move was the North Church in Salem, Massachusetts, which voted in 1772 to build a meetinghouse on a "church plan."[42] This was a newly created, wealthy, well-connected parish looking to make its mark in Essex County. The main entrance was at the gable end of the building, a reversal of its usual place on the long or eave side, making it resemble many Anglican churches in North America where parishioners were obliged to step through the bell tower before entering the sanctuary. Two other congregations—the Brattle Street in Boston and the First Baptist in Providence—tried the same thing in 1773 and 1774, but the approach of the American Revolution put an end to virtually all building activity. It was not until five years after the Revolution that these ideas again found substance when Charles Bulfinch was hired to design a new structure for the Hollis Street congregation in Boston in 1788 whose meetinghouse had been destroyed by fire. Like his seventeenth-century predecessors, Bulfinch drew on Atlantic sources—only this time more directly. According to Abbott L. Cummings, the design was inspired by the parish church in Mistley, Essex, erected in 1776—a twin-towered structure in the Adamesque tradition.[43] The new Hollis Street meetinghouse was soon imitated by Kingston, Massachusetts; and Bulfinch's sequel in Pittsfield, Massachusetts, in 1790, so impressed New England that both of these became the new Federal models. Otis, Massachusetts, was among nine that copied Pittsfield. The gable end of these buildings now faced the street; entry was through the base of a bell tower, which also served as a stairwell porch going to the gallery. Towns after 1795 had to choose between meetinghouses and churches. Typically, building committees hired architects like Bulfinch, Timothy Palmer, and Lavius Fillmore to submit plans well before the votes; some architects like Asher Benjamin published plans for builders to follow. Granted, some towns retained aspects of the old ways: the third-period style Methodist meetinghouse raised in Lynn, Massachusetts, retained the old yellow paint, as did the meetinghouse in Rindge, New Hampshire. But over time, towns that had originally painted their meetinghouses yellow turned to more Georgian hues, primarily "stone colors." Soon even this gave way, and everything became Greek revival white.

What was driving the transformation from meetinghouse to church? Who was advocating architectural change? Who was resisting it? My own hypothesis is that meetinghouse architecture—like liturgy and psalm singing—communicated ecclesiological values. We start with the larger premise that New England's Protestant history consisted of a prolonged struggle between those who wanted to maintain a "pure primitive Church" and those who wished to see it broadened and modernized—data that can be analyzed to indicate how far a given parish had changed.[44] In this framework, "conservative" points of view, most often championed by church communicants and their chosen officers, wished to keep the service as an intellectual or Calvinist event, to retain control over the selection of the minister, to preserve the role of elders, to appoint deacons for their lifetimes, to require written "relations" from prospective church members; to retain separate gender divisions in seating; and to maintain authentic (meaning untrained) musical and ecclesiological practices. The congregation at large, however—that is, the majority of people who attended church services but were not necessarily communicants—supported "progressive" practices. They expected greater and more immediate access to the sacraments (the so-called halfway covenant or the Anglican model) and a more visual or "church-like" experience in the service; to share in the appointment of the minister, to disband the role of elders, and to read Scripture in the service. They supported private pewing and instituted rules allowing families to sit together at an early date. In musical terms, they favored "regular singing" and hoped to improve musical education through singing schools and the use of new translations of the psalms by Tate and Brady and Isaac Watts. They voted to end "lining out" of the psalms at an early date, and they approved setting aside special seats for trained singers, the use of the bass viol, and ultimately voted to install an organ.[45]

In Boston the "hardliners" were the First Church and the Second or North

Church, led among others by several generations of Mathers. These churches resisted ecclesiological change and kept to their old meetinghouses such as the Old North and the Old Brick, which together served from 1677 to 1808. The progressive group advocating change was the Brattle Square Church led by Reverend Benjamin Colman — the same congregation that raised an "Anglicanized" meetinghouse ushering in the second-period style in 1699. This congregation read the Bible during the church service; it recited the Lord's Prayer ("all the Words of it together as it stands in the New-Testament").[46] Equally important was their disavowal of a "Publick Relation" to qualify admission for church membership as outlined in chapter twelve of the Cambridge platform. They also broadened participation by allowing "every Baptized Adult Person who contributes to the Maintenance" (apparently both male and female congregants) the right to elect the minister — thus extending the process to pewholders. The Brattle was the first congregation in New England to omit the deaconizing of psalms (1699), the first to accept an organ given by one of its parishioners (1713), and the first to organize a singing school (1721). It was supported by a group of younger societies in Boston that included the New North, the New South, and the New Brick; eventually they were joined by Boston's Third Church.

A similar standoff between conservative and progressive parishes can be found in New Haven. Here the "hardliners" were the First Church who occupied William and Nathan Andrews's 1639 and 1668 first-period meeting-houses over a period of 118 years. By contrast, the "innovators," led by Guilford, along with the towns immediately adjacent to it in Fairfield and New Haven Counties, passed a succession of votes between 1705 and 1747 that placed five of the first six bell towers erected in Connecticut before 1750 in a tight arc around New Haven (Madison, Wallingford, Milford, Stratford, and Fairfield). They converted to "flat" roofs, seated parishioners in their own pews, hired music teachers, and ended the practice of lining out at an early date to make psalm singing become more "ornate" and melodic. Guilford in particular stands out as a liturgically progressive parish and one that remained in touch with its Atlantic origin. The same year that this town completed its 1712 meetinghouse, the community voted for a majority of men and women to sit together in the pews — perhaps the first in New England to do so. By contrast, New Haven continued to separate men from women. Guilford parish voted to discontinue lining out the psalms in the service in 1748 — the fourth church body in New England to do so (after Boston's Brattle, King's Chapel, and New Brick) and the first in Connecticut. Guilford was the first parish in Connecticut to introduce a pitch pipe and the first in Connecticut to accompany its psalms with a bass viol (in 1796), following up with flutes, violincello, and double bass viol. To this day there are parish loyalists who keep alive the inclusiveness and progressivism of Guilford's church polity and the broad Atlantic perspective on which it was based.

NOTES

1. For a larger discussion, see Peter Benes, *Meetinghouses of Early New England* (Amherst: University of Massachusetts Press, 2012).

2. Most early studies have relied on survivals such as those in Edmund W. Sinnott's, *Meetinghouse and Church in Early New England* (New York: Bonanza Books, 1963). Those based on records include J. Frederick Kelly, *Early Connecticut Meetinghouses*, 2 vols. (New York: Columbia University Press, 1948); Anthony N. B. Garvan, *Architecture and Town Planning in Colonial Connecticut* (New Haven: Yale University Press, 1951); Marian C. Donnelly, *New England Meeting Houses of the Seventeenth Century* (Middletown, Conn.: Wesleyan University Press, 1968).

3. Kevin M. Sweeney, "Meetinghouses, Town Houses, and Churches," *Winterthur Portfolio* 28, no. 1 (Spring 1993): 61, sees meetinghouses as "basically an original architectural expression"; Sinnott, *Meetinghouse and Church*, 16, sees in seventeenth-century meetinghouses "no close resemblance to any communal or ecclesiastical structure of the Old World." Brian Powell and Andrea Gilmore, *Old Ship Meetinghouse, First Parish, Hingham, Massachusetts: Historic Structure Report*, 4 vols. (Dedham, Mass., Building Conservation Associates, 2007), 1:9–11, state that both the term and the idea were essentially American.

4. David H. Fischer, *Albion's Seed: Four British Folkways in America* (New York: Oxford, 1989), 117, indicates that meetinghouses were "constructed on the model of secular buildings in East Anglia." Edgar P. Dean, review of Donnelly, *New England Quarterly* 43, no. 1 (1970): 158–59, reports that meetinghouses "originate more in residential than ecclesiastical architecture."

5. Donnelly, *New England Meeting Houses*, makes the strongest case for a European origin, but admits that a systematic study had yet to be written; Garvan, *Architecture and Town Planning*, 141. John Coolidge, "Hingham Builds a Meetinghouse," *New England Quarterly* 34, no. 4 (1961): 460–61, is the first American scholar to suggest that meetinghouses imitated a European idea, citing Per Gustaf Hamberg's, *Tempelbygge för Protestanter [Temples for Protestants]* (1955. Göteborg: Acta Universitatis Gothoburgensis, 2002).

6. The "four-square" meetinghouse is named after the "4:square roof" cited in a Cambridge document in 1649. *Records of the Town of Cambridge* (Cambridge, Mass.: Privately printed, 1901), 85. See also Hollis R. Bailey, *Beginning of the First Church* (Cambridge, Mass., 1932), 1. Evidence from the Chesapeake area suggests that "4:square" may also signify a "true pitch" of forty-five degrees.

7. *Records of the Colony and Plantation of New Haven, from 1638 to 1649*, ed. C. J.

Hoadly (Hartford, Conn.: Case, Tiffany, and Co., 1857), 25, 145, 304, 388, 427. *New Haven Town Records, 1649–1769*, 3 vols., ed. F. B. Dexter (New Haven, Conn.: New Haven Colony Historical Society, 1917-1962), 1:49, 115, 274. Kelly, *Early Connecticut Meetinghouses*, 2:3–10.

8. Andrew Spicer, *Calvinist Churches in Early Modern Europe* (New York: Manchester University Press, 2007), 57–60. Archbishop William Laud dismisses the Burntisland kirk as a "square theatre."

9. Dean B. Lyman, *An Atlas of Old New Haven, or "The Nine Squares" as Shown on Various Early Maps* (New Haven, Conn.: Scranton, 1929); Richard S. Kirby, *Inventors and Engineers of Old New Haven* (New Haven, Conn.: New Haven Historical Society, 1939). Garvan, *Architecture and Town Planning*; Elizabeth M. Brown, "John Brockett of New Haven, the Man and the Myth," *Journal of the New Haven Colony Historical Society* (1981).

10. The phrase is taken from Jacques Perret, *Des Fortifications et Artifices: Architecture et Perspective de Jacques Perret* (1601), quoted in Hamberg, *Temples for Protestants*, 37.

11. J. Rupert Simonds, *A History of the First Church and Society in Branford, Connecticut* (New Haven, Conn.: Tuttle, 1919), 48.

12. Frances M. Caulkins, *History of New London, Connecticut* (New London, Conn.: Utley, 1895), 9.

13. Sylvanus Newman, *Rehoboth in the Past* (Pawtucket, R.I.: Sherman, 1860), 17.

14. One of the meanings of the term "barn" in Catherine Soanes and Angus Stevenson, eds., *Oxford English Dictionary*, 2nd ed. (2010), is a "building for worship" (1689). European associations between barns and early Protestant houses of worship are cited in John Craig, *Reformation, Politics, and Polemics: The Growth of Protestantism in East Anglican Market Towns, 1500–1610* (Aldershot, UK: Ashgate, 2001), 125; Hélène Guicharnaud, "An Introduction to the Architecture of Protestant Temples Constructed in France before the Revocation of the Edict of Nantes," in *Seeing beyond the Word: Visual Arts and the Calvinist Tradition*, ed. Paul Corby Finney (Grand Rapids, Mich.: Eerdmans, 1999), 135, 143; Spicer, *Calvinist Churches*, 97, 115, 179, 199.

15. Christopher Stell, "Puritan and Nonconformist Meetinghouses in England," in *Seeing beyond the Word*, 51.

16. Alexander Hamilton, *Itinerarium* (Chapel Hill: University of North Carolina Press, 1948), 167.

17. Ibid.; Donnelly, *New England Meeting Houses*, 77–78; Elizabeth Schenck, *The History of Fairfield, Fairfield County, Connecticut*, 2 vols. (New York: privately printed, 1889-1905), 1:8, 41, 48; 2:126, 134, 160, 172. Frank S. Child, *Fairfield, Ancient and Modern* (Fairfield, Conn.: Fairfield Historical Society, 1909), 5–7.

18. Joshua Hempstead, *The Diary of Joshua Hempstead* (New London, Conn.: New London County Historical Society, 1999), 519.

19. Nathaniel Prime, *History of Long Island* (New York: R. Carter, 1845), 341.

20. Henry R. Stiles, *History of the City of Brooklyn* (Brooklyn, N.Y.: Published by subscription, 1867-1870), 355.

21. Hamberg, *Temples for Protestants*, 22-23, 36-43, 126-29.

22. Martin Zeiller, *Topographia Galliae* (1655-1661), Section 7, between pages 60-61, University of Delaware Library, Newark, Del.

23. Rick Kennedy, "Thomas Brattle, Mathematician-Architect in the Transition of the New England Mind, 1690-1700," *Winterthur Portfolio* 24, no. 4 (Winter 1989): 231-45 (241).

24. Kennedy, "Thomas Brattle," 241-42.

25. Claes Van Visscher's *View of London, 1616; Civitas Londinum*, 1663.

26. Edgar W. Tucker, "The Meeting Houses of the First Parish," in *The Meeting House on the Green* (Concord, Mass.: First Parish, 1985), 306-28. It is not known why the Concord townsmen called the "flat" roof an "English Built" roof, though the term "bevel" seems to indicate that the older gathered or four-square design was regarded as a European "Protestant" style of roof associated with the Netherlands and France.

27. Charles Hudson, *History of the Town of Lexington, Middlesex County, Massachusetts* (Boston: Wiggin and Lunt, 1868), 57.

28. Quotation taken from Annie H. Thwing, *Inhabitants and Estate of the Town of Boston* (CD, Boston: New England Historic Genealogical Society, 2001), entry 46760.

29. George F. Ellis, *Commemorative Discourse on the New South Church, December 25, 1864* (Boston: Dutton, 1865), 7.

30. Samuel Sewall, *The Diary of Samuel Sewall, 1674-1729*, 2 vols., ed. M. Halsey Thomas (New York: Farrar, Straus and Giroux, 1973), 24 June 1717 (2:857).

31. Quotations taken from Kelly, *Early Connecticut Meetinghouses*, 1:172.

32. Ibid.

33. Ibid.

34. Ibid.

35. Adin Ballou, *History of Milford, Massachusetts* (Boston: Franklin, 1882), 70.

36. William Miller, *Historical Discourse of the Congregational Church in Killingworth, Connecticut* (New Haven, Conn.: Hoggson and Robinson, 1870), 31.

37. *One Hundred Fiftieth Anniversary of the Organization of the First Church in Pomfret, Connecticut* (Danielson, Conn.: Transcript Press, 1866), 41-42.

38. Clarence M. Waite, *First Trinitarian Congregational Church, Scituate, Massachusetts* (Scituate, Mass., 1967), 41.

39. Watercolor mourning picture, Joseph Joy (1784-1812), in the collection of the Gore Place House Museum, Waltham, Mass. See also, Richard Joy, *Thomas Joy and His Descendants* (New York: privately printed, 1900), 92.

40. Henry T. Blake, *Chronicles of New Haven Green from 1638 to 1862* (New Haven: Tuttle, Morehouse and Taylor, 1898), 93-94; Mary H. Mitchell, *The History of New Haven County, Connecticut* (Boston: Pioneer Historical, 1930), 290.

41. Silvanus Hayward, *Address Delivered at the Centennial Celebration of the Congregational Church, Gilsum, New Hampshire* (Dover, N.H.: Goodwin, 1873), 19.

42. *First Centenary, the North Church and Society, Salem, Massachusetts* (Salem, Mass.: North Church and Society, 1873), 21-23, 183.

43. Abbott L. Cummings, "Meeting and Dwelling House: Interrelationships in Early New England," *New England Meeting House and Church, 1630–1650. The Dublin Seminar for New England Folklife: Annual Proceedings, 1979* (Boston: Boston University Scholarly Publications, 1979), 10–12.

44. Benes, *Meetinghouses of Early New England*, Tables 2 and 3, 282–83.

45. "Lining out" consisted of a church officer, usually a deacon or precentor, temporarily stopping the singing in order to read the next line of the psalm. The shift from "lining out" to "singing all the way through" may have marked the most significant liturgical change in eighteenth-century congregational practice.

46. *The Manifesto Church: Records of the Church in Brattle Square* (Boston: Benevolent Fraternity, 1902), 4.

6

THE PRAYING INDIAN TOWNS

ENCOUNTER AND CONVERSION THROUGH

IMPOSED URBAN SPACE

Alison Stanley

A key element in the New England missionary strategy for converting Native Americans to Christianity was the founding of "Praying Towns," where converts could live together and be prepared for church membership by an English minister. Alternatively argued to be sites for the final destruction of traditional Algonquian culture or refuges offering traumatized survivors of war and plague the opportunity to rebuild their lives and cultures, the praying towns were ideologically significant spaces. While the praying-town project has been much analyzed, the implications of the specific form imposed on the settlements, and particularly the earliest, Natick, have been little discussed. Established in response to Christian Indian requests for land, and constructed according to the design of the principal New England missionary of the period, John Eliot, Natick embodies the encounter of Puritan and Native American cultures. An interrogation of contemporary Puritan texts allows us to reexamine the first praying town in light of the history and cultural associations of town spaces in both Native American and colonial Puritan thought, and offers the opportunity for new insights into the foundation and development of Natick and the contested meanings of urban space in the British Atlantic world.

"COME OVER AND HELP US"

One of the reasons the Massachusetts Bay Company gave for its colonization of New England was a duty to convert its Native American inhabitants to Christianity, a claim reinforced by their adoption of an official seal picturing an Indian man pleading with the English to "come over and help us" (Fig. 6.1). The message that this was a key aim of settlement continued into the next generation: in 1676 Increase Mather looked back on "the professed

FIGURE 6.1. *The seal of the Massachusetts Bay Colony (1629). Image courtesy of the Massachusetts Archives.*

pious, and a main design of the *Fathers* of this *Colony,* viz. *To propagate the Gospel and Kingdome of Christ among these Indians.*"[1] But despite these protestations, few attempts were made by the English colonists to convert the Algonquian Indians living in the area, with the notable exception of the missionary work done by the Mayhew family on Martha's Vineyard, who largely acted without official support or notice. This lack of proselytization was a source of reproach in England, where interest in and sympathy for the "heathen Indians" tended to increase in proportion with distance from the colonies. As a result, when John Eliot's preaching began arousing interest among local Native groups from around October 1646, the authorities actively publicized developments in a series of texts, which have become known as the Eliot Tracts.[2] Written largely by colonists, but aimed at an English audience, these presented evidence for the success of the missionary work, including eyewitness accounts, letters, and transcriptions of statements of faith made by the Praying Indians. The majority of the tracts were collated and printed by the New England Company, established by Parliament in 1649 to publicize and support missionary work in the region; by 1653 the organization had raised £4,500 for this purpose.[3] Those involved were therefore under great pressure to demonstrate that the reported conversions were genuine and sincere.

The ultimate goal of Eliot's missionary efforts was for the Praying Indians to be accepted as full church members by the colonial churches. This was eventually achieved by a group of Praying Indian men in 1659, who went on to gather their own Native American church congregation in Natick. The process by which they achieved this, however, was a long and complex one, in which both Eliot and the Christian Indians had to persuade observers in New England and across the Atlantic that the Praying Indians were motivated by genuine spirituality, and not the prospect of material gain. Until the Praying Indians had enough biblical and theological knowledge to construct convincing narratives of God's influence on their souls, however, they and their chroniclers were unable to use accounts of their spiritual experiences as persuasive material. In the early stages of missionary work, material signs of salvation were used to suggest the presence of an inner change in converts. Such signs were many and varied, ranging from emotional reactions to preaching to the wearing of English clothes. The most ambitious was the founding of a praying town at Natick. That this town was regarded as effective is suggested by the fact that by 1674, it had been used as a model for a further ten Praying Indian communities. These towns were marked not only by the gathering of converts together and the presence of regular preaching, but also by their construction as "civilized," ordered spaces, where Praying Indians could adopt a lifestyle that would act as a material sign corresponding to their claims of inner spiritual change. Historians have debated why Eliot felt it necessary to demand such radical cultural adaptation from the Christian Indians, but there has been little discussion of the implications of the design that he imposed on this site of religious transformation. Those historians who approach the problem in detail, in particular Holstun and O'Brien, discuss the ideology and symbolism of space involved in the requirement for an "ordered" town, but neither of them discuss Natick in terms of seventeenth-century ideas about the significance and conventions of urban space.[4] By investigating the details of how the praying towns were established, we can examine the process by which Praying Indians and English missionaries used this urban space in order to present its inhabitants as serious candidates for church membership.

WHY A TOWN?

It is rarely emphasized by historians that it was specifically a praying *town* that Eliot designed at Natick. Nevertheless, there were powerful ideological associations concerning towns and their inhabitants in seventeenth-century New England. In particular, colonial thought created a dichotomy between towns, marked as English spaces, and unsettled wilderness, associated with Native Americans. Grounded in a traditional association — the word *savage* derives from the Latin word for "woodland" — this dichotomy was emphasized by the fact that in New England "town" referred not only to houses and public

ALISON STANLEY

buildings, but also the fields surrounding them, so it included the majority of the land visibly marked by colonization.[5] On the other hand, local Indians were depicted as being at home in the unchanged part of the American landscape: "These ranging foresters . . . are as welacquainted with the craggy mountaines, and the pleasant vales, the stately woods, and swampie groves, the spacious ponds, and swift running rivers, and can distinguish them by their names as perfectly, and finde them as presently, as the experienced Citizen knows how to finde our Cheape-side crosse, or *London* stone."[6]

As the urban space of London is to the Englishman, so the landscape of New England is to its native inhabitants; as the city is to the European, so the wilderness is to the Indian. The seal of Massachusetts Bay positions its Indian figure outside, between trees and standing on grass; he even appears to be wearing an Adamic costume of leaves, suggesting he is associated with a postlapsarian but preurban phase of civilization (Fig. 6.1). Similarly, in a 1675 map of New England during King Philip's War (Fig. 6.2), the mapmaker carefully marks the location of each English town with symbols representing houses. The Indian settlements, on the other hand, are not marked at all: instead, the names of the Native groups— "Naraganset," "Nipmuck," "Pequid Country"—are written across open countryside, marked only by images of trees and wild animals. The Indian villages, which changed size and shape and composition as well as location at fixed intervals throughout the year, could not be mapped using the conventions for marking fixed English settlements. Native American groups are therefore marked visually not by the locations of their villages, but in terms of their inhabitation of an area of wilderness.

Given this New England colonial association of Indians with wilderness and themselves with urban space, the decision to establish Praying Indians in a town has important ideological connotations. Merely living in a town was seen to be a significant step on the way to becoming Europeanized Christians. "What more hopeful way of doing them good then by cohabitation in such Townes, neare unto good examples, and such as may be continually whetting upon them, and dropping into them of the things of God? what greater meanes at least to civilize them?" asked one contemporary observer, making it clear that even if the good examples continually "dropping into them of the things of God" did not achieve their spiritual regeneration, the sheer experience of town life would be "meanes at least to civilize them."[7]

Contemporary New England observers of the Praying Indians repeatedly suggest that the very process of living in a town would change the relationship of its inhabitants to the environment around them. This is not an idea

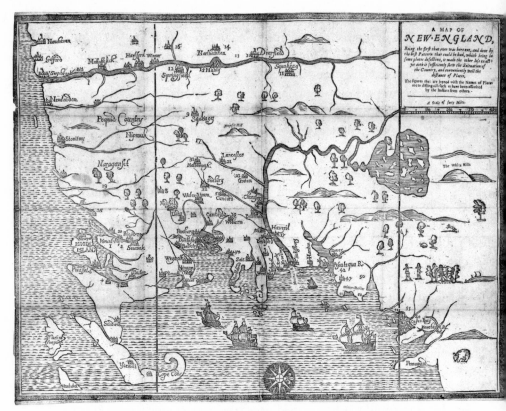

FIGURE 6.2. *"A Map of New England." Originally published in William Hubbard,*
A Narrative of the Troubles with the Indians in New-England *(Boston, 1677).*
Collection of the Massachusetts Historical Society.

unique to them, but one that has influenced, and continues to influence,
thinking about urban space and its implications. As Kostof argues, cities are
both products of the society that creates them, reflecting its preoccupations
and ways of thinking, and also the stage on which life in a culture is enacted.[8]
Furthermore, the colonists' belief that the influence of an English-style town
environment would lead directly to a change in the culture of its inhabitants
was not a purely ideological one. As well as having symbolic associations, life
in a geographically static town necessarily changed the ways that its inhabitants related to their environment.

The traditional lifestyle of the Algonquian-speaking peoples of the region
relied on movement between different food-producing areas in order to maxi-
mize the collection and production of food. Families and larger groups would
assemble at their planting grounds in spring (which would be abandoned for

new land as the ground lost its fertility, every ten years or so), near streams and fishing weirs during fish-spawning season, and lived in isolated groups during the lean months of winter when game was scarce.[9] The adoption of a town fixed in a single location effectively made this lifestyle impossible. Natick's inhabitants now had to rely on the same fields indefinitely, finding ways to rest or fertilize them when they became exhausted. They erected fences to protect crops from roaming cattle, a colonial innovation in a region that had not known domesticated farm animals until the arrival of English settlers. Even the presence of laid roads, noted as an important part of the town development by early observers, confirmed the permanence of both the town's location and its structures, a concept alien to the traditional lifestyle of local Algonquian Indians, who would occasionally move a wigwam purely to escape the irritations of a flea infestation.[10]

Moreover, the permanent division of the land within Natick into individually owned housing lots and fields demanded a complete change in the way that ownership of the land was understood by Native cultures in the region. Traditionally, it had been the right to use the products of the land, rather than the land itself, that Native communities had given, exchanged, or fought over. A wigwam, tools, and utensils might belong to one person or family, but ground where the wigwam was set up at any particular moment was not the property of the family living on it.[11] This conception of the ownership of the land was already under pressure in the period, due to relentless colonial demand for space; now the inhabitants of Natick became part of the English system of land ownership, with the patriarchal head of each family able to buy, sell, and bequeath their land as they wished. Not only did such a significant change have implications for farming, but also for the social relationships among the town's inhabitants.[12] For the Praying Indians, then, the adoption of an English colonial town lifestyle had far-reaching implications. Historians have debated their motivations in accepting such a change. It seems clear that for some of them, at least, the change of lifestyle was regarded as a necessary adaptation if they wanted to remain in their traditional homelands under the new pressures of colonial expansion.[13] Others, who had to leave their homes when they moved to Natick, may have been looking for a secure location and new social structures upon which to rebuild lives devastated by the disease, war, and changing environment brought by the English colonists.[14] Others may have agreed to relocate because it was required by the minister of a new religion they had sincerely adopted.[15]

Whatever their motivations, the Praying Indian inhabitants of Natick wanted to be accepted as Christians and gain the status of full church membership. We can therefore understand their adoption of an English-style town environment at Natick as a demonstration of sincerity and dedication to their new faith. And unlike many of the signs of salvation, which were subtle and not articulated directly to the converts, Eliot told the Praying Indians explicitly that he would not put them forward as candidates for spiritual examination until they had proved themselves materially in a town environment: "These *Indians* (the better and wiser sort of them) have for some years inquired about Church-Estate, Baptism, and the rest of the Ordinances of God, in the observation whereof they see the Godly English to walk. I have from time to time, delayed them on this point, That until they were come up unto Civil Cohabitation, Government, and Labor, which a fixed condition of life will put them upon, they were not so capable to be betrusted with that Treasure of Christ, lest they should scandalize the same, and make it of none effect."[16]

For the Praying Indians, then, agreeing to adopt a fixed town lifestyle was the prerequisite for being taken seriously as Christians; that they did so can be seen as their pledge of sincerity to their observers.

WHY NATICK?

In addition to its status as a town, the way that Natick was laid out and developed reveals much about both Eliot's missionary ideology, and the requirements of the town's Native American inhabitants. Unfortunately, we have only limited knowledge about the original layout of the town, most of it gleaned from accounts written in the period. The number of inhabitants, for example, is not entirely clear from the sources; estimates of the population in 1674 range from 70 to 145.[17] Several contemporary observers, however, note the general layout of the town: "They have laid out three long faire streets there, two on this side the River, and one on that, and have severall house-lots apportioned severally to every one, which doe or be to inhabite there, and in many of them there are fruit trees already planted, and they are building *English* houses for themselves, meane while living in *Wigmoones*, whereof there is good store neere the hill side."[18]

There is evidence that the Praying Indians laid out their agricultural land in the English style, with large "common fields" divided into strips of land located outside the central cluster of houses in the village. Fields were laid out on the south side of the Charles River; the presence of two out of three of the streets on the north side, where the residential area was located, suggests that the house lots were clustered together rather than scattered across farmland.[19] As well as surveying the town and its fields, the Praying Indians constructed several "publicke works," as Eliot calls them. A fort, which Wilson notes "the *Indians* have made of whole trees very hansome and firme," was near a "faire house which the *Indians* have built after the *English* manner high and large," which was used as a guesthouse for colonial visitors and to store furs.[20] A "firme high foote-bridge archwise" was built across the river, connecting the two parts of the town; a fish weir was constructed, and a sawmill was built by the early 1660s.[21] Perhaps most significantly of all, from the point of view of contemporary observers, the Natick inhabitants built "a very sufficient Meeting-House, of fifty foot long, twenty five foot broad, neer twelve foot high betwixt the joynts, wel sawen, and framed," which was the final evidence Eliot required of their spiritual sincerity: "Now my argument of delaying them from entering into Church-Estate, was taken away."[22]

The exact layout and relationship of these buildings within Natick is not clear from the sources. In Gookin's 1674 survey of the praying towns, most of the page describing Natick has been lost, and there is a lack of definitive archaeological evidence. However, some elements at least are clear: the town was laid out on both sides of the Charles River, with fenced common fields on the south side, and "long faire" roads on both sides, two on the north and one on the south. House lots were located to the north of the river, presumably along the two roads, and some Natick residents built English-style houses on them. Many others, however, continued to live in wigwams. Gookin commented in 1674 that most of the houses "are generally after their old mode," while an order passed during King Philip's War in 1675 refers to "the setting of their wigwams."[23] A fort containing a meetinghouse was located on the north side of the river near a large English-style house, with a schoolhouse standing somewhere nearby.[24]

The location of the town is less in dispute than its internal arrangements, and itself offers insights into the multiple ideologies and practicalities contributing to the settlement of Natick. Eliot had difficulty finding a site for his proposed praying town. Specifically, it had to be close, but not too close, to the colonial settlements—"some what remote from the English," as Eliot put it.[25] This requirement has been quoted by historians as marking Eliot's reluctance to integrate the Praying Indians wholly into the English Christian community, but in fact the remoteness was at the request of the Praying Indians themselves.[26] For their part, the missionaries believed that it would be beneficial for the Praying Indians to live near the English, so that being "neare unto good examples, and such as may be continually whetting upon them, and dropping into them of the things of God," they would be more likely to adopt an English mentality, morality, and religion.[27] The Praying

Indians, on the other hand, refused to live among the English, if for no other than purely practical reasons. Eliot noted before Natick was founded that "to come to live here among or neer to the *English*, they are not willing," because their unfenced crops were destroyed by straying English cattle.[28] In the end, Natick was located close to an English settlement, Dedham—too close, in fact, because the two settlements were in constant conflict over the next generation over land claims, and the Indians were forced to adopt the colonial innovation of fencing their fields to protect them from colonists as well as from cattle.

Beyond these practicalities, the location of the town had ideological implications for both English colonists and Praying Indians. For some of the latter, as previously discussed, it allowed them to remain on their ancestral land; there is also a suggestion that they used their symbolic separation from traditional Native groups to discontinue treaty payments to local sachems.[29] For Eliot, on the other hand, the primary significance of the location was its proximity to his home and ministerial responsibilities in Roxbury, which allowed him and other colonial observers to oversee and control the social and spiritual lives of the Praying Indians more effectively. Such surveillance was expected from a minister, whose duties included imposing spiritual discipline on his charges, and was openly acknowledged to the Praying Indians. Before the foundation of Natick, Eliot had lamented that he could make no steady progress with conversions because of his inability to provide continuous teaching and oversight: "Few come to dwell at the neer places where I ordinarily teach, onely some strangers do come to hear, and away again."[30] And as Cogley argues, part of the intention in collecting the Christian Indians into a town was to allow them to observe each other and impose a communal discipline.[31]

One of the first English-style structures erected at Natick was a guest house for Eliot and other colonial visitors who had come to witness and report on the activities of the town's inhabitants; from the start, the missionary desire to facilitate English observation was built into the very fabric of the town. Other surveillance was more circumspect, and indeed disturbing to modern readers. Wilson notes that "Mr Eliots brother . . . had purposely sometimes In the darke walked the Round, as it were alone, and found them in their severall Families as devout in prayer, &c. as if there had been any present to observe."[32] Because of the fear of hypocrisy raised by the need to rely on external "signs of salvation" to indicate inner change, eavesdropping on prayers intended to be private allowed the witness to demonstrate the sincerity of the Praying Indians more effectively than mere witnessing of their public performance. Such eavesdropping would have been difficult, if not impossible, before the settlement of Natick, which was conveniently close to English settlements, contained a guest house from which visitors could come and go unobserved, and whose inhabitants relied on their observers for material goods and support.

A HOLY CITY

The location of Natick is also significant because it was, according to Eliot, a site selected by God. This is not to say that the site itself held mystical or religious significance, but that he saw in its very existence the hand of God. He claimed the location was "of Gods providing, as a fruit of prayer . . . the Lord did both by his providence then, and by after more diligent search of the place, discover that there it was his pleasure we should begin this work."[33] His choice of an undeveloped site for Natick, a *tabula rasa* on which he could impose his model design for a Christian Indian town, suggests that he intended to establish a form of "ideal city," a city of God. Natick has been discussed by critics as a utopian site, but rarely in terms of the structure of the town itself, despite a long tradition linking utopias to the imagined orderly layout of urban space.[34] In his important discussion of the praying towns as a utopian project, James Holstun focuses largely on the millennial structure of their government, although Holstun also acknowledges the ideological implications of integrating the Praying Indians into the space of the "newly gridded, enclosed, and rationalized New England landscape."[35]

Although Eliot seems to have seen Natick as a city of God, ruled by a millennial government drawn from biblical sources, he did not attempt to represent this in the urban space through an elaborate geometric or symbolic layout, as is often the case with ideal cities.[36] Instead, he reserved his interest in significant patterns and numbers for the structure of government.[37] It is not even certain that Eliot imposed straight roads on Natick's plan, and there is no question of a grid given that there were only two roads north of the river. The assumption that the opposite was the case speaks to our continuing association of Euro-American culture with the urban and manufactured, and Native American with the natural and spontaneous. The only description we have of Natick's town plan refers to its "long faire streets," and "faire" cannot be taken to imply straightness, in a period when there is little evidence that this was considered preferable by the colonists. In seventeenth-century New England town planning some towns were surveyed with straight streets, but others were laid out according to their location, for example following a riverbank — something which was a possibility at Natick, given its location by the Charles.[38] However, the lack of a grid system or complicated geometric patterns does not mean that Eliot's layout of Natick was unplanned or lacked ideological implications. In fact, it seems to have been deliberately planned, not to showcase an unusual biblical or millennial model, but the opposite: to blend in, by following the same rules as the layout of other seventeenth-century colonial New England towns.

Unlike other European colonial projects of the period, New England's towns were not built according to a specific design or complex rules. As Reps comments, "It was a characteristic of the New England communities that the elements used in their planning were limited in number and elementary in nature."[39] The only contemporary commentary on town planning that survives from New England in this period, the "Essay on the Laying out of Towns," does not specify a preferred town plan or street pattern, as does the Spanish equivalent, *The Laws of the Indies*.[40] Instead, as Kostof notes, the "Essay" imagines the town as a series of concentric circles with the meetinghouse at the center; houses and gardens surround the meetinghouse, and surrounding them is a ring of farms, with farther out the potential for additional clusters of farmhouses among the fields.[41] The author of the "Essay" assumes that houses will always be built in groups, "for compforte in vicinitye," but beyond this is unprescriptive about the details of the layout.[42]

It is not clear how widely circulated the "Essay" was, but this understanding of colonial towns as a series of concentric circles does seem consistent with reality. As Reps's summary confirms: "Many, though not all, New England villages centered around some form of central open space—the village green or common. . . . The green often served as the site of the meetinghouse and later for other public buildings as well. . . . [It was] a space into which cattle from the common pasture could be herded in case of a threatened Indian attack. . . . Another feature of the New England village community was the sharp break between village and countryside . . . The earlier villages exhibited a compact group of houses and home lots quite apart from the surrounding farm lands."[43]

Reps also notes that most New England villages were either a "compact, 'squared' community in which the home lots were usually small in comparison with farm fields and where several streets led outward from a central green or square," or they were arranged in a "linear pattern, where a single street forms the spine of the settlement"—although they varied endlessly in their particulars.[44] What we know of Natick's layout is consistent with these general rules. The cluster of public buildings—meetinghouse, guesthouse, fort—at the center, and the indications that the home lots were located in a

ALISON STANLEY

group, echoes the compact village structure of contemporary colonial towns. It is possible that the area around the meetinghouse, inside the fort, played a similar role to the central open space of the green in other colonial settlements. Eliot's intent, then, was not to make Natick stand out by its design, but rather to make it blend in; as with other signs of salvation, it was its very similarity to colonial English norms that made it convincing.

"WEL SAWEN" BUILDINGS, WIGWAMS, AND "PUBLICKE WORKES"

This reading of Natick's layout is confirmed by the design of the buildings Eliot planned. The majority of the "publicke workes"—the meetinghouse, the visitors' house, the bridge—were all constructed in English rather than traditional Algonquian style. Eliot demanded the erection of the guesthouse specifically because "we must also of necessity have an house to lodge in, meet in and lay up our provisions and clothes, which cannot be in *Wigwams*."[45] The European style of the buildings, and the quality of their construction, impressed contemporary observers. For example, John Wilson described the visitors' house, "which the *Indians* have built after the *English* manner high and large no *English*-mans hand in it, save that one day or two they had an *English*-Carpenter with them to direct about the time of rearing, with chimneys in it."[46]

Eliot himself gave a similar final proof of the Praying Indians' "Civil Order" and readiness to be considered for church membership, after they succeeded "in building, without any English Workmans help, or direction, a very sufficient Meeting-House, of fifty foot long, twenty five foot broad, neer twelve foot high betwixt the joynts, wel sawen, and framed (which is a specimen, not only of their singular ingenuity, and dexterity, but also of some industry)."[47]

As previous historians have commented, it was the fact that the Praying Indians produced an English-style house without English assistance that was significant; they had proved that they were not merely mimicking colonial forms, but could reproduce them independently.[48] Their adoption of this architectural style also had evident ideological and practical implications. As with town form on a larger scale, how a building is laid out and constructed signals some of the intentions of its designer, and in turn will partly determine the living patterns of its users. The architectural differences between the English-style buildings constructed at Natick and traditionally constructed wigwams demonstrate fundamentally different ways of understanding family life and social space.

Although the focus of this argument is not on the form of Algonquian vernacular architecture but on the ways that Praying Indians adapted colonial English forms, it is worth setting out briefly the traditional construction and appearance of Algonquian wigwams. William Wood describes their form in *New Englands Prospect*:

> [Their] frames are formed like our garden-arbours, something more round, very strong and handsome, covered with close-wrought mats of their owne weaving, which deny entrance to any drop of raine, though it come both fierce and long, neither can the piercing North winde finde a crannie, through which he can conveigh his cooling breath, they be warmer than our *English* houses; at the top is a square hole for the smoakes evacuation, which in rainy weather is covered with a pluver; . . . Their houses are smaller in the Summer, when their families be dispersed, by reason of heate and occasions. In Winter they make some fiftie or threescore foote long, fortie or fiftie men being inmates under one roofe; and as is their husbands occasion these poore tectonists are often troubled like snailes, to carry their houses on their backs sometime to fishing-places, other times to hunting-places, after that to a planting place, where it abides the longest.[49]

The local Native American culture and environment was inscribed in their wigwams. Often dismissed as architecture by the colonists, largely because of their impermanence, wigwams were designed to suit their environment and their inhabitants' needs. Warmer than English houses in the cold New England climate, they were easy to move to the locations where their inhabitants gathered food at different times of year. They were also highly adaptable to suit the weather and the space needed, reflecting the way units of the Indian community moved apart or came together in different seasons. Sieur de Champlain's images of Massachusetts Indian houses (Fig. 6.3) illustrate this—most of the wigwams depicted are round, but one is a longer oblong. A similar method of construction can be seen in John White's watercolor observations of the related culture of the Algonquian Indians in Virginia. Although there were some differences in the design, White's paintings convey in close detail the structure of New England Algonquian wigwams (Fig. 6.4).

Adopting an English-style building meant a fundamental change in thinking not only about relationship to place and property—houses that last for generations can be inherited or sold in a way that wigwams cannot—but also about social relationships. Puritan New England houses were designed to be inhabited by a nuclear family; although servants or dependent relatives might

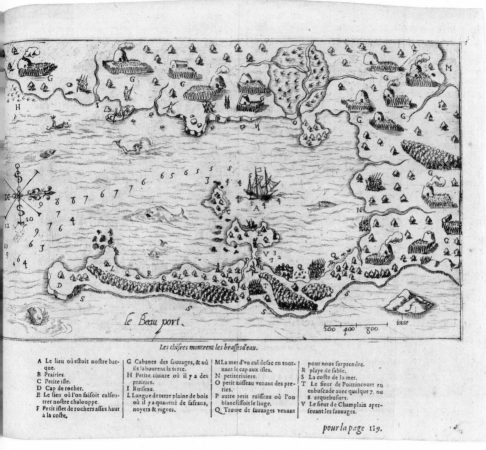

Les chifres montrent les brasses d'eau.

A Le lieu où estoit nostre bar- | G Cabanes des sauuages, & où | M La mer d'vn cul desac en tour- | pour nous surprendre.
que. | ils labourent la terre. | nant le cap aux isles. | R playe de sable.
B Prairies. | H Petite riuiere où il y a des | N petite riuiere. | S La coste de la mer.
C Petite isle. | prairies. | O petit ruisseau venant des pre- | T Le sieur de Poitrincourt en
D Cap de rocher. | I Ruisseau. | ries. | enbuscade auec quelque 7. ou
E Le lieu où l'on faisoit calfeu- | L Langue de terre plaine de bois | P autre petit ruisseau où l'on | 8 arquebusiers.
trer nostre chalouppe. | où il y a quantité de safrans, | blanchissoit le linge. | V Le sieur de Champlain aper-
F Petit islet de rochers assez haut | noyers & vignes. | Q Troupe de sauuages venant | ceuant les sauuages.
à la coste.

pour la page 119.

FIGURE 6.3. *Champlain's chart of "Le Beau Port" (modern-day Gloucester, Massachusetts), from* Les Voyages *(Paris, 1613). Courtesy of the John Carter Brown Library at Brown University.*

also be sheltered, they were clearly owned by the head of the family, usually a patriarchal male. For local Native groups, on the other hand, housing was much less identified with the separation of the nuclear family unit. Roger Williams notes that "two Families will live comfortably and lovingly in a little round house of some fourteen or sixteen foot over, and so more and more families in proportion."[50] Similarly, a law imposed on the Praying Indians in the 1640s required that "every young man if not anothers servant, and if unmarried, . . . shall be compelled to set up a *wigwam* and plant for himself, and not live shifting up and downe to other *wigwams*," implying that this had previously been the norm.[51]

The towne of Pomeiock and true forme of their howses, couered and enclosed some wth matts, and some wth barcks of trees. All compassed abowt wth smale poles stock thick together in stedd of a wall.

FIGURE 6.4. *Watercolor drawing of the Algonquian "Indian Village of Pomeiooc" by John White (created 1585–1586).* © *The Trustees of the British Museum.*

RESISTANCE AND ADAPTATION

Unlike their acceptance of the movement to the urban site of Natick, however, the Praying Indians never fully adopted an English architectural style for their homes. While the large community buildings—the school, the meeting-house, and the guesthouse—were built in imitation of English forms, some if not all of the Praying Indians continued to live in wigwams. Gookin describes how "their other houses in this town [Natick] are generally after their old mode before described; though some they have built in this and other of

ALISON STANLEY

the praying villages, after the English form. But these being more chargeable to built and not so warm, and cannot be removed so easily as their wigwams, wherein there is not a nail used, to avoid annoyance by fleas, and themselves being generally artists in building and furnishing their own wigwams: for these and like reasons, they do incline to keep their old fashioned houses."[52]

Moreover, although they planted orchards on their lots, the evidence suggests that they continued to locate their wigwams in a traditional location away from the surveyed grounds; an observer refers to them "living in *Wigmoones*, whereof there is good store neere the hill side."[53]

It is interesting that once the Praying Indians had moved on to being examined spiritually to see if they were ready for church membership, both Eliot and Gookin (Superintendent of the Indians in Massachusetts from 1656) seem to have accepted the Natick residents' preference for retaining their own traditional architecture. As several historians have noted, Eliot had demanded, even before the founding of Natick, that Puritan social hierarchies and sexual morality be represented in the internal space of converts' homes: "the *Wigwams* of the meanest of [the Praying Indians] equallize any *Sachims* in other places, being built not with mats but barks of Trees in good Bignesse, the rather that they may have their partitions in them for husbands and wives together, and their children and servants in their places also, who formerly were never private in what nature is ashamed of, either for the sun or any man to see."[54]

Once wigwams were partitioned to enforce sexual modesty, social hierarchy, and the nuclear family, however, their external structure seems to have been of less interest to Eliot. And the Praying Indians, though clearly willing to adopt English town forms when required in order to demonstrate their sincerity and achieve their goal of full church membership, made it clear to Gookin that in this case, at least, they regarded their own traditional architecture as superior to that of the English colonists. As a result, despite Eliot's original plan, Natick did not develop into a simple copy of other colonial New England towns, a community sign of salvation, a familiar setting for English observers against which individual performances of spiritual conversion would be performed. Instead, as several historians have argued, it was marked by its culturally mixed appearance. As O'Brien concludes, "It was unmistakably an Indian place" as well as a colonial English town.[55] Kostof notes that "in all 'ideal' cities, the diagram will remain inviolate as long as its inhabitants are denied freedom of action."[56] The movement away from Eliot's original plan, toward a more culturally mixed architecture and form, suggests the ways in which the Praying Indian inhabitants of Natick progressively asserted their freedom of action and its congruence with their profession of Christian belief. Natick was clearly a place of cultural adaptation by not only the Praying Indians, but also Eliot and other colonists involved in the missionary work.

Nevertheless, such cultural continuity and adaptation of Eliot's plans does not negate the colonial English elements of Natick. Although it is useful to emphasize the ways in which the Praying Indians were able to actively assert their preferences as the town developed, nevertheless their adoption of a permanent town site, and the allocation of the land into individual ownership, implied a fundamentally different way of responding to the environment and community around them. Perhaps the most useful way to understand the urban space of conversion at Natick was the symbolism at its center. At the metaphorical—and probably geographical—heart of the community was the meetinghouse, an English-style building erected without English assistance, in which the first Native American congregation in the region eventually worshipped independently. But the meetinghouse was enclosed within a fort built in the traditional Algonquian style, "of whole trees very hansome and firme."[57] The combination of the two architectures suggests how Natick was a place of acculturation rather than purely transculturation, a mingling of traditions rather than the remaking of Native Americans wholly in the English Puritan image.

But there is also a darker way to read this symbol. The Praying Indians located their meetinghouse within the defensive structure of the fort, but never had to defend it against military attack. Despite this, they were forced to leave Natick during King Philip's War (1675–76), not because of an attack from outside, but due to the actions of their allies. The English colonists, refusing to trust them, ordered the Natick Praying Indians to be taken by a military escort and imprisoned in what was effectively a concentration camp on Deer Island, in Boston Harbor. Gookin tells us that "good Mr. Elliot, that faithful instructor and teacher of the praying Indians, met them . . . exhorting them to patience in their sufferings, and confirming the hearts of those disciples of Christ; and exhorting them to continue in the faith, for through many tribulations we must enter into the kingdom of heaven."[58] The Praying Indians went "submissively and Christianly and affectionately," but the praying towns were never to recover to their antebellum form.[59] The fort defending the heart of Natick had effectively been betrayed by the meetinghouse within it.

NOTES

1. Increase Mather, "A Brief History of the War," in *So Dreadful a Judgement: Puritan Responses to King Philip's War, 1676–1677*, ed. Richard Slotkin and James K. Folsom (Middletown, Connecticut: Wesleyan University Press, 1979), 55–206. Originally published as Increase Mather, *A Brief History of the Warr with the Indians in New-England* (Boston and London, 1676).

2. Ola Elizabeth Winslow, *John Eliot, "Apostle to the Indians"* (Boston: Houghton Mifflin Company, 1968), 131.

3. William Kellaway, *The New England Company, 1649–1776: Missionary Society to the American Indians* (London: Longmans, 1961), 15, 34, 50.

4. James Holstun, *A Rational Millennium: Puritan Utopias of Seventeenth-Century England and America* (Oxford: Oxford University Press, 1987), 102–65; Jean M. O'Brien, *Dispossession by Degrees: Indian Land and Identity in Natick, Massachusetts 1650–1790* (Cambridge: Cambridge University Press, 1997).

5. John W. Reps, *Town Planning in Frontier America* (Columbia and London: University of Missouri Press, 1980), 101.

6. William Wood, *New Englands Prospect* (London, 1634), 80–81.

7. Thomas Shepard, *The Clear Sun-Shine of the Gospel Breaking Forth Upon the Indians in New-England* (London, 1648). Reprinted in Michael P. Clark, *The Eliot Tracts With Letters from John Eliot to Thomas Thorowgood and Richard Baxter* (Westport, Conn., and London: Praeger, 2003), 114.

8. Spiro Kostof, *The City Shaped: Urban Patterns and Meanings Through History* (London: Thames and Hudson, 1999), 16.

9. William Cronon, *Changes in the Land: Indians, Colonists, and the Ecology of New England* (New York: Hill and Wang, 1983), 34–53.

10. Ibid., 45.

11. Ibid., 54–81.

12. Ibid., 72–73.

13. Jean M. O'Brien, *Dispossession by Degrees*, 52–53.

14. James Axtell, *After Columbus: Essays in the Ethnohistory of Colonial North America* (New York and Oxford: Oxford University Press, 1988), 47–57; Richard Cogley, *John Eliot's Mission to the Indians before King Philip's War* (Cambridge: Harvard University Press, 1999); Harold W. van Lonkhuyzen, "A Reappraisal of the Praying Indians: Acculturation, Conversion, and Identity at Natick, Massachusetts, 1646–1730," *New England Quarterly* 63, no. 3 (1990): 396–428; Dane Morrison, *A Praying People: Massachusetts Acculturation and the Failure of the Puritan Mission, 1600–1900* (New York: Peter Lang, 1995); O'Brien, *Dispossession by Degrees*, 52–53.

15. James Axtell, *After Columbus*, 100–121; Hilary Wyss, *Writing Indians: Literacy, Christianity and Native Community in Early America* (Amherst: University of Massachusetts Press, 2000), 17–51; David Murray, *Forked Tongues: Speech, Writing and Representation in North American Indian Texts* (London: Pinter Publishers, 1991), 126–57; Kristina Bross, *Dry Bones and Indian Sermons: Praying Indians in Colonial America*

(Ithaca and London: Cornell University Press, 2004); Linda Gregerson, "The Commonwealth of the Word: New England, Old England and the Praying Indians," in *British Identities and English Renaissance Literature*, ed. David Baker and Willy Maley (Cambridge: Cambridge University Press, 2002), 191.

16. John Eliot and Thomas Mayhew, *Tears of Repentance: Or, A Further Narrative of the Progress of the Gospel amongst the Indians in New-England* (London, 1653). Reprinted in Clark, *The Eliot Tracts*, 268.

17. Cogley, *John Eliot's Mission*, 165; Daniel Gookin, *Historical Collections of the Indians in New England* (1792), Special Collections Publications Paper, 195, http://digital commons.uri.edu/sc_pubs/13 (May 17, 2015).

18. Anon. [Henry Whitfield?], *Strength out of Weaknesse; Or, a Glorious Manifestation of the Further Progresse of the Gospel among the Indians in New-England* (London, 1652). Reprinted in Clark, *The Eliot Tracts*, 231–32.

19. Henry Whitfield, *The Light Appearing More and More towards the Perfect Day* (London, 1651). Reprinted in Clark, *The Eliot Tracts*, 202.

20. Anon. [Henry Whitfield?], *Strength out of Weaknesse*, 231.

21. Cogley, *John Eliot's Mission*, 106.

22. Eliot and Mayhew, *Tears of Repentance*, 268.

23. Gookin, *Historical Collections of the Indians*, 181; order quoted in Daniel Gookin, *An Historical Account of the Doings and Sufferings of the Christian Indians in New England, in the years 1675, 1676, 1677* (Cambridge, Mass.: Transactions and Collections of the American Antiquarian Society, 1836), 450.

24. Cogley, *John Eliot's Mission*, 32.

25. Edward Winslow, *The Glorious Progress of the Gospel amongst the Indians in New England* (London, 1649). Reprinted in Clark, *The Eliot Tracts*, 152.

26. Alden T. Vaughan, *New England Frontier: Puritans and Indians, 1620–1675* (Boston and Toronto: Little, Brown and Company, 1965), xvi–xviii; Bross, *Dry Bones and Indian Sermons*, 23.

27. Shepard, *The Clear Sun-shine of the Gospel*, 114.

28. Winslow, *The Glorious Progress of the Gospel*, 152.

29. Whitfield, *The Light Appearing More and More towards the Perfect Day*, 202–3.

30. Winslow, *The Glorious Progress of the Gospel*, 152.

31. Cogley, *John Eliot's Mission*, 79.

32. Anon. [Henry Whitfield?], *Strength out of Weaknesse*, 233.

33. Whitfield, *The Light Appearing More and More towards the Perfect Day*, 201.

34. Kostof, *The City Shaped*, 161–63.

35. Holstun, *A Rational Millennium*, 108.

36. Kostof, *The City Shaped*, 162.

37. Holstun, *A Rational Millennium*, 152.

38. Reps, *Town Planning in Frontier America*, 109–24.

39. Kostof, *The City Shaped*, 258, 105.

40. Ibid., 114.

ALISON STANLEY

41. Ibid., 182.

42. *Winthrop Papers*, 476.

43. Reps, *Town Planning in Frontier America*, 106.

44. Ibid., 107-9.

45. Whitfield, *The Light Appearing More and More towards the Perfect Day*, 201.

46. Anon. [Henry Whitfield?], *Strength out of Weaknesse*, 231.

47. Eliot and Mayhew, *Tears of Repentance*, 268.

48. Bross, *Dry Bones and Indian Sermons*, 24; Holstun, *A Rational Millennium*, 122-24.

49. Wood, *New Englands Prospect*, 105-6.

50. Roger Williams, *A Key into the Language of America* (London, 1643), 33.

51. Anon. [Edward Winslow], *The Day-Breaking, if Not the Sun-rising of the Gospell with the Indians in New-England* (London, 1647), 98.

52. Gookin, *Historical Collections of the Indians*, 181.

53. Anon. [Henry Whitfield?], *Strength out of Weaknesse*, 232.

54. Bross, *Dry Bones and Indian Sermons*, 24; Axtell 1986, 169; van Lonkhuyzen, "A Reappraisal of the Praying Indians," 414-15. Quotation taken from Shepard, *The Clear Sun-Shine of the Gospel*, 133.

55. O'Brien, *Dispossession by Degrees*, 44; Bross, *Dry Bones and Indian Sermons*, 146-47; Cogley, *John Eliot's Mission*, 107-8.

56. Kostof, *The City Shaped*, 167.

57. Anon. [Henry Whitfield?), *Strength out of Weaknesse*, 231. For an example of such a fort, see Fig. 6.4.

58. Gookin, *An Historical Account of the Doings and Sufferings of the Christian Indians*, 473-74.

59. Ibid., 474.

PART III
Commerce, Traffic, and Trade

7

TOOLS OF EMPIRE

TRADE, SLAVES, AND THE BRITISH
FORTS OF WEST AFRICA

Christopher DeCorse

The British forts and trade posts of sub-Saharan West Africa afforded Britain the ability to control access to resources—including slaves—and laid the foundation for empire. Between the mid-seventeenth and late nineteenth centuries Britain or British companies established or occupied more than fifty forts and outposts in West Africa stretching from the Senegambia to the Bight of Benin (Fig. 7.1). Their establishment, design, use, and ultimate disuse varied through time, indicating changes in both regional and global political alliances and economic needs. The principal function of the vast majority of these outposts was commercial. They served as bases for trade, providing places to store and gather trade goods, and to exclude other European competitors. The first forts were established to control access to gold, ivory, and raw materials, and trade in these items remained important. However, during the seventeenth century the need for labor on the plantations of the Americas led to an increasing trade in enslaved Africans, and the forts played a key role in this human traffic. With the abolition of the slave trade in the nineteenth century the commercial viability of the forts dramatically decreased and many fell into disuse. Often poorly built, vernacular in plan, and at times ill-suited to the tropics, the British forts and outposts of West Africa nonetheless collectively delineated an expanding sphere of economic influence that ultimately culminated with the imposition of colonial rule in the late nineteenth century. This chapter considers British forts in the wider Atlantic context and how their establishment, construction, and use reflect the varied cultural, political, and economic landscapes of which they were part.

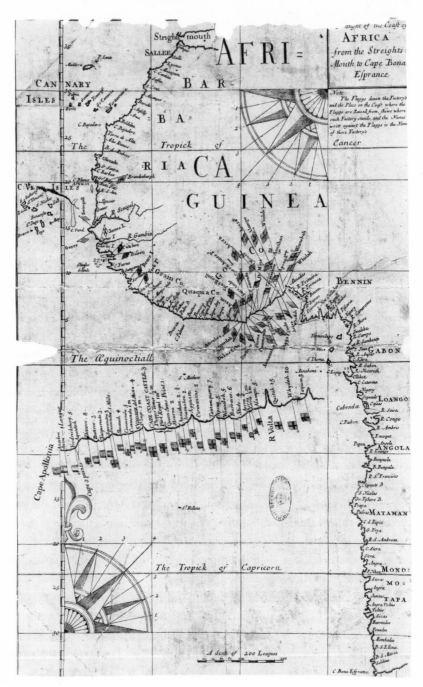

FIGURE 7.1. *An eighteenth-century British map of West and Central Africa with flags marking the locations of the forts of different European nations. The inset, dating circa 1773, shows the detail of coastal Ghana. The National Archives UK, Ref. MPK45.*

Britain was not the first European nation to arrive in sub-Saharan West Africa or the first nation to establish permanent outposts there. European expansion began with the Portuguese, who likely reached coastal Sierra Leone by 1450, the coast of modern-day Ghana by the 1470s, and the Horn of Africa by the end of the century. They subsequently built the first forts on the West African coast.[1] The first and largest of these was *Castelo São Jorge da Mina* (now known as Elmina Castle) founded in 1482.[2] Through forts, military action, royal decree, and Papal sanction, the Portuguese attempted to maintain a monopoly on West African trade. However, within fifty years of the founding of Elmina their control had started to wane. French, Dutch, and English vessels were trading on the West African coast by the 1530s. A dozen or so English voyages were recorded during the 1550s and 60s.[3] These accounts provide relatively detailed information, in some respects more informative (or perhaps more accessible) than contemporary Portuguese sources.

While the English maintained an early and continuous presence on much of the West African coast, during the first half of the seventeenth century they lagged behind the French and especially the Dutch in the extent of their trading networks and in establishing permanent bases. The possibility of constructing a fort in West Africa was periodically raised in England beginning in the 1550s, but no plans were realized until the founding of a small outpost at Kormantin in coastal Ghana in 1631. In contrast, references to Dutch outposts in the Senegambia begin in the 1590s.[4] The French were maintaining a small factory on Gorée Island off the coast of Senegal by 1606. The island was purchased by the Dutch in 1617, who subsequently established the forts Nassau and Orange (later occupied by the French). In coastal Ghana, the Dutch founded Fort Nassau at Mori in 1612, and also occupied the former Portuguese forts at Elmina in 1637 and Shama circa 1639.

The British forts of West Africa date between 1631, when the English founded the fort at Kormantin in coastal Ghana, and the 1890s, when the British established a number of outposts in the West African hinterland. Notably, however, these fortifications were—with the exception of a handful of later installations—all "pre-Colonial," the vast majority having been established between 1660 and 1800. While the arrival of the Europeans on the West African coast in the late fifteenth century enmeshed Africa in an increasingly global economic system dominated by Europe, the political annexation and overt control of West Africa did not begin until the late nineteenth century with the partition of Africa into colonial spheres of influence. The Gold Coast Colony was established in coastal Ghana in 1876; The Gambia became a Crown colony in 1889; the Sierra Leone Protectorate was established in 1896; and the annexation of what is now northern Nigeria was completed in 1914.[5]

The period during which the majority of the British forts of West Africa were established was one of dramatic change. Britain emerged as a fully industrialized nation with an economy that was increasingly aimed at and increasingly dependent upon transoceanic trade. Following the Restoration of Charles II and the House of Stuart in 1660, relative political stability and support for trade fostered expansion into widening markets. It is more than coincidental that the establishment of the majority of British outposts, forts, and lodges in West Africa corresponds to a period that witnessed both domestic mercantile expansion and technological advances ranging from coal extraction to textile and brass manufacture, all of which rested on a commercial and middling sector that was more developed than any other European country.[6] This period also witnessed the emergence of the plantation economies of the Americas and the increasing Americanization of the Atlantic world. At the time of the English Civil War the principal English colonies consisted of Barbados, the Leeward Islands of Antigua, Nevis and St. Christopher in the Caribbean, and Virginia, Maryland, and Massachusetts in North America. By 1776 the British Empire in the Americas included a dozen Caribbean colonies, as well as Belize, the thirteen colonies in the nascent United States, and a number of Canadian provinces. The plantations in these colonies were largely dependent on African slave labor and British merchants established far-flung trade networks connecting the Americas, the Caribbean, and West Africa.

With the emergence of the plantation economies of the Americas during the seventeenth century the trade in slaves became increasingly important. Slaves had been traded in the West African savanna and Sahel for centuries, perhaps from the beginnings of the trans-Saharan trade in the first millennium AD. However, historical evidence for a trade in slaves in the coastal regions of West Africa prior to the arrival of the Europeans in the fifteenth century is limited.[7] The trade in enslaved Africans became progressively important, a consequence of the labor needs of the developing plantations of the Americas.[8] By the second half of the seventeenth-century slaves had eclipsed gold as the primary trade item on the Gold Coast—modern-day Ghana.

The period between 1660 and 1800 was also a period of dramatic innovation in terms of military architecture.[9] European fortifications of the later seventeenth and eighteenth centuries were dramatically different from those of earlier periods. Owing to increasingly powerful and sophisticated artillery, castles that could have comfortably withstood sieges lasting months during the Middle Ages could be reduced to rubble in a matter of days. Fortifications had to be designed to better withstand bombardment with innovations that considered flanking fire, placement of enfilading batteries, and wall construction designed to minimize damage from cannon fire.

Despite these innovations in military architecture, the majority of the British forts and other European outposts in West Africa were typically ill-designed, quickly built, and frequently in disrepair. Often they had small European staffs, for the most part exclusively men, who faced disease, high mortality rates, and poor supply. Some, such as Yamyamacunda, founded on the Gambia River in the 1730s, were little more than small dwellings, simply and expediently built of timber and clay in the style of local African buildings (Fig. 7.2). Others, such as Cape Coast in modern Ghana, grew into substantial fortifications, well deserving of their popular appellation "castles" (Fig. 7.3). While some of the forts incorporated new innovations in military construction, the majority were modest in scale and few presented the classic, fully designed defensive features seen in Europe. In West Africa, it was common practice to establish a small lodge or fort first and gradually expand and strengthen it if the trade proved successful. Consequently, the plans of many forts reflect the expansion and redesign of earlier structures. Lawrence suggested that the strongest fortifications of the West African forts generally faced the sea, as defense against the possibility of European naval bombardment, which was the greatest threat.[10] While this is true in many instances, there were certainly exceptions, and in some cases the strongest fortifications were on the landward side.[11] Forts were also frequently captured and recaptured, experiencing multiple episodes of remodeling and reconstruction in the process. In terms of their construction, the forts of West Africa can be contrasted with some of those built in the British colonial spheres of the Americas and even South Africa, where striking, almost textbook, examples of Vauban-style fortifications can be found.[12]

The establishment of forts, their roles, and construction also reflected varied interactions with African polities. The majority of British forts, as well as those of other European nations, were located on the coast, with the notable exception of the Senegambia where the Gambia and Senegal Rivers are navigable well into the interior. Forts were not established in most of West Africa, and in many areas trade was conducted directly from ships. In many other cases only small factories or unfortified lodges were built. The major forts were established in the Senegambia, Sierra Leone, Benin, and particularly coastal Ghana. More European forts and outposts — and more

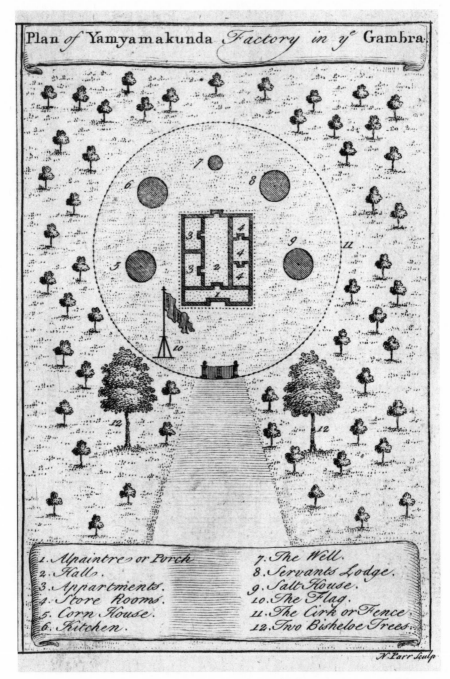

FIGURE 7.2. *Francis Moore's 1738 plan of the Royal Africa Company outpost of Yamyamakunda on the Gambia River. The primary structure and the four outbuildings were built of timber and clay in African style. C. R. DeCorse collection.*

FIGURE 7.3. *Photograph of Cape Coast Castle. The slave dungeons were located beneath the seaward battery on the left. Author.*

British forts—were built in coastal Ghana than in any other part of Africa: there are in fact more European forts in coastal Ghana than all of the other pre-nineteenth-century European outposts in West Africa combined. Coastal Ghana initially became important because of the gold trade, but the concentration of forts also reflects the coast's strategic importance. The relatively stable relations with local African polities in Ghana provided places for established bases that could provide security for both goods and slaves that were often brought from other parts of the West African coast. Forts and outposts were established with the permission, sometimes at the request, of local African states. While African-European relations were sometimes strained and there were conflicts, the need to have African agreement and participation was integral to the commercial success of a fort.[13] In coastal Ghana, European nations often paid ground rent to African rulers in exchange for the use of a fort or at the onset of trade. In reality, while it might have proven difficult for the Africans to oust European traders, it is equally true that Europeans had to maintain cordial relations with local populations as they were the key to maintaining trade.

Elsewhere on the West African coast, states closely restricted the European presence. The most dramatic examples of this are provided by the kingdoms of Hueda and Dahomey in coastal Benin, which closely regulated and

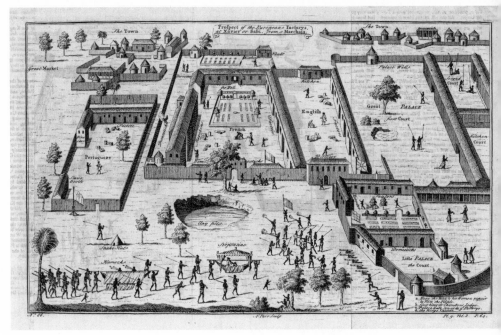

FIGURE 7.4. *An interpretation of European factories at Sabi (Savi),
coastal Benin in the 1720s. The English, French, and Portuguese factories were all
located adjacent to the king's palace. The image is probably from Jean Labat,* Voyage
du chevalier Des Marchais en Guinée, isles voisines, et à Cayenne, fait en 1725,
1726, and 1727, *2nd edition, Amsterdam, 1731. C. R. DeCorse collection.*

manipulated the Europeans powers with which they interacted.[14] European
traders were not granted exclusive trading rights, but rather representatives
of different nations were dealt with at the same time. At Savi, the Hueda
capital, the unfortified factories of the British, French, and Portuguese were
attached to the royal court (Fig. 7.4). Following the defeat of Hueda by Dahomey in 1727, the Europeans relocated to Glewhe (modern Ouidah) some
three kilometers from the coast. Here they built separate fortifications, but
were isolated in factories three hundred meters from one another and forbid-
den to visit the Dahomean capital.[15]

THE FIRST ENGLISH FORTS

Beginning in 1618, English trade in West Africa was, by royal charter, placed
in the hands of the Company of Guynney and Binney. The company was not
particularly successful or profitable. The outpost at Kormantin (Abanzi) in
Ghana was established in 1631 with the help of Arent Goote, a former Dutch

CHRISTOPHER DECORSE

West India Company employee, and with the permission of a local chief. This outpost—the first English fort in West Africa—began as a fortified lodge that was gradually expanded, serving as the English headquarters on the coast.[16] The original building was destroyed by fire in 1640, possibly having been sabotaged by the Dutch. The English subsequently built a more substantial fort at Kormantin, the construction of which may have been completed by 1647.[17] The bastion located at the southwestern corner of the fort was hollow and was used to hold slaves, access having been gained through the ceiling— a trap door in the bastion's platform. This may have been the first slave dungeon built on the African coast.[18] Although enslaved Africans made up an increasing portion of the trade in the mid-seventeenth century, facilities built specifically to house them were still not typical.[19] Indeed, many slaves continued to be accommodated in areas outside of the forts throughout the eighteenth century. The Kormantin fort remained the English headquarters until 1665 when it was captured by the Dutch (and renamed Fort Amsterdam) and the English headquarters was moved to Cape Coast.

The Restoration of the Stuart monarchy in 1660 witnessed an expansion of English interests in West Africa. The origins of most of the more substantial English or British (following Acts of Union in 1707) forts in West Africa can be traced to this period. The earlier Company of Guynney and Binney was replaced by the Company of Royal Adventurers of England Trading to Africa, which would in turn be replaced by the Royal Africa Company in 1672. The British were not, however, alone in their quest for West African trade. During the second half of the seventeenth century an expanding Atlantic economy fueled increasing competition among European powers and a scramble for West African outposts. Forts provided a means of securing trade interests from rival nations. By the end of the seventeenth century the Portuguese, Dutch, French, Courlanders, Swedes, Danes, Brandenburgers, and English had all established fortified outposts in West Africa with varying success.

A series of European conflicts punctuated the second half of the seventeenth century, including the first (1652–54) and second Anglo-Dutch Wars (1665–67), which were specifically aimed at securing dominance in trade. In West Africa, a number of forts were captured and recaptured. An English fleet under Admiral Holmes sailed along the coast taking in succession the Dutch forts and outposts at Goreé in Senegal, Sierra Leone, and Takoradi, Shama, Mori, Anomabu, Carolusburg, and Egyaa in coastal Ghana.[20] This success was, however, short-lived as a Dutch fleet under Admiral de Ruyter sacked a number of English forts and retook the Dutch outposts in Goreé, Sierra Leone, and Takoradi, and also captured Kormantin.[21] In accordance with the Peace of Breda in 1667, the Dutch and English retained their various conquests. These conflicts made the need for strong fortifications clear, and English fortifications, as well as those of other European nationalities, became increasingly sophisticated, at least in comparison to those found before.

The most notable addition to the English forts during this period was Swedish Fort Carolusburg, located on the headland known to the Portuguese as Cabo Corso. Taken from the Swedes in 1664 it was expanded into Cape Coast Castle, which after the loss of Kormantin in 1665 served as the British headquarters on the coast until 1876, briefly functioning as the capital of the nascent Gold Coast Colony. The castle's massive walls and dungeons have become emblematic of a trade that brought millions of enslaved Africans to the Americas.[22] The castle, however, began as a small Swedish fort in 1653, after which it underwent a turbulent decade changing hands several times including a brief (1661–1664) occupation by the *Dey* (King) of Fetu.[23] It was taken and retained by the English following its capture from the Dutch in 1664.

In the 1670s, the newly formed Royal Africa Company dramatically expanded the rectangular Swedish structure to the south and southeast making Cape Coast one of the largest forts in West Africa. This gave the fort its present triangular layout on its eastern side, though features of the castle would continue to be redesigned and modified during the following century.[24] In the second half of the century the British also established or occupied a dozen or so smaller forts and lodges on the Ghanaian coast, of which few if any traces survive. The Royal Africa Company was also busy on other parts of the coast. A number of other forts or fortified lodges were established by the end of the seventeenth century, including outposts in coastal Sierra Leone and The Gambia; areas that would later become Crown colonies.[25]

An example of what some of these small, unfortified outposts may have looked like is illustrated by a site at Egyaa, east of Cape Coast, which was the site of both English and Dutch lodges.[26] Foundations, perhaps relating to an early British lodge, indicate a small structure, consisting of six rooms surrounding a central hall (Fig. 7.5).[27] The northern side of the building may have had two additional rooms or a veranda. It was built of well-laid, but unmortared stone, with a standing stone arch on the northern side that probably marks the location of the main entrance.

A further idea of the appearance of an early factory is provided by Barbot's description of the English fort built at Anomabu in 1679. Barbot notes, "The external walls of this castle are of little importance, consisting merely of a turf circle, 7–8 feet high. Inside it are various lodgings built of the same material, for the paid blacks and the slaves. The English garrison and the commandant

CHRISTOPHER DECORSE

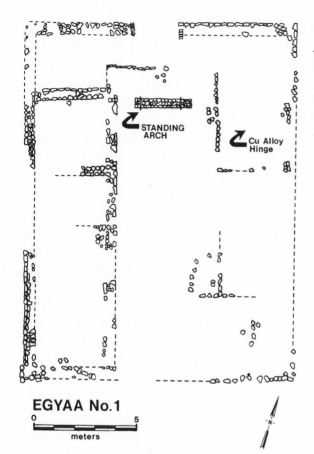

FIGURE 7.5. *Plan of the foundations of a European lodge at Egyaa, coastal Ghana. The structure may represent the foundations of an early English lodge. Author.*

STANDING ARCH

Cu Alloy Hinge

EGYAA No.1

0   5

meters

occupy the large dwelling-house, and it is here that all the merchandise and provisions are kept."[28] This description is reminiscent of Moore's 1738 account of Yamyamakunda on the Gambia River (Fig. 7.2). Smaller structures such as those at Egyaa, Anomabu, and Yamyamakunda likely represent the plan and construction of many of the smaller forts and lodges of the seventeenth and eighteenth centuries that, indeed, were more common than the larger forts. Small and insubstantial, however, they were short-lived and have largely vanished from the landscape. Consequently, it is the larger European outposts that have received the majority of modern-day attention.

THE EIGHTEENTH CENTURY

The eighteenth century was characterized by consolidation, with nations seeking to secure their trading enclaves. Many old forts were rebuilt, redesigned, and expanded. Cape Coast was expanded and other lodges in coastal

Ghana were substantially enlarged. The case of British Komenda is interesting as it illustrates a rather unique means of expanding a fort. The English established a short-lived lodge at Komenda in 1663, but a lasting outpost was not begun until 1686. This was a small stone fort with four corner bastions.[29] In 1708 plans for new fortifications were prepared. However, rather than demolish the earlier structure, the old fort was completely enclosed within a new fort of much greater size. Lawrence suggests that the practice of enclosing an older fort within a new fortification was unique to the British, this having been done in the case of Cape Coast Castle (as noted above) and also a few years later at Sekondi. [30] It may also have been done in the case of Bunce Island, Sierra Leone.

By the beginning of the eighteenth century, the slave trade had become the major focus of trade, and provision had to be made to hold enslaved Africans. Slaves sometimes were held on the coast for months until a ship arrived or, alternatively, had to be kept until a sufficient number had been gathered for a ship's cargo. Slaves were housed in a variety of ways. However, the information on slave housing has not been thoroughly examined, and some of the data are unclear. Many plans of European forts provide little indication of where slaves were housed. There are also instances of enslaved Africans being held in enclosures outside of forts throughout the seventeenth and eighteenth centuries.[31] Notably, however, in these cases the areas around the forts were relatively secure, including examples located on islands and another positioned at the end of a narrow peninsula. It is also possible, perhaps likely, that these areas outside of the forts are referring to housing for castle slaves who worked on the coast, rather than enslaved Africans awaiting shipment to the Americas.

Forts, in some cases initially constructed as places to store goods and to provide housing for garrison staff, were modified to accommodate slaves. The use of the bastion interiors to house slaves, such as in the case of the early Kormantin fort, is also seen in other fortifications. For example, plans of the British forts at Dixcove and Komenda dating to 1756 show slave rooms beneath corner bastions, though these were apparently accessed through doors at the same level as the cell floors rather than through the ceiling. These areas are clearly differentiated from rooms occupied by soldiers and the castle slaves.[32] These slave dungeons were relatively small: the area identified as the "slave hole" in a 1756 plan of the Komenda fort only measures a few square meters.[33] This is of note as at the time Komenda was the largest Royal Africa Company fort on the Gold Coast after Cape Coast Castle.

During the eighteenth century, Cape Coast Castle was further expanded and renovated. Van Dantzig notes that the late eighteenth-century reconstructed dungeons of Cape Coast Castle, as horrible as they were, nevertheless were an improvement over earlier structures that were located beneath the parade ground and accessed through the ceiling (as in the case of the Kormantin fort discussed above).[34] These openings consequently had to be closed when it rained, leaving the slaves in a dark, airless, below-ground enclosure. The renovated castle was a structure specifically designed for the needs of the slave trade. Vaulted dungeons were placed beneath the massive gun platform against the sea wall, providing space to accommodate hundreds of slaves for shipment to the Americas, primarily the British plantations of the Caribbean (Fig. 7.3).

In The Gambia, the principal British fortification was established some twenty miles up the Gambia River on James Island. Control of this site, located much further in the interior than most European forts, theoretically allowed the occupiers to control trade with the hinterland. While ideally situated in this respect, the tiny island, barely above the river's surface, was plagued with problems of maintenance and poor supply. The first fortifications were built on the island (then called St. André) in 1652 by the trading company of the Duke of Courland, now the area occupied by Latvia.[35] However, the fort traded hands numerous times. The English first occupied the island in 1661 and renamed it in honor of the heir to the throne, James II. Barbot describes James Fort as the "next best" Royal African Company fortification on the West African coast after Cape Coast Castle.[36] Through the early 1690s the island's fortifications apparently remained much the same as they were in Barbot's time.[37] Despite the supposedly impressive fortifications, the fort was lost to the French—who spiked the cannon and breached the walls—in 1695 and again in 1702. Captured, sacked a number of times, and accidentally blown up in 1725, Fort James was again reoccupied and reconstructed by the Royal Africa Company in 1726.[38] Although it now approximated its final form—a small square fort with triangular bastions at each corner—it was still somewhat eclectic in plan. A plan dating to 1755 shows bastions and curtain walls that were still ill-designed to provide covering fire. Notably, many of the activity areas were located outside of the fort.[39] A gun platform with seven twelve-pound cannon flanked by two half-moon bastions, each with five guns, was positioned on the western side of the fort facing downriver. This unusual plan is similar to that seen at Bunce Island, Sierra Leone.[40] The remaining portions of the small island, at times protected by a palisade, were occupied by the slave house, various service buildings, and the huts of the castle slaves.

By the end of the eighteenth century all of the major European forts of West Africa had been established. The nineteenth century was a period of reevaluation, consolidation, and abandonment. In The Gambia, James Fort was not reoccupied after its destruction by the French in 1778. Bunce Island in the Sierra Leone Estuary fell into disuse following Britain's abolition of the slave trade in 1808. On the Gold Coast, only three nations continued to maintain outposts in the nineteenth century: Britain, the Netherlands, and Denmark. Only Britain would remain on the coast by 1872.

The abolition of the slave trade was a major precipitator of these changes. The moral and economic rationale for slavery was debated throughout Europe in the eighteenth century. After 1772, slaves reaching England were progressively deemed to have free status. Denmark outlawed the importation of slaves in 1803. Other European nations and finally the United States (in 1865) and Brazil (1888) followed suit. New areas of commercial opportunity were seized, and it was Britain that was in the best position to do this. By the nineteenth century Britain had developed as the economic nexus of Europe. Birmingham brass, Manchester cotton, and Staffordshire pottery increasingly dominated markets on a worldwide scale. During the nineteenth century the gross tonnage of British shipping to West Africa burgeoned, climbing from about 57,000 tons in 1854 to over 500,000 tons in 1874.[41] Even as a crude measure such figures illustrate the increasing volume of trade and commercial growth.

Economic competition was never more intense and the rationale for West African outposts never more carefully scrutinized. Forts were no longer needed to secure trade from other European nations. Their economic value increasingly unclear, many European companies abandoned their outposts.[42] Treaties between European nations sought to consolidate holdings as a means of securing revenue through tariffs and duties on goods traded within spheres of influence.[43] There were increasing claims for territorial rights beyond the confines of the small coastal enclaves where European powers had previously operated. These initial efforts to regulate exchange were largely unsuccessful. Perceptions of political authority and economic gain nonetheless became the rationale for European territorial claims that would typify the end of the nineteenth century. Ultimately, the commercial value of the West African trade would be important in justifying colonial expansion in the late nineteenth century. Yet in the preceding decades the economic worth of the West African outposts was far from obvious.

With the increasing imposition of British political authority over portions of the West African coastal hinterland during the nineteenth century, the surviving forts increasingly took on administrative functions, as well as providing housing for military garrisons—protection from African polities who challenged European territorial claims. A series of conflicts punctuated the nineteenth century, including conflicts with the Asante and, in the late nineteenth century, the Samori State.[44] The small, outlying defensive works of forts William, McCarthy, and Victoria surrounding Cape Coast, Ghana date to this period. During the 1890s and the early twentieth century, the British also established a number of small, unfortified—or lightly fortified— outposts in the West African hinterland, including West African Frontier Force outposts in The Gambia, northern Sierra Leone, northern Ghana, and in Nigeria. More police posts than forts, these structures were likely built of local timber and clay. They are, however, poorly described and no traces survive.[45] To these may be added a few new, smaller fortifications, such as those on the Banana Islands in coastal Sierra Leone established in connection with the West Africa Squadron during the nineteenth century. Created in 1808 to suppress the slave trade, the squadron liberated some 150,000 enslaved Africans between its inception and 1860.[46] The squadron's success can at least partly be attributed to the existence of effective bases for refitting and resupply, some of which included former slave forts on the African coast.

FORT THORNTON AND THE PROVINCE OF FREEDOM

Ironically, the first purely military and specifically colonial British fort in West Africa was Fort Thornton, built in Freetown, Sierra Leone as protection for the settlement of liberated Africans, initially founded by Granville Sharp in 1787. Sharp's vision was of a perfect society in West Africa that would be based on reason. This Province of Freedom was to be independent but under the protection of Britain.[47] Beginning in 1790, the development of the settlement moved forward under the direction of the St. George's Bay Association, which the following year was chartered as the Sierra Leone Company. Although allegedly maintaining Sharp's original vision, the chairman of the new company was businessman Henry Thornton. While the resettlement of free Africans remained the colony's supposed rationale, the development of commercial enterprises and economic return were primary concerns.[48] Several groups of formerly enslaved Africans were resettled. These included the original settlers of London's "black poor" in 1787, the Nova Scotians who arrived in 1792, and resettled Maroons from Jamaica in 1800. Added during the nineteenth century were sixty to seventy thousand liberated Africans saved by Britain's West Africa Squadron who were settled in Sierra Leone.

The plans for a lush paradise established for freed slaves went far from smoothly, and the newly arrived settlers faced a variety of vicissitudes, including conflict with the local African population, European ship captains, and the French.[49] The original settlement at Granville Town was destroyed by the Temne chief King Jimmy in 1789.[50] It was reestablished and renamed Free Town [Freetown] in 1792.[51] The main settlement was again entirely destroyed in 1794, this time by French warships. From a commercial standpoint the Sierra Leone Company was a dismal failure. The slave trade was prohibited from the onset and little income came from other sources. The company subsequently requested that Parliament assume responsibility, and Sierra Leone (then solely consisting of the Western peninsula) became a Crown colony on January 1, 1808.[52] A settlement established for freed slaves thus became the first British colony in West Africa.

Following its destruction by the French in 1794, Freetown was rebuilt following a plan more consistent with American or European settlements of the nineteenth century.[53] The houses, positioned on regular lots, were of wood-frame construction, the architectural design showing similarities to the houses of New England. There were also new efforts to protect the settlement. The establishment of a fort was apparently intended to be undertaken as early as 1791, but plans were not drawn up until 1793, and the fort was not built until the following year.[54] A plan of Thornton Hill dated October 6, 1796 shows a fort of unique, rectangular design, enclosing a series of buildings (Fig. 7.6). The front of the fort is shown with a curtain wall without gun embrasures, flanked by triangular bastions. The side curtain walls are parallel and extend back to matching bastions. The backsides of these bastions form exterior walls that enclose a triangular area at the rear of the fort. These back walls are broken by two matching, triangular salients. The fort would eventually become the seat of government and the state house of an independent Sierra Leone.

CONCLUSION

The establishment, expansion, and success of the European forts of West Africa during the seventeenth and eighteenth centuries must be viewed as essential parts of an expanding global trade network. The forts were first and foremost business ventures; their function commercial. Their establishment was necessitated by the drive to obtain resources in increasing amounts and across ever-expanding territories. The role of British West African outposts in securing trade, including markets that brought slaves to the plantations of the Americas, laid the foundation for British dominance in world markets

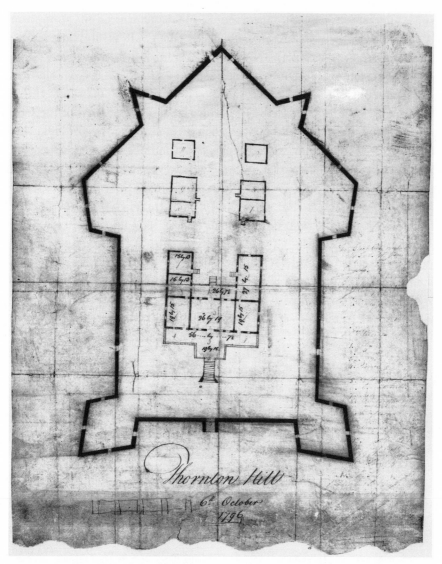

FIGURE 7.6. *Plan of Thornton Hill, Freetown, Sierra Leone, October 6, 1796. The fort's main entrance is at the bottom of the illustration. The National Archives UK, Ref. MPH 797.*

and economic ascendancy. While these enterprises included forts built by private traders, companies with Royal charters, and the British government, they all shared the objective of securing trade and the promise of economic return. In contrast to British colonial ventures in other world areas that were characterized by European settlement, immigration, and the development of associated plantations and industries, the West African forts were staffed by small numbers of men who remained largely dependent on the support of African labor. Castle gardens and industries, such as brick and lime mortar production, were developed. These activities were, however, relatively small-scale.[55] To a large extent, the agricultural production that did take place was dependent on slave labor, and so was also curtailed with abolition.[56]

The changing functions, disuse, and eventual abandonment of the forts during the nineteenth century reflect changes in economic needs. Following abolition, trade in gold, ivory, foodstuffs, and wood was still conducted at the forts, which offered security.[57] There were, however, new markets for British manufactured goods in the vast African hinterlands. The interior trade, far from the old coastal trading centers, became increasingly important.[58] The few military outposts built during the nineteenth century secured authority over hinterland populations and set the stage for much more direct European involvement in African societies. These were small and insubstantial compared to the forts of the preceding centuries. European-style dwellings were also built, but the earliest surviving examples date to the late eighteenth and early nineteenth centuries, a period when the era of the trade castles and forts had waned.

The majority of the forts and pre-nineteenth-century European outposts that once dotted the West African coast have now disappeared from the landscape. Those that survive were extensively remodeled and repurposed, serving as government buildings, prisons, post offices, lighthouses, schools, and rest houses. Nonetheless, the European forts and castles of West Africa are the oldest, most numerous, and best preserved European structures in sub-Saharan West Africa. Collectively, the forts stand as the most permanent architectural survivals of Africa's intersection with the expanding Atlantic world. As such, they remain as iconic symbols of the trade that created them.

NOTES

1. Christopher R. DeCorse, "Early Trade Posts and Forts of West Africa," in *First Forts: Essays on the Archaeology of Proto-colonial Fortifications*, ed. Eric Klingelhofer (Leiden: Brill, 2010), 209–33; Christopher R. DeCorse, Liza Gijanto, William Roberts, and Bakary Sanyang, "An Archaeological Appraisal of Early European Settlement in The Gambia," *Nyame Akuma* 73 (2010): 55–64; Arnold Walter Lawrence, *Trade Castles and Forts of West Africa* (London: Jonathan Cape, 1963).

2. Paul Edward Hedley Hair, *The Founding of the Castelo de São Jorge da Mina: An Analysis of the Sources* (Madison: African Studies Program, University of Wisconsin, 1994).

3. John William Blake, *West Africa: Quest for God and Gold, 1454–1578* (London: Curzon Press Ltd, 1977), 155; Paul Edward Hedley Hair, ed., *Hawkins in Guinea, 1567–1568*,

University of Leipzig Papers on Africa, History and Culture Series, no. 5 (Leipzig: Institut für Afrikanistik, 2000); A. Teixeira da Mota and Paul Edward Hedley Hair, *East of Mina: Afro-European Relations on the Gold Coast in the 1550s and 1560s*, African Studies Program University of Wisconsin-Madison, Studies in African Sources, no. 3 (Madison: University of Wisconsin Press, 1988).

4. Guy Thilman, "Sur l'Existence, fin XVIe, de Comptoirs Néerlandais à Joal et Portudal (Sénégal)," *Notes Africaines* 117 (1968): 17–18; Raymond Wood, "An Archaeological Appraisal of Early European Settlement in the Senegambia," *Journal of African History* 8 (1967): 39–64.

5. Thomas Pakenham, *The Scramble for Africa: 1876–1912* (New York: Random House, 1991).

6. Peter Mathias, *The First Industrial Nation: An Economic History of Britain, 1700–1914* (New York: Routledge, 2001); Kenneth Morgan, *Slavery, Atlantic Trade and the British Economy, 1660–1800* (New York: Cambridge University Press, 2000).

7. Paul E. Lovejoy, *Transformations in Slavery: A History of Slavery in Africa* (New York: Cambridge University Press, 2012), 15–18; Patrick Manning, *Slavery and African Life: Occidental, Oriental, and African Slave Trades* (Cambridge: Cambridge University Press, 1990). Some African oral traditions, as Perbi has noted with regard to the Fanti of coastal Ghana, suggest a trade in slaves prior to the arrival of the Europeans. However, it is unclear if the oral traditions recorded refer to practices predating the late fifteenth century or are conflations with more recent history. See Akosua Adoma Perbi, *A History of Indigenous Slavery in Ghana* (Accra: Sub-Saharan Publishers, 2004), 18–20.

8. See Ivana Elbl, "The Volume of the Early Atlantic Slave Trade, 1450–1521," *Journal of African History* 38 (1997): 31–75; David Eltis, "The Relative Importance of Slaves and Commodities in the Atlantic Trade of Seventeenth-Century Africa," *Journal of African History* 35 (1994): 237–49.

9. Christopher Duffy, *Fire and Stone: The Science of Fortress Warfare 1660–1860* (Edison, N.J.: Castle Books, 2006); Jean-Denis G. G. Lepage, *Vauban and the French Military under Louis XIV: An Illustrated History of Fortifications and Strategies* (Jefferson, N.C.: McFarland, 2010).

10. Lawrence, *Trade Castles*, 77.

11. A clear example is the Brandenburg Fort Dorothea in coastal Ghana, which is protected on the landward side by a curtain wall flanked by two bastions, while the seaward side was surrounded by a wooden or earthen palisade.

12. In addition to lacking well-planned bastions and well-sighted lines of fire, the British forts of West Africa often lacked glacis and ditches, which were key aspects of many other contemporary defensive works. In contrast, many of the late colonial, pre-Revolutionary War forts built in North America incorporated many Vauban-style concepts.

13. For example, Christopher R. DeCorse, *An Archaeology of Elmina: Africans and Europeans on the Gold Coast, 1400–1900* (Washington, D.C.: Smithsonian Press, 2001), 17; Teixiera da Mota and Hair, *East of Mina*, 4.

14. Kenneth Kelly, "Indigenous Responses to Colonial Encounters on the West African Coast: Hueda and Dahomey from the Seventeenth through the Nineteenth Century," in *The Archaeology of Colonialism*, ed. Claire L. Lyons and John K. Papadopoulos (Los Angeles: J. Paul Getty, 2002), 96–120.

15. Kelly, "Indigenous Responses," 109–11. Traders stored their goods in tents on shore and then transported them to the forts. Today, only the Portuguese fort at Ouidah survives. This, however, has been extensively reconstructed in the past fifty years, and it is unclear to what extent the current structure represents the plan of the original fort. In 1726, William Smith described the English fort at Whydah [Ouidah] as a strong fort with mud walls located a musket shot from the French outpost. He also noted that the fort was surrounded by a deep moat, a feature not frequently noted of other British forts in West Africa. A plan of the English fort at Whydah [Ouidah] dated 1749 shows a square fort roughly 350 feet on a side, with three triangular bastions and one circular tower at the northwest corner. The plan was done "According to a Survey made by the Order of Tho's Pye Esq: commander of his Majesty's Ship Humber the 27th Day of February 1749." The plan further notes that: "This fort is gone to decay in every part, and is falling down, and must be rebuilt." See William Smith, *A New Voyage to Guinea* (London: Frank Cass, 1967).

16. Lawrence, *Trade Castles*, 245–49; Albert Van Dantzig, *Forts and Castles of Ghana* (Accra: Sedco Publishing Limited, 1980), 21–23.

17. Lawrence, *Trade Castles*, 245; for later correspondence see Margaret Makepeace, *Trade on the Guinea Coast, 1657–1666: The Correspondence of the English East India Company*, African Studies Program, University of Wisconsin–Madison African Primary Texts 4 (Madison: University of Wisconsin, 1991).

18. Van Dantzig, *Forts and Castles*, 22.

19. In 1646 a ship's captain arriving at Elmina with forty slaves from Ardra requested that a barracoon for slaves be constructed, apparently no space being available in the massive castle (ibid.).

20. Ibid., 33–34.

21. Ibid., 34; Jean Barbot, *Barbot on Guinea: The Writings of Jean Barbot on West Africa, 1678–1712*, translated and edited by Paul Edward Hedley Hair, Adam Jones, and Robin Law (London: Hakluyt Society, 1992), 182.

22. Katharina Schramm, *African Homecoming: Pan-African Ideology and Contested Heritage* (Walnut Creek, California: Left Coast Press, 2010).

23. Barbot, *Barbot on Guinea*, 391; see comments by editors on the fort's history page 403, n. 3. Also see Lawrence, *Trade Castles*, 183; Erick Tilleman, *A Short and Simple Account of the Country of Guinea and Its Nature*, translated and edited by Selena Axelrod Winsnes (Madison: African Studies Program, University of Wisconsin, 1967), 23. Also see William St. Clair, *The Grand Slave Emporium: Cape Coast Castle and the British Slave Trade* (London: Profile, 2006).

24. Lawrence, *Trade Castles*, 183–98; Van Dantzig, *Forts and Castles*, 59–63.

25. Barbot, *Barbot on Guinea*, 144, 235.

26. Ibid., 417, 422, note 12; Willem Bosman, *A New and Accurate Description of the Coast of Guinea* (London: Frank Cass, 1967), 57; Tilleman, *A Short and Simple Account*, 24. Egyaa is variously referred to as Adja, Agga, Aggia, or Egya.

27. These foundations were cleared and planned in 1993 and resurveyed in 2012. Surface artifacts at the site included material from the seventeenth through the nineteenth centuries. A few red bricks were also present, with none of the ubiquitous yellow bricks found on most Dutch sites. This may suggest the Egyaa site is an English rather than a Dutch lodge, but this requires more evaluation.

28. Barbot, *Barbot on Guinea*, 416–17. Describing the fort in the early eighteenth century, Bosman noted it as a "small, but very neat compact fort," Willem Bosman, *A New and Accurate*, 56.

29. The main enclosure of the original fort only measures about twenty by fifty feet. This may have been the initial size of the smaller English forts: the extant ruins of the English fort at Tantumquery (Otuam) in coastal Ghana suggest it was similarly compact.

30. Lawrence, *Trade Castles*, 288.

31. This was the case at James Island in The Gambia discussed below, circa 1708–9 (Ibid., 253–56, 260). For non-British examples of slave housing located outside of the forts, see Fort Vermandois, Gorée circa 1680 (Lawrence, *Trade Castles*, 79) and Gross-Frederichsburg 1708 (Lawrence, *Trade Castles*, Plate 52). In the case of Gross-Frederichsburg, the 1708 plan also indicates a "prison" under the eastern bastion. It is possible that this indicates storage for slaves awaiting shipment.

32. Ibid., 289, 306.

33. The interior of the slave dungeon at the English Komenda fort was excavated in 2007. This revealed no artifacts that might relate to the period of the slave trade. A portion of the fort is still used as a bar and the area specifically associated with the slave dungeon has continued in use as a wash yard. Christopher R. DeCorse, Greg Cook, Rachel Horlings, Andrew Pietruszka, Samuel Spiers, "Transformation in the Era of the Atlantic World: The Central Region Project, Coastal Ghana 2007–2008," *Nyame Akuma* 72 (2009): 85–93.

34. Van Dantzig, *Forts and Castles*, 60; Lawrence, *Trade Castles*, 190–91. Barbot (*Barbot on Guinea*, 392, 404 note 11) noted that the subterranean dungeons made for good security against insurrections. In the nineteenth century, the original Cape Coast Castle dungeons were converted into cisterns (Lawrence, *Trade Castles*, 196).

35. Barbot, *Barbot on Guinea*, 151–52; John Milner Gray, *A History of the Gambia* (Cambridge: Cambridge University Press, 1940), 60, 65, 116. For discussion of the origins of the name St. André and the fort's early history see comments by the editors in Barbot, *Barbot on Guinea*, 155–56, note 6.

36. Barbot, *Barbot on Guinea*, 152. Barbot never visited James Fort and this assessment possibly relies on a 1698 account by Froger (see comments by the editors in Barbot 1992: 156–57 notes 7, 13).

37. Lawrence, *Trade Castles*, 252.

38. Ibid., 257–61; William Smith, *A New Voyage*, 32–33.

39. A plan "According to a Survey made by the Order of Tho's Pye Esq: commander of his Majesty's Ship Humber the 19th Day of October 1749" shows a square fort roughly one hundred feet on a side, with triangular bastions at each corner. The specific details of the interior of the fort shown in the 1749 plan and the 1755 plan reproduced by Lawrence (*Trade Castles*, 258) are difficult to reconcile, and the former is probably inaccurate with regard to the shape of the bastions. For more recent work on the site see Flordeliz Bugarin, "James Island: Reflections of a Gambian Slave Trading Site through GIS and 3D Modeling" (Paper presented for the *Society for Historical Archaeology Conference*, Williamsburg, Va., 2007).

40. The fort also had a four-storied tower similar to Bunce Island.

41. Edward Reynolds, *Trade and Economic Change on the Gold Coast, 1804–1874* (London: Longman, 1974), 119.

42. Coombs notes that by the mid-nineteenth century neither the Dutch nor the British possessions on the Gold Coast were self-supporting. See Douglas Coombs, *The Gold Coast, Britain and the Netherlands, 1850–1874* (London: Oxford University Press, 1963).

43. Ibid., 14–49.

44. Samori Touré's Islamic state expanded across the West African savanna from the Futa Jallon in Guinea eastward through Mali and Burkina Faso, to northern Ghana in the 1880s and early 1890s. See A. K. Koroma, "Samori Toure and the Colony and Hinterland of Sierra Leone: Diplomatic and Military Contacts, 1880–1892," *Journal of the Historical Society of Sierra Leone* 1 (1977): 2–17.

45. One of the major colonial outposts in northern Ghana, the fort at Wa, remained in use as a government office until the 1980s when it was demolished, sadly without being documented. See Benjamin W. Kankpeyeng and Christopher R. DeCorse, "Ghana's Vanishing Past: Development, Antiquities and the Destruction of the Archaeological Record," *African Archaeological Review* 21 (2004): 89–128.

46. Christopher Lloyd, *The Navy and the Slave Trade* (New York: Routledge, 1968); E. H. G. Kingston, *Blue Jackets or Chips of the Old Block* (London: Grant and Griffith, 1854).

47. John Peterson, *Province of Freedom: A History of Sierra Leone, 1787–1870* (Evanston: Northwestern University Press, 1969).

48. Ibid., 35–36; Anna Maria Falconbridge, *Narrative of Two Voyages to the River Sierra Leone, during the Years, 1791-2-3* (London), 152, 165, 168. Although many settlers arrived with promises of having necessary tools provided for them, they were forced to buy inferior tools from the company store (Falconbridge, *Narrative*, 184, 213–15).

49. Peterson, *Province*, 27.

50. Ibid., 26. The site of Granville Town was supposedly on the low hill later occupied by Fort Thornton. See Alexander Peter Kup, *A History of Sierra Leone, 1400–1787* (New York: Cambridge University Press, 1961), 119.

51. Falconbridge, *Narrative*, 137.

52. Peterson, *Province*, 36.

53. Ibid., 32; Also see Falconbridge, *Narrative*, 184.

54. In fact, the company planned to establish a fort in 1791 and sent out six cannon, but they were sent without carriages (Falconbridge, *Narrative*, 68). The fort had not been started by January 1793, as it was only then that a palisade was begun as a temporary defensive measure. The fort was apparently still not completed by the time Anna Maria Falconbridge left the coast in October 1793 (Falconbridge, *Narrative*, 190, 202). However, a stylized plan of Fort Thornton and Freetown appears in Wadström. See Carl Bernhard Wadström, *An Essay on Colonization Particularly Applied to the Western Coast of Africa with Some Free Thoughts on Cultivation and Commerce* (London: Darton and Harvey, 1794). It is presently unknown if the 1796 plan reproduced here is the same plan as drawn up in 1793 by the company's surveyor (Falconbridge, *Narrative*, 188). It is possible that portions of the fort and some of the interior buildings existed earlier and were enclosed by later construction.

55. Edward Reynolds, *Trade and Economic Change on the Gold Coast, 1804–1874* (London: Longman, 1974), 63–69.

56. Ibid., 46.

57. Ibid., 53.

58. For example, see Joseph Dupuis, *Journal of a Residence in Ashantee*, 2 vols. 2nd edition, introduction and edited with notes by W. E. F. Ward (London, 1824), i, 167.

8

THE FALMOUTH HOUSE AND STORE

THE SOCIAL LANDSCAPES OF CARIBBEAN
COMMERCE IN THE EIGHTEENTH CENTURY

Louis P. Nelson

Edward Barrett—the British sugar planter in Trelawney Parish, Jamaica, and the primary urban developer of Falmouth, that parish's port town—died in 1799, leaving his town lots and his wharf to his son-in-law and grandson together with a substantial financial endowment. This inheritance built a grand house and shop that stood at the foot of Market Street in town. The house filled the front of the lot in its entirety with a substantial masonry ground floor that served as shop, warehouse, and counting office. Above this substantial construction stood a timber-frame upper floor that projected out over the sidewalk in front of the shop/warehouse. With segregated access, the upper family residence was an elite social space sitting above a commercial space with which it had very little communication. Supported by a march of columns along the street, the upper story created a pleasant shaded space for potential customers to gaze in through the enlarged shop windows to see the wares on offer. With similar buildings cheek by jowl along the whole street, the new Barrett House was a participant in the formation of a new urban space in the Caribbean, the shaded commercial street, a more socially and physically comfortable space than the warehouses that lined the city's wharves.

This chapter begins with the Barrett House in Falmouth, Jamaica, to examine the emergence of the merchant shop/residence as a building type across the British Caribbean in the closing years of the eighteenth century and the early nineteenth century. Mixed-material merchant houses with projecting upper stories that shade the pedestrian space below appear not only in Falmouth, but also in Kingston and other cities in Jamaica in these same years. They can also be found in other British Caribbean contexts, especially St. John's, Antigua, where a number still survive. Significantly, major French

FIGURE 8.1. *Adolphe Duperly, "Market Street, Falmouth," 1844.*
National Library of Jamaica.

Caribbean port towns of the same era offer an alternative strategy, carrying substantial balconies on wrought iron brackets rather than fully projecting the enclosed floor plan of the upper floor out over the pedestrian walkway. In 1844 traveling German artist Adolphe Duperly published a hand-colored lithograph of Market Street in the town of Falmouth, on the north coast of Jamaica (Fig. 8.1).[1] As the principal commercial street in town, Market originated at the wharves and passed through town and south toward the many sugar plantations of the north coast. Looking southward down the street in the late morning, Duperly's view captures a wealthy white couple arriving in town by carriage while a number of black Jamaicans proceed through town on foot undertaking various tasks, and small groups of men and women socialize along the side of the street. On both sides of this major thoroughfare stands a line of buildings, closely built, whose collective form distinguished Market from other streets in town: ground floor shops sit back from the street while upper-story residences carried by a march of columns reach out over the sidewalk, creating a public space that was both sheltered from the elements and elevated above the dirt of the street.[2]

Most of these buildings were built in the short season between the foundation of the town in 1769 and emancipation in the 1830s. In these six short decades Falmouth expanded from a waterside hamlet to one of Jamaica's premier port towns.[3] The remarkable growth of Falmouth was noted as early as 1793 by commentator Bryan Edwards: "The rapid increase of this town and neighborhood in the last sixteen years is astonishing. In 1771, the three villages of Martha-Brae, Falmouth, and the Rock, contained together but eighteen houses." But only two decades later, Falmouth alone boasted 150 houses. Edwards continued by noting that the town's growth was tied directly to the commerce of Falmouth's harbor: "Vessels which entered annually at the port of Falmouth [in 1771] did not exceed ten. At present it can boast upward of thirty capital ships, which load for Great Britain, exclusive of sloops and smaller craft."[4] Writing in 1793, however, even Edwards would not see the town's most explosive growth, which happened in the first decades of the early nineteenth century, especially after 1809 when Falmouth became a free port.[5] By 1810 Falmouth was Jamaica's busiest port after Kingston.

Serving as the commercial spine of Falmouth, Market Street boasted a number of large and well-stocked stores. The commercial spaces of these buildings were distinctive enough to warrant comment by a Scotsman visiting Falmouth in 1802:

> There appeared to be several large shops, or in Jamaican parlance, "stores" all open in front, and apparently filled with an *omnium gatherum*, consisting of silk mercery, woolen and linen drapery, hardware, saddler, groceries, etc. I observed in some of the larger of the stores several gentlemen, who I opined were leading men in the country, carrying on a lively conversation, which, doubtless, was increased by potations of sansgaree, which was freely circulating among them. Their costume was of an airy and light description, consisting of white trousers and waistcoats, with coatees of nankin and other light fabrics. They all wore hats with large broad brims, and in one or two cases, the crown was raised above the brim by a light wire or whalebone, thus admitting the air freely to the top of their caputs.[6]

As understood by this visitor, these "stores" were richly stocked with a wide range of goods; they were impressive commercial spaces. But they were also spaces occupied by "leading men" who used these stores as places of social gathering for drink, conversation, and a chance to escape the intense heat of the Caribbean sun. So these stores were also social spaces, dominated by elite men who enlisted the environment of rich and abundant imports as a stage for performing the embodied dispositions that differentiated them as elites, performing of course for each other, but also for those laboring in and around these spaces, and for all who might come shopping.[7]

The urban store is not the predominant building type in the scholarly or popular conception of preemancipation Jamaica. Jamaica is primarily understood through the lens of the sugar plantation—scores of enslaved blacks laboring in cane fields or sugar works while the white plantation owner enjoys a breeze from the piazza of the great house. And rightly so. As Ralph Davis has argued, sugar consumption in England expanded rapidly over the first half of the eighteenth century. If sugar was consumed by only the most elite in late seventeenth-century England, "by 1750 even the poorest English farm laborer's wife took sugar in her tea."[8] England's importation of sugar rose from 3,000 hogsheads in 1660 to 110,000 by 1753, and consumption would only increase into the early nineteenth century.[9] This massive consumption was largely fed by Jamaica, England's largest producer. In 1805, Jamaica's peak year for production, the island produced 100,000 tons of sugar; the following year Jamaica exported 6,760,000 gallons of rum, a byproduct of sugar and a strong secondary export.[10] Jamaica's plantation economy generated extraordinary wealth. In his recent assessment of wealth in Jamaica, Trevor Burnard has suggested that in the years just before the American Revolution, the average white Jamaican was 36.6 times wealthier than the average white person in the thirteen mainland colonies.[11] That wealth, of course, depended on the most extreme conditions of enslavement anywhere in the British colonial world; Jamaica was Britain's greatest consumer of slaves, and, as a result, enslaved Africans outnumbered whites ten to one. Jamaica was very much a plantation economy.

Even so, the coastal towns of Jamaica played a crucial role as points of export for sugar and other plantation products and as markets for goods consumed in both towns and on the plantations. The greatest concentration of colonial merchants was the capital city of Kingston, where extremely wealthy merchants competed with one another for transatlantic partnerships and with local planters for control of the Colonial Assembly.[12] Mercantilism and commercial activity was so important in Kingston, in fact, that almost one-half of the labor in the city was in some way related to maritime activity. By comparison, maritime-related work comprised only one-fourth of the total labor in early nineteenth-century Boston and New York.[13] But Jamaica's smaller port towns, like Falmouth, had more fluid boundaries. Unlike Kingston, where the lines between merchant and planter were often clearly drawn and politically loaded, those roles in smaller towns were less distinct. As his-

FIGURE 8.2. *Barrett House shell, Falmouth, Jamaica, 1799. Jeff Klee.*

torian Barry Higman has demonstrated, Jamaica's port towns were closely connected to the immediate plantation context and the hinterland of pens that provided meats and local produce.[14] In these situations, families were often by necessity both planters and merchants.[15] And so, when our traveling Scot commented on the social life in the interior of Falmouth's stores he rightly noted that they were occupied by "the leading men in the country," of both town and plantation.

One of the earliest and largest examples of the merchant store in Falmouth was the grand house that stood at the foot of Market Street from its construction in 1799 to its near demolition by Hurricane Danny in 1997. The house was likely built by Charles Moulton, son-in-law to Edward Barrett, who had owned and developed more than half of the town in the preceding decades. Barrett had also conveyed a significant inheritance to his grandson (Charles Moulton's son) in his 1799 will, under the condition that his grandson change his last name to Barrett. Surviving on the site today is the seven-bay masonry shell of the ground floor shop, with three tall doors originally opening into a single large store, and footings at the street line marking the locations of the columns that carried the frame upper-story residence (Figs. 8.2 and 8.3). Inside the masonry shell a transverse partition divided the large open store at the front from a shallow range of chambers behind. A single door centrally located in the cross partition led into a rear stair chamber that also gave access to the rear yard. A more prominent double door opened through that same partition from the large front storeroom into a smaller rear chamber that likely served as a back store or counting room. Pre-1997 drawings of the building

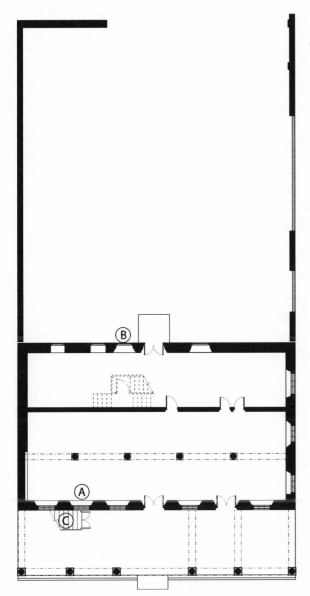

reveal the clear contrast between the fine neoclassical finishes of the upper-
story residence and the starkly plain finishes of the shop on the ground floor.
Preliminary archaeological investigation of the deep back lot suggests that
this large yard also had a complex of outbuildings (now completely lost) that
supported the residential functions of the upper story.[16] And finally, an 1844
plan illustrates the large wharf complex immediately across Market Street

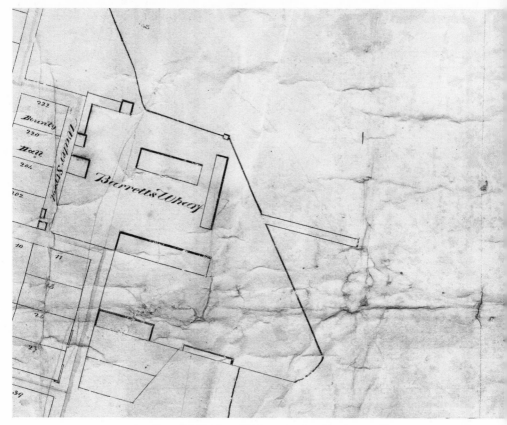

FIGURE 8.4. *Detail, plan of Falmouth, 1844. The Barrett House stood on lot 11. National Library of Jamaica.*

from the house, a complex leased and managed by Charles Moulton as early as 1786 (Fig. 8.4).[17]

The Barrett family house, store, and wharf at the foot of Market Street was the nexus of numerous interdependent social and economic landscapes.[18] Through differences in building materials and the clear segregation of floors via the rear staircase, the merchants, clerks, and customers of the ground floor commercial space were removed from the family in the residential spaces of the building's second floor. Cut another way, the refined spaces of family dining and elite entertaining upstairs depended on the service provided by enslaved laborers working in the back lot. And finally, the customers entering the store from the sheltered sidewalk on Market could probably hear from the wharf across the street the bawdy conversations of sailors unwinding from lengthy voyages and the groans of slaves unloading heavy crates of stock. But if these three are social landscapes that segregated and differentiated, others conspired to unite. The Barrett store's street colonnade was made all the more effective when considered alongside similar colonnades that ran down the rest of Market Street. Together they created a collective space that was far greater than the sum of its parts. The Barrett store was also in conversation with merchant houses elsewhere in the Caribbean, as later portions of this essay will demonstrate, as merchants from different corners of the Caribbean responded to the demands of leisure shopping.

Individuals who experienced this store and its associated residence, back lot, street, and wharf were united or differentiated in many ways: local or visitor; enslaved or free; black, mulatto, or white; elite, aspiring, or common; male or female; merchant, sailor, or day laborer. The space of the store, then, was both a space of intense and diverse human interaction and a space directly dependent on the work (social and physical) of many other spaces. This essay enlists the Falmouth house, store, street, and wharf as evidence of complex social and economic landscapes. As the published literature on merchant houses of this period has focused on the domestic and service functions of such buildings around the British Atlantic, this article will instead focus on the architecture of the store, the street, and the wharf, to demonstrate that these buildings and landscapes actively shaped the culture of consumption at the turn of the nineteenth century.[19] The article also positions the Barrett house, store, and wharf in the context of the major commercial centers in the "Greater British Caribbean," a region that expanded from South Carolina to Barbados and from Jamaica to the Leeward Islands.[20]

WHARVES

Located directly opposite Barrett's house and store was Barrett's wharf, which predated the construction of the house by at least thirteen years, and possibly predated the foundation of the town in 1769. The detail of the 1844 town plan of the wharf shows the strong diagonal stroke of the seawall interrupted only by the projecting dock. Dominating the middle of the wharf are four massive rectangular buildings that likely served as warehouses that stored the many thousands of barrels of sugar that were produced on Barrett plantations.[21] Great houses surviving at Cinnamon Hill and Greenwood plantations are two surviving material reminders of the thousands of acres of sugar plantations owned by the Barrett family and worked by many hundreds of slaves in the eighteenth and early nineteenth centuries.

But those warehouses were also used to store imports. Factors often rented space on private wharves to store the many items recently unloaded from ships and not yet transferred elsewhere for sale. While detailed records of imported items are rare, one very lengthy 1794 inventory of English goods shipped to Falmouth on board the Jamaican vessel the *Martha Brae* by merchant John Stogdon has recently come to light.[22] The list includes an astonishing array of English-made items. In addition to textiles, buckles, thimbles, buttons, and huge sums worth of ready-made clothes, the manifest included a wide range of hats for men, women, and children, including four blue beaver hats with elegant feathers, and a large assortment of shoes and slippers. So if Barrett's warehouses were filled with Jamaican sugar for export, they were also filled with the many imported goods made possible by the wealth generated from that very same sugar.

If the small buildings lining the streets were booths or small shops, the shallow ranges of buildings on the wharf itself were probably shops as well, if more substantial. Shops on wharves were often let to ship captains whose cargo was not consigned to a particular merchant's store.[23] This use of the space of the wharves for the sale of goods was a strategy that competed directly with more established Falmouth merchants who, in 1798, presented a formal complaint to the House of Assembly. They argued that "transient traders . . . have been enabled to dispose of their goods and merchandise on lower terms than the resident traders"; they were enabled to do so, these merchants argued, because they were not "subject to public and parochial taxes, store rent, and other expenses and charges."[24] With individual sailors hawking fine goods, slaves selling local products from pushcarts, and captains selling goods from small shops, the wharves were spaces of lively commerce and exchange.

This complex landscape of social and economic interactions, of course, was not unique to Jamaica. In 1743, the front pages of the *South Carolina Gazette* published the report of a special commission dedicated to assessing the condition of Charleston's wharves, a report that gives insight into the architectural conditions of early modern wharves.[25] All of the wharves had buildings, most of which were being used as shops and a few as dwellings. For example, Elizabeth Jeny's wharf boasted no less than three houses and a cooper's shop. William Elliott's wharf contained one house, three large stores, a smith's shop and store complete with a chimney, and a silversmith shop with a chimney. Such an arrangement created a commercial alley offering a wide range of utilitarian and fine goods in that narrow space between the wharf and the city.

Mid-eighteenth-century advertisements in the *South Carolina Gazette* give further evidence of the shops and stores on Charleston's eighteenth-century wharves.[26] By far the most prominent category of item for sale on the wharves was foodstuffs followed thereafter by spirits and beer. The predominance of foodstuffs and spirits suggests that Charleston's shopkeepers sought to capitalize on the high demand for supplies for the many ships that passed through the harbor. The majority of craftsmen who worked from shops on the wharves offered services associated with shipping and the maintenance of ships: sailmakers, coopers, blacksmiths, and ship carpenters and painters were the majority. There were a few exceptions. William Wright was a gold- and silversmith working on Trott's wharf in the early 1740s. Benjamin King worked on Simmons wharf in the 1760s as a survey instrument maker and mender, and Thomas Floyd was a clockmaker on Burn's wharf in the same years. While offering high end and fancy items, each of these artisans might also have benefited from working on the wharves. Most of these shops offered their wares directly through the falling shutter of a shop front window much like the booths erected at Falmouth's racetrack, a form identified by Dell Upton as the earliest form of Euro-American storefront. In both cases, a simple wooden shutter hinged at the bottom could be raised and secured from within at night and then lowered and braced from below to become a display surface during operating hours.[27]

STORES

Differentiating themselves from the shops and the people of the wharves, Falmouth's elite erected stores along Market Street for the sale of both fancy goods and utilitarian staples in a far more respectable venue.[28] Measuring almost sixty feet wide and twenty-five feet deep, the ground floor store of the Barrett House was among the largest commercial spaces in town. The only apparent ornamentation of the interior of this space was a range of four turned classical columns that helped to carry the ceiling framing across the depth of the chamber. The two elevations facing Market and Lower Harbour Streets were perforated with large windows, while the other two walls were almost entirely solid, likely mounted with shelving for the display of finer goods. With the absence of any other physical or documentary evidence, it seems reasonable to assume that the store included a number of stock display strategies, ranging from shelves to open crates in the middle of the floor. Surely Barrett's store was among the many visited by our traveling Scotsman when he commented in 1802, only three years after the construction of the Barrett store: "There appeared to be several large shops, or in Jamaican parlance, 'stores' all open in front, and apparently filled with an omnium gatherum, consisting of silk mercery, woolen and linen drapery, hardware, saddler, groceries, &c."[29] Significantly, Jamaicans' preference for the term "store" over the term "shop" clearly differentiated these wholly retail spaces from the smaller-scale retailing of shops on wharves and from the labor undertaken in an artisan's house-shop.

The "omnium gatherum" noted by the Scot is quite clear in various contemporary records. In 1815, Arnold's Repository in Falmouth advertised for sale in the *Cornwall Chronicle* a remarkably wide range of goods just imported from London. Customers could purchase diverse books, looking glasses, musical instruments, hair combs and powder boxes, fabric, lace, and other materials for sewing, and ready-made clothes, including either black or brown beaver hats for ladies, and shoes for men, women, and children. Most fine goods were imported from Britain and her colonies. As a result of the Navigation Act, more than three-quarters of the imported goods sold in Jamaican stores were of British origin, and another 16 percent were from Canada and the United States.[30] In terms of their goods for sale, these stores differed little from the stores in any town in England.

While it seems clear that the large open-fronted stores of early Falmouth offered a wide range of stock, the means of organization and display within the store is entirely unknown. The complete absence of any interior store fittings in a townscape with a remarkably high level of architectural survival, in fact, suggests that Falmouth's stores were not entirely unlike the large open shops of mid-eighteenth-century merchants in larger cities like Charleston, South Carolina. Consider a late eighteenth-century plat of the house and shop erected in the 1740s on Broad Street—the major commercial district of that city—for Benjamin Smith, one of the city's wealthiest merchants. A single door opened through the Broad Street elevation into a very large shop room, not dissimilar from the large shop rooms of Falmouth. A single door through the rear wall of this shop opened into a central stair hall, which then gave access to two heated chambers that likely served as offices or counting rooms. The staircase, of course, rose to second and third floors that were reserved as residential spaces.

The 1764 probate inventory of Charleston merchant William Wilson sheds light on the spatial organization of an eighteenth-century merchant's house and shop.[31] The inventory opens with a listing of items that appear to be stored on twenty-one shelves along the walls. These include textiles, tin wares, ceramics, collections of small items like thimbles, buckles, and buttons, and specialized items like spectacles, compasses, and weights and scales. The next section is a series of specialized items displayed in the "shew glass," which was likely standing in the shop window. These range from silver buttons and silver-edged cloth, sugar and almonds, to a box of Dutch toys. The remaining items in the inventory are all contained in six fairly large boxes and one trunk, likely filling the shop floor or positioned along the walls under the shelves. Some of these were differentiated by contents, strictly textiles, for example, while others were diverse, including everything from tobacco to decanters to looking glasses. As was the case for most late eighteenth-century merchants, luxury goods were sold from the same spaces as every-day wares. After writing the inventory of the shop, the appraisers moved to the (presumably other) "room below stairs." Equipped with a tea table, a mahogany dining table, and a desk and corner cupboard, this back room was well appointed for the necessary blending of business and entertaining that was so much a part of eighteenth-century commerce. The walls were hung with five large maps and a looking glass, further communicating the worldliness and refinement expected of an eighteenth-century merchant. Above the stairs was a single room with three bedsteads for the merchant and his family and floor bedding for their slaves, among sundry other items. The integration of the shop into the space of the residence had been common for centuries in English practice and remained common practice through the eighteenth century.[32]

While counters and shelves had been commonplace in Charleston shops since the early eighteenth century, the increasing significance of "show glass" in Charleston shops by the late eighteenth century is made clear in the day-book of Charleston painter and glazier Alexander Crawford.[33] His 1785 to 1795 daybook has regular notations of repairs to show glasses or the replacement of a regular window with a "bow window" to physically project store goods into the space of passersby. Some show glasses were also finely finished to especially draw the eye; in 1793 Crawford painted a show glass with faux mahogany finish on the outside and a black interior. A similar process of increasingly sophisticated shop interiors and more prominent front windows, or show glasses, is evident in eighteenth-century towns across England as well. As scholars of the English shop have demonstrated, these increasingly refined spaces of the later eighteenth century accommodated new "polite" modes of shopping that included women as prominent consumers and that encouraged "window shopping" and browsing through goods.[34]

Just across Broad Street from Benjamin Smith's 1740s house and shop stands the Geiger House, constructed in the 1770s as a shop and residence, but with the rare survival of a partially intact shop space dating from about 1800 (Fig. 8.5). The deep shop space is trimmed with a fashionable neo-classical cornice that stepped out from the wall on the right to accommodate

FIGURE 8.5. *Shop interior, Broad Street, Charleston, South Carolina, ca. 1800. Author.*

now-missing shelves and/or fixed cupboards. The cornice curved toward the back of the shop room as it moved toward the spectacularly framed glass-filled door with fanlight that gave access to the slightly elevated and heated back-shop or counting room.[35] In addition to participating in the growing significance of leisure shopping as a polite activity, this more elaborate interior highlights the emergence of the specialty shop in the later eighteenth century as a retail space selling a particular subset of finery, differentiated from the shop or storerooms of merchants carrying a wide range of goods.[36] The large front chamber has a far higher level of refinement than do the larger open storerooms of Falmouth, which seem to be more a warehouse space by comparison. And, by extension, the absence of such spaces from Falmouth reinforces the documentary evidence that specialty retail shops like the Geiger shop in Charleston were not a common fixture in Falmouth.

Thus far, the surviving architecture and documentary record of Falmouth offer no indication of such refined retail interiors.[37] Rather than bow windows and show glasses, merchants in Falmouth chose to keep their shops "all open in front."[38] The street fronts of Falmouth's surviving stores all seem to have had multiple large double doors and shuttered windows between; show

LOUIS P. NELSON

glasses are nowhere to be seen. This opening of the front façade of stores in Falmouth parallels display practices among wholesale merchants in major port cities like New York and Philadelphia, but also among retail merchants in smaller ports across the Caribbean and in British-dominated port towns in Southeast Asia.[39] The lack of retail store display windows and finished interiors in Falmouth and other small towns across the British colonial world might be a result of those towns' small size. As Claire Walsh has argued, shops in London were burdened with the responsibility of influence on the customer's judgment of the shop and of the reputation of the shopkeeper. Architecture did not carry such burdens in smaller markets where the reputations of both merchants and most consumers were well known in the community.[40] Falmouth's small size, the practice among Jamaican merchants for the importation of a wide range of English-made goods, and the general Jamaican preference for the importation of refined goods over the local generation of such goods, as in South Carolina, all seem to have conspired against the emergence of refined specialty stores like the Geiger store in Charleston.[41]

The lack of transparent storefronts might also be a result of the general anxiety about security that marked everyday life in colonial centers like Jamaica. There is, of course, a direct correspondence between the transparent display of goods and shoplifting; visibility and ease of access created retail risk.[42] It is clear that solid masonry walls and heavy shutters locked from the inside are all that faced Market Street in nighttime hours. But such apparent impermeability was not enough to provide constant protection. At least one ingenious thief broke into a Falmouth store "by removing the bricks from under the sill of the window by means of a knife," while working from the inside of a barrel.[43] The burglar had positioned a barrel on its side under the windowsill with himself inside and "quietly carried on his work within it, so that had a person passed at the moment, they could have seen nothing but the barrel."[44] The growing volume and value of goods available in shops became an increasing temptation to those who had not the means to participate in legitimate leisurely consumption, and Falmouth's large, masonry stores were an attempt to deter such theft.

STREETS

One of the most distinctive features of Falmouth's stores is the projecting piazzas or colonnades along the street that sheltered the storefronts from the Caribbean sun, and when positioned cheek by jowl, created a shaded shopping street. As early as 1774, Edward Long noted that the fronts of most buildings in Kingston, Jamaica, "are shaded with a piazza below, and a covered gallery above."[45] While many are heavily altered, examples of colonnaded house-stores survive along the major commercial street in St. John's, the capital and port city of (English) Antigua. And a handful of similar buildings appeared along Waterfront Street in (Dutch) Paramaribo, Suriname, on the north coast of South America, after a major fire in 1821. This practice of sheltering the public way in front of the ground-floor shops, of course, is hardly unique to the early Caribbean. In more monumental form, arcaded commercial streets and squares—called *portales*—are found throughout southern Europe and across the Mediterranean, where they are also a response to climate. Similar arcaded streets appeared in the newly developed sections of expanding seventeenth-century London such as Covent Gardens. Nineteenth-century examples exist throughout colonial port towns in Southeast Asia, where buildings accommodate a "five foot way" on the ground floor that creates a public walkway right along the street and sheltered from the elements by the second floor.[46] Via Spain, this form is manifest in Mexico and in the Spanish Caribbean, where merchants preferred to build masonry arcades; the Plaza Vieja in Havanna, Cuba, for example, is ringed with commercial/residential buildings supported by recessed ground floor arcades.[47] Sheltered walkways in front of shops appear throughout the western United States in the middle and late nineteenth century. And, as Spiro Kostov has suggested, the arcaded commercial street reaches as far back as the ancient Roman Empire as an important component of urban commercial districts. [48] The notion of sheltering the public space along primary commercial streets is a longstanding practice found across the globe, resulting in a fairly wide range of formal strategies.

The colonnaded commercial front of Falmouth's stores was not the only resolution to the problem of shading potential customers from the tropical sun. The installation of a balcony that allowed outside access to residents of a second floor also created a shading device for the shop elevation and the public right of way below, much like canvas awnings would on fully commercial nineteenth-century buildings in Philadelphia, New York, and elsewhere.[49] Merchants in Marigot, the capital of French St. Martin, erected two-story masonry buildings fronted by covered balconies that were both cantilevered from the building and supported by spectacular iron brackets (Fig. 8.6). Those in Bridgetown, Barbados, appear to have preferred the balconies as well, although they are shallower and carried by scrolled wooden brackets, probably not unlike those erected in early Charleston. Interestingly, the commercial streets of Rosseau, Dominica, have examples of both balconied and colonnade shop fronts; most Caribbean urban centers demonstrate a par-

LOUIS P. NELSON

FIGURE 8.6. *House-shop on Rue de la République, Marigot,*
St. Martin, early nineteenth century. Author.

ticular preference for one or the other. The effect of shading the sidewalk and
the front of the store, of course, was the same in all these places, if the architectural solution differed. In all cases, the buildings that stood along emerging commercial streets of Caribbean towns in the late eighteenth and early
nineteenth centuries collaborated to create physically comfortable spaces.
This variation of forms makes clear that merchants in many diverse locations
across the Caribbean were responding to the shared impulse to create comfortable and convenient shopping environments. But it also demonstrates
that merchants in any locale tended to collectively agree on a shared strategy,
reflecting the broader impulse among early modern merchants to create an
ordered and unified commercial sphere.[50]

If merchants serving people of means were erecting buildings that shared
a physical form, they were doing so in rows, creating streets dedicated to
elite consumption.[51] As Martha Zierdon's research has demonstrated, Broad
Street in Charleston emerged over the course of the eighteenth century as the
preferred address for merchants in that city, and, as a result, Broad became
Charleston's polite shopping strip.[52] John Stobart has completed a similar
analysis of Chester, England, and has noted the clustering of shops serving
the "better sort" on the town's two major streets, centered on the town's theater and public assembly rooms.[53] Merchants lobbied to have old and shabby

medieval buildings torn down and replaced by new and regular (i.e. Georgian) façades.

In addition to lobbying for better pavement and improved street lighting, merchants in Chester lobbied effectively in the last decades of the eighteenth century to have fairs and markets removed from the town's main streets, creating a more orderly and respectable commercial district.[54] In the late eighteenth century, for example, the city of Basse-Terre on Guadeloupe built a public promenade as part of a larger urban redesign.[55] As shops migrated toward greater material refinement and display, the streets they faced followed suit. In Falmouth and across the Caribbean, this move toward order and refinement was manifest in the formation of colonnaded commercial streets. If fashionable uniformity was the order of the day, the uniformity of the Caribbean commercial street was not a series of similarly proportioned shop windows under and between aligned belt courses and cornices but the regular march of columns down each side of the street. The result was a street-side colonnade, an architectural strategy that not only claimed the public way as semiprivate display space for merchandise, but that also sheltered potential customers from the intensity of the Caribbean sun.[56]

The importance of physical protection from the sun was particularly keen for elite women in the Caribbean, who were in these same years becoming a significant factor in the culture of consumption.[57] The colonnaded streets of Falmouth and other Caribbean towns protected white women from the sun (distinguishing them from the black and other nonwhite members of the colonial workforce). Projecting balconies and, even more effectively, fully projecting upper floors functioned as sun screens and prevented the direct rays of the sun from penetrating the store interior, keeping it cooler. Shaded store interiors became comfortable places for gathering among the "leading men in the country," whose costume was of an "airy and light description," some even with hats "admitting the air freely to the top of their caputs."[58] The colonnades allowed potential customers, especially women, to stroll leisurely along the street, also shaded from the rays of the sun.[59]

As demonstrated by a number of historians, the eighteenth century saw the slow decline of traditional markets and the increase of shops and stores as a response to growing consumerism and the emergence of shopping as a leisure activity.[60] But shops could be located in a variety of places in a cityscape, from wharves to main streets. If wharves were important commercial zones, they were also morally disreputable. In response, merchants in Falmouth and other towns in the greater British Empire worked to create an alternative, more respectable, commercial zone in socially "safer" spaces in the city. In Falmouth these shaded sidewalks worked to resist the common perception that the streets were beyond the bounds of polite society.[61] Market Street worked to be everything that the wharves and the market in Water Square were not: clean, attractive, and fashionable. Mirroring similar shifts in English towns, the sheltered colonnades of Market Street's stores created a fashionable promenade where "parading and shopping could combine as status-acquiring activities in an environment free from heat and rain."[62] In the Caribbean, they also created spaces where elite men could convene in the deep shade of a cool store, reinforcing their distinction as elites differentiated from others in the public sphere. They also allowed women to avoid the sun and preserve their fashionably pale complexion.

As a result, Falmouth's colonnaded commercial street was not just about physical comfort but social comfort as well. Offering access to that deep shade, Falmouth's stores became sites where these same leading men could segregate themselves from public space and engage in "lively conversation."[63] Such conversations were claims on space; others—women, nonlocals, non-elites, and nonwhites—who surely came into stores were exposed as interlopers by their unwillingness or inability to participate. Similarly, the shaded and elevated space behind the colonnades created zones where women could participate in the burgeoning practice of leisure shopping safe from the intense racial and social intermixing of the wharves, and be protected from the darkening rays of the sun. In this way, the Barrett family house and store was an exemplar of architectural and social design in the Caribbean. It stood at the intersection of many landscapes and its physical form and location in the townscape helped those who used the store, the wharf, and the street to understand their place in Falmouth's complex social, racial, and economic hierarchy.

In 1799, the Barrett family began the construction of a house in Falmouth that would become a model for others of its type in town. Built by one of the town's leading families at the foot of that town's most prominent commercial street, the Barrett house and store would also be among the largest of its kind. The building faced the warehouses of its own wharf, demonstrating the clear connectivity of wharf and store. But at the same time, it stood apart from that wharf, segregating itself from a social landscape of sailors and slaves. And if it distanced itself from the wharf just across the street, it actively embraced the similar houses and stores that stood along the rest of the street. Working collaboratively, these buildings created a socially safe and physically comfortable streetscape that allowed elite men and women of the Caribbean to participate in the leisure activity of shopping. And as a result, the Barrett

House was the nexus of diverse interdependent social, racial, and economic landscapes each working to align or differentiate individuals in particular—if perpetually repeated—encounters. But if the wharves, shops, and streets of the Barrett House were spaces not at all unique to the Caribbean, they were in conversation with merchant houses throughout the Caribbean betraying regionally distinctive solutions to international impulses. The emergence of a shared response by merchants in the Caribbean—at least in the non-Spanish Caribbean—suggests that merchants were engaged in trans-Caribbean social and economic networks; they were not isolated outposts looking always to the metropole, but a community of individuals engaged in collective identity formation between Caribbean port cities. And, finally, this series of spaces built by the Barrett family but occupied by many reminds us that early modern stores and their associated streets and wharves realized a complex network of social and economic landscapes enlisted by a few to manage many.

NOTES

1. This lithograph is derived from a daguerreotype taken by Duperly in 1843. For information on Adolphe Duperly, see Tim Barringer, Gillian Forrester, and Barbaro Martinez-Ruiz, *Art and Emancipation in Jamaica: Isaac Mendes Belisario and His Worlds* (New Haven: Yale University Press, 2007), 420. See also Allister Macmillan, *The West Indies Illustrated: Historical and Descriptive, Commercial and Industrial Facts, Figures, and Resources* (London: W. H. and L. Collingridge, 1909).

2. Buildings with a striking resemblance can be found in Anglo-colonial port cities in Southeast Asia as well. See Lee Ho Yin, "The Singapore Shophouse: An Anglo-Chinese Urban Vernacular," in *Asia's Old Dwellings: Tradition, Resilience, and Change*, ed. Ronald G. Knapp (New York: Oxford University Press, 2003), 115–34, and Mai-Lin Tjoa-Bonatz, "Shophouses in Colonial Penang," *Journal of the Royal Asiatic Society* 71, no. 2 (1998): 122–36.

3. The significance of Caribbean port cities in the early modern Atlantic world has become increasingly recognized among historians. As early as 1991, for example, a volume on Atlantic port cities included five essays that address Caribbean port cities, four on Central and South American port cities, and only one on a port city in North America. See Franklin Knight and Peggy K. Liss, *Atlantic Port Cities: Economy, Culture, and Society in the Atlantic World, 1650–1850* (Knoxville: University of Tennessee Press, 1991).

4. Bryan Edwards, *The History, Civil and Commercial, of the British Colonies in the West Indies* (London: J. Stockdale, 1793), 263–64.

5. B. W. Higman, "Jamaican Port Towns in the Early Nineteenth Century," in *Atlantic Port Cities: Economy, Culture, and Society in the Atlantic World, 1650–1850*, ed. Franklin W. Knight and Peggy K. Liss (Knoxville: University of Tennessee Press, 1991), 125.

6. Phillip Barrington Ainslie, *Reminiscences of a Scottish Gentleman*, reprinted in

Georgian Society of Jamaica, *Falmouth, 1791–1970* (Jamaica: Lithographic Printers Limited, 1970), 28.

7. This social formulation is informed by sociologist Pierre Bourdieu's conceptions of habitus and cultural capital. For habitus, see Pierre Bourdieu, *Outline of a Theory of Practice* (Cambridge: Cambridge University Press, 1977), and for cultural capital see Bourdieu, *Distinction: a Social Critique of the Judgment of Taste* (Cambridge, Mass.: Harvard University Press, 1984).

8. Ralph Davis, *The Rise of the Atlantic Economies* (Ithaca: Cornell University Press, 1973), 251.

9. Sidney Mintz, *Sweetness and Power: The Place of Sugar in Modern History* (New York: Penguin, 1985), 39.

10. Higman, "Jamaican Port Towns," 120.

11. Trevor Burnard, "'Prodigious Riches': the Wealth of Jamaica before the American Revolution," *Economic History Review* 54, no. 3 (August 2001): 506–24.

12. For a discussion of the political competition between merchants in Kingston and planters in Spanishtown, see George Metcalf, *Royal Government and Political Conflict in Jamaica, 1729–1783* (London: Longmans, 1965), 122–40. For a discussion of that contest's impact on urban history, see James Robertson, *Gone is the Ancient Glory: Spanish Town, Jamaica, 1534–2000* (Kingston, Jamaica: Ian Randle Publishers, 2005).

13. Higman, "Jamaican Port Towns," 119.

14. Ibid., 133.

15. Evidence for such overlap appears as early as the late seventeenth century. See Richard Dunn, *Sugar and Slaves: The Rise of the Planter Class in the English West Indies, 1624–1713* (Chapel Hill: University of North Carolina Press, 1972), 182–83. Emma Hart has offered a similar assessment of the economic interdependence of plantations and city trades and services in her discussion of later eighteenth-century Charleston. See chapter 2 of Emma Hart, *Building Charleston: Town and Society in the Eighteenth-Century British Atlantic World* (Charlottesville: University of Virginia Press, 2010).

16. Kit W. Wesler, "Excavations at the Barrett House, Falmouth, Jamaica, 2006, Preliminary Report" (unpublished report for the Jamaica National Heritage Trust, November 2006). Archaeology also revealed heavy deposits of fine early nineteenth-century tableware but light deposits of utilitarian wares used in the preparation of meals. This suggests the possibility that the site was a full-time commercial space—possibly selling the very same fine tableware—and only a part-time residence. This migration toward full-time commercial functions in domestic buildings is addressed in the Philadelphia context by Dell Upton. See Upton, "Commercial Architecture in Philadelphia Lithographs" in *Philadelphia on Stone: Commercial Lithography in Philadelphia, 1828–1878*, ed. Erika Piola (Pennsylvania State University Press, 2011).

17. This history of the house depends heavily on archival research completed by Emilie Johnson and published in the VAF Falmouth Field Guide, 2011.

18. This formulation of social and economic landscapes depends on models offered by both Dell Upton and Bernard Herman. For landscapes of race, see Dell Upton,

"White and Black Landscapes in Eighteenth-Century Virginia," reprinted in *Material Life in America, 1600–1860*, ed. Robert Blair St. George (Boston: Northeastern University Press, 1988), 357–69, and for embedded social and economic landscapes see Bernard Herman, "The Embedded Landscapes of the Charleston Single House," *Perspectives in Vernacular Architecture* 7 (1997): 41–57. "House and store" is a phrase used in the period to describe this building type, and so it will be used in this article. For example, see the rental advertisements in the *Cornwall Chronicle*, Montego Bay, Dec 27, 1854, for "the house and store on the corner of Duke and King Streets, Falmouth."

19. Bernard Herman, *Townhouse: Architecture and Material Life in the Early American City, 1780–1830* (Chapel Hill: University of North Carolina Press, 2005).

20. By grouping together those British colonies that were a source of tropical produce, such as sugar, rice, and tobacco, and by distinguishing these from colonies that provided a market for manufactures and reexport, Immanuel Wallerstein was among the first to group the colonies of the "Greater British Caribbean." Not only were these colonies ecologically suited for the production of staple crops, they also depended on a coerced or enslaved labor source to reduce production costs. See Immanuel Wallerstein in *The Modern World System*, vol. 2: *Mercantilism and the Consolidation of the European World Economy, 1600–1750* (New York: Academic Press, 1974), 103. See also Peter Hulme, *Colonial Encounters: Europe and the Native Caribbean, 1492–1797* (London: Methuen, 1993), 4–5, and Matthew Mulcahy, *Hurricanes and Society in the British Greater Caribbean, 1624–1783* (Baltimore: Johns Hopkins University Press, 2006).

21. These warehouses were probably not unlike the historic warehouses that have survived along the careenage in Bridgetown, Barbados.

22. Special thanks to Emilie Johnson for bringing this document to my attention.

23. See David Geggus, "Major Port Towns of Saint Domingue in the Later Eighteenth Century," in *Atlantic Port Cities*, 99.

24. Nov 7, 1798, a petition of the merchant, traders, and other inhabitants of Trelawny presented to the House of Assembly. Quoted in Carey Robinson, *The Rise and Fall of Falmouth: Urban Life in 19th Century Jamaica* (Kingston, Jamaica: LMH, 2007), 14.

25. "Report of laws regarding wharves," *South Carolina Gazette*, May 16, 1743.

26. Data extracted from Jeanne Calhoun, Martha Zierden and Elizabeth Paysinger, "The Geographic Spread of Charleston's Mercantile Community, 1732–1767," *South Carolina Historical Magazine* 86, no. 3 (July 1985): 183–220.

27. For examples of these in Philadelphia, see John Watson, *Annals of Philadelphia and Pennsylvania in the olden time* 3 vols. (Philadelphia: E. Stuart, 1900), 1:221. For Upton, see Dell Upton, "Commercial Architecture."

28. This phenomenon of merchants retreating from wharves happened in port cities across the early modern world. For an extensive discussion of the emergence of dedicated commercial spaces in early nineteenth-century Philadelphia, see Dell Upton, "Commercial Architecture." For a discussion of the same in New York, see David M. Scobey, *Empire City: The Making and Meaning of the New York City Landscape* (Philadelphia: Temple University Press, 2002).

29. Ainslie, *Reminiscences*, 28.

30. Higman, "Jamaican Port Towns," 135.

31. Inventory reprinted as Appendix A in Lisa R. Hudgins, "The Probate Record of William Wilson, Charleston Merchant" (unpublished report, Museum of Early Southern Decorative Arts, 2008). On the integrated house and shop of eighteenth-century merchants and artisans see Dell Upton, "Commercial Architecture."

32. Jon Stobart, Andrew Hann, and Victoria Morgan, *Spaces of Consumption: Leisure and Shopping in the English Town, 1680–1830* (London: Routledge, 2007), 117.

33. Show glasses were cabinets with glass tops fitted out for display, often positioned in the shop window. For early eighteenth-century shop counters and shelves see Elizabeth Sindry Account Books, SCHS. See also Alexander Crawford *Daybook*, South Carolina Historical Society.

34. Stobart, et. al., *Spaces of Consumption*, 16, 126–27, and chapter 5. On fittings in English shops, see Claire Walsh, "Shop Design and the Display of Goods in Eighteenth-Century London," *Journal of Design History* 8, no. 3 (1995): 157–76; Jon Stobart, "Shopping Streets as Social Space: Leisure, Consumerism and Improvement in an Eighteenth-Century County Town," *Urban History* 25, no. 1 (May 1998): 19. For a discussion of bulk windows in early Philadelphia, see Dell Upton, "Commercial Architecture."

35. Such shop refinement and differentiation was common in London through the eighteenth century. See Walsh, "Shop Design," 160.

36. See *Spaces of Consumption*, 128, for English examples. For a detailed discussion of refined retail spaces in early nineteenth-century Philadelphia, see Dell Upton, "Commercial Architecture." On the rise of specialization, see Glenn Porter and Harold C. Livesay, *Merchants and Manufacturers: Studies in the Changing Structure of Nineteenth-Century Marketing* (Baltimore: Johns Hopkins University Press, 1971).

37. For a discussion of the differentiation between wholesale and retail shop interiors, see Upton, "Commercial Architecture."

38. Ainslie, *Reminiscences*, 28.

39. For Philadelphia, see Upton, "Commercial Architecture." For New York, see Ellen Fletcher Rosebrock, *Counting-House Days in South Street: New York's Early Brick Seaport Buildings* (New York: South Street Seaport Museum, 1975), 27. For examples of open shop fronts in Southeast Asia, see examples in Penang, Malaysia and elsewhere. Special thanks to Dell Upton for bringing these examples to my attention.

40. See Walsh, *Shop Design*, 167.

41. On the significance of artisans in early Charleston, see Emma Hart, *Building Charleston*, especially chapter 2.

42. *Spaces of Consumption*, 136–38.

43. *The Falmouth Gossip*, June 14, 1826. National Library of Jamaica.

44. Ibid.

45. Edward Long, *History of Jamaica: Reflections on its Situation, Settlements, Inhabitants, Climate, Products, Commerce Laws, and Government*, 3 vols. (London, 1774), 2:21.

46. See Lee Ho Yin, "The Singapore Shophouse: An Anglo-Chinese Urban Vernacular," in *Asia's Old Dwellings: Tradition, Resilience, and Change*, ed. Ronald G. Knapp (New York: Oxford University Press), 2003, 115–34.

47. The Spanish *Laws of the Indies*—sixteenth-century guidelines intended to govern city planning in the Spanish New World—dictated that new cities should have arcaded streets.

48. See Spiro Kostof, *The City Assembled: Elements of Urban Form Through History* (Bulfinch, 1992), 216–18.

49. See Upton, "Commercial Architecture."

50. Jon Stobart, et al. *Spaces of Consumption*, chapters 3 and 4.

51. Joan H. Geismar, "Patterns of Development in the Late-Eighteenth and Nineteenth-Century American Seaport: A Suggested Model for Recognizing Increasing Commercialism and Urbanization," *American Archeology* 5 (1985): 175–84.

52. Jeanne Calhoun, Martha Zierdon, and Elizabeth Paysinger, "The Geographic Spread of Charleston's Mercantile Community, 1732-1767," *South Carolina Historical Magazine* 86 (July 1985): 183-219. For a detailed discussion of the merchants positioned along the early nineteenth-century waterfront of Philadelphia, see Abraham Ritter, *Philadelphia and Her Merchants, as Constituted Fifty to Seventy Years Ago* (Philadelphia: Published by the author, 1860). For a discussion of this phenomenon in Philadelphia, see Upton, "Commercial Architecture."

53. Stobart, "Shopping Streets as Social Space."

54. Ibid., 16. On the quest for urban order, see Dell Upton, *Another City: Urban Life and Urban Spaces in the New American Republic* (New Haven, Conn.: Yale University Press, 2008), 133–44. For a discussion of the broader remaking of the refined English town, see Peter Borsay, *The English Urban Renaissance: Culture and Society in the Provincial Town, 1660–1770* (Oxford: Oxford University Press, 1989).

55. Anne Perotin-Dumon, "Cabotage, Contraband, and Corsairs: The Port Cities of Guadeloupe and Their Inhabitants, 1650–1800," in *Atlantic Port Cities*, 75.

56. Stobart, "Shopping Streets as Social Space," 18.

57. For more on consumption by women in this period, see Clair Walsh, "Shops, Shopping, and the Art of Decision Making in Eighteenth-Century England," and Ann Smart Martin, "Ribbons of Desire: Gendered Stories in the World of Goods," in John Styles and Amanda Vickery, *Gender, Taste, and Material Culture in Britain and North America, 1700–1830* (New Haven: Yale University Press, 2006).

58. Ainslie, *Reminiscences*, 28.

59. On this point, I differ from William Chapman, who argues that genteel women were constrained to the spaces of the parlor through the day and were allowed access to the social spaces of the street only in the evening. See William Chapman, "Irreconcilable differences: urban residences in the Danish West Indies, 1700–1900," *Winterthur Portfolio* 30 (Summer–Autumn 1995): 129–72.

60. For the emergence of a consumer society, see Neil McKendrick, John Brewer, and J. H. Plumb, eds., *The Birth of a Consumer Society: The Commercialisation of Eighteenth-*

Century England (London: Hutchinson, 1982), and Daniel Miller, ed., *Acknowledging Consumption: A Review of New Studies* (London: Routledge, 1995), 164–62; John Brewer and Roy Porter, eds., *Consumption and the World of Goods* (Routledge: London, 1993); on the increasing number of shops see S. Mitchell, "The Development of Urban Retailing 1700–1815," in *The Transformation of English Provincial Towns*, ed. Peter Clark (London: Hutchinson, 1984), 259–83.

61. Chapman, "Irreconcilable Differences," 167.

62. Stobart, "Shopping Streets as Social Space," 14–15.

63. Ainslie, *Reminiscences*, 28.

9

BUILDING BRITISH ATLANTIC PORT CITIES

BRISTOL AND LIVERPOOL IN THE

EIGHTEENTH CENTURY

Kenneth Morgan

The growth of port cities was an essential component of building the eighteenth-century British Atlantic world as British overseas trade became "Americanized" in the volume and value of goods traded across the Atlantic.[1] Such urban centers flourished with the growth of oceanic shipping lanes and the activities of merchants and their agents. Demographic growth and the stimulus provided by commercial exchange led to a reconfiguration of the urban environment and the provision of port facilities. Thus the economic and urban development stimulated by Atlantic trade was reflected in the built landscape of British cities from London to Glasgow.[2] The size, shape, and economic functions of such port cities were transformed during the Georgian era. As the metropolis and one of the largest port cities in Europe, London's overseas commerce gained significant advantages from increased shipping and trade with the Americas.[3] But London was such a large port city, trading throughout the world, that it is difficult to pin down the precise contribution made by expanding Atlantic trade to its urban environment. By contrast, the impact of growing Atlantic trade on the built environment of major west coast outports can be more readily established. This chapter addresses this theme by focusing on the changes in urban space and buildings that accompanied the transatlantic trade connections of Bristol and Liverpool—the two major English port cities with a clear geographic connection to the Atlantic trading world.

Bristol and Liverpool benefited considerably from the growth of Atlantic trading connections in the eighteenth century. Bristol had pursued overseas commerce since the Middle Ages, and had quickly established trade with the Americas in the 1650s. By 1700 Bristol, then the second largest city in England with 20,000 people, was regularly trading with North America and the Caribbean, as well as continuing older lines of trade with Ireland and Europe.[4] In 1700 Bristol was the second largest port in England. Bristol's dominance of her hinterland for the supply and distribution of goods was such that in the eighteenth century the port was dubbed "the metropolis of the west."[5] The tonnage of merchant shipping owned at Bristol rose from 15,500 in 1709 to 19,000 in 1751 and to 43,000 in 1792.[6] Bristol's transatlantic trade expanded during the eighteenth century, though it experienced relative decline. It was the premier English port in the slave trade in the 1720s and 1730s before Liverpool overtook it as a result partly of entrepreneurial drive by merchants who carved out dominance in slave supplies in Africa and slave sales in the Americas. By the 1740s Bristol's tobacco trade was outcompeted by Glasgow's as the Scottish port tapped the important tobacco reexport business to a much greater extent than Bristol. By 1800 Bristol had a population of 60,000 but had slipped to sixth place among British cities.[7] Bristol's transatlantic trade was then dominated by the West India trade and the city's commercial elite included rich sugar merchants and planters.[8]

Liverpool, by contrast, was virtually a small fishing port in 1700, with a population of 7,000. Liverpool ships traded coastwise and carried goods to and from the Isle of Man and Irish ports. They conducted commerce with European destinations, and increasingly adopted an Atlantic outlook, with ships sailing between the River Mersey and African and transatlantic destinations. Liverpool's vessels delivered slaves, manufactured wares, and provisions to North American and West Indian markets, and brought home sugar, tobacco, and industrial raw materials.[9] Liverpool owned 6,400 tons of shipping in 1709, less than half the volume of shipping owned at Bristol. By 1792 Liverpool owned 92,100 tons of shipping, more than twice the level of Bristol.[10] From circa 1745 onward Liverpool expanded its commerce in the slave trade, becoming the leading port in the world for this nefarious commerce on the eve of British slave trade abolition in 1807. Liverpool's other transatlantic trading interests also flourished during the eighteenth century, notably in the Chesapeake and West Indian trades. From the 1760s onward, Liverpool was connected via canals with industrializing areas of south Lancashire. The city's population doubled between 1780 and 1801, when it totaled 78,000. This made Liverpool the second largest town in England.[11]

Contemporary comments drew attention to a direct connection between success in the slave trade and the growth of the built environment in Bristol and Liverpool. Of Bristol it was claimed, anonymously, that "there is not a brick in the city but what is cemented with the blood of a slave."[12] An almost identical insult was made by an actor in a Liverpool theatre. Faced with hissing from the audience, he told them "there is not a brick in your dirty town but what is cemented by the blood of a negro."[13] These colorful anecdotes are overstatements of reality, but plenty of evidence points to the connection between the growth of Atlantic-based trades and the built landscape of Georgian Bristol and Liverpool. This chapter shows that the concentration on Atlantic trade and shipping was an integral part of the urban and commercial culture of each city in the eighteenth century, and that expanding trading arrangements influenced the growth of the built environment. The first section examines the provision of wharves, quays, docks, and other harbor facilities that were an essential part of the infrastructure of Bristol and Liverpool. The second section discusses the main new commercial buildings that were constructed in the eighteenth century to reflect civic pride in trade, and the location and style of merchant housing in Bristol and Liverpool in relation to the "urban renaissance" of Georgian England. This was a revival in the planning and architecture of provincial towns that displayed their civic pride and status through new buildings, squares, and streets that emphasized their growing sophistication as urban centers.[14]

HARBOR AND DOCK DEVELOPMENT

In Bristol and Liverpool extensive capital works accommodated the expanding volume and wider geographical distribution of overseas trade. In both ports, harbor improvements were connected to expanding transatlantic trade, the deployment of larger vessels, and an increased volume of shipping. Vessels registered in the English outports grew threefold in number and fourfold in tonnage during the eighteenth century.[15] Such growth required a response from port cities with overcrowded existing harbor facilities. The scale and nature of the harbor and dock improvements differed, however, in Bristol and Liverpool. This resulted partly from the different locations and topography of each city, especially the characteristic features of the main rivers—the Avon and Mersey—that stretched into the center of each port. But it was also the result of differing attitudes on the part of those charged with initiatives for urban improvement.

By the mid-eighteenth century most port installations, trades, and industries in Bristol were clustered in the city center between the River Avon and its tributary the River Frome, with very little development downstream.[16] The increased volume of shipping at Bristol, and the topography of its port area, indicated the need for harbor and dock improvement. Ships entering the Avon from the Bristol Channel contended with seven miles of winding river, fast currents, and an exceptional tidal range of forty-five feet before

KENNETH MORGAN

reaching quays in the city center. Spillage of industrial waste into the Avon and Frome from glass houses, sugar refineries, and other works situated near the riverbank, hindered the navigation of larger vessels. Ships were damaged by grounding on mud banks at low tides, or immobilized by lack of water at neap tides. Pilots and towboats were needed to help large ships pass up and down the river.[17] Shipping congestion was common. Alexander Pope noted on a visit to Bristol in 1739 that there were "as far as you can see, hundreds of ships, their Masts as thick as they stand by one another."[18] Overcrowding continued for the rest of the century, as Nicholas Pocock's marine sketches and paintings of Georgian Bristol show.[19]

The responsibility for making port improvements at Bristol lay with the Society of Merchant Venturers, a private body of merchants who (from 1661) leased the wharves and quays from the corporation of Bristol. Changes made by the Merchant Venturers to port facilities, however, were piecemeal, often delayed, and did not solve the problem of port congestion. By 1712 they had extended the quay wall along the Frome and had erected cranes. A decade later they built a wharf on Welsh Back for loading corn and other goods from market boats and constructed a separate quay on St. Augustine's Back, in the center of the port, for timber and naval stores. A wet dock was built at Sea Mills between 1712 and 1717 on the Gloucestershire side of the Avon, but merchants considered it too far from the city center and so it was little used except by privateers and whalers. The Merchant Venturers' lease to operate the port was renewed in 1764 on condition that further improvements were made. They extended existing quays and built a new quay at the Grove and on St. Augustine's Back. In 1770 they purchased William Champion's dock, built alongside the Avon near Rownham five years earlier. Shipbuilding yards were constructed at Wapping. Yet none of these changes provided a safe anchorage at a time when, with expanding trade, it was crucial for Bristol to cope with a larger volume of shipping.[20]

Many schemes were mooted for improving the port of Bristol. In 1767 the merchant William Champion suggested that a floating harbor should be built to enable large vessels to use the port with ease. This would be constructed by building lock gates across the Avon at its confluence with the Frome. Anticipated costs delayed this and other schemes, though Bristol did not lack capital for investment. Opponents of port improvement, including influential members of the Merchant Venturers and the corporation, stated that the costs would be prohibitive. The proposals were dropped. Plans for port improvement stalled as the Merchant Venturers found their finances stretched by the upkeep of the existing port. In the 1780s the outlook seemed brighter:

the Bristol merchant Richard Bright noted the "spirit for improvement" to make access to Bristol's quays easier for large vessels and for keeping those ships constantly afloat.[21] A spate of port improvement schemes proposed between 1787 and 1793, however, encountered reluctance by the corporation and the Merchant Venturers to fund the projects and opposition to change.[22]

A partial solution to port congestion only came after much procrastination. In 1803 William Jessop's revised scheme for the creation of a Floating Harbor in Bristol's center and the digging of a New Cut or course for the Avon was accepted by the Bristol Corporation. The high water level within the Floating Harbor was maintained by the construction of a feeder canal from the Avon. The construction of this huge seventy-acre dock between 1804 and 1809 had a capital cost of £580,000. This large-scale enterprise transformed the built environment of the harbor and city center, enabling ships to reach the city's wharves regardless of the tides; but it did not entirely remove the cramped accommodation for shipping in the port of Bristol.[23]

Liverpool was a relatively small port in 1700, with a much lower level of shipping and trade than Bristol. "Here," wrote Defoe, "was no Mole or Haven to bring in their Ships and lay them up . . . for the Winter; nor any Key for the delivering their goods."[24] During the eighteenth century, however, Liverpool's commercial ventures and dock improvements surged to new heights. The increased volume of shipping at Liverpool placed pressure on port facilities, but the challenges were met more satisfactorily than at any other British port. Liverpool had a deepwater estuary frontage and access to the Irish Sea, but before 1700 it consisted of a large but shallow pool subject to shoals, sandbanks, and awkward winds and tides. The Pool, a former tidal creek, was marshy and restricted to more or less a moat to the south and east. Liverpool lacked a natural haven and had an inadequate tidal basin. Ships therefore had difficulty in finding a place to moor or lie. The fast-flowing River Mersey had the biggest tidal variation of any English port after Bristol. These factors constrained the port's development. Many ships lay aground on the Mersey foreshore and only one quay existed at Liverpool before 1700.[25] However, during the eighteenth century five wet docks were constructed in the channel of the Mersey, within easy reach of the city center; these greatly increased the space for ships to moor, load, and unload cargoes. A sustained program of capital works and dock building occurred in the city center along the Mersey.[26]

The first wet dock, the Old Dock, was constructed at Liverpool between 1709 and 1715. This dock compounded the Pool by constructing a seawall and enabled ships to berth away from the tidal frontage on the Mersey. It was the first commercial dock ever built in Britain. Probably around £50,000 was spent on building the dock and its warehouses and ancillary works. Four more docks were constructed before 1800, and a new tidal basin of four acres was completed. Salthouse (originally South) Dock was begun in 1738 and opened in 1753. This was followed by George's (originally North) Dock, constructed between 1762 and 1771; Duke's, begun in 1762 and completed in 1773; King's, built in the years 1785–88; and Queen's, started in 1785 and finished in 1796. All except George's Dock were situated to the south of the Old Dock. King's Dock and Queen's Dock together comprised 14¼ acres. The construction of docks was accompanied by the erecting of shipbuilding yards and warehouses.[27] The total cost to the Liverpool Corporation of the ninety acres of docks created between 1709 and 1835 was £4 million.[28] This dock construction attracted contemporary admiration. In 1776 an American Quaker visiting Liverpool referred to the city's "noble docks" that were "admirably calculated for the reception of 3 or 4000 ships, which may lie with perfect ease and Safety afloat."[29] In 1793 William Vaughan, a London merchant, considered that "Liverpool owes everything to its docks and spirit of enterprise."[30]

Liverpool was able to afford these docks because it was exceptionally well endowed financially. This made it unusual in terms of corporate governance. The local town council raised money for the improvements through bonds purchased by the public. Liverpool's corporation consolidated property from 1700 onward. A mercantile oligarchy dominated the town council from 1695 until the reform of municipal corporations in 1835. Three-quarters of the councilors in 1709, when the plan for the first wet dock on the Mersey was mooted, were heavily involved in the tobacco and sugar trades. The improvement of dock facilities was undertaken more effectively at Liverpool than at any other British port. Liverpool's promoters of port improvement were fortunate because there were no vested interests that claimed the Pool where the Old Dock was constructed.[31]

THE URBAN RENAISSANCE

Merchants at Bristol and Liverpool played a central role in the development of harbor and dock facilities that changed the physical layout of both ports in the eighteenth century, but they also influenced the built environment of the two port cities in other ways. Merchants equated improvements to the built environment with civic pride. Closely involved in buying and occupying fine urban residences that reflected their status and wealth achieved through commerce, they were sufficiently wealthy to sustain cultural development in the city. Civic pride was linked to the building of commercial exchanges and customs houses in the center of the cities, which were intended to serve as a public display of prosperity. Fine town houses were either built close to the city centers, within walking distance of quays, wharves, and mercantile counting houses, or they were built in new suburbs as the population of both Bristol and Liverpool expanded into areas that had previously been rural outskirts. Both types of development were part of the urban renaissance identified by Peter Borsay, a phenomenon closely connected to the rise of polite, middle-class culture in English cities.[32]

Bristol's urban infrastructure developed considerably in the years between the publication of the first two city maps in 1673 and 1742. The Bristol mercer Jacobus Millerd's map, *An Exact Delineation of the Famous Citty of Bristoll and Suburbs* (1673), depicted a fairly compact city in which most buildings were contained within the medieval city walls. Merchants conducted business under the Tolzey, a covered walkway in Corn Street; many streets and buildings were clustered near the confluence of the Avon and Frome Rivers; the area at the edge of the harbor — "the Marsh" — was little developed; and there were few suburbs. The Society of Merchant Venturers had their headquarters in the midst of commercial Bristol — at their Merchants' Hall in King Street near Broad Quay.[33] The Hotwell spa, situated near the port area, developed as a focal point for leisure and consumption connected with urban development.[34]

Bristol's urban topography had undergone considerable change by the time the French Huguenot émigré John Rocque compiled *A Geometrical Plan of the City and Suburbs of Bristol with Vignettes of Brandon Hill* (1742). Rocque's map was probably the first accurately measured survey of Bristol. It shows signs of increased industrial activity, with glass houses and sugar refineries included, as well as new streets where commercial activity flourished, such as Guinea Street and Prince's Street, and residential squares, such as Queen Square, where the Custom House was situated.[35] Buildings had been constructed in the early eighteenth century on the Marsh, around College Green, and on streets stretching northwest from St. Augustine's Back, including Denmark Street, Hanover Street, and Orchard Street.[36] Most of this increased building development lay within Bristol's urban space as it existed in 1700, especially north of the River Avon; there was little suburban extension into the surrounding countryside.[37] Rocque noted on his map that Bristol was enlarged "by the addition of so many fair streets and stately edifices on every side, that at present it is near a third bigger than it was forty years ago."[38]

As Madge Dresser has shown, this urban development occurred in exactly

KENNETH MORGAN

the period that Bristol's transatlantic trade sector burgeoned: some of the wealth accrued from the slave trade and West India commerce was funneled into genteel housing, streets and squares, and public buildings.[39] Already by 1700 slave-based wealth was stimulating urban development with new gentry houses built between Park Row and St Michael's Hill, near the modern University of Bristol precinct.[40] William Matthew, involved in the slave trade and West India trade, was selling plots on St Michael's Hill to merchants in the 1730s.[41] Warehouses, residential dwellings, and public buildings in Prince's Street all had connections with investors in the slave trade. Prince's Street had an African House, tavern, and coffee house as well as Assembly Rooms, financed by merchant capital, and constructed in 1755.[42] Nearby, on the corner of Marsh and King Streets, the Merchant Venturers built a new hall between 1719 and 1721 that served as their headquarters. Bristol's expanding trade meant that the crowded, inconvenient Tolzey was replaced by a new exchange on Corn Street, designed by John Wood the Elder, with an impressive Palladian façade.[43] This large covered building symbolized the wealth and civic pride of Bristol's mercantile and political community. Its opening ceremony was accompanied by a ringing of bells, firing of guns, bonfires, and a procession of the mayor, Merchant Venturers, and Bristol's corporation from the Exchange to the Council House and Merchants' Hall. Wood emphasized how the Exchange testified to urban improvement: "That the trade of this city may flourish and increase, and the prosperity and reputation of it be daily advanced, are the ardent wishes of the corporation, this noble pile, raised by their liberal hand more eminently testifies than words can express."[44] Rocque advertised on his map cartouche for subscriptions to the Exchange, and emphasized the architectural splendor of the new building.[45]

The most striking urban development that combined the business of transatlantic merchants in Bristol with the reorganization of urban space in the city was Queen Square, built in an area known as the Mead between the Avon and the Frome. Planned in 1699 and completed thirty years later, this was modeled on fashionable London squares. It was the largest city square in England in the early eighteenth century, and the site of the new customs house, completed by 1710. Bristol's corporation leased out surrounding building plots for genteel residences. By 1750 town houses had been built there mainly as homes for Bristol's merchants. These included mansion houses fronted in brick, with three stories and an attic.[46] Leading merchants lived there while carrying out their commercial affairs in the slave trade and the trades with Virginia, South Carolina, and the Caribbean. Ten of the leading twenty-four ratepayers in the square were involved in the African trade by 1730.[47] By 1789 the antiquarian writer William Barrett noted that Bristol's "great repute in the commercial world" had led to the construction of new streets, squares, and public buildings, with "every year almost . . . productive of improvements."[48]

Fashionable suburban development in Georgian Bristol was also closely linked to the residential patterns of Bristol merchants involved in transatlantic trade. The most socially prestigious of these suburbs was the hilly area of Clifton, which was incorporated into the city of Bristol in 1835. Bristol's African and West Indian merchants were widely represented among householders at Clifton. The Society of Merchant Venturers owned much of the property in this suburb. They promoted the construction of elegant terraces and crescents. The erection of fashionable streets and buildings in Clifton transformed it from a village to an elegant outer suburb of a commercial city. Clifton's Royal York Crescent, designed in 1782 and completed in 1820, was conceived as a project by six merchants, most of whom had African or West Indian trading connections.[49] The speculative building development that flourished in Bristol in the decade after the American Revolution, notably in and around Park Street, Brandon Hill, and College Street, also involved investment by Bristol West India merchants.[50] William Paty's neoclassical Georgian House was built in 1790 in Great George Street as an urban residence for the merchant-planter John Pinney and his family.[51] Bristol merchants in the Africa and West Indian trades also bought properties in the countryside surrounding Bristol. Dresser has shown, for example, that thirty of the sixty-five houses on Benjamin Donne's 1769 map of the country within eleven miles of Bristol were linked to wealth derived from the African and West India trades or to the ownership of slave plantations.[52]

Liverpool's built environment also benefited from commercial vigor in the eighteenth century. Defoe noted that early eighteenth-century Liverpool was visibly increasing in wealth, people, business, and buildings. He considered that no other town outside London could equal Liverpool "for the fineness of the streets, and beauty of the buildings."[53] Liverpool had no guilds, regulatory institutions, or organizations, such as Bristol's Merchant Venturers, with a private interest in land and building development in the city center. The corporation was therefore free to play a major role in urban development. It fulfilled that task vigorously. Civic leaders, dominated by the merchant community, invested in property that complemented the port's dock-building program.[54] In the late seventeenth century, the main streets in Liverpool were Tithebarn Street, Dale Street, Chapel Street, Water Street, and Castle Street. Half of the overseas traders resided in the latter three streets. The town only had seven main streets altogether, with houses extending three hundred yards from north to south.[55] From 1672 onward new streets could be built because Liverpool's corporation bought all the rights over the town. It became ground landlord of around nine hundred acres of central and south Liverpool by acquiring a lease of a thousand years on heathlands and wastelands south of the Pool. This became the area into which the central part of the town could expand.[56]

Liverpool's corporation became easily the largest corporate promoter of building land in England in this period.[57] An excise office was constructed on Paradise Street; a dock office was built on Brook Square; and a Sun Fire insurance office opened on Fenwick Street. These buildings, vital for the commercial life of Liverpool, were concentrated near the Old Dock. Private capital between £100,000 and £120,000 was invested in new buildings in a cluster of streets beyond the Pool, running from Hanover Street to Ranelagh Street. F. E. Hyde estimated that some £572,000 was invested in warehouses, ships, industrial plants, and housing in Liverpool between 1710 and 1750. Substantial merchants, including slave traders, leased land from the corporation estate and retained their holdings until demand for housing stimulated construction. Already by 1720, leading merchants had made significant investments in the town center and in nearby undeveloped lands. Arthur Heywood, Henry Hardar, and Thomas Seel, all listed as Africa merchants in 1752, built large homes on Hanover Street, then the most fashionable street in Liverpool.[58] Merchants investing in new buildings in Liverpool took advantage of the growth of an expanding town center.[59]

In the second half of the eighteenth century, Liverpool underwent an urban renaissance comparable to that at Bristol. The building of fine new streets and houses reflected the commercial wealth of the town: economic development and polite urban culture were intertwined. By 1766 the town had over two hundred streets, but most of the corporation lived on twenty streets within two hundred meters of the Town Hall. In that year, Gore's street directory for Liverpool showed merchants living in fashionable parts of the town such as Duke Street, Cleveland Square, and Hanover Street.[60] By 1798 leading slave merchants had a considerable investment in land, houses, offices, and warehouses in Liverpool. As at Bristol, merchants possessed property in suburbs beyond the immediate borough of Liverpool at places that are now part of the modern city, such as Everton, West Derby, Wavertree, and Kirkdale.[61] Some significant cultural institutions built as part of Liverpool's urban renaissance were directly connected to merchants involved in transatlantic trading activities. The Royal Institution building — intended to encourage the arts, literature, and science — was built in 1799 on Colquitt Street as the home of the Liverpool slave merchant Thomas Parr. Several slaving merchants contributed to the investment in Liverpool's infirmary, opened in 1749.[62]

The Liverpool Corporation also embarked on a building program that expressed commercial confidence, wealth, and success in structures such as John Wood the Younger's classical construction of the Town Hall, the Exchange, and the Assembly Rooms, erected between 1749 and 1754, at a cost of around £14,000. The Exchange was adorned with arches and massive columns. Its imposing exterior suggested that the success of Liverpool's trade demanded a grand commercial building to signify civic and mercantile prosperity.[63] The inauguration of the Exchange, in Jane Longmore's words, "reinforced the importance of the civic authority in a successful provincial port."[64] The building had ornamental carvings of foreign trade with, in a specific acknowledgment of the slave trade, busts of blackamoors, elephants' teeth, and similar emblematic figures representing African trade. The construction firm that built the Exchange was owned by the Liverpool slave trader Joseph Brooks. Liverpool's corporation paid for an extension of the Town Hall in the 1780s by the fashionable architect James Wyatt.[65] A contemporary description of Liverpool in 1793 noted that the town had expended "large sums in improvements in streets and buildings."[66]

Liverpool's physical growth during the eighteenth century was characterized by a shift in the center of gravity from the medieval location in and around Castle Street, which originally formed the location for most of the city's administrative and commercial activities, to the area surrounding the new docks to the south, and by a significant increase in the urbanized area. Between the 1720s and 1760s, Liverpool almost doubled its built-up area. These were the years when the port's commitment to the slave trade and to commerce with North America and the West Indies increased significantly. Physical growth was accompanied by the erection of buildings connected with manufacturing and the wholesale trade in goods as well as residential quarters and public and semipublic institutions such as hospitals. A new customs house was built on the east side of the Old Dock. In the 1750s sugar refineries, shipbuilding yards, and warehouses were added to the area north and south of the docks.[67] The Liverpool Improvement Act of 1786 trebled the breadth of the main thoroughfare of Castle Street and widened a number of surrounding streets.[68]

A Plan of Liverpool (1765) by John Eyes, surveyor to the corporation, shows three glass houses, two silk mills, two breweries, a sugar house, a salt house, thirteen roperies, three white roperies, a dye house, a pot house, and twelve ship- or boat-builders' yards. By the same decade urban squares imitating fashionable squares in London were constructed to the south of the Old Dock by merchants leasing land from the Liverpool Corporation.[69] Street improvements largely "removed the reproach which formerly attached to the town for its mean and crowded appearance."[70] Liverpool's housing growth in the late eighteenth century received stimulation from the proliferation of maritime workers in and around the docks needing dwellings near their place of work.[71] Charles Eyes's *Survey of Liverpool* (1785) shows the town extended over a radius of fourteen hundred meters. The corporate elite mainly lived in an inner circle of the city within walking distance of the docks and the Town Hall. But, as in Bristol, wealthier merchants were beginning to acquire residences in villages adjoining Liverpool and country houses by the beginning of the nineteenth century.[72]

Bristol and Liverpool are good examples of the connection between economic development and urban growth in Georgian England. In both cases considerable changes to the physical layout of the urban environment occurred as a result of trading growth and the aspirations of civic leaders and the merchant class. By 1800, both cities had thriving trade connections with Ireland (via the ports of Dublin and Belfast), Scotland (especially west-coast Glasgow), Europe, and the Americas, a well-established merchant class, improved port facilities, commercial buildings with a civic presence, and an expanding urban environment that had a denser topographical presence than a century earlier. Though differences occurred in the pace of development in both cities with respect to population growth, dock provision, and the construction of new buildings and streets, Bristol and Liverpool both participated in the urban renaissance of eighteenth-century England. The desire for improvement and progress is the key to understanding the changing built environment of both port cities; and both of those factors were connected to the desire for upward social mobility among the urban professional class. Merchants and other traders who worked hard to establish and maintain a flourishing overseas commerce wished to live in cities that reflected the prosperity they had achieved. This gave impetus to the construction of new buildings, streets, and commercial exchanges, often designed according to the latest architectural fashions. These changes in the urban built environment embodied this spirit of improvement.

The economic development of eighteenth-century Bristol and Liverpool therefore provided a major impetus for urban change. Such change in the topography of the urban environment was influenced considerably by the mercantile influence on civic politics. In Liverpool, the policies pursued by merchants on the corporation had a critical effect on the provision of these facilities through the construction of docks and the lease of land bought up by the town council. In Bristol, the Merchant Venturers and the city council helped to shape the provision of wharves and quays and the building of new streets in many parts of the city. Though Liverpool's corporation was more proactive in pursuing these developments than the Bristolians, in both cities the wealth entering the ports from overseas, notably from across the Atlantic, was an important factor in building the urban environment of England's two most important west-coast outports during the eighteenth century. Changes in the urban landscape of eighteenth-century Bristol and Liverpool therefore reflected commercial growth and notions of improvement and civic identity.[73]

NOTES

1. Ralph Davis, "English Foreign Trade, 1700–1774," *Economic History Review*, 2nd series, 15 (1962–63): 285–303, and Ralph Davis, *The Industrial Revolution and British Overseas Trade* (Leicester: Leicester University Press, 1979).

2. Stephen J. Hornsby, "Geographies of the British Atlantic World," in *Britain's Oceanic Empire: Atlantic and Indian Ocean Worlds, c.1550–1850*, ed. H. V. Bowen, Elizabeth Mancke, and John G. Reid (Cambridge: Cambridge University Press, 2012), 24.

3. Nuala Zahedieh, *The Capital and the Colonies: London and the Atlantic Economy, 1660–1700* (Cambridge: Cambridge University Press, 2010), and Christopher J. French, "'Crowded with Traders, and a Great Commerce': London's Domination of Overseas Trade, 1700–1775," *London Journal* 17 (1992): 27–35.

4. David Harris Sacks, *The Widening Gate: Bristol and the Atlantic Economy, 1450–1700* (Berkeley: University of California Press, 1991); Richard G. Stone, "The Overseas Trade of Bristol in the Seventeenth Century" (Ph.D. diss., University of Bristol, 2012), 105–89.

5. W. E. Minchinton, "Bristol — Metropolis of the West in the Eighteenth Century," *Transactions of the Royal Historical Society*, fifth series, 4 (1954), 69–89, and David Hussey, *Coastal and River Trade in Pre-Industrial England: Bristol and its Region, 1680–1730* (Exeter: Exeter University Press, 2000).

6. P. J. Corfield, *The Impact of English Towns, 1700–1800* (Oxford: Oxford University Press, 1982), 40.

7. Kenneth Morgan, *Bristol and the Atlantic Trade in the Eighteenth Century* (Cambridge: Cambridge University Press, 1993), and "The Economic Development of Bristol, 1700–1850," in *The Making of Modern Bristol*, ed. Madge Dresser and Philip Ollerenshaw (Bristol: Redcliffe Press, 1996), 48–75; David Richardson, "Slavery and Bristol's 'Golden Age,'" *Slavery and Abolition* 26 (2005): 35–54.

8. Kenneth Morgan, "Bristol West India Merchants in the Eighteenth Century," *Transactions of the Royal Historical Society*, sixth series, 3 (1993): 185–208.

9. Diana E. Ascott, Fiona Lewis, and Michael Power, *Liverpool, 1660–1750: People, Prosperity and Power* (Liverpool: Liverpool University Press, 2006), 9; Paul G. E.

Clemens, "The Rise of Liverpool, 1665–1750," *Economic History Review*, second series, 29 (1976): 211–25.

10. Corfield, *The Impact of English Towns*, 36, 40; M. K. Stammers, "Ships and port management at Liverpool before the opening of the first dock in 1715," *Transactions of the Historic Society of Lancashire and Cheshire* 156 (2007): 30–31.

11. F. E. Hyde, *Liverpool and the Mersey: An Economic History of a Port, 1700–1970* (Newton Abbot: David & Charles, 1971), 10–42; Kenneth Morgan, "Liverpool's Dominance in the British Slave Trade, 1740–1807," in *Liverpool and Transatlantic Slavery*, ed. David Richardson, Suzanne Schwarz, and Anthony Tibbles (Liverpool: Liverpool University Press, 2007), 14–42; and Sheryllynne Haggerty, *The British-Atlantic Trading Community, 1760–1810: Men, Women, and the Distribution of Goods* (Leiden: Brill, 2006).

12. J. F. Nicholls and John Taylor, *Bristol Past and Present*, 3 vols. (London and Bristol: J. W. Arrowsmith, 1881–82), 3:165.

13. Ramsay Muir, *Bygone Liverpool* (Liverpool: Henry Young and Sons, 1913), 59. In 1797 the Rev. William Bagshawe Stevens similarly stated that "throughout this large-built Town every Brick is cemented to its fellow Brick by the blood and sweat of Negroes:" see Joseph Sharples, *Liverpool* (New Haven: Yale University Press, 2004), 10.

14. Peter Borsay, *The English Urban Renaissance: Culture and Society in the Provincial Town, 1660–1770* (Oxford: Oxford University Press, 1989).

15. R. C. Jarvis, "The Appointment of Ports," *Economic History Review*, second series, 11 (1958–59): 464.

16. Alan F. Williams, "Bristol Port Plans and Improvement Schemes of the Eighteenth Century," *Transactions of the Bristol and Gloucestershire Archaeological Society* 81 (1962): 143. For good maps of Georgian Bristol, see M. D. Lobel and E. M. Carus-Wilson, *Bristol Historic Towns Atlas* (London: Scolar Press, 1975).

17. Grahame Farr, "Bristol Channel Pilotage: Historical notes on its administration and craft," *Mariner's Mirror* 39 (1953): 27–44.

18. Morgan, *Bristol and the Atlantic Trade*, 29–31, 33 (quotation).

19. Francis Greenacre, *Marine Artists of Bristol: Nicholas Pocock 1740–1821, Joseph Walter 1783–1856* (Bristol: City of Bristol Museum and Art Gallery, 1982).

20. W. E. Minchinton, *The Port of Bristol in the Eighteenth Century* (Bristol: Bristol branch of the Historical Association, 1962); Patrick McGrath, *The Merchant Venturers of Bristol: A History of the Society of Merchant Venturers of the City of Bristol from Its Origin to the Present Day* (Bristol: The Society of Merchant Venturers, 1975), 150–69; G. E. Farr, "Sea Mills Dock, Bristol," *Mariner's Mirror* 35 (1939): 349–50.

21. Richard Bright, "Draft of Particulars of the Trade of Bristol, 1788," in *The Bright-Meyler Papers: A Bristol-West India Connection, 1732–1837*, ed. Kenneth Morgan (Oxford: Oxford University Press, 2007), 664.

22. Williams, "Bristol Port Plans and Improvement Schemes," 138–88.

23. R. A. Buchanan, "The Construction of the Floating Harbour in Bristol, 1804–9," *Transactions of the Bristol and Gloucestershire Archaeological Society* 88 (1969): 184–204.

24. John McVeagh, ed., Daniel Defoe, *A Tour Thro' the Whole Island of Great Britain (1724–6)*, 3 vols. (London: Pickering & Chatto, 2001), 3:126.

25. Gordon Jackson, *The History and Archaeology of Ports* (Tadworth: World's Work, Surrey, 1983), 46–48.

26. N. Ritchie-Noakes, *Liverpool's Historic Waterfront: The World's First Mercantile Dock System* (Liverpool: HMSO, 1984).

27. Jackson, *The History and Archaeology of Ports*, 47–48; Hyde, *Liverpool and the Mersey*, 10–15; Michael Power, "Creating a Port: Liverpool 1695-1715," *Transactions of the Historic Society of Lancashire and Cheshire* 149 (2000): 51–71.

28. Jane Longmore, "Liverpool Corporation as Landowners and Dock Builders, 1709–1835," in *Town and Countryside: The English Landowner in the National Economy, 1660–1860*, ed. C. W. Chalklin and J. R. Wordie (London: Routledge, 1989), 139.

29. Kenneth Morgan, ed., *An American Quaker in the British Isles: The Travel Journals of Jabez Maud Fisher, 1775–1779* (Oxford: Oxford University Press, 1992), 232.

30. [William Vaughan], *On Wet Docks, Quays, and Warehouses for the Port of London: with Hints respecting Trade* (London, 1793), 2.

31. Longmore, "Liverpool Corporation as Landowners and Dock Builders," 116–46; Michael Power, "Councillors and Commerce in Liverpool, 1650-1750," *Urban History* 24 (1999): 301–23; and Michael Power, "Politics and Progress in Liverpool, 1660-1740," *Northern History* 35 (1999): 119–38.

32. Borsay, *The Urban Renaissance*, 108–9; Jon Stobart, "Culture versus Commerce: Societies and Spaces for Elites in Eighteenth-Century Liverpool," *Journal of Historical Geography* 28 (2002): 471–85.

33. Millerd's map of Bristol is reproduced at http://www.buildinghistory.org/bristol /millerd.shtml (June 1, 2015).

34. Vincent Waite, *The Bristol Hotwell* (Bristol: Bristol branch of the Historical Association, 1962); David Hussey, " 'From the Temple of Hygeia to the Sordid Devotees of Pluto.' The Hotwell and Bristol: Resort and Port in the Eighteenth Century" in *Resorts and Ports: European Seaside Towns since 1700*, ed. Peter Borsay and John K. Walton (Bristol: Channel View Publications, 2011), 50–65.

35. For the location of sugar refineries, see Kenneth Morgan, "Sugar Refining in Bristol" in *From Family Firms to Corporate Capitalism: Essays in Business and Industrial History in Honour of Peter Mathias*, ed. Kristine Bruland and Patrick O'Brien (Oxford: Oxford University Press, 1998), 144.

36. Lobel and Carus-Wilson, *Bristol Historic Towns Atlas*, 23.

37. Carl B. Estabrook, *Urbane and Rustic England: Cultural Ties and Social Spheres in the Provinces 1660–1780* (Manchester: Manchester University Press, 1998), 44–46.

38. Quoted in Lobel and Carus-Wilson, *Bristol Historic Towns Atlas*, 23.

39. Madge Dresser, *Slavery Obscured: The Social History of the Slave Trade in an English Provincial Port* (London: Continuum, 2001), 96–118.

40. Roger H. Leech, ed., *The St Michael Precinct of the University of Bristol: Medieval*

and Early Modern Topography, Bristol Record Society's Publications, 52 (Bristol: Bristol Record Society in association with the University of Bristol, 2000), 26, 31, 115.

41. J. H. Bettey, *The Royal Fort and Tyndall's Park: The Development of a Bristol Landscape* (Bristol: Bristol branch of the Historical Association, 1997), 9.

42. Dresser, *Slavery Obscured*, 97–105.

43. Walter Ison, *The Georgian Buildings of Bristol* (London: Faber & Faber, 1952), 95–104; Andor Gomme, Michael Jenner, and Bryan Little, *Bristol, An Architectural History* (London: Lund Humphries, 1979), 115, 143–48; Timothy Mowl, *To Build the Second City: Architects and Craftsmen of Georgian Bristol* (Bristol: Redcliffe Press, 1991), 45. Defoe had pointed out the inadequacies of the Tolzey; see McVeagh, ed., Defoe, *A Tour*, 2:158.

44. John Wood, *A description of the Exchange of Bristol; Wherein the Ceremony of Laying the First Stone of that Structure; together with that of opening the Building for Publick Use, is particularly recited* (Bath, 1745), 7, 33–34 (quotation), 36.

45. Eric Frederick Gollannek, "'Empire Follows Art:' Exchange and the Sensory Worlds of Empire in Britain and its Colonies, 1740–1775" (Ph.D. diss., University of Delaware, 2008), 58–59.

46. Andrew Kelly, *Queen Square Bristol* (Bristol: Redcliffe Press, 2003).

47. Dresser, *Slavery Obscured*, 105–8.

48. William Barrett, *The History and Antiquities of the City of Bristol* (Bristol: W. Pine, 1789), 84.

49. Dresser, *Slavery Obscured*, 108–11; Donald Jones, *A History of Clifton* (Chichester: Phillimore, 1992). See also McGrath, *The Merchant Venturers of Bristol*, 182–96.

50. J. R. Ward, "Speculative Building at Bristol and Clifton, 1783–1793," *Business History* 20 (1978): 3–19.

51. Mowl, *To Build the Second City*, 112.

52. Dresser, *Slavery Obscured*, 110–13.

53. McVeagh, ed., Defoe, *A Tour*, 3:124, 126 (quotation).

54. Longmore, "Liverpool Corporation as Landowners and Dock Builders," 116; Jane Longmore, "Residential Patterns of the Liverpool Elite, c.1660–1800" in *Living in the City: Elites and their Residences, 1500–1900*, ed. John Dunne and Paul Janssens (Turnhout, Belgium: Brepols, 2008), 176, 180.

55. C. W. Chalklin, *The Provincial Towns of Georgian England: A Study of the Building Process 1740–1820* (London: Edward Arnold, 1974), 98–100; Perry Gauci, *The Politics of Trade: The Overseas Merchant in State and Society, 1660–1720* (Oxford: Oxford University Press, 2001), 57.

56. Hyde, *Liverpool and the Mersey*, 5, 8–9.

57. Chalklin, *The Provincial Towns of Georgian England*, 100.

58. Hyde, *Liverpool and the Mersey*, 14–15, 21–22; Jane Longmore, "'Cemented by the Blood of a Negro'? The Impact of the Slave Trade on Eighteenth-Century Liverpool," in *Liverpool and Transatlantic Slavery*, ed. Richardson et al., 233–35.

59. Gauci, *The Politics of Trade*, 59, 61.

60. Jane Longmore, "The Urban Renaissance in Liverpool 1760–1800" in *Joseph Wright of Derby in Liverpool*, ed. Elizabeth E. Barker and Alex Kidson (New Haven: Yale University Press, 2007), 5, 7; Longmore, "Residential Patterns of the Liverpool Elite," 184.

61. David Pope, "The Wealth and Social Aspirations of Liverpool's Slave Merchants of the Second Half of the Eighteenth Century," in *Liverpool and Transatlantic Slavery*, ed. Richardson et al., 172–74, 219–22.

62. Sharples, *Liverpool*, 201; George McLoughlin, *A Short History of the First Liverpool Infirmary, 1749–1824* (London: Phillimore, 1978).

63. W. Enfield, *An Essay towards the History of Liverpool* (Warrington, 1773), 58–59.

64. Longmore, "The Urban Renaissance in Liverpool 1760–1800," 5, 7.

65. Ascott, Lewis, and Power, *Liverpool, 1660–1750*, 149–50; Sharples, *Liverpool*, 43; Jane Longmore, "Civic Liverpool: 1680–1800," in *Liverpool 800: Culture, Character and History*, ed. John Belchem (Liverpool: Liverpool University Press, 2006), 148.

66. [Vaughan], *On Wet Docks*, 2.

67. François Vigier, *Change and Apathy: Liverpool and Manchester during the Industrial Revolution* (Cambridge, Mass.: Harvard University Press, 1970), 48, 51; Ascott, Lewis, and Power, *Liverpool, 1660–1750*, 160 n61.

68. Longmore, "The Urban Renaissance in Liverpool," 9.

69. Longmore, "'Cemented by the Blood of a Negro'?," 240; Longmore, "Civic Liverpool," 158.

70. J. A. Picton, *Memorials of Liverpool Historical and Topographical, including a history of the Dock estate*, 2 vols. (Liverpool: Howell, 1907), 1:223.

71. I. C. Taylor, "The Court and Cellar Dwelling: the Eighteenth-Century Origin of the Liverpool Slum," *Transactions of the Historic Society of Lancashire and Cheshire* 122 (1971): 81 n49.

72. Longmore, "Residential Patterns of the Liverpool Elite," 186, 189; Jane Longmore, "Rural Retreats: Liverpool slave traders and their country houses" in *Slavery and the British Country House*, ed. Madge Dresser and Andrew Hann (London: English Heritage, 2013), 30–45, 159–61.

73. Katie McDade, "Bristol and Liverpool Port Improvements in the Latter Half of the Eighteenth Century: The Case for Liverpool's Entrepreneurial Success," *International Journal of Maritime History* 24 (2012): 201–24.

PART IV

Houses and the Home

10

BUILDING STATUS IN THE
BRITISH ATLANTIC WORLD

THE GENTLEMAN'S HOUSE IN THE ENGLISH
WEST COUNTRY AND PENNSYLVANIA

Stephen Hague

In the mid-1680s, young John Elbridge set off from the Massachusetts Bay Colony bound for England. John's family hailed from the port of Bristol, but some years previously his father had taken them to the Pemaquid settlement in the modern-day state of Maine and then, in the aftermath of King Philip's War, on to Massachusetts. His mother and father had lately departed for Jamaica to manage a sugar plantation the family owned on the Caribbean island. Accompanied only by an older sister and leaving behind several siblings, John Elbridge traveled to England to serve as an apprentice to his cousin, merchant and customs official Thomas Moore of Bristol. He would spend the rest of his life in England's second port city.[1] A few years later, another young man arrived in Bristol. Born in Ireland to Scottish Quaker parents, James Logan had traversed the British Isles to join Bristol's thriving Quaker community. There his father opened a school where James quickly developed a reputation as a teacher. Not long after, William Penn, founder of the colony of Pennsylvania, engaged Logan as his secretary to accompany him on his second voyage to America. Arriving in 1699, Logan took on myriad political and administrative tasks for the Penn family that eventually established him as a leading citizen in the American colony. Logan would spend the rest of his life in Philadelphia.[2]

The stories of John Elbridge and James Logan illustrate the transatlantic character of life in the British Atlantic world for those with the means or ambition to experience it. They were from similar "middling" backgrounds, were entrepreneurial, and willing to take the dangerous transatlantic crossing, consequently rose in social rank through positions in public life, and accumulated fortunes through a range of trade activities and investments.

FIGURE 10.1. *Cote, ca. 1720, Westbury on Trym. Author.*

Like many "new men" throughout the British Atlantic in the late seventeenth and eighteenth centuries, they negotiated a series of overlapping and intersecting networks to establish their positions within the social fabric of the British world.

Critically important in affirming their hard-earned social status was their choice of dwelling. Relatively late in their respective lives, Elbridge and Logan both acquired a small classical house as a home and, more importantly, as a statement of their gentility. Elbridge's house, Cote, is located in Gloucestershire in England's West Country (Fig. 10.1). This five-bay, hip-roofed stone structure reinforced Elbridge's membership in the mercantile and professional elite of nearby Bristol. Five miles from Philadelphia in Pennsylvania, Logan's house, Stenton, represented genteel houses built in the American colonies. A "large brick house . . . of 51 ft by 40," erected between 1723 and 1730, its ample size would have impressed eighteenth-century Pennsylvanians and provincial Britons alike (Fig. 10.2).[3] Despite separation by the Atlantic Ocean, the Logan and Elbridge houses were remarkably similar: two-and-a-half-story boxes roughly fifty feet across by forty feet deep. Neither, so far as can be determined, was designed by a professional architect but relied instead on craftsmen for planning and construction. While built of different

STEPHEN HAGUE

FIGURE 10.2. *Stenton, 1723–1730, Philadelphia. Stenton, NSCDA/PA.*

materials available locally, each displayed classical symmetry on the main façade, had a compact, double-pile, or two-room deep, floor plan, and ancillary service buildings to the rear of the main structure. Four principal rooms with a center hall and staircase comprised the first floor. The upper floors accommodated chambers for family, servants, and visitors. Noted in one sales advert as "fit for a gentleman," in their similarities, houses like Cote and Stenton represent a house form associated with genteel owners in various parts of the British Isles and colonial America.[4]

These two houses erected in the 1720s in different parts of Britain's Atlantic world model the process of building status for individuals on the peripheries of elite society. By examining gentlemanly housebuilding, arrangement of space, furnishings, and social action in the domestic setting, this chapter argues that despite geographic distance, regional variation, and local condition, genteel standards of taste cohered in and around such gentlemen's houses. Replicated in varying situations throughout the British Atlantic world, small classical houses were a carefully calibrated strategy used by minor landed gentry, merchants, early industrialists, and professional men as a universal marker of genteel status.[5] Moreover, such "gentlemen's houses" reflected and shaped the social interactions of their inhabitants, enabling them to project their status through cultural practices and sociable routines. Gentlemen's houses illuminate the important link between buildings, possessions, and social position, suggesting a moderate and incremental pace of social change.[6]

Few symbols were as potent in delineating status as building a small classical house, which pushed builders and owners over the threshold of politeness so important in the eighteenth century, even if it did not entirely resolve the contested nature of their identity within British society.[7] A comparison of Cote and Stenton provides one specific example of the cultural exchanges and relations that emerged in the British Atlantic world. Although they are not, in themselves, representative of that world as a whole, they are important illustrations of broader processes at work. Modest by comparison with great country houses, houses like these played a pivotal role in building status for lesser elites throughout Britain and its North American colonies until the American War for Independence.

BRITISH IDENTITY AND GENTEEL BUILDING

A transatlantic perspective focused on genteel houses elucidates thorny issues of architecture, social mobility, and consumption and helps to reconceptualize how and in what ways people shaped identity. Imperial expansion framed the identity of Britons across the geographic boundaries of "Greater Britain."[8] Individuals living in provincial England and the American colonies could be at once English or American, provincial, and British.[9] Indeed, in the century after 1680 *colonial* Americans adopted symbols of British culture that increasingly transformed them into *provincial* Britons.[10] In London up to the American War, for instance, Americans might easily be taken for British provincials.[11] In this way, Britain's empire offered provincial and colonial elites like Elbridge and Logan, "a sense of belonging, identity and order."[12]

Within this Atlantic world, the purchase of a landed estate and the building of a country house has been interpreted as a precise indicator of aspirational motivation.[13] Building or buying a house and furnishing it entailed considerable expenditure and were noteworthy acts of consumption.[14] The adaptability of the compact classical house to the needs of different social groups, however, cautions against a narrative that links status and building with an ambitious, linear "ascent into the realm of the gentleman" that included the acquisition of large country houses, the doing of good works, and the collecting of art.[15] Some, but not all, gentlemen in the Atlantic world invested in land, and gentlemen's houses stood in situations ranging from a few acres to large landed estates or plantations, although genteel builders were increasingly inclined to build on small estates or in suburban settings.[16]

STEPHEN HAGUE

Indeed, new men who derived wealth from mercantile activity often did not seek to acquire a landed estate and country house at all, content instead to reside in cities or choose more modest residences.[17] Their houses and relatively small contiguous estates were often supported by significant property investments elsewhere. John Elbridge owned a number of estates in the west of England, as well as part of a plantation on Jamaica, incomes from which were supplemented with salary and fees arising from his post as deputy controller of customs in Bristol. Stenton comprised a five-hundred-acre estate, but Logan's widespread landholdings reached about eighteen thousand acres in Pennsylvania and New Jersey by his death in 1751, and he made significant sums from his involvement in the American fur trade.[18]

Classical gentlemen's houses developed as an important architectural type across the British Atlantic world from the late seventeenth century, but architectural historians have largely neglected their importance as social and cultural indicators in an Atlanticist context.[19] Terminology used to describe compact classical houses has raised definitional problems of whether these houses were characteristic of the middle class, the minor gentry, or the aristocracy.[20] The distinctions between a country house, a house in the country, and the villa blur when examining social status through the lens of a particular kind of house, which could be built in a range of situations. Small classical houses, built in both urban and rural settings, ideally suited individuals like Logan and Elbridge who represented a dynamic segment of society that supplied much of the civil and imperial administration, commercial control, and social direction in Britain and its colonies.[21]

THE GENTLEMAN'S HOUSE IN THE WEST COUNTRY AND THE MID-ATLANTIC

The construction of compact classical houses in the west of England and the British North American colonies became particularly widespread in the second quarter of the eighteenth century. In Gloucestershire, for instance, owners built or substantially altered at least eighty compact classical houses in the century after 1680, but especially between 1720 and 1770, nearly three-quarters of those who built in Gloucestershire hailed from commercial or professional backgrounds, mostly funded by the proceeds of commerce in Bristol or cloth manufacturing in the Stroudwater valleys. [22] The onset of this building trend in the 1720s occurred during a period when the number of larger country houses built in England declined.[23] Concurrently in the North American colonies, two- and three-story elite houses proliferated along the eastern seaboard.[24] The timing and location of these robust gentlemanly housebuilding trends suggest a strong tie between the financial success of commercial centers like Bristol and Philadelphia and the dynamism of a variegated but genteel group of merchants, government officials, professionals, and minor gentry.

John Elbridge's house, Cote, illuminates the relationship between architecture and status. After arriving in England in 1682, Elbridge embarked on a career as a merchant and government official. Appointed deputy controller of the customs in 1708, over the next three decades Elbridge became a well-established figure in the commercial world of Bristol, with extensive social, professional, and business networks as far-flung as London, the Caribbean, and New England.[25] In 1728, nearly sixty years of age, Elbridge inherited the Cote property and came into possession of a newly built gentleman's residence a few miles from Bristol described as "a good house, with a suitable estate, pleasantly situated."[26] A single man, he adopted Cote as his primary residence and had at least three servants living with him at the time of his death.[27] Despite a substantial fortune and status as a leading citizen, it was only with the acquisition of Cote that Elbridge secured a house removed from the urban center of Bristol, commodious and suitably equipped for a gentleman of his standing.

A similar combination of personal interaction, business, public service, and house acquisition occurred as colonial elites forged identities, often with an eye firmly on the British Isles. After emigrating to Pennsylvania in 1699, James Logan quickly became a central figure in the colony's political life, invested in property, and made a fortune in the fur trade. Even as a leading figure in colonial administration, Logan's construction of a gentleman's house was not without its uncertainties. Early in his time in Pennsylvania, Logan remarked that he was "firmly resolved never to set up a gentleman."[28] Shortly thereafter, however, he began to acquire the land that became Stenton, commenting that he was "about purchasing a plantation to retire to, for I am heartily out of love with the world."[29] Logan began erecting a brick classical mansion in the 1720s with specific criteria in mind that combined aesthetics and status projection (and the accepted social limits of that projection), writing to a friend, "My wife . . . fears I should build too fine."[30]

Stenton reinforced Logan's social and political power. The building required widespread use of hired and enslaved labor that imposed Logan's identity on the landscape and the psyches of the myriad people associated with its creation between 1723 and 1730.[31] Craftsmen were engaged to finish the interior, installing fine fielded paneling and wainscoting in a number of rooms, and adorning the entrance space with substantial fluted pilasters and

STEPHEN HAGUE

three drop pendants carved with a small heart motif, a possible allusion to the Logan family coat of arms.[32] By November 1727, as work continued on the house, Logan firmly decided to "change the town for the country."[33] Stenton also played an important role in building status in England with those above him on the social scale. The following year he told Thomas Penn, one of the proprietors of the colony, that he was soon "to retire with my family into the countrey, where I have for sometime been building a handsome house, tho' very leisurely."[34] After moving to their new house in 1730, Logan wrote his brother in Bristol that he had named the house Stenton after the ancient village in Scotland where their father had been born, an allusion to their gentrified ancestors.[35] Stenton's construction also coincided with the increasing frequency with which Logan appeared in Pennsylvania tax records listed as "gentleman" or "esquire."[36]

Logan's primary intent in removing to Stenton was to retire from public service, an objective that was not fully accomplished until the 1740s. Yet this was not a colonial version of the villa; rather, Stenton functioned as a primary, year-round residence for the Logan family. No less a figure than Benjamin Franklin called Stenton "a country seat," indicating a level of physical and symbolical removal that reinforced in a literal way Logan's lofty position in colonial Pennsylvania.[37] In this way, Stenton reflected many gentlemen's residences in other parts of the British world after about 1730, not entirely rural but rather existing in relationship to an urban environment.

Although such properties have been linked with the aspirational qualities of "new men" from commercial and professional worlds, gentlemen's houses were built not so much as an effort to seek status but rather as a strategic move to confirm status already conferred. Elbridge and Logan both acquired their houses after the age of fifty, having been engaged in commerce and public service for many years. In Virginia, leading planters, although somewhat younger, often delayed building until after marriage or an inheritance.[38] By about 1730, then, gentlemen from nonlanded backgrounds increasingly opted for a compact classical house as a secure architectural choice to confirm their position within an established hierarchy.

The compact, double-pile floor plan seen at Stenton and Cote had wide appeal to a range of builder-owners in the British Atlantic world. In America, the "classic Georgian plan of four rooms on a floor," has attracted much interest, but far less attention has been paid to this plan in Britain.[39] Despite arguments that compact Georgian houses were built on a smaller scale in England than in America, sizes were in fact comparable.[40] Taken as an example, Stenton's slightly awkward six-bay façade accommodated a four-room plan

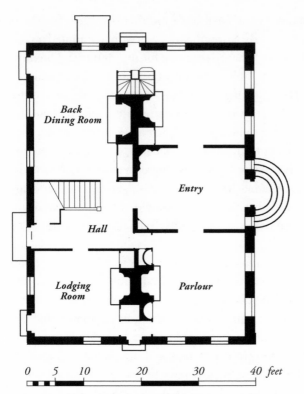

FIGURE 10.3.
Stenton first-floor plan.
Mary Agnes Leonard.

Back
Dining Room

Entry

Hall

Lodging
Room

Parlour

0   5   10   20   30   40 *feet*

(Fig. 10.3). Although he intended to construct a "plain, cheap Stone farmer's house," Logan was "forced to build in brick" because his "quarries failed him entirely."[41] Transatlantic networks proved useful in securing building materials difficult to obtain in America in the early eighteenth century. Several orders to leading Bristol merchant Nehemiah Champion included a clock jack for cooking, nails for construction of Logan's new country house, a large order for locks, a thousand squares of window glass, and fifteen squares "to cover a doz flower prints."[42] Champion in Bristol literally and figuratively helped Logan in Philadelphia to build his status. In terms of design, architectural pattern books played a limited role for gentlemen builders until after 1730.[43] James Logan's library, for instance, one of the finest in the American colonies, contained only four books of architecture, and there is little indication that any of them inspired Stenton, although it is possible the second edition of Richard Neve's *The City and Country Purchaser* arrived in time to be of some use.[44] Gentlemanly building was not therefore architecture in emulation of aristocratic practice but rather a response that combined classical vocabulary and imported goods with local, vernacular materials and methods.

By the middle of the eighteenth century, most gentlemen's houses contained fifteen to twenty spaces in total. The four primary rooms on the ground floor included a hall and stair, a best parlor, a common parlor, and a final space, occasionally a third parlor, study, or other room. Throughout the period, the main spaces on the floor above invariably served as bedchambers, which might include an attached or smaller subdivided room such as a closet or cabinet that served as private space within the household.[45] Third stories or garrets, in most instances the domain of the servants' rooms, were smaller, tucked under the eaves, and more numerous. Sometimes these spaces served as chambers for children, other members of the family, or visitors. Basements or attached offices or wings accommodated additional rooms for storage and service functions. Spaces were much less differentiated than in larger houses, but the typical four rooms per floor of a gentleman's house enabled vertical and horizontal arrangements of public, private, and service spaces — rooms for all the functions that genteel status demanded.[46]

Location, access, and interior finishes signaled room importance and function. The stair hall and the parlor, as discussed in Bernard L. Herman's chapter, particularly distinguished gentlemen's houses from those lower down the social scale on both sides of the Atlantic.[47] The construction, ornamentation, and space allocated to the main stair highlighted it as a status symbol that governed movement. Staircases are a central feature at Cote and Stenton, framed by arches that visually emphasized their importance (Figs. 10.4 and 10.5). Most often, secondary staircases were used for service functions or personal access by members of the household. Parlors functioned as a primary space of sociability. Wood paneling was common to better rooms in most grand houses until about 1750.[48] Gentlemen's houses invariably had at least one paneled parlor, although subsequent decorating campaigns have obscured whether paneling in most houses was originally painted and, if so, in what color.[49] The "Great Parlour" at Cote had "dark paneling like the hall."[50] In the Stenton parlor, an elaborate shell-carved buffet cupboard, a feature common to many gentlemen's houses, housed Logan's substantial 329 ounces of plate (i.e. silver). Worth £148 in Pennsylvania currency, this display offered a clear indication of prosperity.[51]

Interior finishes conveyed important meanings for gentlemen and their audiences. Early eighteenth-century decorating schemes are well documented for many larger houses in Britain, but technical investigation is virtually unknown for gentlemanly houses. Surviving evidence and research has been much more robust for American examples of this type, offering useful comparative data.[52] The use of wood paneling, painted walls, tapestry

FIGURE 10.4. *The hall at Cote. Author.*

FIGURE 10.5. *Stenton entry hall, with arched double doors leading to the stair hall. Stenton, NSCDA/PA.*

hangings, other textiles, and wallpaper all contributed to color and texture in rooms.[53] As the most expensive category of domestic good after precious metals, textiles especially constituted a visible way of adorning a room with color at the same time that they conveyed messages about the intended importance of the space.[54] In grander houses, color hierarchies placed red or crimson as the highest color, followed by green and then blue. Yellow fabrics and yellow-painted rooms appeared infrequently before 1740 in larger houses. [55] Such rules were less stringently followed in gentlemen's houses. The best bedchamber at Elbridge's Cote house had a mix of textiles and colors, predominantly yellow and green, whereas the second most expensively furnished bedchamber was decorated in crimson. In Pennsylvania, the Logans' "Yellow Lodging Room," adorned with yellow wool damask bed hangings and window curtains and painted yellow, was the best chamber despite the stricture that yellow was uncommon.[56]

Room furnishings from well-documented houses like Cote and Stenton provide additional layers of evidence suggesting that genteel houses functioned similarly in Britain and America. The household contents at Cote were valued at £290.8.10. Elbridge left a fortune of nearly £80,000, an indication that Elbridge furnished Cote handsomely but not ostentatiously given his resources.[57] Logan's 1752 inventory cataloged contents worth £415.0.6 Pennsylvania currency (roughly £250 sterling), with an additional £900 Pennsylvania in books.[58] These were typical sums, indicating that the contents of gentlemen's houses were worth a few hundred pounds. Considerable by most measures, these costs were substantially lower than in many larger houses of the gentry and peerage, where several thousand pounds might be spent on furnishing.[59]

Rich evidence from Cote provides a guide to the furnishing of a gentleman's house and how it functioned as a social unit (Fig. 10.6). A procession route circulated from public to more private spaces. The fully paneled hall governed entry to the house and was equipped with "8 Turkey Worked Chairs" — named for the fabric that imitated Turkish carpets that covered their seats and backs — that had their peak popularity in the seventeenth century.[60] Movement on the ground floor might then have led to the "Great Parlour." Fully paneled with the fireplace highlighted by a marble surround, bold bolection molding, large ionic pilasters, the room's size, interior fittings, the large number of chairs, and several tables indicated a formally fashionable space to receive guests (Fig. 10.7). The "Parlour" behind was less elaborate. Leather upholstery in the "Great Parlour" and "Parlour" indicated that

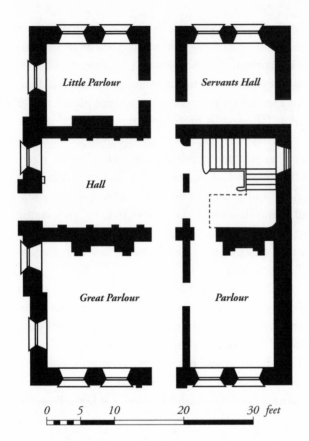

FIGURE 10.6.
Cote first-floor plan.
Mary Agnes Leonard.

Little Parlour

Servants Hall

Hall

Great Parlour

Parlour

0   5   10   20   30 *feet*

meals eaten in these more public rooms required hard-wearing coverings for furniture. The "Little Parlour," by contrast, had one table and seating covered in matte bottoms. Although a small room, the "tobacco tonges," decanters, glasses, and punchbowl suggest that it was a predominantly masculine space.[61]

Buildings, objects, and people interacted in the gentleman's house to highlight the fine gradations of status and indicate how these houses functioned as social spaces. The exercise of political authority was one act inherent in building a gentleman's house. As settings for the exercise of power, genteel houses amply fulfilled a role as theaters for status enactment.[62] Stenton's spaces impressed callers ranging from other colonial and provincial elites to representatives of Native American groups. Guests were frequent, seeking counsel, talking politics, and especially viewing the library. Benjamin Franklin first visited Stenton to take advice from Logan, whom he called, "a Gentleman of universal learning, and the best Judge of Books in these parts."[63] His frequent returns and long correspondence with Logan saw status enacted in the

FIGURE 10.7. *The "Great Parlour" at Cote. Author.*

domestic setting on a recurring basis. Over time the relationship between the two men changed, Franklin becoming more preeminent as Logan grew older, a shift that coincided with the falling off of Franklin's visits to Stenton. Late in life, a frail and elderly Logan complained to Franklin, "I have expected to see thee here for several weeks."[64] Stenton captivated other colonial leaders; William Black, who visited Philadelphia in 1744 with Thomas Lee of Stratford Hall in Virginia, called it a "beautiful house."[65] John Smith, eventually to become Logan's son-in-law, made frequent reference to gatherings at Stenton, including "many Friends dining" and being "Genteelly treated."[66] This sociability extended across cultural boundaries, as Logan formed his identity among the indigenous peoples of North America. In the 1730s and 1740s, by which time Logan was a respected but calculating diplomat, Stenton hosted large gatherings of Native Americans from the Iroquois confederation, or Haudenosaunee, complete with exchanges of wampum and other goods, an indication of the house's role in impressing the Native populace and projecting the power of the colonial government.[67] The number of dishes and serving pieces at Stenton offer guidance to the level of entertaining. The house thus functioned almost as a public building, a meeting place for European colonists and Native Americans alike.

Gentlemen's houses in America displayed a parallel mix of fine furnishings, most often situated in public spaces, and older, less stylish objects present in back rooms. The contents of Stenton typified the combination of old and new English furnishings and locally produced objects.[68] Several pieces, such as a desk and bookcase, and two sets of India-back chairs, were made in Philadelphia, while others, especially ceramics and textiles, continued to be imported from England.[69] The presence of numerous chairs throughout the house—seventy-four in total—speaks to the level of the Logan family's social interactions, as does the number and variety of dishes and serving pieces indicated by documents and surviving archaeological evidence.[70] Like Cote, visitors ascending the stairs to Stenton's first floor encountered two significant chambers that straddled a public/private divide. The yellow lodging room, which had a bed with curtains, window curtains, and bed cloths in yellow wool damask worth thirty pounds, was comparable to the best chambers of gentlemen's houses in England.[71] A second bedchamber cum library filled with 2,651 books constituted one of the great collections in North America. One visitor noted that, "After the tea table was removed we were going to take leave, but it appeared we must first view his library, which was customary with him to any persons of account."[72] By the mid-eighteenth century, the presence of books in even high-status households in England was far from universal, and their use to convey intellectual power also set off the gentleman's house.[73] The household possessions of Elbridge and Logan were particularly important as status markers for the genteel.[74] Following the classical doctrine of decorum, although Elbridge and Logan had the wherewithal to adorn their houses more lavishly, the objects that they owned were finely graded indicators of their conceptions of self and their social status; marking the height to which they had climbed but also the ceiling they had reached.

The commonality between these two houses in the English West Country and the mid-Atlantic colonies of British America suggests significant cultural links between similar social groups in different parts of Britain's Atlantic world. In the years preceding the American Revolution, colonial elites in North America developed characteristic attitudes that diverged from their British counterparts in important ways.[75] However, for much of the eighteenth century there was considerable continuity in genteel attitudes, material life, consumption, and status across Britain and its empire.[76] In certain key behaviors such as the construction and use of houses, colonial elites negotiated many of the same complex relationships as their British equiva-

STEPHEN HAGUE

lents. This is part of what Cary Carson has termed "international gentrification."[77] Provincial and colonial Britons like John Elbridge of Bristol and James Logan of Philadelphia confirmed their position within British society by building and inhabiting compact, classical houses.

Evaluating houses and their genteel inhabitants through an Atlantic lens reincorporates American elites and their domestic buildings into a wider British framework. The numerous compact classical houses spread across Britain's Atlantic empire underscore the connections between commercial interests, landed wealth, public service, transatlantic trade, and architecture. Gentlemen and their houses stood at the leading edge of cultural relations and social change. From Philadelphia to Bristol, from the frontier in the Mohawk Valley of New York to the Stroudwater valleys of Gloucestershire, this adaptable form presented gentlemen with a specifically calibrated material choice to exert authority, reinforce their power, and put social practice in motion. Many successful government officials, merchants, and landowners alike engaged in this form of building status. Although their efforts could be contested, the possession of a "gentleman's house" was an indicator of admittance to Britain's polite governing class.

NOTES

1. See especially Bristol Record Office/AC/WO/10-20: Elbridge Papers. Also, Donald Jones, "The Elbridge, Woolnough and Smyth Families of Bristol, in the Eighteenth Century; with Special Reference to the Spring Plantation, Jamaica" (Ph.D. diss., University of Bristol, 1972). [BRO/34328/a].

2. Frederick Tolles, *James Logan and the Culture of Provincial America* (Boston, 1957); Albright G. Zimmerman, "James Logan, Proprietary Agent," *Pennsylvania Magazine of History and Biography* (April 1954): 143–76.

3. James Logan to Thomas Story, 29 September 1729, James Logan Letterbook, 4 vols. The Historical Society of Pennsylvania (hereafter HSP), 3:245.

4. *Gloucester Journal*, 11 February 1755.

5. The geographic diversity of houses as keys to genteel status is suggested in R. G. Wilson, *Gentlemen Merchants: The Merchant Community in Leeds, 1700–1830* (Manchester: Manchester University Press, 1971), 203–6; T. M. Devine, *The Tobacco Lords: A Study of the Tobacco Merchants of Glasgow and Their Trading Activities, c. 1740–90* (Edinburgh: John Donald, 1975); P. Jenkins, *The Making of a Ruling Class: The Glamorgan Gentry, 1640–1790* (Cambridge: Cambridge University Press, 1983); A. Vickery, *The Gentleman's Daughter: Women's Lives in Georgian England* (New Haven and London: Yale University Press, 1998), 25, 35; J. Longmore "Rural Retreats, Liverpool Merchants and the British Country House" (unpublished paper, *Slavery and the English Country House*

Conference, London School of Economics, November 2009); B. B. Mooney, *Prodigy Houses of Virginia: Architecture and the Native Elite* (Charlottesville: University of Virginia Press, 2008); Lorena Walsh, *Motives of Honor, Pleasure, and Profit: Plantation Management in the Colonial Chesapeake, 1607–1763* (Chapel Hill: University of North Carolina Press, 2010), 239–42, 413–17; Trevor Burnard, *Creole Gentleman: The Maryland Elite, 1691–1776* (New York and London: Routledge, 2002), 213–30.

6. Amanda Vickery and John Styles, *Gender, Taste, and Material Culture in Britain and North America, 1700–1830* (London and New Haven: Yale University Press, 2006); K. Harvey, ed., *History and Material Culture: A Student's Guide to Approaching Alternative Sources* (London: Routledge, 2009). Some architectural historians have led the way in developing a material culture approach to history, such as Bernard L. Herman, *Town House: Architecture and Material Life in the Early American City, 1780–1830* (Chapel Hill: University of North Carolina Press, 2005).

7. L. E. Klein, "Politeness and the Interpretation of the British Eighteenth Century," *The Historical Journal* 45, no. 4 (Dec. 2002): 869–98; R. W. Brunskill, *Vernacular Architecture: An Illustrated Handbook* (London: Faber and Faber, 4th edition, 2000), 27–30.

8. David Armitage, "Greater Britain: A Useful Category of Historical Analysis?," *American Historical Review* 104, no. 2 (April 1999): 427–45. On the imperial construction of identity, see Linda Colley, *Britons: Forging the Nation, 1707–1837* (London: New Pimlico edition, 2003); Kathleen Wilson, *The Sense of the People: Politics, Culture and Imperialism in England, 1715–1785* (Cambridge, 1995); Kathleen Wilson, ed., *A New Imperial History: Culture, Identity, and Modernity in Britain and the Empire 1660–1840* (Cambridge, 2004); For an alternative view, see Marie Peters, "Early Hanoverian Consciousness: Empire or Europe?," *English Historical Review* CXXII, 497 (June 2007): 632–68.

9. P. T. Marcy, "Eighteenth-century views of Bristol and Bristolians," in *Bristol in the Eighteenth Century*, ed. P. McGrath (Newton Abbot, 1972), 11–40; Michal J. Rozbicki, "The Curse of Provincialism: Negative Perceptions of the Colonial American Plantation Gentry," *Journal of Southern History* 63, no. 4 (November 1997): 727–52; Michal Rozbicki, *The Complete Colonial Gentleman: Cultural Legitimacy in Plantation America* (Charlottesville: University of Virginia Press, 1998), especially 28–29; Burnard, *Creole Gentleman*, 1–2.

10. Ned Landsman, *From Colonials to Provincials: American Thought and Culture 1680–1760* (Ithaca, N.Y.: Cornell University Press, 1997).

11. J. Flavell, *When London Was Capital of America* (New Haven and London: Yale University Press, 2010), 166. For political attitudes toward the American colonies as part of Britain, see P. J. Marshall, *The Making and Unmaking of Empires: Britain, India, and America c. 1750–1783* (Oxford: Oxford University Press, 2005), 172–74. The difficulty Americans encountered in jettisoning their connection with Britain is treated in Kariann Yokota, *Unbecoming British: How Revolutionary America Became a Post-Colonial Nation* (Oxford: Oxford University Press, 2011).

12. H. V. Bowen, *Elites, Enterprise and the Making of the British Overseas Empire, 1688–1775* (London: Macmillan, 1996), 103.

13. Mark Girouard, "The Power House," in *The Treasure Houses of Britain: Five Hundred Years of Private Patronage and Art Collecting*, ed. Gervase Jackson-Stops (New Haven: Yale University Press, 1985), 23.

14. The vast literature on consumption has developed from the landmark study, Neil McKendrick, John Brewer, and J. H. Plumb, *The Birth of Consumer Society: The Commercialization of Eighteenth-Century England* (London: Europa Publications, 1982). Of particular relevance are Carole Shammas, *The Pre-Industrial Consumer in England and America* (Oxford: Oxford University Press, 1990); Lorna Weatherill, *Consumer Behavior & Material Culture, 1660–1760* (London: Routledge, 2nd edition, 1996); Maxine Berg, *Luxury and Pleasure in Eighteenth-Century Britain* (Oxford: Oxford University Press, 2005); T. H. Breen, "An Empire of Goods: The Anglicization of Colonial America, 1690–1776," *Journal of British Studies* 25 (1986): 467–99; Cary Carson, Ronald Hoffman, and Peter J. Albert, eds., *Of Consuming Interest: The Style of Life in the Eighteenth Century* (Charlottesville: University of Virginia Press, 1994).

15. David Hancock, *Citizens of the World: London Merchants and the Integration of the British Atlantic Community, 1735–1785* (Cambridge: Cambridge University Press, 1995).

16. In Gloucestershire, landholdings associated with small classical houses ran from less than ten to about a thousand acres. See Stephen Hague, "'A MODERN-BUILT house . . . fit for a Gentleman': Elites, Material Culture and Social Strategy in Britain, 1680–1770" (D.Phil. diss., University of Oxford, 2011), chapter 4. In Pennsylvania William Penn constructed Pennsbury Manor on 8,431 acres and some Virginia plantations stretched to thousands of acres. See Figures 2–5 in Clare Lisa Cavicchi, "Pennsbury Manor Furnishing Plan, Morrisville, Penn." (unpublished MS, 1988), 58 ff.

17. Stephen Hague, *The Gentleman's House in the British Atlantic World, 1680–1780* (Basingstoke: Palgrave Macmillan, 2015); Lawrence and Jeanne Fawtier Stone, *An Open Elite? England, 1540–1880* (Oxford: Oxford University Press, 1984).

18. James Logan Will, 1751, file copy at Stenton. James Logan's ledger books are at the Historical Society of Pennsylvania.

19. John Summerson, *Architecture in Britain, 1530–1830* (New Haven, Conn.: Yale University Press, 9th edition, 1993); Giles Worsley, *Classical Architecture in Britain: The Heroic Age* (New Haven, Conn.: Published for the Paul Mellon Centre for Studies in British Art by Yale University Press, 1995) 10–12, 29–31, 169–73; Cooper, *Houses of the Gentry*. For North America, see Hugh Morrison, *Early American Architecture* (Oxford: Oxford University Press, 1952); and James Deetz, *In Small Things Forgotten: An Archaeology of Early American Life* (New York: Anchor, expanded and revised, 1996), 156–58.

20. Kevin Sweeney, "High Style Vernacular: Lifestyles of the Colonial Elite," in *Of Consuming Interest*, 1–58, 11, 24.

21. Paul Langford, *A Polite and Commercial People: England, 1727–1783* (Oxford: Oxford University Press, 1989), 76. Accounts that discuss the gentry-bourgeois conjunc-

tion include Wilson, *Gentlemen Merchants*; Amanda Vickery, *The Gentlemen's Daughter: Women's Lives in Georgian England* (New Haven and London: Yale University Press, 1998); Susan Whyman, *Sociability and Power in Late-Stuart London: The Cultural World of the Verneys, 1660–1720* (Oxford: Oxford University Press, 1999).

22. Hague, "'A MODERN- BUILT house . . . fit for a Gentleman,'" chapter 2.

23. See especially Figure 2 and Table 4 in Richard Wilson and Alan Mackley, *Creating Paradise: The Building of the English Country House, 1660–1880* (London, 2000), 205–7. Kingsley, *The Country Houses of Gloucestershire*, 8.

24. Richard Bushman, *The Refinement of America: Persons, Houses, Cities* (New York: Vintage, 1992), xi, 5.

25. Jones, "The Elbridge, Woolnough and Smyth Families of Bristol, in the Eighteenth Century." [BRO/34328/a]; "Entry Book: December 1694," 10 Dec. 1694, *Calendar of Treasury Books*, vol. 10: *1693–1696* (1935); "Warrant Books: December 1708, 1–10," *Calendar of Treasury Books*, vol. 22: *1708* (1952), 451–58; Patrick McGrath, *Records relating to the Society of Merchant Venturers of the City of Bristol in the Seventeenth Century*, BRS vol. XVII (1952), 33; GA/CMS/202: Justices of the Peace of 1736 [Transcription of GA/Q/JC/3]; BRO/04356/9: Apprentice Book, 1709–1719.

26. Samuel Rudder, *A New History of Gloucestershire* (Cirencester, 1779), 796.

27. BRO/AC/WO/10/14/b-d: Copy wills of John Elbridge.

28. Quoted in Tolles, *James Logan*, 93.

29. James Logan Letterbook 1712-1715, James Logan to Thomas Story, 26 June 1714, 199. Reed Engle, "Historic Structures Report: Stenton" (unpublished report, 1982), 1–4, 9–10.

30. James Logan Letterbook, James Logan to Thomas Story, 10 November 1721, 209.

31. James Logan's ledger books documenting, *inter alia*, the construction of Stenton are at the Historical Society of Pennsylvania. See also Engle, "HSR: Stenton," Table 2.

32. The Logan family crest includes a heart with three passion nails ("three piles sable conjoined in point in a heart gules"). Laura Keim, "Stenton Room Furnishings Study" (unpublished manuscript, 2012), on file at Stenton, 37.

33. Tolles, *James Logan*, 186.

34. James Logan to Thomas Penn, *Penn Manuscripts: Official Correspondence, 1728–1734*, 2:41, HSP.

35. James Logan letterbook, 4:208, James Logan to William Logan, 15 December 1730, HSP.

36. "Guide to the Philadelphia Exemption Series, Being True Copies of Philadelphia County Land Records in the Master of Rolls Office and its Successors, 1669–1838," prepared by James Duffin (Philadelphia, 1994), 238–39.

37. Benjamin Franklin, *Papers of Benjamin Franklin*, vol. 4, 207 (*Pennsylvania Gazette*, 7 November 1751).

38. Barbara Burlison Mooney, *Prodigy Houses of Virginia* (Charlottesville: University of Virginia Press, 2008), 87–92.

39. Bushman, *The Refinement of America*, 7; Moody, *Prodigy Houses of Virginia*. See

also A. Gomme and A. Maguire, *Design and Plan in the Country House: From Castle Donjons to Palladian Boxes* (New Haven and London: Yale University Press, 2008), which deals relatively briefly with plans of four rooms per floor, favoring instead analysis of larger houses.

40. For the former view, see Worsley, *Classical Architecture in Britain*, 171, and Daniel Reiff, *Small Georgian Houses in England and Virginia: Origins and Development through the 1750s* (London, 1986), 323, Appendix 2, Table 6. More recent investigation appears in Hague, "'A MODERN-BUILT house,'" 149–151.

41. Engle, "HSR: Stenton," 10.

42. Ibid., 16–17; Raymond V. Shepherd, "James Logan's Stenton: Grand Simplicity in Quaker Philadelphia" (Unpublished Winterthur M. A. thesis, 1968), 177, 179.

43. Janice G. Schimmelman, *Architectural Books in Early America: Architectural Treatises and Building Handbooks Available in American Libraries and Bookstores through 1800* (New Castle, Del.: Oak Knoll Press, 1999).

44. Edwin Wolf, *The Library of James Logan of Philadelphia, 1674–1751* (Philadelphia: Library Company of Philadelphia, 1974), 336. A review of James Logan's ledger at the Historical Society of Pennsylvania suggests that Wolf misinterpreted the conventional dating system in the ledger. I would argue that the date recorded is more likely 12 Mo 29 1727 (i.e., 29 March 1728). This would place the Neve volume in Philadelphia two years earlier than previously thought and possibly of more use in the building of Stenton.

45. See for example, R. B. St. George, "Reading Spaces in Eighteenth-Century New England," 90–103 and K. Lipsedge, "'Enter into thy Closet': Women, Closet Culture, and the Eighteenth-Century Novel," 107–22, especially 109–12, in *Gender, Taste, and Material Culture*, ed. John Styles and Amanda Vickery; Amanda Vickery, "An Englishman's Home Is His Castle? Thresholds, Boundaries and Privacies in the Eighteenth-Century London House," *Past and Present* 199 (2008): 147–73; John Bold, "The Design of a House for a Merchant, 1724," *Architectural History* 33 (1990): 75–82, 80.

46. Gomme and Maguire, *Design and Plan in the Country House*, 140–47. For further consideration of floor plans see Mark Girouard, *Life in the English Country House: A Social and Architectural History* (New Haven and London: Yale University Press, 1978), especially chapter 7, "The Social House"; J. Bold, "The Design of a House for a Merchant, 1724," is a useful consideration of a merchant's house in Bristol; for the evolution of floor plans of "villas," see especially Patricia Smith, "Plain English or Anglo-Palladian? Seventeenth-Century Country Villa Plans" in *The Renaissance Villa in Britain 1500–1700*, ed. Malcolm Airs and Geoffrey Tyack (Reading: Spire Books, 2007), 89–110.

47. Bushman, *The Refinement of America*, 114–22; Hall, "Yeoman or Gentleman?," 2–19; Gomme and Maguire, *Design and Plan*, 152–72; James Ayres, *Building the Georgian City* (New Haven and London: Yale University Press, 1998), 120.

48. Ian Bristow, *Architectural Colour in British Interiors, 1615–1840* (New Haven and London: Yale University Press), 53; John Cornforth, *Early Georgian Interiors* (New Haven and London: Yale University Press, 2004), 40, 113.

49. Surviving unpainted wainscot can be seen at Cote, Goldney House, Frampton

Court, and Eastbach Court in Gloucestershire. In Pennsylvania, several rooms at Fairhill were denoted by their wood; see Norris Family Papers, vol. 2, 40, HSP.

50. Elisabeth Robinson, "Some Notes about Cote" (unpublished manuscript, April, 1971), 7. Typescript on file at Cote House.

51. James Logan inventory, August 1752, file copy at Stenton.

52. For Stenton, for example, see Matthew J. Mosca, "Historic Paint Finishes Study" (Unpublished report, 31 March, 2000); Peggy Olley, "Stenton Paint Analysis" (Unpublished manuscript, 2004); Peggy Olley, "Stenton and Mount Pleasant: Revisiting the Finish Histories of Two of Philadelphia's Most Treasured 18th-Century Houses," in *Architectural Finishes in the Built Environment*, ed. M. A. Jablonski and C. R. Matsen (London: Archetype Books, 2009), 56–67. A useful overview of paint analysis at Stenton is in Keim, "Stenton Room Furnishings Study," 11–19.

53. Bristow, *Architectural Colour in British Interiors*; H. Hughes, ed., *Layers of Understanding: Setting Standards for Architectural Paint Research* (London: English Heritage, 2002); Jablonski and Matsen, *Architectural Finishes in the Built Environment*.

54. E. S .Cooke Jr., ed., *Upholstery in America and Europe from the Seventeenth Century to World War I* (New York and London: Norton, 1987); Peter Thornton, *Authentic Décor: The Domestic Interior, 1660–1920* (New York: Crescent, 1984), especially 57 and 100 for window curtains. F. Montgomery, *Textiles in America, 1650–1840* (New York: W. W. Norton, 1984) has much to say of relevance to England.

55. On color, see Cornforth, *Early Georgian Interiors*, 113–21; Amanda Vickery, *Behind Closed Doors: At Home in Georgian England* (New Haven and London: Yale University Press, 2009), 172–175; Bristow, *Architectural Colour*. Blue particularly became more popular during the eighteenth century, Cornforth, *Early Georgian Interiors*, 120.

56. James Logan inventory.

57. BRO/AC/WO/10/19: 2 April 1739, Inventory of the goods of John Elbridge at his house at Stoke, Westbury (Cote House).

58. The rough equivalent was £100 sterling to £168 Pennsylvania, valuing Logan's inventory at £250. His books added an extraordinary £540 to the value of his possessions. On currency exchange, see John J. McCusker, *Money and Exchange in Europe and America, 1600–1775: A Handbook* (Chapel Hill: University of North Carolina Press, 1978), especially 175–88; 185, Table 3.7.

59. Compare, for example, Weatherill, *Consumer Behavior and Material Culture*; Shammas, *The Pre-Industrial Consumer*; and Mark Overton, Jane Whittle, Darron Dean, and Andrew Hann, *Production and Consumption in English Households, 1600–1750* (London: Routledge, 2004), with the aristocratic inventory amounts listed in Cornforth, *Early Georgian Interiors*; Tessa Murdoch, ed., *Noble Households: Eighteenth-Century Inventories of Great English Households: A Tribute to John Cornforth* (Cambridge: J. Adamson, 2006); and J. Collett-White, ed., *Inventories of Bedfordshire Country Houses, 1714–1830*, Publications of the Bedfordshire Record Society, vol. 74 (Bedford: Bedfordshire Record Society, 1995).

60. Thornton, *Authentic Décor*, 24, 59; Charles Saumarez Smith, *Eighteenth-Century Decoration and the Domestic Interior in England* (New York: Harry N. Abrams, 1993), 175, plate 163; Adam Bowett, *English Furniture, 1660–1714: from Charles II to Queen Anne* (Woodbridge, UK: Antique Collectors Club, 2009), 76–79.

61. K. Harvey, "Barbarity in a Tea Cup? Punch, Domesticity and Gender in the Eighteenth Century," *Journal of Design History* 21, no. 3 (Autumn 2008): 205–21.

62. Rhys Isaac, *The Transformation of Virginia, 1740–1790* (Chapel Hill: University of North Carolina Press, 1982, new edition, 1999), xxxi.

63. Minutes of the Library Company of Philadelphia, 29 March 1732.

64. Franklin, *Papers of Benjamin Franklin*, vol. 3, 146.

65. "The Journal of William Black," June 1, 1744, *Pennsylvania Magazine of History and Biography* 1, no. 4 (1877): 406.

66. Albert Cook Myers, ed., *Hannah Logan's Courtship* (Philadelphia, 1904), 86, 114, 160, 178, 180, 185, 190, 209, 293.

67. Paul A. Wallace, *Conrad Weiser, 1696–1760: Friend of Colonist and Mohawk* (Philadelphia: Wennawoods Publishing, 1945), 71–75, 126; James H. Merrell, *Into the American Woods* (New York: Norton, 1999), 119–20; *Colonial Records of Pennsylvania* (1736–1745), 4:575, 580; Edwin Wolf II, *The Library of James Logan* (Philadelphia: Norton, 1974), 50, documents Logan's ownership of the 1663 Indian Bible translation by John Eliot.

68. James Logan inventory. Raymond V. Shepherd, "James Logan's Stenton: Grand Simplicity in Quaker Philadelphia" (M.A. thesis, Winterthur, 1968) has been supplemented and corrected in parts by Laura Keim, "Furnishing Stenton: Quaker Grandeur in Philadelphia," in *The Philadelphia Antiques Show Catalogue 2002* (Philadelphia, 2002), 49–80, and Philip D. Zimmerman's series of articles: "Philadelphia Case Furniture at Stenton," *The Magazine Antiques* (May 2002): 94–101; "Eighteenth-Century Chairs at Stenton," *The Magazine Antiques* (May 2003): 122–29; and "Early American Tables and Other Furniture at Stenton," *The Magazine Antiques* (May 2004): 102–9.

69. Maxine Berg, *Luxury and Pleasure in Eighteenth-Century Britain* (Oxford: Oxford University Press, 2005), chapter 8.

70. Deborah Miller, "Archaeology at Stenton" (M.A. thesis, Pennsylvania State University, 2006) and Dennis Pickeral, "The Proper Equipage: Tea, Coffee, and Chocolate at James Logan's Stenton" (M.A. thesis, Pennsylvania State University, 2008). Barbara Liggett, "Archeological Notes on Stenton" (unpublished manuscript at Stenton, 1983[?]). See also, John L. Cotter, Daniel G. Roberts, and Michael Parrington, *The Buried Past: An Archaeological History of Philadelphia* (Philadelphia: University of Pennsylvania Press, 1993), 332–36.

71. Cornforth, *Early Georgian Interiors*, 84–92.

72. "The Journal of William Black," 407.

73. Weatherill, *Consumer Behavior and Material Culture*, Tables 2.1, 5.1, and 8.1. Overton et al, *Production and Consumption in English Households*, Table A4.1.

74. Vickery, *The Gentleman's Daughter*, 229. See also Deborah Cohen, *Household Gods: The British and Their Possessions* (New Haven, Conn.: Yale University Press, 2006), 86.

75. Burnard, *Creole Gentleman*, 256–57; Rozbicki, *The Complete Colonial Gentleman*, chapter 5.

76. Berg, *Luxury and Pleasure*, chapter 8; Ann Smart Martin, *Buying into the World of Goods* (Baltimore: Johns Hopkins University Press, 2008).

77. Cary Carson, "The Consumer Revolution in Colonial America: Why Demand?," in *Of Consuming Interest: The Style of Life in the Eighteenth Century*, 483–697, 687.

11

PARLOR AND KITCHEN IN THE BORDERLANDS OF THE URBAN BRITISH AMERICAN ATLANTIC WORLD, 1670–1720

Bernard L. Herman

Borderlands map edge and threshold. They are locations of indeterminacy, performance, conflict, and uneasy negotiation. Borders are never resolved and always policed in some fashion. Borders are places of exchange where identities are questioned and passage regulated. In some instances, borderlands are discovered in hindsight; in others, they are fully present at the frayed edges of territory. To be at the border is to occupy a place, however transitory, between two iterations of belonging. The border is a place of checkpoints and guards—and yet a place that is porous and the site of smuggling and contraband, where tariffs are levied and manifests checked and stamped, where expressions of integrity are most hotly articulated and vigorously defended. Borders are simultaneously visible and invisible. They are like the intertidal world where land and sea overlap, never entirely separated and never entirely merged—a place where the properties of one place or the other are forever in flux—and where some species flourish in the littoral zones that borders always entail. Borders are the places where our suspicions are aroused and where we pose questions, often indelicate and sometimes ill-advised. A borderland is thin ice over dark water. Imagining borderlands, I think of liminal places, places that exist between two or more identities. Borderlands in this sense are locations for colonization, resistance, disputation, and invention. Because borderlands are uncertain places, they make the conditions of certainty discernible. Critical borderlands are where old paradigms and canons falter and new explanations and categories emerge.

The borderland I map in this essay focuses on the changing architectural landscape and mentalité of London in the decades following the Great Fire with a particular emphasis on the location of parlors and kitchens in houses. The proposition of London as a borderland may at first blush appear counter-intuitive, but, if we accept the idea of a border as a liminal space, the booming metropolis in the last third of the seventeenth century was exactly that. The rebuilding of London following the Great Fire in 1666 and the rapid expansion of its suburbs into the eighteenth century reveal the urban heart of emergent empire in a defining moment of architectural and social transformation. Significantly, London as borderland was coeval with urban developments around the north Atlantic world, exemplified by parallel developments close to home in places such as Bristol and Deal and across the ocean in Philadelphia, Charleston, and Boston. By shifting our focus from London as the wellspring from which vernacular architectural practices flowed to an urban place in flux and conversation with its many contemporaries, we deepen our perspective on the place of the great conurbation in the imagination of the Atlantic world. To do this, we look briefly at the as-told trajectory of London's vernacular housing and then turn to the problem of how builders and residents negotiated the domestic core of the house through the late seventeenth and early eighteenth century.

A prevailing notion of Georgian London derives from Summerson's influential work that offers a compelling master narrative that links the rise of the post-Fire metropolis to the phoenix-like appearance of a great conurbation (the city and its suburbs) marked by values of regularity, taste, and economy.[1] In the ruins of mid-twentieth-century Europe, Summerson's Georgian London optimistically spoke to destiny, order, and architectural triumph. Provocative recent works recast the rise of the Georgian city in more nuanced terms. Elizabeth McKellar offers a fresh narrative that looks to complex changes in land transfers and leases, the systematization of building practices, and the standardization of building types.[2] The London she describes lurches uncertainly, but somehow inexorably toward modernity. In McKellar's history the purposeful, confident stride into the future that inflects Summerson's story becomes more provisional, conflict-ridden, and tentative. Peter Guillery addresses the multitude of dwellings that fell by the wayside in Summerson's architectural history.[3] Even as Londoners, especially those building and living on its eighteenth-century edges in suburbs exemplified by Deptford, Hackney, and Spitalfields, engaged the "new" architectural values of the Georgian moment, they erected countless small houses that reflected sensibilities that had little to do with bookish taste. The "smaller" houses of London were not some sort of minor anomaly, but instead the architectural sinew that filled the minor streets, courts, and alleys, and even lined major thoroughfares such as Kingsland Road. What unites these histories and many more investigations into the architectural course of London in the decades following the Great Fire through the eighteenth century is an understated sense of process. The architectural renewal and expansion of the post-Fire urban landscape is about the progress of rank redefined by wealth, professionalism in the building trades, and the ebb and flow of communities of sensibility. Summerson, McKellar, and Guillery offer a set of portraits of the rise of eighteenth-century London. In each, London as subject changes through the construction of context and interpretive purpose. Together these representations of the metropolis invite a continuing consideration of urban housing and city living.

The history of the Great Fire of London in 1666 is well and often told, as are the narratives surrounding the rebuilding of the burned areas where over thirteen thousand houses vanished in the conflagration. In a three-day period, a large swath of London became an architectural ash heap smoldering at the very heart of an empire taking form. The problem that confronts us, though, is how that wasteland emerged as a borderland—a space between territories of sensibility, identity, and image—and subsequently metamorphosed over nearly forty years into the Georgian city celebrated by Summerson and nuanced by McKellar, Guillery, and others. A central problem that confronts us at the outset is the relative scarcity of urban housing from the period between 1666 and 1700. Scattered examples survive to be sure, but their numbers are modest. The situation improves for the first two decades of the eighteenth century, but even then the instances of existing dwellings are defined by the exception of their survival. Victorian and early twentieth-century architectural surveys add to our knowledge of the range of building diversity, but again the evidence is uneven and trends toward the mid-eighteenth century and later.

All of this is complicated by the facts that the Great Fire did not consume the metropolis in its entirety, and that housing reflecting earlier practices survived on the periphery. At the same time, though, those peripheral areas were in the process of being consumed by the rapidly expanding architectural fabric at the city's ever-expanding margins. The geometry of destruction and expansion resulted in the creation of two architectural borderlands: one in the burned districts, one on the urban periphery. Certainly, grasping a sense of the organization of housing in the post-Fire decades is central to an interpretation of the larger cultural process that gave shape to Georgian London. Third, the period of roughly 1670 to 1720 constitutes the extended generation of London as an architectural borderland—a time period coincident with the emergence of a much larger new architectural urbanism underway in the many provincial cities in the capital's economic, political, and cultural orbit from Bristol, Hull, and Lancaster to Philadelphia, Charleston, and the seaport towns of northern New England as well as urban settlements in the Caribbean, South America, Asia, and Africa. In short, the architectural ideas that shaped post-Fire London were instrumental in shaping the urban domestic landscapes of the British Atlantic world.

My goal here is fourfold. First, I marshal the evidence from three distinct bodies of documentation that describe London in the post-Fire period from very different perspectives. The reconciliation of these records suggests a London that was very much an architectural borderland in a period when provincial towns and cities were also in the process of dramatic change. Second, the observations on London after the Fire raise questions not only about the diversity of architectural form and usage, but also query the explanatory conventions of standardization and regularity often deployed in interpretations of the rise of the Georgian city. Third, by conjoining the graphic evidence of architectural form with the enumerative record of household possessions and the action statements found in criminal prosecutions, I provide a sense of the fluidity of borderlands—both within the city and its far-flung urban satellites. Finally, I offer the hypothesis that the provincial domestic architectures of the late seventeenth-century British Atlantic world owe as much to the preconditions of experimentation and innovation epitomized by the builders and residents of London's vernacular dwellings after the Fire as they do to influences such as regionalism, creolization, and contemporary fashion. The evidence for these claims lies not in period narratives, but in the material fact of the houses people occupied, furnished, and inhabited.

Begun in the 1680s and concluded in the 1720s, two manuscript volumes cataloged as the *Bridge House and City Lands Properties* recorded lease details for properties owned by the Corporation of London.[4] The books consist of ground floor plans for houses with notations on the lessee, location, building material, and room use. In rare instances the surveys offer plans for multiple stories in a particular structure. The plans depict grand houses, such as the premises of the Lutestring Company, as well as clusters of buildings organized in rows, courts, and alleys. Among the many dwellings represented are a number built against the old city wall including at least two residences that captured the base of turrets as domestic spaces (Fig. 11.1). The plans unfortunately do not bear individual dates nor is there notation about why they have been collected in bound books, although we can surmise that these volumes

BERNARD L. HERMAN

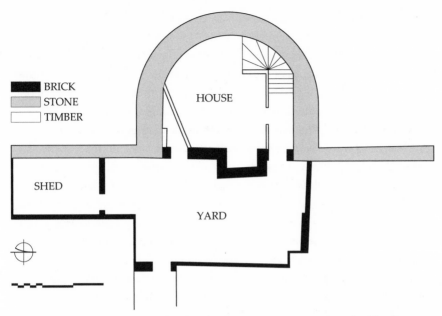

BRICK
STONE
TIMBER

HOUSE

SHED

YARD

FIGURE 11.1. *Lease in Mugwell Street. Books of Plans of City Lands and Bridge House Properties (ca. 1680–1720), CLA/008/EM/03/018 and CLA/008/EM/03/019. Drawing by Jeff Klee after the original in the City of London, London Metropolitan Archives.*

constitute a ledger that records the range of properties under management and their disposition. The dates of individual plans might be recoverable by reuniting the plats with their leases, but there is no guarantee that the bound plan is coeval with the lease date. Thus, we are compelled to approach the Bridge House records as a chronologically ordered aggregate of assets.

The Archdiocese of Middlesex probate inventories run through the last third of the seventeenth century into the early decades of the eighteenth. Notable for the large number of room-by-room listings, these documents provide a sense of how Londoners furnished houses that ranged from dwellings with shops to at least one house of assignation. Where rooms are named (parlors or kitchens, for example) we are able to recover a sense of how the occupants defined their residences through personal possessions. The level of detail in the inventories is such that we gain a sense of both the vertical and horizontal organization of houses and how that changed over time. The chief limitations of the inventories are first that they record the estate of the decedent and not necessarily the totality of the dwelling's contents, and, second, that although they identify rooms by name and notation they do not describe the physical relationships between different domestic spaces. Thus, the inventories yield insight into domestic proximity discerned through objects and named (or numbered) rooms.

The proceedings of the *Old Bailey Online* constitute the third source that informs this discussion of post-Fire London as an architectural borderland. The trial records often specify the details of a crime, recording where people and objects were in the house, how actors (victims, malefactors, and witnesses) moved, and times of day. The architectural content of an individual trial record is never comprehensive, but in the aggregate the proceedings suggest much about how Londoners from across the social spectrum understood, exploited, and defended the spaces they occupied through their descriptions of the actions that transpired within the house. Cases involving breaking and entering may not tell us much about the overall organization of the house, but they do convey significant information on how people moved in and out of rooms, how they thought about security and vulnerability, and the etiquette and conventions of peeking, locking, and sneaking. In these accounts, we hear voices calling out for help and we see who harkens and who responds. We envision how household residents secured themselves, where they were lax in their precautions, and how they were betrayed not just by behavior but also by the ways in which particular kinds of domestic spaces afforded venues for misfortune.

Because of the immensity of this material I focus in this abbreviated discussion on the parlor, a room that appears in all three sources with some degree of regularity and was clearly in the process of entering the post-Fire architectural lexicon. Finally, although these three sources do not overlap in any intentional or even predictable way beyond the business and institutions they represent, together they do provide a suggestive glimpse into the transformation of a rapidly evolving Atlantic urban world under unceasing negotiation through individual and collective action. The borderland we see here is one that in retrospect is provisional, opportunistic, and far from representing the qualities of order and regularity ascribed to the Georgian city.

Elizabeth Symbole of St. Ann's Westminster stood trial with her sisters for her husband's murder in February 1695. Symbole listened as the witnesses to the crime testified how she together with her two sisters and Jacob Regnier accomplished a deed that, due to its violation of conjugal relations, achieved the status of petty treason. Regnier, in a separate trial, claimed self-defense, protesting that he stabbed Symbole a mere eighteen times in response to the victim cursing him, striking him with his fist, and threatening him with a fire fork. What interests us, however, is the architectural dimension of the testimony. Jane Williams, the Symboles' servant described how Elizabeth Sym-

BERNARD L. HERMAN

bole's sisters and Regnier, bottle of wine in hand, came to visit. Mrs. Symbole, who was in the kitchen with Williams, ordered her servant upstairs "to make a Fire in the Parlor" where the guests convened, "drank, and were merry." Isaac Symbole returned home late in the evening from the neighboring alehouse and found his wife, sisters-in-law, and Regnier playing the card game Bone Ace. Isaac Symbole joined in the festivities, ordering "a Supper to be drest" followed by an apparently spirited continuation of card playing. Williams retired back downstairs to her post in the kitchen where she dozed off only to be awakened by the watchman's knock at the door and the discovery of her master mortally wounded and "sunk down in his Chair behind the Table." The watchman corroborated her story, adding that when he called upon the Symbole house "some Woman answer'd him out at the Window."[5]

Several details emerge from this late seventeenth-century account. The parlor was upstairs, but how many flights of stairs is unknown. If the kitchen was underneath the house, the likelihood is that the parlor stood on the ground floor slightly above sidewalk level. The hallooing for the watchman, however, indicates the parlor's position in an upper story and at the front of the house. The merriment fueled by wine, cards, a late supper, and more cards identifies a room closely associated with an emergent culture of polite sociability. The facts that the room was not in general use and a fire had to be set and lit to warm it for the evening further suggest the occasional nature of sociability and the summoning forth of its amenities. The Symboles' parlor was in essence a space defined by circumstance and by the rapidly evolving etiquette associated with conviviality and polite ritual made visible in this instance through its violation epitomized by the appearance of Regnier "standing in the Room with a Naked sword in his Hand, all bloody, which he wiped upon his Coat."[6]

Although we might be interested in the fate of Elizabeth Symbole and her sisters (all acquitted), our architectural interests focus on the parlor and the place it occupied and defined in the evolving London landscape. Parlor (in various spellings) appears in the proceedings of the Old Bailey a dozen times between 1674 and 1695 and in forty-two cases from 1696 through 1720. Significantly, no mention of parlors occurs prior to 1687 and twenty-one or nearly 40 percent of the total crop up in the last five years. By the early 1730s, the term parlor had been codified as "a fair lower Room design'd principally for the Entertainment of Company."[7] Parlors in this iteration, it seems, were a late development—but what was the nature of the understanding and the social practices that lent these rooms significance?

In the aggregate, parlors were understood as rooms that housed valued objects like plate and textiles. Evidence given in housebreaking and theft trials often place parlors on the ground floor in a manner where their contents could be seen from the street and their sanctity violated by thieves nimble enough to shimmy in and out of windows or wily enough to take advantage of unlocked doors. Thus, on a winter's day in 1688 Thomas Smith "came in at the Window and the Casement was open, and the Coat was brought down one pair of the Stairs and laid in the Parlour" from whence it disappeared from the house of widow Mary Callamy in St. Mary Aldermanbury, or Thomas Fenchly's "Maid going into the Parlor to see what it was a Clock, the Room being somewhat dark, she opened the pin [pane] of the window for light; and going up stairs, heard a noise below, upon which she lookt over the window, and saw two persons going away from the House with clothes in their arms, and coming down stairs found the window open, and the Goods missing."[8] In these two accounts and numerous others, the parlor emerges as something other than a space for sociability and more in line with the general usage associated with a common room.

Servants and householders routinely used this room as an occasional staging area where soiled laundry, clothing, and other objects were left en route to other destinations within the house: "Richard Whiting alias Jones, was Indicted for stealing on the 25th of April, three pair of Holland Sheets value 30 s. from Henry Baldwin; The Linning lay foul in a lower Parlor, in Baldwins House, and the Prisoner took his opportunity to go into the House and take it away under his Arm; and the Woman of the House, espying his shadow going out of the door ran after him, crying, stop Thief, and he being pursued, dropt them in the Street."[9] The parlor in post-Fire London houses was a place defined by varying associations and practices that ranged between polite and porous, secure and vulnerable, public and private. They were rooms secured with hasps, locks, and, in some instances, string—and yet they were also rooms where members of the household left doors ajar and windows cracked open. Even as late as 1717 when Mary Townsend sat down in her parlor to her supper on a warm July evening, thieves seeing "Things lying in the Windows" lifted the sash and made off with a hat, cane, and silver spoon.

The location of the parlors mentioned within the proceedings of the Old Bailey varies, but the general pattern (at least as far as criminal proceedings go) is that they were generally found on the ground floor at the front of the house. The Bridge House surveys, however, suggest that parlor locations within London houses were quite variable. Thomas Hoxton's dwelling near The Postern consisted of three principle ground floor spaces: an

BERNARD L. HERMAN

entry and passage containing the stair, a front parlor, and a back kitchen (Fig. 11.2). In its arrangement, Hoxton's house resonates with the central-chimney house illustrated in Moxon's *Mechanick Exercises* of 1702, a dwelling form still found with considerable frequency in London's southern and eastern suburbs.[10] Samuel Wilson's premises placed the parlor behind his shop in Pudding Lane and the domestic work spaces of kitchen and washhouse in separate structures at the back of the work-yard behind the house (Fig. 11.3). William Andrews located his parlor in Old Bethlem even further back from the street placing it third in a progression of shop, kitchen, parlor, and foundry (Fig. 11.4). Notable in these houses is the degree of variation not only in the location of the parlor but also in the placement of chimneys, stairs, and attendant service spaces. Similarly, the absence of parlors in many of the City Lands plans does not indicate that these rooms were lacking, but that, if parlors were present, they were likely to be found in the story above the ground floor rooms. The relative frequency with which upper story parlors occupied the front or the back of the house is unrecorded.

Parlors appeared in a host of configurations where the exigencies of the leased property compelled novel solutions. A modest house on the "Passage to the Church" stood backed against the London wall with its parlor pushed to the rear and access gained either from the entry or the kitchen. Admitting natural light and air into this space appears to have been a secondary consideration. A premises in Cripplegate, for example, wraps around another store in a progression from the shop, an unnamed and unheated room with a stair and parlor. In contrast to the other ground floor spaces, the parlor is notable not only for its brick fireplace but also for its flanking closets hinting at storage and possibly the display of valued objects including plate or decorative ceramics. At its core the architectural knot of Ann Howard's Hounds-ditch premises held an orderly dwelling unit with the parlor overlooking a garden (Fig. 11.5). Peter Monger's considerably more complex and socially ambitious brewhouse compound in Minories placed the parlor so that it offered a view of the work-yard and cooper's shop (Fig. 11.6). Houses attached to stables situated their parlors at the furthest remove from the earthy pungency of manure and trampled urine-sodden straw. The experience of Howard's privileged prospect of the garden, Monger's brewery vista, and the sound and smell of stableyards impel us to query the relative degree of polite sensibility associated with these rooms.

Variation in the arrangements of London houses after the Fire suggests something of a distinction between the placement of parlors within houses and evolving conventions of what those domestic spaces signified. The de-

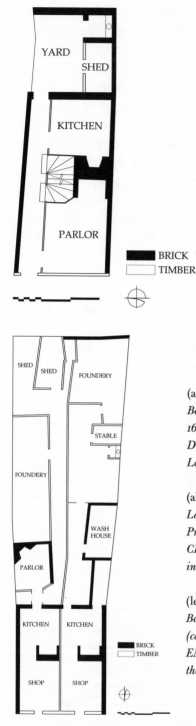

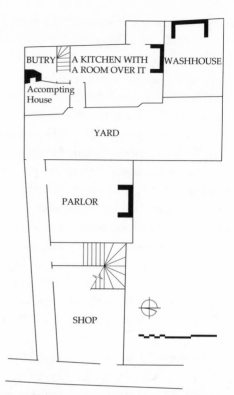

BRICK
TIMBER

BRICK
TIMBER

(above left) FIGURE 11.2. *Thomas Hoxton Lease, The Postern. Books of Plans of City Lands and Bridge House Properties (ca. 1680–1720), CLA/008/EM/03/018 and CLA/008/EM/03/019. Drawing by Jeff Klee after the original in the City of London, London Metropolitan Archives.*

(above right) FIGURE 11.3. *Samuel Wilson Lease, Pudding Lane. Books of Plans of City Lands and Bridge House Properties (ca. 1680–1720), CLA/008/EM/03/018 and CLA/008/EM/03/019. Drawing by Jeff Klee after the original in the City of London, London Metropolitan Archives.*

(left) FIGURE 11.4. *William Andrews Lease, Old Bethlem. Books of Plans of City Lands and Bridge House Properties (ca. 1680–1720 CLA/008/EM/03/018 and CLA/008/ EM/03/019. Drawing by Jeff Klee after the original in the City of London, London Metropolitan Archives.*

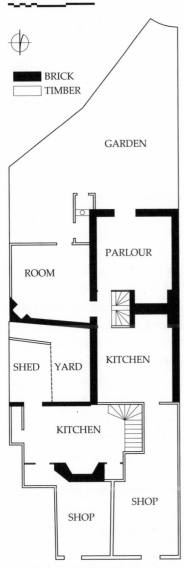

FIGURE 11.5. *Ann Howard Lease, Houndsditch. Books of Plans of City Lands and Bridge House Properties (ca. 1680–1720), CLA/008/EM/03/018 and CLA/008/EM/03/019. Drawing by Jeff Klee after the original in the City of London, London Metropolitan Archives.*

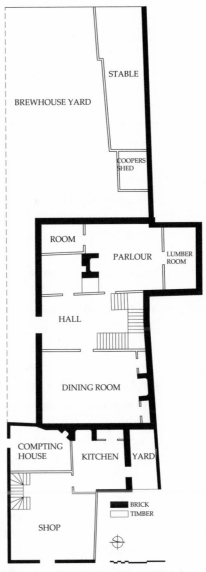

FIGURE 11.6. *Peter Monger Lease, Minories. Books of Plans of City Lands and Bridge House Properties (ca. 1680–1720), CLA/008/EM/03/018 and CLA/008/EM/03/019. Drawing by Jeff Klee after the original in the City of London, London Metropolitan Archives.*

gree of variability in position describes a noteworthy flexibility for how these rooms could be incorporated into the fabric of the house. Certainly, the larger operations of the house, lot contours, preexisting conditions, and commercial functions ranging from retail to workshop were all factors. Still, the quality of irresolution surrounding the parlor speaks to a realization that it was not the location of the parlor that mattered so much as the fact that it existed at all. But, questions remain as to how these rooms were understood, how they changed over time, and how they assist our understanding of London as an architectural borderland in the decades following the Fire and as a wellspring for architectural thought around the North Atlantic periphery.

A sampling of room-by-room probate inventories from the archdiocese of Middlesex yields something of a sense of how parlors were furnished. Unlike the City Lands surveys that describe the physical organization of the house and the proceedings of the Old Bailey that narrate extraordinary events within ordinary spaces, the inventories provide a listing of a decedent's possessions. Although inventories seem to follow the enumerators' progress through the house, the physical geometry of rooms remains vague beyond notations that record story and front or back locations. Thomas Gadbury of St. Clement Danes, for example, occupied a house in 1691 that was inventoried in the order of garret, a room up two pair of stairs, a room up one pair of stairs, a shop, parlor, and kitchen.[11] The sequence of named spaces also raises the question about the number of rooms per floor. Gadbury's house appears to have been three stories high with a garret under the roof and a kitchen located either in a cellar or behind the dwelling. The fact of two rooms—shop and parlor—on the ground floor in contrast to the single room in the first and second stories introduces two possibilities: the upper story rooms were either quite large or there were unenumerated rooms in the tenure of lodgers.

When the inventory takers visited William Bernnard's house in St. James, Westminster, in 1700, they began their listing with the "back" and "fore" parlors.[12] The back parlor, they noted, contained a fully outfitted bed with curtains and bedding along with three cane chairs, a glass case, a fireplace grate, and nothing more. The fore parlor contained the best bed in the house along with a trundle bed, a wainscot chest of drawers, six cane chairs, a looking glass, a fully equipped fireplace, and the "king and queen's picture." The kitchen and shop followed the parlors. There is no mention of relative position in terms of stories—and there is the problem of missing rooms, most notably garrets, cellars, and stairs. The placement of the parlor in Bernnard's house corresponds to any one of a number of possibilities recorded in the City Lands leases. The designation of rooms in Bernnard's house conforms

BERNARD L. HERMAN

to an established practice of terming chambers, especially the best chamber, as parlors. When the inventory takers visited the house of the late Evan Jones in St. James in 1691 they noted: a "Parlour" with "one table bed & table six old chairs some other things." A garret, back room, kitchen, dining room, and bed chamber completed their list. The distinction between chamber and parlor in Jones's residence speaks to a hierarchy of use. Jones's parlor with both bed and a table and six chairs hints at a space where practices of sociability (that extended to the dining room) kept company with displays of wealth through textiles.[13] Nearly thirty years later, London parlors continued to display the same constellation of tables, chairs, and beds. When Thomas Phill, a joiner and coffin maker died in 1717, his parlor held a fully outfitted press bed, a half dozen cane chairs, a table, a walnut chest of drawers, a looking glass, a corner cupboard, fireplace equipment, "some old pictures," a kettle, and earthenware.[14]

Widow Jane Borden's front and back parlors, apparently located on the ground floor of her house in St. James, operated *en suite* with the back parlor outfitted as a private sitting and dressing room. Her front parlor with two curtained windows overlooking the street contained an elaborate bed and bedding, cane chairs and an oval table, a wainscot chest, sconces and pictures on the wall, and, significantly, thirty pieces of china and delftware. Borden's front parlor looked to older usage. Her dining room, however, engaged newer rituals of sociability. Located above the front parlor, Borden's dining room contained her walnut desk, two card tables, a tea table, and "matted" chairs. Two pier glasses, eight pictures, "Indian prints," sconces, and more graced the walls.[15] Significantly, Borden's dining room held none of the objects we associate with dining. In fact, she outfitted her dining room in the fashion of an eighteenth-century town house parlor. What Borden's inventory reveals is the fluidity of the designation "parlour" in a kind of nuanced specificity. Her "parlours" are little different from the legions of front and back rooms identified in other estate listings from the 1670s well into the second decade of the eighteenth century. At issue in discussions of borderlands, then, is not so much the designation of a room as a parlor, but what that term may have meant in the popular imagination.

Derived from the French *parler*, the parlor was nominally understood first of all as a room for private conversation.[16] Over time, the material conditions of that conversation evolved with the changing sensibilities of polite sociability and its attendant etiquette and rituals. The transition of the parlor from the best room in the house furnished with the most valuable and elaborate bedding as well as chairs and table for company to a room equipped with specialized tables for cards, tea, displays of ceramics and pictures, and an array of chairs, settees, and couches did not follow a straightforward trajectory. From the outset, though, the parlor elicited associations with privacy, privilege, and prestige. The material representation of those values, however, was in flux. When we link household contents listed in probate inventories to the many possibilities for the physical placement of rooms detailed in the Bridge House surveys to the actions incisively limned in criminal court proceedings, we see that the decades after the Fire were characterized by a somewhat inchoate and changing domestic social imagination—and that this period of transformation extended across several decades.

The evolution in displays of wealth (beds being the most valuable object in a house) shifted unevenly to displays of ability linked to emergent idioms of social performance (for example, card tables and tea tables with their related objects). Simply, it was not enough to furnish parlors with key objects; you had to know how to use them. The fact that many individuals struggled with the mastery of certain forms of social performance provided artists and writers from the 1720s onward with ample material for the satirization of ambition and rank. As the parlor increasingly became a space inviting new forms of polite enactment, its place in narratives of architectural borderlands shifted from what a parlor meant to whom it defined. Variations in the location and furnishing of these spaces mapped a community of sensibility that operated within continuous and dynamic conversational fields and enacted social exchanges that relied on the material circumstances of their occasions.[17] Thus, the changing material conditions of social and cultural exchange define London as a borderland in the post-Fire decades.

Nor was this phenomenon limited to London. Peter Cooper's circa 1720 prospect of Philadelphia (founded in 1682) depicts a host of building forms that dropped from the repertoire of local builders through the later decades of the eighteenth century. The fact that fewer than six pre-1740 dwellings are known to survive from the first sixty years of the city's existence speaks in retrospect to the borderland qualities in a manner consonant with London in the same period. The same can be said for Charleston, South Carolina, where the architectural diversity of housing that defined the city from its origins as a walled town in the 1670s steadily evaporated, resulting in the emergence of the dominant form of the single house at the close of the eighteenth century. In English provincial towns, for example, St. Albans, older architectural fabric dating to the sixteenth century and earlier typically received a brick veneer of modernity and the modification of interior arrangements through the insertion of floors and partitions. In English seaport towns ranging from Deal to Whitby to Whitehaven, regional inflection accented the larger urbanism epitomized by London. The borderlands of streetscape, architecture, and sensibility that defined London in the extended turn of the eighteenth century were certainly transatlantic if not global.

Finally, we return to the problem of borderlands. The parlor where Isaac Symbole received his mortal wounds was a place of conviviality where friends (up to a point) convened in the warmth of the fireplace, chatted and laughed over cards, drank wine, dined, and ultimately quarreled. The trial narratives speak selectively to objects central to the event, but almost certainly elide others. The witnesses in Elizabeth Symbole's trial repeatedly specified the parlor by name; those who took the stand for Jacob Regnier did not. We cannot know if Isaac and Elizabeth Symbole were in the vanguard of Londoners who embraced the new materiality of sociability on the rise, or if they played cards, supped, and drank in a room where the best bed stood as a physical connection to older, more familiar sociable modes. What we recognize, though, is that the Symboles occupied a larger liminal landscape where parlors appeared in various places in houses reflecting legion possibilities in the layout and design of their apartments, where borderlands entailed the interiority of the spatial imagination and the exteriority of the street, where objects served as signposts marking new territories and old assumptions. In the borderlands of London after the Fire, in the urban hinterlands, and around the North Atlantic network of cities and towns, the Symboles were not alone.

NOTES

1. John Summerson, *Georgian London* (New York: Scribner's, 1946), 22–35.

2. Elizabeth McKellar, *The Birth of Modern London: The Development and Design of the City, 1660–1720* (Manchester: Manchester University Press, 1999).

3. Peter Guillery, *The Small House in Eighteenth-Century London* (New Haven, Conn.: Yale University Press, for the Paul Mellon Centre for Studies in British Art, 2004), 38–77.

4. Book of Plans of City Lands and Bridge House Properties: vol. 1; ca. 1680–1720, CLA/008/EM/03/018 and Book of plans of City Lands and Bridge House Properties: vol. 2; c. 1680–1720, CLA/008/EM/03/019. City of London, London Metropolitan Archives.

5. "Elizabeth Symbole, Killing>Petty Treason," *The Proceedings of the Old Bailey Online*, reference number t16950220-18 (February 20, 1695), www.oldbaileyonline .org (July 8, 2015); and "Jacob Regnier, Killing>Murder," *The Proceedings of the Old Baily Online*, reference number t16950403-18 (April 3, 1695), www.oldbaileyonline.org (July 8, 2015).

6. "Elizabeth Symbole, Killing>Petty Treason."

7. "Parlour," *The Builder's Dictionary: or, Gentleman and Architect's Companion*, vol. 2 (Washington, D.C.: Association for Preservation Technology, 1981 facsimile reprint of the 1734 edition), n.p.

8. "Thomas Smith, Theft," *The Proceedings of the Old Bailey Online*, reference number t16880222-1 (February 22, 1688), www.oldbaileyonline.org (July 8, 2015); "John Adshed alias Davenport, Theft," *The Proceedings of the Old Bailey Online*, reference number t16980720-17(July 20, 1698), www.oldbaileyonline.org (July 8, 2015).

9. "Richard Whiting, Theft," *The Proceedings of the Old Bailey Online*, reference number t16880425-15 (April 25, 1688), www.oldbaileyonline.org (July 8, 2015).

10. Joseph Moxon, *Mechanick Exercises or the Doctrine of Handy-Works* (Scarsdale, N.Y.: Early American Industries Association, 1979 facsimile reprint of the 1703 edition), 265–67; Bernard L. Herman and Peter Guillery, "Negotiating Classicism in Eighteenth-Century Deptford and Philadelphia," *Articulating British Classicism: New Approaches to Eighteenth-Century Architecture (Reinterpreting Classicism: Culture, Reaction & Appropriation)*, ed. Elizabeth McKellar and Barbara Arciszewska (Oxford: Ashgate, 2004), 187–225.

11. Thomas Gadbury, Probate Inventory, Archdiocese of Middlesex, 1691, London Metropolitan Archives. Gadbury's parlor contained old leather chairs, a table, an old chest of drawers, a grate, a looking glass, household linen, and the deceased's clothing.

12. William Bernnard, Probate Inventory, Archdiocese of Middlesex, AM/PS (2) 1701/1707, London Metropolitan Archives, London.

13. Evan Jones, Probate Inventory, Archdiocese of Middlesex, 1691, London Metropolitan Archives, London.

14. Thomas Phill, Probate Inventory, Archdiocese of Middlesex, 1717/1718, London Metropolitan Archives, London.

15. Jane Borden, Probate Inventory, Archdiocese of Middlesex, 1717/1718, London Metropolitan Archives, London.

16. Definitions for parlor along with its etymology can be found at http://www.memidex.com/parlor (July 8, 2015).

17. David Shields, *Civil Tongues and Polite Letters in British America* (Chapel Hill: University of North Carolina Press for the Omohundro Institute of Early American History and Culture, 1997). For conversational fields, see Bernard L. Herman, "On Being German in North America," *Winterthur Portfolio* 45, no. 2/3 (Autumn 2011): 195–97.

12

PALLADIANISM AND THE VILLA
IDEAL IN SOUTH CAROLINA

THE TRANSATLANTIC PERILS
OF CLASSICAL PURITY

Lee Morrissey

Built between 1738 and 1742, Drayton Hall, outside Charleston, South Carolina, is an ideal subject for a book on the architecture of the British Atlantic world, as it illustrates tensions inherent in the transatlantic approach to early modern American and British history. The house was built for an English family who had moved to Carolina from Barbados; the family had been plantation owners in both colonies. In this way, Drayton's creation would seem to represent a classic transatlantic story for the British Atlantic world, combining as it does England, Africa, the Caribbean, and the southeastern edge of North America on the Atlantic coast. The house was built under the influence of English architectural publications and pattern books to an Anglo-Palladian standard (Fig. 12.1). It speaks, therefore, to a clear transatlantic effect expressed in architecture and design. But it also reveals the underlying regional complexities that accompany transatlantic approaches. This home was built with unpaid and racialized slave labor, on the edge of a swampy tidal marsh, in an area given to malaria outbreaks on the banks of the Ashley River (a principal waterway leading to Charleston and the Atlantic) (Fig. 12.2). While the home is impressively designed in the English Palladian style, it is done so relatively late compared to the English Palladian building boom for homes of its size and type. This delay, too, is part of the transatlantic experience, but it also needs to qualify how we understand transatlantic connections. Finally, as a home based on Palladian precedents, Drayton raises questions about the politics of such transatlantic forms. In this case, we are looking at an English colonial home derived from neo-Palladian books, published in England, but reworking neoclassical antecedents from an area outside republican Venice. Through Drayton, we can also see the limits of think-

FIGURE 12.1. *Drayton Hall, Ashley River, South Carolina. Daniel Maudlin.*

ing transatlantically about architecture, although that is also part of the value of Drayton, and of thinking transatlantically.

Rather than an exhaustive catalog of transatlantic Palladian buildings, I am interested in the dynamics within Palladianism that point to larger processes of the transatlantic experience in the early modern era. I begin, then, with an overview of the intellectual history and context for eighteenth-century transatlantic English Palladianism. There is, first, the delayed reception of the Italian architect, Andrea Palladio (1508–80), who died fifty years before the first English pioneering Palladian building was started. There is nearly another century before Palladian domestic architecture makes it to the western edge of the Atlantic, or the eastern seaboard of today's United States. This additional delay has many causes, including the English Civil Wars and Interregnum and the relatively slow circulation of English Palladian texts. There is, finally, a larger story of transatlanticism at issue, though, in the later arrival of English Palladianism in English-speaking North America: colonialism. Palladio's interpretation of Roman architecture carries with it a series of important associations; the purity of classical form and the independence of the villa are both reimagined in Palladio's works. During the seventeenth century in England, these associations added to Palladio's influence, initially

LEE MORRISSEY

FIGURE 12.2. *Rice fields on the Ashley River, Drayton plantation, South Carolina. Daniel Maudlin.*

for the easy importation of a classical ideal into an England that saw itself as culturally lagging behind the Continent, and, later, for an England concerned with the growing power of a centralized government and thus interested in an architecture of self-sufficiency.

But English Palladianism goes transatlantic as part of a colonial project; Drayton, for example, was built not only in one of Britain's colonies, but, even more specifically, as the manor house for a plantation relying on slave labor. By the time it gets to the New World, that is, the villa ideal requires exploitation of racialized unpaid workers. Of course, many landed estates in the British Isles were also made possible with money raised from slave plantations in the New World; Drayton was built with slave labor directly. The villa's independence, then, and its classical purity, take on new associations. For the architecture, the questions would focus on the extent to which the colonial use of Palladian architecture was consistent with, say, the Italian sense of it. But that focus would raise related questions about the transatlantic experience. Palladio had been working to imagine a mathematical architectural purity, one that could be potentially transferred universally. His architecture is transplanted, to England, and to the English colonies, and thus seems to achieve a universality, or at least an applicability outside Italy. Such a cultural transfer is consistent with transatlanticism. But insofar as the transfer coincides with the slave-owning plantations of the colonies, Palladian architecture raises the most important question of early modern English transatlanticism: to what extent was it a colonial project? To this end the cultural meanings embedded within a plantation house such as Drayton must be understood within the specific history of Carolina.

CAROLINA AND THE ATLANTIC WORLD

By focusing on a certain area of the British Atlantic, the coast of what is today South Carolina (but which was simply Carolina at the early part of the period covered by this book), I hope that this chapter might contribute to a metahistory of transatlantic history. For at least five hundred years trade routes have existed across the huge expanse of the Atlantic. Related to this transatlantic cross-fertilization, there is also an element of multiculturalism to the interest in transatlantic approaches to cultural history. A comparative approach to both sides of the Atlantic reveals a persistence of cultural patterns that belie familiar binaries between Europe and the Americas, or between Africa and the Americas. There is a process of identity politics and discovery that can follow from these revelations, that is, that the Atlantic is a space of cultural hybridity.[1]

Seventeenth- and eighteenth-century Carolina subverts many of the expectations that make transatlantic approaches feel as fresh as they do. From transatlantic wars to transatlantic globalization to multiculturalism, seventeenth- and eighteenth-century Carolina has it all and has it long before the post-World War II period that is thought to have sparked the current interest in transatlantic issues. Much of the attention in transatlanticism focuses on New England, the Northeast of today's United States, and the mid-Atlantic states, such as Pennsylvania and Virginia. From the eastern side of the Atlantic, this makes a certain amount of sense. Virginia and Massachusetts can each rightly vie for being the first English colony, with just a little more than a decade between their most famous English settlements, and with Plymouth, Massachusetts, offering the U.S. national narrative an origin story on the basis of which thanks are given on an annual holiday.[2] But it is to Carolina, or later the Carolinas, that we should look if we are to find the earlier examples of a fuller sense of transatlantic Britain, including a fuller sense of architecture in the British Atlantic world. Within the shape of today's Carolinas — a shape that was still being adjusted by the United States Supreme Court as recently as 1990 — there were the Native American populations, of course, and, in the sixteenth century, French and Spanish exploration and settlement, at Port Royal and Saint Helena. (Both settlements were abandoned, although the diseases that Europeans brought with them stayed and decimated the Native American population). These complexities within Carolina point to the wider complexities in transatlantic approaches to history. As Bernard Bailyn points out in *Atlantic History: Concepts and Contours* (2005), historians might be attracted to the possibility of reconsidering the Atlantic in a way similar to the approach Fernand Braudel took for the Mediterranean in his influential work, *The Mediterranean and the Mediterranean World in the Age of Philip II*.[3] However, a thoroughgoing transatlanticism would need to extend from the Cape of Good Hope on the southeastern side to the Arctic on the northeastern, and from Tierra del Fuego on the southwestern side to the Canadian maritime provinces and Arctic on the northwestern. In addition to the Native American and African histories thus involved, there would also need to be at least Dutch, English, French, Irish, Portuguese, Scottish, and Spanish perspectives on the Atlantic considered as a whole (not to mention, say, the Italian contribution to countries not governed from Italy). Through this diversity and complexity has arisen the practical need to subdivide Atlantic history into more specific histories—as in the parameters of subject, nation/empire, and time set for this book.

Today's North and South Carolina are two states within the north-south boundaries of a 1665 land grant Charles II made to eight Lords Proprietors, a grant originally intended to stretch westward to the Carolina Pacific. In the earlier seventeenth century, Royalist Sir John Colleton had gone to Barbados during the English Civil Wars and established a sugar plantation there using slave labor. Upon the Restoration of the Stuarts in 1660, Colleton returned to London, and was appointed to the Council for Foreign Plantations, through which he made influential contacts and, with them, a successful pitch for an English settlement on the southeastern coast of North America. In 1663, Charles II "granted a charter for the colony of Carolina that made the eight petitioners the 'true and absolute lords and proprietors' of the province."[4] The capital of this settlement would be on a peninsula between two rivers, named the Ashley and the Cooper (after Sir Anthony Ashley Cooper, one of the Lords Proprietor); and the town between them would be named Charlestown after the king (from whom the colony also took its name). The first constitution of Carolina was written for the Lords Proprietors, quite likely by a young John Locke. We shall see more of that constitution shortly, but for now I would point out that Carolina was the first of the English colonies to write racialized African slavery into its constitution. "Within the first year of colonization, enslaved Africans arrived in South Carolina via the West Indies."[5] By 1775, or over the next century, "forty percent of the Africans imported into North America came through Charleston."[6] At the same time, with a religiously tolerationist Constitution, open to "Jews, heathens, and other dissenters," Carolina would welcome Huguenots forced to flee France after the revocation of the Edict of Nantes and what would soon become the largest Jewish population in England's American colonies.[7] The result was "one of the more heterogeneous European populations in British North America," and an African population "coming from more than two dozen ethnic groups and speaking forty different languages."[8] This seventeenth-century history of Carolina has been obscured by the earlier experiments in, say, Virginia or the Massachusetts Bay Colony. In the process, though, we have misplaced another new England, which, in the seventeenth century could not have been Boston or Providence, both of which, filled with religious radicals, might as well be called New London (which, it turns out, is the name of towns in both Connecticut and New Hampshire). To find a place that replicated the seventeenth-century land, agricultural, and class systems of the late feudalism that characterized life outside the largest English metropolis, look to Carolina.

SLAVERY, LOCKE, AND THE
CONSTITUTION OF CAROLINA

The English moral philosopher John Locke (1632–1704) is probably most famous for his *Second Treatise of Government*, a text that circulated in manuscript form at the same time that Parliament was confronting James II in what has come to be known as The Glorious Revolution of 1688. However, considering Locke transatlantically raises important questions about the subsequent history of the two English-speaking sides of the Atlantic. With the *Second Treatise*, Locke explained how it was that a monarch could be chosen, rather than born. His argument has long been understood as providing a vision of modern social contract theory preferable to that offered four decades earlier by Thomas Hobbes. For Hobbes, the state of nature is a state of war; because we are equal, we have an equal chance of killing each other for our individual survival. And thus, according to Hobbes, we created a government, a sovereign, who can overawe us into a peaceful submission. In the *Second Treatise*, by contrast, Locke begins with a state of nature in which we lived peacefully, until, of course, someone accumulated too many acorns and thereby threatened the overall acorn supply. For Locke, we need government, then, to protect property, but also to create an artificial nature, in which we

LEE MORRISSEY

are peaceful again. For Hobbes, equality is the problem the sovereign solves; for Locke, government restores us to a peaceful, agreed-upon, and natural inequality. For this Locke, the Locke of the *Second Treatise*, Hobbes's state of nature is actually the state of war, and slavery. Government is created to restore, prosthetically, a state of nature in which we can live *agreeably*, and freely.

In short, the Locke we have come to know through the *Second Treatise* is read as part of England's development toward a modern democratic state, as a major theorist of property, participation, and choice. Largely overlooked in this portrait is the Locke of the transatlantic exchange, the Locke who worked with the Lords Proprietor of the colony of Carolina. *The Fundamental Constitutions of Carolina* begins, for example, by claiming that it had been written so as "to avoid erecting a numerous democracy" (211), a sharp contrast from the familiar Locke of modern democratic theory. Now, it may be that this claim is just a generic requirement in a preamble to a constitution for land that—Native Americans aside, of course—was a grant in a royal charter; the context might explain the initial avoidance of democracy, and the stated preference for a form of government "most agreeable to the monarchy" (211). But this is not merely a "rhetorical" gesture. With Charles's charter, the Lords Proprietors are taking their titles very seriously—they will be the Lords of Carolina: "The whole province shall be divided into counties; each county shall consist of eight signories, eight baronies, and four precincts; each precinct shall consist of six colonies" (211). Each of these titles— signories, baronies, and colonies—represented a related portion of land, twelve thousand acres apiece. They were to be arranged in a ratio, with one fifth for the proprietors, another for the "hereditary nobility" (211), leaving the remaining "three-fifths, amongst the people" (211).[9] From signories to baronies to the hereditary nobility, this is the vocabulary of feudalism, with power tied to the size of an individual's landholdings. For some commentators, *The Fundamental Constitutions* "is a cleverly written document designed to attract settlers," in which case, the "numerous references to land . . . would have been attractive to individuals in England and in the already crowded English West Indies" (Edgar, 43). That may be, but it does not, on the one hand, change the fact that the remaining three-fifths would be subdivided into smaller and smaller parcels by the increasing number of "the people," while the hereditary nobility would start with a substantial acreage advantage.

In a dramatic divergence from the familiar Lockean argument that slavery is the state of war continued, this constitution goes on to write slavery, slave-ownership, and voluntary multigenerational servitude into what we might call the fundamental constitution of the Carolinas. *The Fundamental Constitutions* includes a category of permanent servitude, the "leet-man," who "shall be under the jurisdiction of the respective lords of the said signory, barony, or manor, without appeal." But it does protect a capacity to choose, albeit a very strange kind of choosing: "Whoever shall voluntarily enter himself a leet-man, in the registry of the county court, shall be a leet-man." That is, *The Fundamental Constitutions of Carolina* protects a person's right to enter voluntarily into servitude, within which there is no appeal. And so agreeing means that "all the children of leet-men shall be leet-men, and so to all generations." Moreover, becoming a leet-man prevents one from leaving the land of one's lord without the approval "under hand and seal" of the lord to whom one can make no appeal (215). This sounds like voluntary feudalism, and an arrangement that creates voluntary slavery for presumably poor white settlers, although a recent history of South Carolina reminds us that "even if a person agreed to become a 'leetman,' or perpetual serf, he would be given 10 acres when married" (Edgar, 43). For these ten acres, he, the person he just married, and all the children their children would ever bring forth would live in continuous servitude to a lord from whom they could seek no appeal.

Having a founding constitution is itself a sharp departure from the history of the Massachusetts Bay Colony, whose Mayflower Compact does not rise to the level of specificity of the *Fundamental Constitutions of Carolina*. It is also profoundly different from the eastern side of the Atlantic, which, after 1776, will be thought not to have a constitution, but which from 1640 to 1660 was involved in a high-level discussion of how to acquire one (e.g., Thomas Hobbes's *Leviathan* [London, 1651], Marchamont Nedham's *The Excellencie of a Free State* [London, 1656], James Harrington's *The Commonwealth of Oceana* [London, 1656], and John Milton's *The Ready and Easy Way to Establish a Commonwealth* [London, 1660], among others), and did have two different ones during the 1650s. Considered transatlantically, or in terms of transatlantic exchanges, the question that comes to mind is why Locke would write slavery and feudalism into a colony on the western side of the Atlantic, while developing a theory of government designed to avoid slavery and to ground democracy on the eastern side of the Atlantic. For some, the difference between these two documents means that Locke's role in the *Fundamental Constitutions* was minimal; for others, it means that Locke learned from the experience and published an improvement two decades later. Others argue that Locke's two positions—one for Carolina and another for England—represent an emerging transatlantic double standard that would keep the bulk of slavery at a distance from the British Isles. By 1740, in "Rule, Britannia," James Thomson might have been summarizing fifty years of the Lockean tradition when he wrote that "Britons never shall be slaves." The question is whether that means Britain as a political entity is opposed to slavery, or whether it is the British as an ethnicity who will always be free.

DRAYTON HALL

Although *The Fundamental Constitutions* was never ratified, "a number of its provisions would be implemented de facto and be responsible for the rapid and successful development of South Carolina."[10] It was in this context that an English-born Barbadian planter named Thomas Drayton arrived in Charleston, in the first few decades of the new colony. By 1700, Drayton had set himself up on Magnolia Plantation about ten miles northwest of Charleston on the Ashley River. His son, John Drayton, purchased 350 acres of land to the south of his father's estate, still on the river. Probably in the late 1730s, John began to build Drayton Hall. By then, John Drayton had inherited a dozen of his father's slaves, and had begun purchasing others. These slaves would have built Drayton Hall, a two-story brick structure with a pitched roof and wings connected to an outbuilding on each side. Whether there was an architect involved is not known. Presumably, Drayton brought in craftsmen from England as well, "for no American-designed mansion could approach Drayton Hall's elegance and style," as one recent commentator on American domestic architecture has put it.[11] But the work of those craftsmen and Drayton's slaves would remain anonymous, visible only in the built result, a building whose first record is for the birth in Drayton Hall of the eldest surviving son of John Drayton's second marriage, September 20, 1742.[12]

Probably built sometime between the late 1730s and the early 1740s, Drayton Hall is considered "the first Palladian house in the United States."[13] In this word, "Palladian," the most visible and, I would add, perplexing transatlantic architectural feature of the house is found. During the first few decades of the eighteenth century, English architecture and English architectural publications underwent a renewed interest in the sixteenth-century Palladian villas of northern Italy, a Palladian revival. There are several interrelated reasons for this interest, all of them relevant for Drayton Hall. First, there is an interest in villas, generally. As we shall see, villas in eighteenth-century Britain were intended to represent independence or liberty. They also, therefore, represent a connection to classical Rome and Roman Augustan civic ideals. Second, by reviving the idea of the villa in the area outside Venice, Palladio confirmed an English interest in Venice as a well-managed republic, and—through Venice and the villa—back to the republican height of classical Rome. Third, there is an eighteenth-century interest in order, simplicity, and symmetry. These features of Palladian architecture were appealing in the early eighteenth century for aesthetic, political, and even scientific reasons. Aesthetically, they pointed to a classicizing way forward, out of the excesses of what we now call the baroque. To its enthusiastic defenders, Palladian architecture offered the same possibility to English politics, then still recovering from the complex consequences of its seventeenth-century civil wars. It is likely not a coincidence that the English two-party system emerges around the same time as the high point of neo-Palladian popularity—both simplified, organized, and provided the polarities that accompany symmetry. Finally, the English neo-Palladian interest in Palladio's stylized reimagining of a classical past also matched developments in Newtonian mechanics. Where Newton offered a reaction for every action, Palladian architecture offered an equal and opposite dimension for every aspect of each building.

THE VILLA IDEAL

In his buildings, Palladio tapped into and reinvigorated an older idea of the villa.[14] At once a building type, a way of siting a building, and a style of living, the villa is a form of domestic and agricultural architecture that is "rooted in the contrast of country and city."[15] Typically, the villa is in a livable, agricultural setting, close to the city, but far enough away from it that there can be a sense (or at least the possibility) of contemplation: "the self-sustaining agricultural estate [and] the villa . . . conceived primarily as a retreat."[16] Related to this sense of contemplation, there is also an idea of independence— the villa owner is apart from the city, and apart, in the English case, from the court politics that would often accompany well-to-do urban living in the seventeenth and eighteenth centuries. This independence built into the idea of the villa is increased by the villa's agricultural base; villas are meant to be agriculturally self-sufficient, ideally producing enough food for their residents. The fact is, of course, that if a villa were too remote, that would not work either. It is actually a certain proximity to the city that conveys the villa's sense of independence. Neither urban nor rustic, the villa's location is already a kind of balance, indicating a combination of the sophistication of the city and the relaxation of the country. The villa offers what J. G. A. Pocock calls "a politics of style accompanied by a morality of politeness."[17]

To its defenders in the neo-Palladian architectural revival, the form of the Palladian villa represented an ideal distance, or disinterestedness. Distinguished by an almost obsessive search for formal simplicity, through both the seeming simplicity of life in the villa and the formal arrangement of its architectural elements, early eighteenth-century British architectural theory focused on Palladio. In early eighteenth-century England, Palladio was not Palladio the builder, and was only sometimes Palladio the author of the *Four Books*; for the neo-Palladian revival, "Palladio" and Palladianism ultimately constituted metonymies for simplifying and standardizing. Palladio's contribution was to reinterpret terms such as Vitruvius's "analogia" and Alberti's "harmony" into what we today call "symmetry," understood principally as reflection on either side of an axis. His villas, arranged around a central vertical axis, on either side of which the rooms "strictly reflect each other," simplified symmetry.[18] At the same time, it was not lost on early eighteenth-century English observers that in Palladio's villas the placement of the living quarters and the farmhouse "emphasized the formal separation of the two domains, which were not to compete against each other in their aesthetic claims, despite their mutual unity."[19] With Palladio, even what was brought together was kept apart, and "symmetry" was one way of achieving this unified separation.

In letters, the eighteenth-century English version of this older villa ideal can be seen in the work of Alexander Pope. In 1724, Pope wrote to Martha Blount about the estate of Lord Digby, where the fifth Lord Digby was then revamping the castle and grounds of his family at Sherborne. Pope's disparaging comments about other castles spring from his embrace of the villa ideal: "I cannot make the reflection I've often done upon contemplating the beautiful Villas of Other Noblemen, rais'd upon the Spoils of plunder'd nations, or aggrandiz'd by the wealth of the Publick. I cannot ask myself the question, 'What Else has this man to be liked? What else has he cultivated or improv'd? What good, or what desirable thing appears of him, without these walls?'"[20] Pope believes that the villa should be part of a benevolent political arrangement, contributing to the civic life of its area. In this, he was not alone, for the villa was seen as a powerful political alternative. Because of its comparatively modest scale, and its potential for agricultural self-sufficiency, "the villa was perceived as one instrument by which the middle class might emulate and challenge the privilege of the aristocracy and gentry."[21] Whereas the seventeenth-century had the larger "Country Seat" as "the physical manifestation of complex political and economic theory and policy," the early eighteenth-century interest in the villa was an architectural expression of a new ideal of balance. [22] They may have been more expensive and more landed than what many people lived in, but during the first decades of the eighteenth century, England recognized that villas such as

Marble Hill, Chiswick House, and Pope's Twickenham were smaller than and therefore preferable to the massive "prodigy houses" such as Blenheim Palace or Houghton Hall; the decision to build a smaller, Palladian villa conveyed an impression of the owner's separation from court politics.[23]

James Gibbs, the English author of an influential eighteenth-century architectural treatise on colonial American public architecture, claims that he can provide *rules for drawing . . . in a more exact and easy manner . . . by which all FRACTIONS . . . are avoided*, according to the title of his 1732 book.[24] It is one thing to offer a method of architectural drawing that supposedly avoids fractions, but it is another thing to claim doing so will be "more exact." Gibbs seems to confuse simplicity and exactness, but his exacting avoidance of fractions is consistent with an implication throughout several of the Palladian publications. Gibbs's Palladian "fractions" figuratively describe political factions, and Palladianism held out the possibility of creating a more uniformly proportioned community that moved beyond fractions. Most explicit in this regard is Robert Morris, who argues for an architecture in which "beautiful and harmonious Productions aris[e] from . . . the agreeable Symmetry and Concordance of every particular separate Member, centred and united on the oeconomy of the Whole . . . regulated . . . in a due Proportion."[25] Although Morris's argument replays the terms of Vitruvian classicism—"harmonious," "Symmetry," "Concordance," and "Proportion"—he significantly adds "the oeconomy as a whole." This version of classicism shifts the focus to the economy, using symmetry as a claim for the appropriate way to organize civil society. The Palladian theory of the simplified and the uniform, "centred and united on the oeconomy of the Whole," offered a standardization of political (and cultural) life that could recreate a national community thought to have been lost in the upheavals of the seventeenth century.

Early eighteenth-century English Palladian preferences circulated widely through books. There were books by English Palladian enthusiasts and a new English translation of Palladio's own book about architecture. Indeed, there was a boom in British architectural publications. Between 1556 and 1700, only fifty-six new architectural titles were published in England—only one new book every three years.[26] Geoffrey Richards's 1663 translation of Palladio refers to "the scarcity of Books of architecture in English."[27] Not only was the output slow, but, as Hanno-Walter Kruft puts it, "Few works of any significance appeared in England in the seventeenth century."[28] In the eighteenth century, however, all that changed. "The eighteenth century was a Golden Age of architectural publications," according to John Wilton-Ely.[29] Fifty-six new architectural titles were published during just the first three decades of the eighteenth century, something that had taken the preceding century and a half; whereas it had previously taken an average of three years for one title, the early eighteenth century saw two new architecture books every year. The first third of the eighteenth century saw such important works as Colen Campbell's *Vitruvius Britannicus* (London, 1715), James Gibbs's *Book of Architecture* (London, 1728), so influential in the American colonies, and Robert Morris's theoretical treatise *Essay in Defense of Ancient Architecture* (London, 1728). It is with reference to such works that Hanno-Walter Kruft has recently argued that "although . . . England's contribution to architectural theory dates only from the beginning of the eighteenth century, it immediately acquired a position of virtual dominance in Europe."[30]

DRAYTON HALL AND THE TRANSATLANTIC APPROACH

In terms of the above publications and the cultural history that shaped it, Drayton is a transatlantic product, and one that can also begin to prompt a reexamination of transatlantic approaches. It is a long-standing and familiar grievance in colonial American history that the so-called New England of the northeastern United States dominates the historical American narrative, overlooking, as a result, the earlier arrival of the Spanish in the Southeast and Southwest, or the French along the Mississippi or the St. Lawrence. Although comparative, such a transatlantic focus would do little to help us reimagine national stories in either the United Kingdom or the United States if the existing tendency to coalesce around London and the "Pilgrims" of the northeastern United States were to continue. A building such as Drayton can redirect transatlantic attention southwards, not only for its Palladian architecture, but also for the political claim that this building makes on the landscape. On the one hand, as a villa, and a Palladian villa at that, Drayton Hall represents a triumph of order, simplicity, and symmetry (maybe more so over the natural forces all around it than would have been the case in northern Italy or London). Moreover, Drayton has that distance from the city suitable for the independence that the villa is meant to represent. Built by a wealthy farmer able both to acquire, transatlantically, the books that were informing the English Palladian movement, and to build a superb Palladian mansion, John Drayton's building taps into the then-current idea of the villa as a place of letters, a setting for urbane conviviality, and a retreat from the urban with views of nature to show for it.

Drayton Hall engages each of these transatlantic developments: in politics, in architecture, and in publishing. To start with the latter, "In 2009, the Drayton Library Catalog was discovered within the Drayton manuscript collection," and it contained "references to seven popular eighteenth-century architectural books."[31] From the handwritten short-title catalog that was discovered, it turns out that the library at Drayton Hall included John Evelyn's *A Parallel of Ancient Architecture with the Modern* (1664), Colen Campbell's *Vitruvius Britannicus* (1715), William Halfpenny's *Art of Sound Building* (1725), James Gibbs's, *A Book of Architecture, Containing Designs of Buildings and Ornaments* (1728), William Salmon's, *Palladio Londinensis* (1734), Isaac Ware's, *The Four Books of Andrea Palladio's Architecture* (1738), and Batty Langley's, *The London Prices of Bricklayers Materials and Works* (1748).[32] That is, this brick building on the edge of a tidal river, surrounded by swamp marshes on the southwestern edge of the British Atlantic, had collected the most popular textbooks of London's Palladian movement (a list that also happens to include some of the largest and most expensive architecture books of the day). Ultimately, we don't know whether any of these particular volumes were consulted in the design of the house. But Drayton seems to have been influenced by illustrations from Ware's 1738 edition of Palladio's *Four Books*. Usually, Drayton is thought to have been modeled on Palladio's *Villa Pisani* (in Montagnana), but there are several examples of two-story pedimented façades in the *Four Books* that might relate to Drayton: Plate XL, and Plate L stand out (Fig. 12.3). Inside the house, further evidence of British architectural publication can be seen, most famously in the overmantel on the first floor, which would seem to be influenced by designs from either William Kent's 1727 *Designs of Inigo Jones* or Gibbs's *Book of Architecture* (1728) (Figs. 12.4 and 12.5).[33]

At the same time, though, there is much about Drayton Hall that serves to accentuate its distance and difference from the English Palladian buildings. First, this extraordinary building was directly built by slave labor: anonymous, racialized slave labor. Of course, fortunes were made on both sides of the Atlantic from the slave trade, and slave labor helped make British great houses possible. However, as Laurie Ossman puts it, "Whether Drayton brought trained craftsmen to the site or hired others to train them on the job, it is certain that Drayton Hall was not only built of bricks molded, fired, and set by enslaved people but also finished with fine carving, carpentry, glazing, plasterwork, and surface treatments created, in large part, by enslaved artisans."[34] Ossman probably means to imply this, but it is worth specifying: those bricks were molded, fired, and set by slaves in the heat and humidity of the South Carolina coast, in which malaria was endemic. Moreover, differences between this building and the Palladian buildings in the British Isles also point to its distance from the center of the Palladian movement, if not

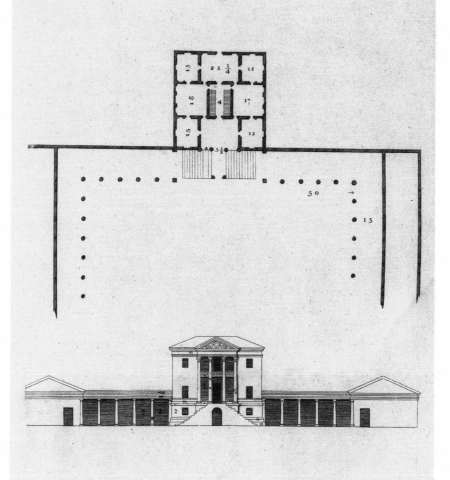

FIGURE 12.3. *Plate XL, Book 2. Isaac Ware's 1738 edition of Andrea Palladio's* The Four Books of Architecture. *Courtesy of the Winterthur Library: Printed Book and Periodical Collection.*

W. Kent invt.   H. Flitcroft Delin.   P. Fourdrinier sculp.

FIGURE 12.4. *Plate 64, William Kent's 1728* The Designs of Inigo Jones.
Courtesy of the Winterthur Library: Printed Book and Periodical Collection.

FIGURE 12.5. *Overmantle after Kent, first floor, Drayton Hall. Daniel Maudlin.*

from the center of the British Atlantic world itself. Archaeological research indicates that the family shared in the eighteenth-century interest in chinoiserie, investing in fine painted porcelain from China. Similarly, the quantity of lead crystal table glass found on the site indicates the wealth of the family.[35] Both collections would have been true of wealthy families in England. However, in the case of Drayton, "trade artifacts are made up exclusively of Colonial-Indian ceramics."[36] That is, the ceramics at Drayton also reflect the home's participation in Native American trade networks.

There are so many of these Native American ceramics that the archaeological report on Drayton records a range of theories, including whether such ceramics were bought only for slaves, or whether they were also for the kitchen (as opposed to the public spaces in the house). But the most obvious point is also the most important and most transatlantic: among early eighteenth-century British Palladian houses, Drayton would be among those few that combine African on-site slave labor and locally acquired Native American ceramics, precisely because it is a Palladian building not in England, but instead on the western side of the Atlantic. Similarly, although the first floor overmantle discussed above was Palladian in design, it was carved from local wood that was then painted; it was not, in other words, fine Italian marble. For Ossman, this imitation "not only had the advantage of style but also tacitly asserted the ability of American craftsmen and materials to 'keep up.'"[37] Actually, though, both the materials and the timing of the building indicate the difficulty of keeping up with architectural developments in England. By 1747, or five years after Drayton Hall is thought to have been completed, Horace Walpole had leased the building at Strawberry Hill, which, by 1750, he would begin to convert into an imitation miniature Gothic castle. That is, the aesthetic and cultural preferences that undergird the Palladian love of order were in the process of being displaced just as Drayton Hall was being completed. In that context, it would be difficult for Lowcountry planters to "keep up." It would take more time for Southern Gothic to develop (although, when it did, it was as successful in its own way as Drayton had been with the Palladian).

Drayton Hall and early South Carolina serve as examples of transatlantic British similarities in the seventeenth and eighteenth centuries—they point toward transatlantic continuities. The same is true, though, in the differences between Drayton and English Palladianism—they point toward transatlantic discontinuities. These differences are also made visible by transatlantic approaches, in the way that comparisons invite contrasts. But those contrasts point to limitations in transatlanticism as well. From the perspective of early

South Carolina—given its important spot on the Atlantic triangle trade—transatlanticism looks a lot like globalization, and its specifically Atlantic character can become effaced, as it emerges as one part of a larger set of global trade patterns. From the perspective of Drayton Hall, a building as Palladian as Horace Walpole's Strawberry Hill is Gothic, the transatlantic approach to architecture invites seeing architectural styles as simulacra, with one participant in the Atlantic facet of a globalizing trade network building what is supposed to be a villa descended from classical Rome. The question, then, is whether the villa ideal has ever been about independence and liberty (as it would be understood in the English discussion of it) or whether it has always been connected to emerging empires, as the example of Rome would suggest. In that sense, then, does Drayton make a claim about a new Roman empire, this one transatlantic?

NOTES

1. For example, in March 2012, a group from Guinea, West Africa, visited Drayton Hall, accompanied by an anthropologist from the University of South Carolina. The visiting delegation reported recognizing the South Carolina sweet grass baskets as similar to ones still used today in West Africa. See George McDaniel, "Guineans Visit the Lowcountry," *The Drayton Hall Diaries: The Official Blog of Drayton Hall*, April 26 2012, http://draytonhall.wordpress.com/2012/04/26/guineans-come-to-the-lowcountry/ (June 23, 2015).

2. There is even an early American architecture and literature connection, as Massachusetts was also home to the first English-language poet in the New World, Anne Bradstreet, who wrote a poem, "Here follows Some Verses Upon the Burning of Our House July 10th, 1666. Copied out of a Loose Paper," in *The Works of Anne Bradstreet*, ed. Jeanine Hensley (Cambridge, Mass.: Belknap Press, 1967), 292–93.

3. Bernard Bailyn, *Atlantic History: Concept and Contours* (Cambridge: Harvard University Press, 2005), 4.

4. Walter Edgar, *South Carolina: A History* (Columbia: University of South Carolina Press, 1998), 39.

5. Ibid., 63.

6. Ibid., 67.

7. John Locke, "The Fundamental Constitutions of Carolina," in *John Locke: Political Writings*, ed. David Wootton (Indianapolis: Hackett, 1993), 210–32 (228). All subsequent citations come from this edition and will be cited parenthetically in the body of the text.

8. Edgar, *South Carolina*, 50, 71.

9. It is difficult not to hear in this ratio the later Constitutional compromise over slavery, which was reached by deciding to count the slaves as three-fifths of a person, so that the disenfranchised blacks of the American South did not outweigh the white popu-

lation of the North. *The Fundamental Constitutions of Carolina* claims that with this particular ratio "the balance of the government may be preserved."

10. Edgar, *South Carolina*, 42.

11. Gerald Foster, *American Houses: A Field Guide to the Architecture of the Home* (New York: Mariner Books, 2004), 152.

12. Lynne G. Lewis, *Drayton Hall: Preliminary Archaeological Investigation at a Low Country Plantation* (Washington, D.C.: Preservation Press, The National Trust for Historical Preservation, 1978), 1.

13. Foster, *American Houses*, 152.

14. On the villa ideal, see Colin Rowe, *The Mathematics of the Ideal Villa* (Cambridge, Mass.: MIT Press, 1982) and James Ackerman, *The Villa: Form and Ideology of a Country House* (Princeton, N.J.: Princeton University Press, 1990). In this section, I draw directly from my 1999 book, *From the Temple to the Castle: An Architectural History of British Literature, 1660–1760* (Charlottesville: University Press of Virginia), particularly pages 6, 64, 67, and 70–71.

15. Ackerman, *The Villa*, 12.

16. Ibid., 15.

17. J. G. A. Pocock, *Virtue, Commerce, and History: Essays on Political Thought and History, Chiefly in the Eighteenth Century* (New York: Cambridge University Press, 1988), 236.

18. George L. Hersey and Richard Freedman, *Possible Palladian Villas: (Plus a Few Instructively Impossible Ones)* (Cambridge, Mass.: MIT Press, 1992), 15.

19. Richard Bentman and Michael Müller, *The Villa as Hegemonic Architecture*, trans. Tim Spence and David Craven (Atlantic Highlands, N.J.: Humanities Press, 1992), 29.

20. Pope to Martha Blount, June 15, 1724, in *The Correspondence of Alexander Pope*, vol. 2, ed. George Sherburn (Oxford: Clarendon Press, 1956), 239.

21. Ackerman, *The Villa*, 214.

22. Jules Lubbock, *The Tyranny of Taste: The Politics of Architecture and Design in Britain, 1550–1960* (New Haven: Yale University Press, 1995), 55, 61.

23. Ibid. For more on eighteenth-century English Palladian architecture, see the third chapter of Morrissey, *From the Temple to the Castle*.

24. James Gibbs, *Rules for drawing the several parts of architecture, in a more exact and easy manner . . . by which all fractions, in dividing the principal members and their parts, are avoided* (London, 1732).

25. Robert Morris, *An Essay in Defense of Ancient Architecture* (London, 1728), 14.

26. See the "Chronological Index of Titles and Editions," in Eileen Harris, *British Architectural Books and Writers, 1556–1785* (Cambridge: Cambridge University Press, 1990), 513–32. This figure includes various editions of translations of works by Continental architects (such as Fréart, Palladio, Scamozzi, Serlio, and Vignola), not to mention the assorted "builder's companions" explaining measurement, such as John Brown, *Description and Use of Joynt-Rule* (London, 1661).

27. Andrea Palladio, *The First Book of Architecture*, trans. Geoffrey Richards (London, 1663), unnumbered preface.

28. Hanno-Walter Kruft, *A History of Architectural Theory: From Vitruvius to the Present* (New York: Zwemmer/Princeton Architectural Press, 1994), 232.

29. John Ely-Wilton, "The Rise of the Professional Architect," in *The Architect: Chapters in the History of the Profession*, ed. Spiro Kostof (Oxford: Oxford University Press, 1977), 188.

30. Kruft, *Architectural Theory*, 229.

31. Patricia Ann Lowe, *Volumes That Speak: The Architectural Books of the Drayton Library Catalogue and the Design of Drayton Hall*. (M.A. thesis, Clemson University, 2010), ii.

32. Ibid., 51.

33. See Laurie Ossman, *Great Houses of the South*, photography by Steven Brooks (New York: Rizzoli, 2010), 28; and Lowe, *Volumes That Speak*, 33-36.

34. Ossman, *Great Houses of the South*, 28.

35. Lewis, *Drayton Hall*, 109.

36. Ibid., 62.

37. Ossman, *Great Houses*, 28.

13

POLITICS AND PLACE-MAKING
ON THE EDGE OF EMPIRE

LOYALISTS, HIGHLANDERS, AND THE
EARLY FARMHOUSES OF BRITISH CANADA

Daniel Maudlin

This final chapter is concerned with place-making in the maritime landscape of Nova Scotia through the very human activities of housebuilding and homemaking. In the eighteenth century, Nova Scotia was a heavily forested peninsula surrounded by the North Atlantic Ocean on the northern edge of the British Empire (Fig. I.1). Yet, the colony was at the center of international politics as a contested territory where the British and French North American empires collided. Accordingly, Nova Scotia was heavily fortified, by the French at Louisburg in Cape Breton, by the British at Annapolis Royal, Halifax, and elsewhere; but it was also settled as farms and small towns were carved out of the forest. Settlement, as managed by the French and British governments in Nova Scotia, was part of a wider political-military strategy to secure the long-term ownership of the province, and was modeled after the Roman system of *coloniae* where settlements were established in conquered territories. The British removed the French troops and French Acadian settlers to establish their own settlements with populations of New Englanders, Highland Scots, and others.

However, this was not place-making. If settlement in Nova Scotia was a government-approved project of dividing the land into lots, gifting or selling that land, and, importantly, registering deeds of ownership, place-making was the subsequent process by which new landowners made their lot their home: turning forests into farms, the unfamiliar into the familiar. Place-making in Nova Scotia was a state of mind, whereby settlers began to think of their square of heavily forested land not as the unknown to be tamed—and feared—but as a home within a community of friends and neighbors doing familiar things and sharing familiar concerns. A first step was to build a house. Building a house on your land was, of course, a practical priority. A house provided shelter for people and, at first, animals and stores. It had to be weatherproof and it had to have a good hearth, because Nova Scotia in winter is extremely cold. However, a house had to do much more than provide shelter; it had to make its occupants feel at home. Feeling at home required the construction of buildings that reflected the identity, the self-image, the values, and the beliefs of their occupants. So, the central question of this chapter is, in the politically tense atmosphere of early modern Nova Scotia, what values did the typical settler choose to express through his or her home? What we find is that while settlement in Nova Scotia was a highly politicized process, place-making as represented in building homesteads was actually dominated by the practicalities of clearing the land, farming, and the social concerns of being modern, fashionable, and demonstrating good taste. By their presence, settlers in Nova Scotia were implicitly engaged with colonial politics, but the home was not the medium by which this was expressed. Whereas a public building such as a courthouse may have flown the flag, carried the royal coats of arms, or displayed portraits of the king, the home, in its forms and furnishings, was genteelly British, reflecting good taste and politeness rather than patriotism or national identity — which did not, however, preclude a tastefully hung wall featuring a rude cartoon of Louis XV or George Washington. Perhaps more so because they lived in a political edgeland, settlers dwelt in modern but modest homes that avoided overt political statements in favor of British good taste and material comfort. Across the province, and from one ethnic and subcultural group to the next, these early modern homes are defined by the sameness of their design, suggesting a high degree of social cohesion. In these Nova Scotian homes eighteenth-century rituals of politeness were acted out in spaces like the parlor where the occupants' good taste was read in the visual language of classical architectural ornament and in objects such as blue-and-white china tea sets.

THE POLITICS OF SETTLEMENT IN
EARLY MODERN NOVA SCOTIA

Notwithstanding the frozen ocean and endless forest, the ordinary houses of Nova Scotia were built in an unusual place. Nova Scotia was the first and last landfall in mainland North America on the northern passage to and from Britain. It was the sentinel guarding the mouth of the St. Lawrence River and access to the Great Lakes and the North American interior. Enclosing the Gulf of Maine, Nova Scotia was only a short distance from the heart of

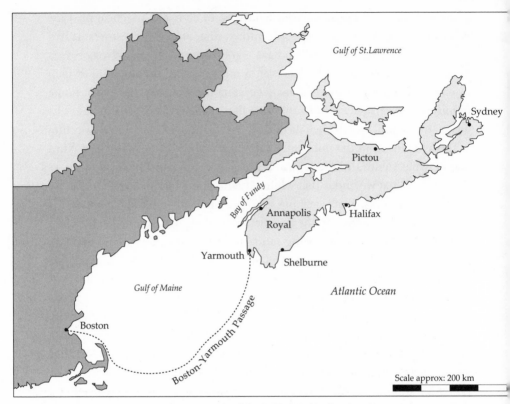

FIGURE 13.1. *Map of the Gulf of Maine showing the passage from Boston to Yarmouth. Author.*

colonial New England (Fig. 13.1). Because of its extraordinary strategic importance, settlement in Nova Scotia was closely related to Britain's political struggles over Canada, first with France and later with the United States. The British under General Wolfe famously defeated the French on the Plains of Abraham before the walls of Quebec City in 1759, heralding the beginning of the end for New France, the birth of British Canada, and an end to the global, European-imperial conflict that was the Seven Years' War. In the Treaty of Paris, the French formally ceded their northern North American territories to the British (while Spain gained Louisiana). For both the French and the British, settlement by pioneer farmers and homesteaders was part of a wider, planned political process of territorial conquest and control of Canada, as farmers and their families threw down deeper roots than soldiers; farmers and homesteaders changed the land, built homes, and turned territories into places as communities were established and grew, making Canada a British place rather than simply contested territory on which British soldiers fought or built fortifications. As such, pioneering farming families in Nova Scotia, the land they worked, and the buildings they built need to be understood as part of a greater equation that included a large, ongoing military presence and extensive military installations, such as the French superfort of Louisbourg on Cape Breton at the northern tip of Nova Scotia (lost to the British in 1758); the British citadel of Fort George that dominated the provincial capital of Halifax; the garrison fort of Annapolis Royal guarding the settled Annapolis Valley and the Bay of Fundy toward New Brunswick and Maine; and numerous smaller forts throughout the province.

The geopolitical consequences of a British victory in the Seven Years' War directly and immediately affected settlement patterns and settlers in Nova Scotia. The disbandment of French forces and the pulling down of Fort Louisbourg was part of the same strategy of conquest and pacification that also saw the expulsion of the French Acadians from Nova Scotia and Isle Saint-Jean (renamed Prince Edward Island), as lamented by Longfellow in the epic poem *Evangeline*. The Acadians, who had first settled in maritime Canada in the early seventeenth century, had extensively cleared and improved the land, building dykes, draining land, and cultivating crops. From the late 1750s they were uprooted and forcibly cleared from their farms by British troops and their lands given to British (often British American) colonists, including military veterans of the Seven Years' War. Many Acadians resettled in Louisiana where they became known as Cajuns. From the North Shore to the Annapolis Valley, almost no trace of Acadian homes, buildings, and material culture were left by the British forces who, through a policy of house-burning, made an apparent *tabula rasa* for new British settlers (Acadian dikes and tilled fields were left and put to use).

After 1763 the Canadian maritime provinces (and Quebec) briefly became Britain's northernmost North American territory, creating an unbroken chain of East Coast colonies down to Florida (ceded to Spain under the Treaty of Paris). Within the Atlantic network of ports, towns, and farmlands, Nova Scotia was an extension of New England with a similar environment, climate, people, and material culture. Beyond North America, Nova Scotia's position within the wider British Atlantic world was reflected in the coverage of newspapers such as the *Halifax Gazette*, which regularly covered stories from locations such as London, Edinburgh, Glasgow, Dublin, Boston, New York, Philadelphia, Williamsburg, Charleston, Bermuda, and the Caribbean. Post-1763 Nova Scotia was settled by a mixture of British subjects including veterans of the Seven Years' War—emigrants from England, Ireland, and Scotland—as well as some Germans, but most of all Nova Scotia was settled by New Englanders expanding northward.

The process of surveying and laying out regular lots in British colonial settlements in Nova Scotia was not an anarchic wilderness land-grab but a well-ordered government-monitored business, often run by British American companies.[1] For example, land in the Pictou area of northern Nova Scotia, was divided into regular lots and sold by the Philadelphia Grant Company. These lots were adjacent to a military veteran settlement owned and run by the British government. Land grants, each of about two hundred acres, were often subdivided and sold to settlers by speculative land developers. Lots were distributed along the coast, along the course of rivers, and around the shores of lakes according to accessibility, as initially the whole region was densely forested and traveling to new grants was only possible by water. However, the period of orderly government-monitored settlement in the 1760s and 1770s was disrupted and overwhelmed by new political instability: the American War of Independence or American Revolutionary War of 1775-1783. American independence fundamentally changed the map of Britain's Atlantic colonies, creating a new nation state between British Canada and the British Caribbean.

American independence had two significant outcomes for settlement in Nova Scotia. First, the loyalist exodus from New England saw thousands of pro-British British Americans emigrating to Nova Scotia in the late eighteenth century, where the scale of migration imprinted a dominant New England material culture on the province's towns and farm settlements into which other migrant groups from Britain were assimilated. Second, subsequent to American independence emigration to North America from Britain meant British maritime Canada was the first option, forging an intensely British frontier identity for settlers in Nova Scotia. The immigration of loyalist political refugees from New England and, later, economic migrants from Scotland plot two distinct migrant pathways within the British Atlantic world: regional or sub-Atlantic coastal migration and transatlantic intercontinental migration—neither of which passed through southern England (and London), the titular center or hub of empire. It is estimated that in 1763 the population of the province of Nova Scotia stood at 13,374, of which over half—in other words the largest cultural group—had come from New England, principally Connecticut.[2] The second largest group were English settlers; for example, in the brief period of 1772-1774, a thousand settlers emigrated from Yorkshire to Cumberland County in central Nova Scotia near the border with New Brunswick.

Therefore, the population of the province was massively swelled by the loyalist exodus from New England in 1783, following American independence. Nova Scotia was a clear choice for loyalists leaving New England as it was by far the closest landfall on British soil. Crossing the Gulf of Maine from Boston to Yarmouth at the southern end of Nova Scotia, a distance of 295 nautical miles, took two and a half days (at an average speed of five knots), a short hop for eighteenth-century sailing times. Between 1783 and 1785, fifteen thousand loyalists landed at Halifax alone. New port towns such as Digby, Shelburne, and Sydney were established by loyalists, with the support of the British government, and the populations here rapidly grew to several thousand strong. From these initial ports of arrival, settlers dispersed within a few years to locations throughout Nova Scotia: to small towns and farms in the Annapolis Valley, to the Bay of Fundy and to northeastern counties such as Pictou and Antigonish (the population of Shelburne, for example, peaked at ten thousand in 1785 but had dwindled to three hundred by 1818). By 1815 the population of Nova Scotia had risen to seventy-five thousand, a six-fold increase from 1763.[3] For the British, loyalists provided a substantial, instant population of fiercely patriotic and experienced settlers from across the social spectrum—farmers, fishermen, builders, furniture-makers, innkeepers, lawyers, doctors: a ready-made society. For the settlers, life in Nova Scotia, where the environment is similar to New England, provided cultural continuity—the continuum of British American culture that had evolved over a century and a half. That there is little distinction between the houses built in Nova Scotia and New England in the decades immediately after 1783 demonstrates the strength of the common anglophone material culture over political divisions. The loyalist exodus to Nova Scotia after 1783 created a New England-style landscape of small independent farms and small towns into which later waves of immigrants were assimilated.

By the early nineteenth century, the shifting political sands that surrounded Nova Scotia had created a place that was singular in terms of its geopolitical significance but which produced a material culture indistinguishable from that of New England and very similar to that produced and consumed throughout the British Atlantic world. After the loyalist exodus from New England had subsided and settlers had dispersed, the second wave of immigrants came from Britain, especially Highland Scotland. Between 1815 and 1838, 39,243 settlers disembarked at the ports of Halifax, Sydney, and Pictou;

of this total, the majority—21,833—had embarked in Scotland.[4] Prior to 1783 pockets of Scottish Highland settlement had been established in Georgia, North Carolina, and the Mohawk and Hudson valleys of New York.[5] Emigration to North America from Scotland increased rapidly in the late eighteenth century.[6] However, settlement by Highlanders—Scottish Gales—increased exponentially in the early nineteenth century as clearances (forced evictions) of Highland estates reached their peak back in Scotland.[7] While—like the English, Irish, and Welsh—Lowland Scots emigrated as lone craftsmen, entrepreneurs, or pioneer family units, Highlanders emigrated *en masse* as clan-based kinship groups dominating the North Shore region of Nova Scotia. In the Scottish Highlands extended family groups of Gaels lived in irregularly clustered settlements known as *clachans*. The clachan was at the center of traditional (though not legally held) communal farms and pasturelands. This contrasted with the legally owned lots (typically owned by the male head of household) of individual settlers in Nova Scotia, forcing to some extent a turn from communal thinking to individual- or family-oriented thinking. Perhaps connected to this shift to property ownership, despite a strong, distinct, even insular Gaelic subculture that continued to be nurtured in language and music, housebuilding Highlanders in Nova Scotia, like the Irish and English, abandoned their traditional forms in favor of the modern house type already established by New Englanders.

THE NEW ENGLAND HOUSE IN NOVA SCOTIA

Overwhelmingly, early Nova Scotian farmhouses are one-and-a-half-story buildings, rectangular in plan and symmetrical in elevation, either three or five bays wide, with a regular arrangement of rectangular windows, door, and chimney.[8] Ross Farm, New Ross, Lunenburg County, in central Nova Scotia to the south of Halifax, is a good example of this standard building type (Fig. 13.2). Ross Farm was built in 1817 by Captain William Ross, born in Nova Scotia, who was one of 172 soldiers disbanded from the Nova Scotia Fencible Infantry at the end of the Napoleonic War in 1816.[9] The typical floor plan, as at Ross Farm, is a rectangle divided into three internal spaces that broadly correspond with the tripartite main elevation (Fig. 13.3). The internal partition walls then further break up these three internal spaces: either into a four-room arrangement, of two rectangular rooms to each outer space—one to the front and one to the back—flanking the central space, which contains the staircase, central chimney stack, and entrance hall; or into a three-room arrangement, with a large kitchen occupying the entire rear of

DANIEL MAUDLIN

FIGURE 13.2. *Ross Farm, New Ross, Lunenburg County, Nova Scotia. Author.*

the house (Fig. 13.4). The stairs are accessed either directly from the lobby to the front, or from a back kitchen whenever the staircase is located to the rear of the chimney stack. The ground floor rooms follow the eighteenth-century "polite" formal arrangement of parlors and kitchen, with livestock removed to a barn or field enclosure. Internal lath and plaster was commonly employed, even in rural regions of Nova Scotia, from the late eighteenth century onward. In addition to this, moldings were applied to internal doors, window frames, fire surrounds, skirting, and dado rails in formal rooms such as the parlor—the central space of British Atlantic domestic life (Fig. 13.5). Many houses also feature a small, single-story extension to the side or rear, known as an "ell," which was used as a summer kitchen. The summer kitchen was a specific adaptation to the environment of Nova Scotia and the extreme temperature differences across the year; that is, too hot to cook—and too many flies—in the main house during high summer while the uninsulated space was too cold for inhabitation in the frozen winters. Most farms also featured a timber-framed barn. These were simple, rectangular-plan, gabled buildings that were erected adjacent to farmhouses. The primary purpose of such barns was to house the farmer's livestock, especially in winter, including chickens,

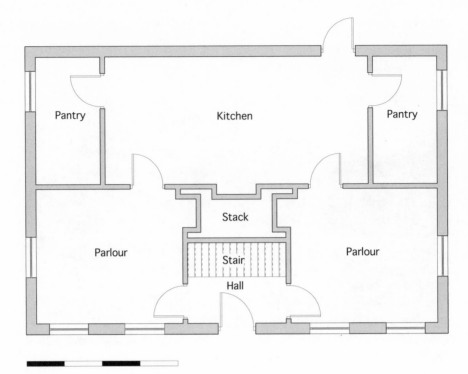

Pantry

Kitchen

Pantry

Stack

Parlour

Stair

Parlour

Hall

Scale: 4 m

FIGURE 13.3. *Sketch plan of ground floor, Ross Farm. Author.*

pigs, horses, and cattle. Barns of this type were commonplace, developed to support the self-sufficient small-scale holding of mixed livestock typical of a self-sufficient, colonial farm. Very few of these early barns remain, although mounds of derelict timber boards frequently point to their former existence, since traditional farming has all but disappeared.

The early establishment of sawmills capable of producing timber boards was vital to the early growth of farming communities and townships, because a local sawmill meant timber-framed houses clad with clapboards or shingles could be built. The first sawmill in Pictou County in northern Nova Scotia was opened by James Patterson in 1786.[10] Sawmills were the next step from log construction and, in the cultural imagination, a step further away from the forest. Timber-framed houses were also imported in "flat-pack" kit-form directly from New England. For example, the five-bay house on the waterfront in Chester, Lunenburg County (circa 1780), shown here was imported from New England and then erected by sea captain David Evans, who later served in the Royal Navy during the Napoleonic Wars (Fig. 13.6).[11] With sawn timber readily available throughout the province, from the South Shore to Cape

DANIEL MAUDLIN

FIGURE 13.4. *Main kitchen, Ross Farm. Author.*

Breton, the everyday Nova Scotia farmhouse was a timber-frame construction composed of posts and beams, and in some techniques diagonal braces,
connected by means of a variety of joint profiles and wooden pegs, with nails
being employed from the mid-nineteenth century onward. The original outer
cladding of shingles or clapboards covered a thick board sheathing attached
to the frame, the board also serving to augment lateral strength. The use today
of modern vinyl siding demonstrates the living character of this vernacular
tradition, of continuously replacing the outer sacrificial layer of cladding. The
majority of roofs were originally covered with wooden shingles, although
they are now usually covered with asphalt tiles. These houses often feature
paneled timber doors, made by the local house carpenter, and twelve- or
four-pane sash windows imported as prefabricated units from Britain or New
England. In the roof, dormer windows of various types, dates, and combi-
nations are also common reflecting the need to gain as much headroom and
light as possible within the confined attic space. Houses typically stand upon
a raised foundation, itself often incorporating a small cellar or crawl space,

FIGURE 13.5. *The parlor, Ross Farm. Author.*

which provides a degree of damp and frost proofing. The majority still stand upon their original stone foundations with a minority standing upon replacement concrete or brick foundations. The chimneystack and foundation were the first parts of the house to be built and provided the formal central axis and architectural plinth for the structure.

The similarity of these early Canadian houses from one township or farm to the next is in part because they were built from the same materials using the same construction methods. However, as in New England, the profound visual impact of their sameness is ultimately derived from the universal adherence to classical design by the producers of domestic architecture in Nova Scotia through to the mid-nineteenth century (and its continued popular consumption). Plan, elevation, and ornament such as door moldings, cornices, or fanlights, are all designed and constructed according to the strict rules of classical architecture as they were understood by British American architects, builders, and house carpenters in the late eighteenth century. The use of a classical system of proportion is widely evident in the consistent use of the ratio of 3:2 in the rectangular form of the elevation, floor plan, and windows of early houses across the province. The extensive use of classical ornament is also evident in both the exterior and interior of houses, principally in the

DANIEL MAUDLIN

FIGURE 13.6. *David Evans House, Chester, Chester County. Author.*

form of simple moldings to openings, such as windows and doors, but this could extend to delicate neoclassical demilune fanlights. These homes were not privately built; house construction of this complexity required settlers to employ highly skilled craftsmen such as house carpenters and stone masons (who were also immigrants and important members of colonial communities).

The high degree of material, formal, and decorative uniformity that can be observed across the early houses of Nova Scotia reflects the dominance of New England building tastes and traditions over those of later emigrant groups. Many loyalist refugee-settlers were able to build New England-style houses immediately upon arrival in Nova Scotia due to the British government's provision of tools and building materials. The architectural link between Nova Scotia and New England was first noted in a 1962 article by historian Alan Gowan, in which he noted that, "If you come to houses . . . from Nova Scotia, they will remind you of something you have seen in Maine or Massachusetts."[12] In New England, the mid-to-late-eighteenth-century house had developed from the English timber-frame and clapboard type introduced there by seventeenth-century emigrants from southern England. Through the eighteenth century, parallel with architectural developments in Britain and disseminated by migrant craftsmen, the apprentice system, and the transatlantic trade in architectural manuals, a classical system of proportion and ornament had become standardized in New England timber-frame house design and build.[13] Research by Abbott Lowell Cummings has established that the earliest architectural text known to have been employed in New England was Joseph Moxon's eminently practical *Mechanick Exercises*, published in London in 1678.[14] Cummings has also demonstrated that the most popular titles available in eighteenth-century New England were William Salmon's *Palladio Londinensis* (London, 1737), Francis Price's *The British Carpenter* (London, 1753), and Batty Langley's *The Builder's Jewel* (London, 1741). Cummings has found evidence that at least 170 different architectural titles, all printed in London, were available in eighteenth-century New England. Among these titles, eighty-four surviving books have been linked with known buildings or house carpenters active in New England in the eighteenth century.[15] In turn, an advertisement placed in the *Nova Scotia Gazette* of 14 July 1772 reveals that alongside the influx of migrant loyalist craftsmen, British architectural titles were also imported from New England to Nova Scotia:

> Just imported via Boston and to be sold by Robert Fletcher; Hoppus' Admeasurement of Timber; Ryland's Mechaniks; Free Mason's Pocket Companion.[16]

While these books were useful, especially those related to timber construction, they were not used slavishly, as British design was adapted to local needs and environmental conditions with, for example, the introduction of the summer kitchen or "ell."

A pattern, therefore, emerges of New England housebuilding traditions, themselves informed by British design, transplanted to Nova Scotia. What this meant for the New Englander in Nova Scotia was continuity. Nova Scotia was similar in landscape and climate to New England but much less developed, turning well-established New England families into pioneers. It was also, as we have seen, not an isolated wilderness but a heavily militarized region, so there was a degree of fear and uncertainty for an already dislocated group. As an entire culture including its craft traditions was transplanted, building homes in the New England style was in part simply a case of how things were done. But, it was also part of the process of place-making, reproducing familiar architectural forms and spaces; and filling those spaces with familiar things helped to make the new and unfamiliar feel like home and visually maintained connections to a wider culture beyond Nova Scotia.

The history of Scottish Highland settlers in Nova Scotia presents a very different experience from that of the loyalists. The first small party of two hundred dred Scottish Gaels, or Highlanders, to land in Nova Scotia departed from Lochbroom in the western Highlands aboard the *Hector*, landing at Pictou Harbour on 15 September 1773. However, it was not until the mid-nineteenth century that Scottish Gaels emerged as the dominant ethnic group in Nova Scotia, long after the characteristics of the province's material culture had been established. Indeed, Gaels aboard the *Hector* arrived to find the land immediately around the town of Pictou already settled by New Englanders, and took grants further inland and further along the coast. Nonetheless, of the 529 extant early farmhouses in Pictou County it is likely that 369 were built for the Scottish families who registered for freehold property; the vast majority of these were of Highland or Scottish Gaelic origin, compared with thirty-nine English, twenty-four American, seventeen Irish, and eighty French Acadian families who returned to the province in the early nineteenth century.

Whereas loyalists experienced continuity and familiarity in their Nova Scotia homes, Highland Gaels experienced newness. This is because loyalists and Highlanders in Nova Scotia built and occupied the same homes, but what was familiar to the former was new to the latter. Recent studies have concluded that the building traditions of later settler groups in Nova Scotia made little impact on the common house type introduced from New England.[17] Loyalists opted for continuity while Highlanders chose change. The Highland Gaels arrived to find Nova Scotia already fairly settled by New Englanders, but they took lands in relatively undeveloped areas in the north of the province so had the pioneer experience of trailblazing, tree felling, and land clearance. However, from this apparent *tabula rasa*, where their house-building options lay open, Highland Gaels chose to reject their native Scottish housebuilding traditions evolved over millennia and copied the New Englanders. This had practical reasons. Nova Scotia was covered in forest, and land clearing produced a lot of lumber; therefore, building with timber made more sense than the stone-and-turf construction used in the often treeless environment of the Scottish Highlands. However, as for the loyalists, the choice of house meant more than shelter; it was part of the process of place-making. Back in Britain, Scottish Gaels in the north of Scotland dwelt in blackhouses (a mistranslation of the Gaelic *tugadh* or thatch). Blackhouses were a form of long house; the external structure, interior space, and east-west orientation

FIGURE 13.7. *Reconstruction of traditional Scottish Highland blackhouses,*
Highland Folk Museum, Kingussie. Author.

had evolved over time to minimize the effects of the Highland environment
and create a warm and dry living space (Fig. 13.7). As described in *The Highland House Transformed*:

> The single-story, low walls of a blackhouse were typically constructed of
> field-cleared stones and turf, often in a double-wall construction with an
> insulated central core in-filled with earth. Earth and rubble walls could
> not support the weight of a roof. Therefore, the roof was supported by
> pairs of cruck frames, known as Highland couples, which were set in the
> ground and rose through the walls to meet overhead to form the apex of
> the roof. The cruck frames were the largest single components in the struc-
> ture of a blackhouse, and the most valuable in a largely treeless environ-
> ment. In some communities the cruck frames were the property of the clan
> chief or other hereditary landowner. The roof was generally comprised of
> turfs covered with a thatch of heather or straw, the whole held in place by
> twisted heather ropes weighed down with stones.[18]

On arrival in Canada, however, the Highlanders were quick to reject the
blackhouse in favor of the New England house with its well-defined parlors, kitchens, and bedrooms. They rejected the dark, earthy interior of the

FIGURE 13.8. *Early nineteenth-century farmhouse, Lower South River,*
Antigonish County. Author.

blackhouse in favor of large sash and case windows, light-flooded rooms with
painted walls, and the visual language of classically molded cornices, doorframes, and fireplaces. This change also required a shift in practice from self-
build to the employment of trained craftsmen. In short, Highlanders chose
modernity and membership of modern British culture. These values can be
read in the typical Antigonish County farmhouse built by a Highland emigrant family near the mouth of the Lower South River in the early nineteenth
century (Fig. 13.8). What we see is a neat white box standing clearly against
a small area of farmland surrounded by forest and water. In this context of
observed forms, 10 Coleraine Street, Pictou Town, is a small but interesting
building that is worth mentioning, reputedly dating from 1796. In this region steeped in Scottish Highland myth and memory, 10 Coleraine Street is
called "The Long House" due to its elongated, rectangular plan, seemingly
reminiscent of traditional blackhouses. The first official record of the building's ownership dates from 1827, when the house was owned by a Scottish
emigrant blacksmith, John McKay. However, the unusual length of the building is simply due to a later timber-framed addition to one end of a typical

FIGURE 13.9. *The parlor, McCulloch House, Pictou County. Author.*

rectangular-plan house, showing the will of later Highland identity-affirming mythologies to see what is not there.

Indoors, the observance of fashionable design standards by Highland emigrants can be seen in the parlor of the McCulloch House—at five bays, a slightly larger than average house in Pictou County built for the educationalist and founder of Dalhousie College, Thomas McCulloch (circa 1820). This polite parlor is decorated with fine neoclassical moldings at the doorframes—fashionable in the grander houses of Britain in the later eighteenth century—and skirting completed with an "Adam style" fire surround and molded arched niche, framing a locally made longcase clock in a similar plain neoclassical style (Fig. 13.9). The parlor was the primary public space of the "polite" British Atlantic home. Like similar rooms throughout the British Atlantic world, the parlor of the McCullochs' house was furnished with a mixture of local, artisan-made versions of fashionable, early nineteenth-century furniture and imported ornaments, tableware, prints, and books as well as the longcase clock.[19] These fashionable objects provided a material focus for the Highland settlers' "social imagination": their sense of belonging to a social group.[20] As a whole, the neat and regular elevations, well-proportioned rooms, and simple neoclassical moldings of the New England house type cre-

DANIEL MAUDLIN

ated an appropriate stage for the practice of a modern eighteenth-century life that embodied "the correlation between one's position in society and one's place in physical space."[21] This was to be part of the Highland settlers' new identity where building similar houses, and filling them with similar things represented a common desire to be British Canadian farmers.[22] A mixture of locally made and imported objects of British material culture similar to those found in the McCulloch House or other early houses in Nova Scotia, such as Ross Farm, could be found in new houses throughout the British Atlantic, whether the modern tenanted farmhouses of the Scottish Highlands, the merchants' houses of Falmouth, Jamaica, or the parlors of London and Philadelphia. Although it is likely that most considered only the immediate social context of their neighbors.

If we look back across the Atlantic to the changes in settlement that were taking place in the Scottish Highlands through the late eighteenth and early nineteenth centuries a wider picture emerges. The large number of Highland emigrants to Nova Scotia was in large part precipitated by their forced eviction from their traditionally held lands in the Highlands as landowners leased their lands to single-tenant sheep ranchers (often Lowland Scots or English).[23] Clachans were abandoned and blackhouses destroyed. Highlanders either resettled in planned villages or crofts (small holdings) elsewhere on an estate, migrated to growing industrial cities such as Glasgow in the south, or, like the Irish, emigrated to North America. In place of the clachan and the blackhouse, sheep ranchers built lone farmhouses. These were typically two-story, three-bay symmetrical houses built of stone and slate: whitewashed neoclassical boxes typical of improved farmhouses built across Britain in this period. It is significant in the Atlantic context that in the early nineteenth century the landowning sheep rancher of the Scottish Highlands and the Highland emigrant in Nova Scotia were choosing to commission and occupy houses that were designed according to the same architectural principles, that were decorated with the same architectural details, and that contained the same spaces furnished in similar ways. While representing opposing forces in Scottish history, in the wider context we can see that given opportunity both groups wanted to belong to the same modern British Atlantic culture. Moreover, the rejection of the blackhouse by Highland settlers in Canada is perhaps most fundamentally an expression of the ability to choose, to act as a modern consumer.

Highlanders employed trained craftsmen to build houses the same as their neighbors from New England. However, behind this architectural conformity Highlanders fiercely guarded Gaeldom's intangible culture of language, literature, music, and dance. The notion of these "hidden" identities expressed through intangible (and often unseen) practices such as language and music can perhaps be interpreted as acts of Gaelic cultural, if not political, resistance to a dominant British Atlantic culture—what James C. Scott describes as the "hidden transcripts" of history.[24] The coexistence of these open and hidden identities suggests a distinction of values between the material and nonmaterial that allowed the Gaels, like many other immigrant ethnic minority groups in North America, to adapt successfully to and assimilate into life within the broader cultural structure of the early modern Atlantic world. The rejection of a redundant and incommodious vernacular architectural tradition expressed a modern and improving attitude within a culturally vibrant Gaelic society when given the freedom of choice brought by relative prosperity and landownership.

THE NOVA SCOTIAN HOME AND BRITISHNESS

For both New England loyalists and Highland Scots, when it came to making a home in Nova Scotia the desire to conform to common British Atlantic standards of taste appears to have been overwhelming. Indeed, loyalist, Highland, English, Irish, and German settlers all chose the architectural forms and ornament of neoclassicism. This reflects the fact that neoclassicism, while often in a simplified form, was the decorative style most associated with good taste, not just in British Canada but throughout the British Atlantic world in the eighteenth and early nineteenth centuries, acting as visual shorthand for good taste itself. This applied as much to furniture and furnishings as it did to the design of the building that framed them. In an imitative, conforming, and aspirational culture neoclassicism was, therefore, the obvious choice in the home because the display of that visual shorthand was a powerful social tool that maintained social distinctions; it included and excluded, and mediated other self-controlling societal notions such as respectability. As such, the early Nova Scotian house can be understood as a representation of peoples' social identity, their position in society, locally, regionally, and, if they were aware of intercontinental commonalities, within the wider British Atlantic world. As the neoclassical material culture of Nova Scotia was for the most part produced and/or designed within the English-speaking world and because—through variations in the style and construction of its designed objects—it is recognizably different from the neoclassical products of other European countries/empires, we can say that the use of distinctly British neoclassical products conferred on Nova Scotians a British Atlantic consumer identity. Indeed, when the British Atlantic world fractured into distinct British and American spaces, places, and interests, the persistence of a common material culture was the beginning of a new transnational Anglo-American or transatlantic culture, which we recognize today. As we have seen, however, what that British consumer identity actually meant to different social groups in Nova Scotia, how it made them feel about their homes, varied enormously.

More broadly and deeply, within most European societies in the late eighteenth century, neoclassicism embodied the aesthetic, cultural, and moral values of a shared post-Renaissance, Enlightenment civilization. Therefore, the occupation of classically designed spaces in North America connected occupants with that larger Western civilization and distanced them from their new environment (physically and culturally). Place-making, for many migrants in a new, alien land, involved observance of one's most valued cultural practices in order to maintain the idea that though we are here, we come from there, and still belong there (or with them). However, housebuilding and home furnishing in early modern Nova Scotia was undertaken by ordinary families making a series of consumer choices: Which door? Which fireplace? Which chairs, tables, plates, and bowls? Though most likely aware that they lived in a British world, which dictated much of their taste and choice, settler families would probably not have reflected on the larger cultural or historical framework within which they discussed design options with their carpenter or tableware with their storekeeper.

It appears, therefore, that for most settlers the everyday process of placemaking through the production and consumption of homes was a matter of cultural identity. However, when considering place-making in early modern Nova Scotia the question of politics must also be addressed. After all, the reason New Englander and Scottish settlers were there was because the British government wanted them there to secure the colony against the French and, later, the Americans. Therefore, all settlers under the British in early British Canada were *de facto* political agents, and while not necessarily politically active most would have been aware of the political significance of the colony, not least through the heavy military and naval presence. Indeed, the politically charged mood of daily life in the colony can be identified in the title of the *Colonial Patriot*, a leading Nova Scotian newspaper of the early nineteenth century. So, was the display of a British Atlantic material culture in Nova Scotia not just a social matter of good taste but also a deliberate political act, a demonstration of a different identity: the patriot? While building British houses on foreign soil is implicitly political, it seems likely that in this political edgeland, as with the *Colonial Patriot*, everyday things were also deliberately given sharp political edges—not least with the French who had only recently been evicted from their new home. In this context the preservation of the neoclassical British American house by New England loyalist refugees or its adoption by royalist Highland Scots can be shaded, in part at least, as a direct expression of belonging to the British Empire as well as to British culture (a side note in this discussion is that when the British Atlantic world fractured following American independence, neoclassicism was recast by early America as a patriotic national style: we say Georgian, you say Federal). Additionally, in some homes alongside samplers, calendars, and occasional prints, occupants may have also gazed upon walls hung with political cartoons (pro-British or anti-British) or china plates on the chimneypiece depicting George III and George Washington. Identity and its expression is complex, layered, and, at times, conflicting, and Britishness in early modern Nova Scotia may have meant different things to different people at the same time. It seems clear that to most subcultural and ethnic migrant groups in Nova Scotia a neoclassical house represented social position in one's immediate community. To members of those groups it probably further represented membership in a wider British Atlantic world as a consumer (though what that precisely meant may have differed from one group to the next). For some it may have also had an additional political meaning in terms of a patriotic national identity. In well-appointed, late eighteenth-century parlors in Nova Scotia and Massachusetts, people sat on similar chairs in similarly shaped rooms framed by similar cornices, chair rails, and washboards, all of which spoke a common visual language that for different reasons made them feel at home.

CONCLUSION

The early history of British settlement, farming, and homemaking in Nova Scotia highlights the complex, overlapping, and, at times, hidden relationships that developed in the British Atlantic world between people and place, architecture and identity. Nova Scotia in the late eighteenth and early nineteenth century was a heavily militarized edgeland where patriotism and loyalty to the British Crown was the dominant public identity. Yet, within that climate settlers established a material culture that could transcend political loyalties. A modern, fashionable house represented wealth, good taste, and a family's social standing within eighteenth-century British Atlantic society; although, the average colonial family in Nova Scotia was more likely simply concerned with getting it right within their immediate social world.[25] For migrants from New England this was a process of recreating the familiar. In

DANIEL MAUDLIN

contrast, for later settlers from the Scottish Highlands, it was a matter of rejecting the familiar and choosing the new. Yet, while their experience of the same house type would have been very different, both migrant groups built, decorated, furnished, and occupied those houses as part of the same process of place-making, of feeling at home in Nova Scotia.

NOTES

1. Eric Richards, "Scotland and the Uses of the Atlantic Empire," in *Strangers within the Realm: Cultural Margins of the First British Empire*, ed. Bernard Bailyn and Philip D. Morgan (Chapel Hill: University of North Carolina Press, 1991), 93–94.

2. James D. Kornwolf and Georgiana W. Kornwolf, *Architecture and Town Planning in Colonial North America* (Baltimore: Johns Hopkins University Press, 2002), 13–33.

3. James Stuart Martell, *Immigration to and Emigration from Nova Scotia, 1815–1838. Prepared by J. S. Martell, under the direction of D. C. Harvey*, Public Archives of Nova Scotia. Publication. no. 6. (Halifax, Nova Scotia: Public Archives of Nova Scotia, 1942), 95.

4. Ibid.

5. David Dobson, *Scottish Emigration to Colonial America, 1607–1785* (Athens: University of Georgia Press, 1994).

6. Daniel Maudlin, "Regulating the Vernacular: The Impact of Building Regulations in the Eighteenth-Century Highland Planned Village," *Vernacular Architecture* 35 (2004): 40–49; Richards, "Scotland and the Uses of the Atlantic Empire," 92.

7. Clearances continued through the nineteenth century, but later emigrants from across Scotland (and indeed Britain in general) set sail for Australia, New Zealand, and South Africa, rather than for Canada.

8. For detailed statistical evidence see Daniel Maudlin, *The Highland House Transformed: Architecture and Identity on the Edge of Empire* (Dundee: Dundee University Press, 2009), 163–67.

9. Information supplied by the Nova Scotia Museum, Halifax, Nova Scotia.

10. Provincial Archives of Nova Scotia (PANS)/MFM/8154: *Nova Scotia Gazette*, 25 November 1787, 3.

11. Information supplied by the Chester Municipal Heritage Society.

12. Alan Gowan, "New England Architecture in Nova Scotia," *Art Quarterly* 25 (Spring 1962): 24–36, 30.

13. Amir H. Ameri, "Housing Ideologies in the New England and Chesapeake Bay Colonies, c. 1650–1700," *Journal of the Society of Architectural Historians* 56, no. 1 (1997): 6–15, 6; Nora Pat Small, "New England Farmhouses in the Early Republic: Rhetoric and Reality," in *Shaping Communities: Perspectives in Vernacular Architecture VI*, ed. Carter L. Hudgins and Elizabeth Collins Cromley (Knoxville: University of Tennessee Press, 1997), 33–45, 36.

14. Abbot Lowell Cummings, "The Availability of Architectural Books in Eighteenth-

Century New England," in *American Architects and Their Books to 1848*, ed. Kenneth Hafertepe and James F. O'Gorman (Amherst: University of Massachusetts Press, 2001), 1–16, 1.

15. Cummings, "The Availability of Architectural Books," 5–8.

16. *Nova Scotia Gazette*, July 14, 1772, p. 2.

17. Peter Ennals and Deryck Holdsworth, *Homeplace: The Making of the Canadian Dwelling over Three Centuries* (Toronto: University of Toronto Press, Scholarly Publishing Division, 1998), 76–79; Daniel Maudlin, *The Highland House Transformed*, 142–43.

18. Daniel Maudlin, *The Highland House Transformed*, 13.

19. Ruth Spicer, ed., and Bruce Berry and Ron Merrick, photography, *Nineteenth-Century Pictou County Furniture* (Pictou, Nova Scotia: Hector Centre Trust, 1977). The 1838 census shows four joiners and eight cabinetmakers active in Pictou town. In the 1870s, the Scots-owned firm of Dewar Bros. ran a large sawmill and furniture factory on Barney's River, Pictou. See Karen E. Mackay, *1838 Census of Pictou County* (Halifax, Nova Scotia, 1995), pp. 176–79 (transcribed from: PANS/RG1/vol. 449/166a-166f). "Dewar Bros. Builders & Manufacturers, Barneys River, Pictou Co. N.S.," illustrated in Sir John Douglas Sutherland Campbell, *Illustrated Historical Atlas of Pictou County, Nova Scotia* (Philadelphia: J. H. Meacham & Company, 1879).

20. Bernard L. Herman, "Tabletop Conversations: Material Culture and Everyday Life in the Eighteenth-Century Atlantic World," in *Gender, Taste, and Material Culture in Britain and North America, 1700–1830*, ed. John Styles and Amanda Vickery (New Haven, Conn.: The Yale Center for British Art, 2007), 44.

21. Hélène Lipstadt, "Sociology: Bourdieu's Bequest," *Journal of the Society of Architectural Historians* 64, no. 4 (2005): 433–46, 434–35.

22. Nicholas Cooper, "Display, Status and the Vernacular Tradition," *Vernacular Architecture* 33 (2002): 28–33, 31.

23. T. M. Devine, *Clanship to Crofters' War: The Social Transformation of the Scottish Highlands* (Manchester: Manchester University Press, 1994), 15–25.

24. James C. Scott, *Domination and the Arts of Resistance: Hidden Transcripts* (New Haven: Yale University Press, 1992).

25. Vickery and Styles, *Gender, Taste, and Material Culture*, 16.

SELECTED BIBLIOGRAPHY

Ackerman, J. *The Villa: Form and Ideology of Country Houses.* The A. W. Mellon Lectures in the Fine Arts. Princeton: Princeton University Press, 1990.

Albertone, M., and A. De Francesco, eds. *Rethinking the Atlantic World: Europe and America in the Age of Democratic Revolutions.* Basingstoke: Palgrave Macmillan, 2009.

Armitage, D., and M. J. Braddick, eds. *The British Atlantic World, 1500–1800,* 2nd ed. Basingstoke: Palgrave Macmillan, 2009.

Armstrong, D. *The Old Village and the Great House: An Archaeological and Historical Examination of Drax Hall Plantation, St. Ann's Bay, Jamaica.* Blacks in the New World. Urbana: University of Illinois Press, 1990.

Bach, R. A. *Colonial Transformations: The Cultural Production of the New Atlantic World, 1580–1640.* Basingstoke: Palgrave Macmillan, 2000.

Bailyn, B. *Atlantic History: Concepts and Contours.* Cambridge, Mass., and London: Harvard University Press, 2005.

Bailyn, B., and P. L. Denault, eds. *Soundings in Atlantic History: Latent Structures and Intellectual Currents, 1500–1830.* Cambridge, Mass., and London: Harvard University Press, 2009.

Bailyn, B., and P. D. Morgan, eds. *Strangers within the Realm; Cultural Margins of the First British Empire.* Chapel Hill: University of North Carolina Press, 1991.

Bauer, R. *The Cultural Geography of Colonial American Literatures: Empire, Travel, Modernity.* Cambridge: Cambridge University Press, 2003.

Benes, P. *Meetinghouses of Early New England.* Amherst: University of Massachusetts Press, 2012.

Benjamin, T. *The Atlantic World: Europeans, Africans, Indians and Their Shared History, 1400–1900.* Cambridge: Cambridge University Press, 2009.

Berg, M. *Luxury and Pleasure in Eighteenth-Century Britain.* Oxford: Oxford University Press, 2005.

Bhabha, H. K., ed. *Nation and Narration.* Oxford: Routledge, 1990.

Blair St. George, R. *Possible Pasts: Becoming Colonial in Early America.* Ithaca: Cornell University Press, 2000.

———, ed. *Material Life in America, 1600–1860.* Seattle: Northeastern University Press, 1988.

Borsay, P. *The English Urban Renaissance: Culture and Society in the Provincial Town, 1660–1770.* Oxford: Clarendon, 1991.

Bowen, H. V. *Elites, Enterprise and the Making of the British Overseas Empire, 1688–1775*. London: Macmillan, 1996.

Bowen, H. V., E. Mancke, J. G., Reid, eds. *Britain's Oceanic Empire: Atlantic and Indian Ocean Worlds, c.1550–1850*. Cambridge: Cambridge University Press, 2012.

Brewer, J., and R. Porter, eds. *Consumption and the World of Goods*. London: Taylor and Francis, 1993.

Burnard, T. *Creole Gentleman: The Maryland Elite, 1691–1776*. New York and London: Routledge, 2002.

Bushman, R. L. *The Refinement of America: Persons, Houses, Cities*. New York: Vintage, 1993.

Canny, N., and P. Morgan, eds. *The Oxford Handbook of the Atlantic World, 1450–1850*. Oxford: Oxford University Press, 2011.

Canny, N., and P. Pagden, eds. *Colonial Identity in the Atlantic World, 1500–1800*. Princeton: Princeton University Press, 1987.

Chalklin, C. *English Counties and Public Building, 1650–1830*. London: The Hambledon Press, 1998.

Chalklin, C. W., and J. R. Wordie, eds. *Town and Countryside: The English Landowner in the National Economy, 1660–1860*. London, 1989.

Chambers, I. *Migrancy, Culture, Identity*. London: Routledge, 1994.

Cooper, N. *The Houses of the Gentry, 1480–1680*. London and New Haven, Conn.: Yale University Press, 1999.

Cronon, W. *Changes in the Land: Indians, Colonists, and the Ecology of New England*. New York: Hill and Wang, 1983.

Crossick, G. *The Artisan and the European Town, 1500–1900*. Aldershot: Scolar Press, 1997.

Cummings, A. L. *The Framed Houses of Massachusetts Bay, 1625–1725*. Cambridge, Mass.: Harvard University Press, 1979.

DeCorse, C. *An Archaeology of Elmina: Africans and Europeans on the Gold Coast, 1400–1900*. Washington, D.C.: Smithsonian, 2001.

———, ed. *West Africa during the Atlantic Slave Trade: Archaeological Perspectives*. New Approaches to Anthropological Archaeology. London: Leicester University Press, 2001.

Dunne, J., and P. Janssens, eds. *Living in the City: Elites and their Residences, 1500–1900*. Belgium: Turnhout, 2008.

Edgar, Walter. *South Carolina: A History*. Columbia: University of South Carolina Press, 1998.

Ellis, C. and R. Ginsburg. *Cabin, Quarter, Plantation: Architecture and Landscapes of North American Slavery*. New Haven, Conn.: Yale University Press, 2010.

Ennals, P., and D. Holdsworth. *Homeplace: The Making of the Canadian Dwelling over Three Centuries*. Toronto and Buffalo: University of Toronto Press, 1998.

Farnsworth, P. *Island Lives: Historical Archaeologies of the Caribbean*. Tuscaloosa: University of Alabama Press, 2001.

Flavell, J. *When London Was Capital of America*. New Haven and London: Yale University Press, 2010.

Fowkes Tobin, B. *Colonizing Nature: The Tropics in British Arts and Letters, 1760–1820*. Philadelphia: University of Pennsylvania Press, 2005.

Gilroy, P. *The Black Atlantic: Modernity and Double Consciousness*. Cambridge, Mass.: Harvard University Press, 1993.

Graham, C. *Ordering Law: The Architectural and Social History of the English Law Court to 1914*. Aldershot: Ashgate, 2003.

Green, A., and R. Leech, eds. *Cities in the World, 1500–2000*. Leeds: Maney, 2006.

Greene, J. P., and J. R. Pole, eds. *Colonial British America: Essays in the New History of the Early Modern Era*. Baltimore: Johns Hopkins University Press, 1984.

Griffin, P. *The People with No Name: Ireland's Ulster Scots, America's Scots Irish, and the Creation of a British Atlantic World, 1689–1764*. Princeton: Princeton University Press, 2001.

Guillery, P. *The Small House in Eighteenth-Century London: A Social and Architectural History*. London: Yale University Press, 2004.

Haggerty, S. L. *The British-Atlantic Trading Community, 1760–1810: Men, Women, and the Distribution of Goods*. Leiden: Brill, 2006.

Hamling, Tara, and Catherine Richardson, eds. *Everyday Objects: Medieval and Early Modern Material Culture and Its Meanings*. Farnham; Ashgate, 2010.

Hancock, D. *Citizens of the World: London Merchants and the Integration of the British Atlantic Community, 1735–1785*. Cambridge: Cambridge University Press, 1995.

Harper, M., and M. E. Vance, eds. *Myth, Migration and the Making of Memory: Scotia and Nova Scotia, c. 1700–1990*. Edinburgh: John Donald Publishers, 2000.

Hart, E. *Building Charleston: Town and Society in the British Atlantic World*. Hartfield: University of Virginia Press, 2009.

Herman, B. L. *Town House: Architecture and Material Life in the Early American City, 1780–1830*. Chapel Hill: University of North Carolina Press, 2005.

Hicks, Dan, and Mary C. Beaudry, eds. *The Oxford Handbook of Material Culture Studies*. Oxford: Oxford University Press, 2010.

Holstun, J. *A Rational Millennium: Puritan Utopias of Seventeenth-Century England and America*. Oxford: Oxford University Press, 1987.

Hornsby, S. J. *British Atlantic, American Frontier: Spaces of Power in Early Modern British America*. Lebanon: University Press of New England, 2004.

Hulme, P. *Colonial Encounters: Europe and the Native Caribbean, 1492–1797*. London: Methuen, 1993.

Jackson, G. *The History and Archaeology of Ports*. Surrey, England: Tadworth, 1983.

Kalman, H. D. *A History of Canadian Architecture*. Vols. 1–2. Oxford: Oxford University Press, 1994–1995.

Klingelhofer, E., ed. *First Forts: Essays on the Archaeology of Proto-Colonial Fortifications*. Leiden, The Netherlands: Brill, 2010.

Knight, F. W., and P. K. Liss, eds. *Atlantic Port Cities: Economy, Culture, and Society in the Atlantic World, 1650–1850*. Knoxville: University of Tennessee Press, 1991.

Kostof, S. *The City Shaped: Urban Patterns and Meanings through History*. London: Thames and Hudson, 1999.

Landsman, N. *From Colonials to Provincials: American Thought and Culture, 1680–1760*. Ithaca: Cornell University Press, 1997.

Lanier, G., and B. L. Herman. *Everyday Architecture of the Mid-Atlantic: Looking at Buildings and Landscapes*. Creating the North American Landscape. Baltimore: Johns Hopkins University Press, 1997.

Levander, C. F., and R. S. Levine, eds. *Hemispheric American Studies*. New Jersey: Rutgers University Press, 2007.

Lounsbury, C. *Essays in Early American Architectural History: A View from the Chesapeake*. Charlottesville: University of Virginia Press, 2011.

———. *From Statehouse to Courthouse: An Architectural History of South Carolina's Colonial Capitol and Charleston County Courthouse*. Columbia: University of South Carolina Press, 2001.

———. *An Illustrated Glossary of Early Southern Architecture and Landscape*. New York: Oxford University Press, 1994.

Lovejoy, P. *Transformations in Slavery: A History of Slavery in Africa*. Cambridge: Cambridge University Press, 2012.

Lubbock, J. *The Tyranny of Taste: The Politics of Architecture and Design in Britain, 1550–1960*. New Haven: Yale University Press, 1995.

MacCubbin, R. P., and P. Martin. *British and American Gardens in the Eighteenth Century: Eighteen Illustrated Essays on Garden History*. Williamsburg, Va.: Colonial Williamsburg Foundation, 1984.

MacMillan, K. *The Atlantic Imperial Constitution: Center and Periphery in the English Atlantic World*. New York: Palgrave Macmillan, 2011.

Mancke, E., and C. Shammas, eds. *The Creation of the British Atlantic World*. Baltimore: John Hopkins University Press, 2005.

Manning, P. *Slavery and African Life: Occidental, Oriental, and African Slave Trades*. Cambridge: Cambridge University Press, 1990.

Massey, D. *For Space*. London: SAGE, 2005.

Masson, K. *Historic Houses of Virginia: Great Plantation Houses, Mansions, and Country Places*. New York: Rizzoli, 2006.

Maudlin, D. *The Highland House Transformed: Architecture and Identity on the Edge of Empire, 1700–1850*. Dundee: Dundee University Press, 2009.

McKellar, E., and B. Arciszewska, eds. *Articulating British Classicism: New Approaches to Eighteenth-Century Architecture (Reinterpreting Classicism: Culture, Reaction & Appropriation)*. Oxford: Ashgate, 2004.

McKellar, E. *The Birth of Modern London: The Development and Design of the City, 1660–1720*. Manchester: Manchester University Press, 1999.

McKendrick, N., J. Brewer, J. H. Plumb. *The Birth of a Consumer Society: The Commercialization of Eighteenth-Century England*. London: Europa Publications, 1982.

McNamara, M. J. *From Tavern to Courthouse: Architecture and Ritual in American Law, 1658–1860*. Baltimore: Johns Hopkins Press, 2004.

Miller, A. *The Empire of the Eye: Landscape Representation and American Cultural Politics, 1825–1875*. Ithaca, N.Y.: Cornell University Press, 1993.

Morgan, K. *Bristol and the Atlantic Trade in the Eighteenth Century*. Cambridge: Cambridge University Press, 1993.

———. *Slavery, Atlantic Trade and the British Economy, 1660–1800*. Cambridge: Cambridge University Press, 2000.

Morrissey, L. *From the Temple to the Castle*. Charlottesville: University of Virginia Press, 1999.

Myers, Fred R., ed. *The Empire of Things: Regimes of Value and Material Culture*. Santa Fe: School of American Research Press, 1997.

Nelson, Louis. *The Beauty of Holiness: Anglicanism and Architecture in Colonial South Carolina*. Richard Hampton Jenrette Series in Architecture and the Decorative Arts. Chapel Hill: University of North Carolina Press, 2009.

Olmert, M. *Kitchens, Smokehouses, and Privies: Outbuildings and the Architecture of Daily Life in the Eighteenth-Century Mid-Atlantic*. Ithaca, N.Y.: Cornell University Press, 2009.

Olwell, R., and A. Tully. *Cultures and Identities in Colonial British America*. Baltimore: John Hopkins University Press, 2006.

Ossman, L. *Great Houses of the South*. New York: Rizzoli, 2010.

Pestana, C. G. *Protestant Empire: Religion and the Making of the British Atlantic World*. Philadelphia: University of Pennsylvania Press, 2009.

Pocock, J. G. A. *Virtue, Commerce, and History: Essays on Political Thought and History, Chiefly in the Eighteenth Century*. New York: Cambridge University Press, 1988.

Relph, E. *Place and Placelessness*. London: Pion Press, 1976.

Reps, J. W. *Town Planning in Frontier America*. Columbia and London: University of Missouri Press, 1980.

Rowe, C. *The Mathematics of the Ideal Villa*. Cambridge: MIT Press, 1982.

Rozbicki, M. *The Complete Colonial Gentleman: Cultural Legitimacy in Plantation America*. Charlottesville: University of Virginia Press, 1998.

Shammas, C. *The Pre-industrial Consumer in England and America*. Oxford: Oxford University Press, 1990.

Shields, D. S. *Civil Tongues and Polite Letters in British America*. Chapel Hill: University of North Carolina Press for the Omohundro Institute of Early American History and Culture, 1997.

———, ed. *Material Culture in Anglo-America: Regional Identity and Urbanity in the Tidewater, Lowcountry, and Caribbean. Carolina Lowcountry & the Atlantic World*. Columbia: University of South Carolina Press, 2009.

Smith, S. D. *Slavery, Family, and Gentry Capitalism in the British Atlantic: The World of the Lascelles, 1648–1834*. Cambridge Studies in Economic History — Second Series. Cambridge: Cambridge University Press, 2010.

Stotz, C. M., and D. Upton. *The Early Architecture of Western Pennsylvania*. Pittsburgh, Penn.: University of Pittsburgh Press, 1994.

Styles, J., and A. Vickery, eds. *Gender, Taste, and Material Culture in Britain and North America, 1700–1830*. New Haven: The Yale Center for British Art, 2007.

Upton, Dell. *Holy Things and Profane: Anglican Parish Churches in Colonial Virginia*. New Haven: Yale University Press, 1997.

Vickery, A. *The Gentleman's Daughter: Women's Lives in Georgian England*. New Haven and London: Yale University Press, 1998.

Vlach, John Michael. *Back of the Big House: The Architecture of Plantation Slavery*. Fred W. Morrison Series in Southern Studies. Chapel Hill: University of North Carolina Press, 1993.

Wahrman, D. *The Making of the Modern Self: Identity and Culture in Eighteenth-Century England*. New Haven: Yale University Press, 2004.

Walsh, L. *Motives of Honor, Pleasure, and Profit: Plantation Management in the Colonial Chesapeake, 1607–1763*. Chapel Hill: University of North Carolina Press, 2010.

Weatherill, L. *Consumer Behavior and Material Culture, 1660–1760*. 2nd edition. London: Routledge, 1996.

Wilson, K. *A Sense of the People; Politics, Culture, and Imperialism in England, 1715–1785*. Cambridge: Cambridge University Press, 1995.

Yates, N. *Buildings, Faith, and Worship: The Liturgical Arrangement of Anglican Churches 1600–1900*. Oxford: Oxford University Press, revised 2000.

Yokota, K. *Unbecoming British: How Revolutionary America Became a Postcolonial Nation*. Oxford: Oxford University Press, 2011.

CONTRIBUTORS

Peter Benes is director of the Dublin Seminar for New England Folklife, a continuing series of conferences, exhibitions, and publications on early American history sponsored by Historic Deerfield, Deerfield, Massachusetts. He is the author of *Meetinghouses of Early New England* (Amherst: University of Massachusetts Press, 2012), which received the Fred B. Kniffen Book Award in 2012 from the Pioneer America Society and the Abbott Lowell Cummings Prize in 2014 from the Vernacular Architecture Forum. His other publications include *The Masks of Orthodoxy: Folk Gravestone Carving in Plymouth County, Massachusetts, 1689–1805* (Amherst: University of Massachusetts Press, 1977), which was awarded the Chicago Folklore Prize by the American Folklore Society and the University of Chicago, as well as four exhibition catalogs, two coedited volumes, and numerous articles on New England history, cartography, art, and culture. His new book, *For a Short Time Only: Itinerants and the Resurgence of Popular Culture in Early America* (Amherst: University of Massachusetts Press, 2016), will be released in spring 2016.

Christopher DeCorse is professor and past chair of Anthropology at the Maxwell School of Citizenship and Public Affairs, University of Syracuse. His research focuses on the archaeology, ethnohistory, and ethnography of sub-Saharan Africa, particularly how archaeology can help us understand the transformations that occurred in Africa during the period of the Atlantic trade. His major field projects include excavations at the African settlement at Elmina, Ghana, the site of the first and largest European trade post established in sub-Saharan Africa, and also Bunce Island, Sierra Leone, a major slave-trading entrepôt during the seventeenth and eighteenth centuries. His principal publications include: *The Record of the Past: An Introduction to Physical Anthropology and Archaeology* (Upper Saddle River, N.J.: Prentice Hall, 2000); *Anthropology: A Global Perspective*, 8th ed., coauthored with Raymond Scupin (Upper Saddle River, N.J.: Prentice Hall, 2016); the edited volume *West Africa during the Atlantic Slave Trade: Archaeological Perspectives* (Leicester: University of Leicester Press, 2001); and *An Archaeology of Elmina: Africans and Europeans on the Gold Coast* (New York: Smithsonian Institution Scholarly Press, 2001).

Peter Guillery is a senior historian for the Survey of London in the Bartlett School of Architecture, University College London. His books on London's buildings cover subjects ranging from seventeenth-century churches to London Zoo and include *The Small House in Eighteenth-Century London* (London: Yale University Press, 2004), *Behind the Façade, London House Plans, 1660–1840* with Neil Burton (Reading: Spire

Books, 2006), and, as editor, *Built from Below: British Architecture and the Vernacular* (Abingdon: Routledge, 2011), and volume 48 in the Survey of London series, on Woolwich (2012). With Bernard L. Herman he has written on links between the houses of Deptford in London and Philadelphia in *Articulating British Classicism: New Approaches to Eighteenth-Century Architecture* (Farnham: Ashgate, 2004).

Stephen Hague is a historian of the British Atlantic world at Rowan University in New Jersey. He is the author of *The Gentleman's House in the British Atlantic World, 1680–1780* (London and New York: Palgrave Macmillan, 2015), which explores the interstitial boundary between the upper-middling sort and lesser landed gentry in eighteenth-century Britain and the British Atlantic world by examining small classical houses in England and British North America. He has published on the gentry house in the Atlantic world, historic buildings and community, and the architects Charles Barry and A. W. N. Pugin. He has held fellowships at the Lewis Walpole Library, the Winterthur Museum and Library, the Athenaeum of Philadelphia, and the Library Company of Philadelphia. He holds a D.Phil. from Oxford University and is also a Supernumerary Fellow of Linacre College, Oxford.

Bernard L. Herman is the George B. Tindall Distinguished Professor of American Studies and Folklore at the University of North Carolina at Chapel Hill, where he also serves on the art history faculty. His books include *Town House: Architecture and Material Life in the Early American City, 1780–1830* (Chapel Hill: University of North Carolina Press, 2005) and *The Stolen House* (Charlottesville: University of Virginia Press, 1992). He is currently completing a book *Quilt Spaces* centered on the quilts and quilt makers of Gee's Bend, Alabama. He has published essays, lectured, and offered courses on visual and material culture, architectural history, self-taught and vernacular art, foodways, culture-based sustainable economic development, and seventeenth- and eighteenth-century material life. He is a 2010 recipient of a John Simon Guggenheim Fellowship for his book-in-progress *Troublesome Things in the Borderlands of Contemporary Art*. His recent exhibitions include contributions as a guest cocurator of *Thornton Dial: Thoughts on Paper* (2011–2012) with an accompanying edited volume and an installation of contemporary quilts and their narratives from The Alliance for American Quilts Quilters' Save Our Stories project (International Quilt Festival, Houston, October 2010).

Carl Lounsbury is senior architectural historian in the Architectural and Archaeological Research Department at the Colonial Williamsburg Foundation and adjunct associate professor of history at the College of William and Mary. His research has focused on English and colonial American public buildings, churches and meetinghouses, theatres, craftsmen, and preindustrial building technology. His extensive publications include: *Architects and Builders in North Carolina: A History of the Practice of Build-*

ings with Catherine W. Bishir, Charlotte V. Brown, and Ernest H. Wood (Chapel Hill: University of North Carolina Press, 1990); *An Illustrated Glossary of Early Southern Architecture and Landscape* (Oxford: Oxford University Press, 1994); and *The Courthouses of Early Virginia* (Charlottesville: University of Virginia Press, 2005), all three of which won the Abbott Lowell Cummings Award from the Vernacular Architecture Forum. Other books include *From Statehouse to Courthouse: An Architectural History of South Carolina's Colonial Capitol and the Charleston County Courthouse* (Columbia: University of South Carolina Press, 2001), and *Essays in Early American Architectural History: A View from the Chesapeake* (Charlottesville: University of Virginia Press, 2011). Most recently, he is the coauthor and a contributor to *The Chesapeake House: Architectural Investigation by Colonial Williamsburg* (Chapel Hill: University of North Carolina Press, 2013).

Emily Mann is an early career researcher at the Courtauld Institute of Art, London. Her research examines English colonial architecture and its representation in the seventeenth and early eighteenth centuries, with a current focus on the construction of defenses and their destruction in both human conflict and natural disasters. Her publications include "In Defence of the City: The Gates of London and Temple Bar in the Seventeenth Century," *Architectural History*, 2006, and an essay on printed views of fortifications in West Africa (Studies in British Art, no. 24, Yale University Press, forthcoming). She has received several research awards including AHRC studentships and a grant from the University of London Central Research Fund towards fieldwork in the Caribbean. She has delivered conference and seminar papers on the fortification of Bermuda, Barbados, Jamaica, and West Africa, and on architectural competition and conflict between the English and French on the island of St. Kitts.

Anna O. Marley is curator of historical American art at the Pennsylvania Academy of Fine Arts, Philadelphia. At PAFA, Marley has curated several exhibitions on the art and material culture of early modern America, including *Public Treasures/Private Visions: Hudson River School Masterworks from the Metropolitan Museum of Art and Private Collections* (2009–2010), *Virgins, Soldiers, Angels, and Saints: Violet Oakley's Religious Art from the PAFA Collection* (2010), *Anatomy/Academy* (2011), *"A Mine of Beauty": Landscapes by William Trost Richards* (2012), as well as the touring retrospective, *Henry Ossawa Tanner: Modern Spirit* (2012), *Modern Women at PAFA: From Cassatt to O'Keeffe and Hidden Treasures Unveiled: Watercolors* (both in 2013), *and Spiritual Strivings: A Celebration of African American Works on Paper* (2014). In addition to her curatorial work she has served as editor and lead author of numerous publications including *Henry Ossawa Tanner: Modern Spirit* (Oakland: University of California Press, 2012). Marley's most recent exhibition at PAFA is the touring exhibition, *The Artist's Garden: American Impressionism and the Garden Movement,*

1887–1920 (2015). She is working on future exhibits on Thomas Eakins's photography and nineteenth-century history painting in the Americas. Marley's professional affiliations include serving as chair of the Association of Historians of American Art.

Daniel Maudlin is professor of early modern history at the University of Plymouth. He has previously worked as an inspector of historic buildings for Historic Scotland and held positions at Dalhousie University, the University of Pennsylvania, and the University of Glasgow. His publications include: *The Idea of the Cottage in English Architecture, 1760–1860* (Abingdon: Routledge, 2015); *Consuming Architecture: On the Occupation, Appropriation and Interpretation of Buildings*, edited with Marcel Vellinga (Abingdon: Routledge, 2015); "Early Colonial Settlement in North America, India and the British Isles" in *Architecture and Urbanism of the British Empire (Oxford History of British Empire)* (Oxford: Oxford University Press, 2016); "British Atlantic Architectures" for *Oxford University Press Bibliographies Online* (2012); and *The Highland House Transformed: Architecture and Identity on the Edge of Empire* (Dundee: Dundee University Press, 2009). Awards and fellowships relating to British Atlantic history include: Leverhulme Trust Major Research Fellowship on the "Inn and the Traveller in the Atlantic World"; John D. Rockefeller Fellowship, Colonial Williamsburg Foundation; Arts and Humanities Research Council Network Grant: "Transatlantic Exchanges"; Leverhulme Trust Fellowship; and the 2008 Jeffrey Cooke Prize awarded by the International Association for the Study of Traditional Environments.

Kenneth Morgan is professor of history at Brunel University where he is director of the Isambard Centre for Historical Research. Educated at the University of Leicester and New College, Oxford, he is a fellow of the Royal Historical Society. He has held fellowships and awards from the University of Sydney, the National Library of Australia, the National Archives of Australia, the British Library, the UK Arts and Humanities Research Council, the Virginia Historical Society, and the Robert H. Smith International Center for Jefferson Studies, Monticello. His published work concentrates mainly on the commercial history of the oceanic trading world in the long eighteenth century. Among his books are *Bristol and the Atlantic Trade in the Eighteenth Century* (Cambridge: Cambridge University Press, 1994), *Slavery, Atlantic Trade and the British Economy, 1660–1800* (Cambridge: Cambridge University Press, 2000), and *Slavery and the British Empire: From Africa to America* (Oxford: Oxford University Press, 2007).

Lee Morrissey is professor and chair of English at Clemson University. At Clemson, he has been a recipient of the Student Government Teacher of Excellence Award, the Gentry Award for Distinguished Teaching in the Humanities, and is one of the university's Alumni Distinguished Professors. Morrissey is author of *From The Temple to the Castle: An Architectural History of British Literature, 1660–1760* (Charlottesville: University of Virginia Press, 1999); and *The Constitution of Literature: Literacy,*

Democracy, and Early English Literary Criticism (Redwood City, Calif.: Stanford University Press, 2007). Morrissey is editor of *Debating the Canon* (New York: Palgrave Macmillan, 2005) and a contributor to *English Literature in Context*, edited by Paul Poplawski (Cambridge: Cambridge University Press, 2007).

Louis P. Nelson is professor in American architecture at the University of Virginia specializing in early modern architecture of the Atlantic, vernacular architecture, and theories and methods of sacred space. The majority of his published work focuses on the early American South and the Greater Caribbean. Nelson is interested in the close examination of evidence—both material and textual—as a means of examining the ways architecture shapes the human experience. *The Beauty of Holiness: Anglicanism and Architecture in Colonial South Carolina*, The Richard Hampton Jenrette Series in Architecture and the Decorative Arts (Chapel Hill: University of North Carolina Press, 2009), his first book, examines the ways Anglican churches in colonial South Carolina express regional identity, social politics, and divergent theologies of the sacred. His interest in the colonial South has led him past the "sacred thirteen," where his fieldwork in Jamaica and the Leeward Islands has resulted in some of the first systematic recording of eighteenth- and nineteenth-century British architecture in the Caribbean. His most recent book, *Falmouth, Jamaica: Architecture as History*, edited with Edward A. Chappell and Brian Cofrancesco (Kingston: University of the West Indies Press, 2014), reveals the significance of urban architecture in the Caribbean and explores the implications of heritage tourism and the cruise ship industry on developing communities.

Alison Stanley is currently an independent scholar, having previously been employed as a teaching fellow in American studies at King's College, London. Her research follows an interdisciplinary approach to seventeenth-century British American history and literature. Her publications include: "'To Speak with Other Tongues': Linguistics, Colonialism and Identity in 17th Century New England" in *Comparative American Studies* (2009); the entry on Roger Williams for the online encyclopedia *The Literary Encyclopedia* (2009); articles on Charles Chauncy, Samuel Davies, Robert Finley, Samuel Hopkins, William Tennent Jr., and the New Divinity for the *Encyclopedia of Revolutionary America*; as well as numerous reviews for the *Journal of American Studies*.

INDEX

Abingdon Town or County Hall (Abingdon, Oxfordshire, England), 56

Acadians, 23, 290, 293. *See also* Cajun; French Canada

Adamesque, 87, 306. *See also* Neoclassicism

Adams, John, 15, 78, 84

Adaptation in building, 104, 402

African: diaspora, 12; enslaved labor, 23, 168, 191, 236. *See also* Black Atlantic; Slavery; West Africa

Alberti, Leon Battista, 47. *See also* Architectural books

Algonquin, 142, 143, 146, 154. *See also* Native Americans

American Revolution, 61, 63, 75, 79, 82, 244, 294

American West, 93

Anabaptists, 108. *See also* Nonconformists

Andrews, Nathan, 124

Andrews, William, 121

Anglicans, 59; churches, 10, 17, 60, 119, 136; High, 108

Anglo-Dutch Wars, 173

Anglo-Palladian. *See* Palladianism

Annapolis Royal, Nova Scotia, Canada, 290

Anne (queen of England), 63, 72

Anthropology, 13

Antigua, 19, 39, 47, 168, 188. *See also* Caribbean

Apprentices, 301

Arcades, 14, 53, 62, 63, 70, 72, 202

Arcadia, 15, 82, 87

Archaeology, 14, 33, 193

Architects, 5, 8

Architectural books, 4, 83, 238, 261, 269, 280, 281, 302. *See also* Alberti, Leon Battista; Campbell, Colen; Gibbs, James; Kent, William; Langley, Batty; Morris, Robert; Moxon, Joseph; Palladianism; Palladio, Andrea; Price, Francis; Salmon, William; Ware, Isaac; Wood the Elder, John; Wood the Younger, John

Architectural history, 13

Architectural patrons, 8

Arctic, 273

Aristocracy, 235

Artisans, 4, 32, 103, 105, 106; artisan-made, 306; churches, 16

Ashlar, 73

Ashley River, S.C., 269, 273, 277

Asia, 82, 83, 201, 256

Assemblies, 14, 63, 65

Assembly room, 55, 58, 65, 75, 203, 219, 222

Assizes, 57, 58

Atkins, Jonathan, 41

Atlantic history, historiography of, 10–12

Augustan culture, 6, 277. *See also* Roman architecture

Avalon Charter, 31

Axe, Samuel, 40

Balconies, 14, 53, 189, 202

Baptists, 17, 59, 119. *See also* Nonconformists

Barbados, 19, 38–40, 44, 47, 168, 195, 202, 269, 273

British, 19, 195, 294. *See also* Antigua; Barbados; Dominica; Jamaica; Leeward Islands; Montserrat; Nevis; St. Christopher; West Indies

Carolina, 5, 8, 272. *See also* Lords Proprietor of Carolina

Carpenters, 5, 53, 108, 113; house carpenters, 4, 32, 33, 299, 300, 301. *See also* Carpentry; Timber

Carpentry, 7. *See also* Carpenters; Timber

Castles, 46, 169, 176, 177. *See also* Forts

Caversham, Berkshire, England, 78

Centre-periphery theory, 4, 11. *See also* Exchange; Networks; Trickledown

Ceremonies, 54, 58, 66, 219

Chapels, 108. *See* Nonconformists

Charles City, Va., 38

Charles Fort, Bermuda, 36

Charles II, 41, 168, 273

Charleston, S.C., 3, 5, 11, 22, 256, 266, 269, 273, 274, 293; assembly room, 75; market house, 63; statehouse, 58, 73; stores, 201; wharves, 196. *See also* South Carolina

Charlotte (queen of England), 70

Charlottesville, Va., 88

Chatham, London, 16, 107, 108

Chelmsford, Essex, England, 75

Chelmsford, Mass., meetinghouse, 130

Chesapeake, 61, 119; plantocracy, 80. *See also* Delaware; Maryland; Virginia

Chester County, Pa., courthouse, 59, 60

Children, 4, 198

Chimneypiece, 80, 241. *See also* Chimneystack; Fireplace; Mantelpiece; Overmantel

Chimneystack, 296. *See also* Chimneypiece

China. *See* Asia

Chiswick Villa (London), 84, 280. *See also* Boyle, Richard; Drayton Hall; Twickenham

Christ Church (Boston, Mass.), 103

Christ Church (Philadelphia, Pa.), 103

Christian groups, 16; converts, 142, 150, 158

Church. *See churches, chapels, and meetinghouses listed by name of building or location*

Cibber, Gabriel Gaius, 112

City, 18, 20, 254; port, 13, 20, 53, 190, 212. *See also* Ports; Square; Street; Suburb; Urban

Civic development, 20; halls, 54; order, 74; pride, 214, 217

Clachan, 296, 307

Clapboard, 299

Classicism/Classical design, 6, 8, 104, 300; British, 5; ideal, 271; ornament, 6, 7, 21, 53, 69, 197, 232, 291, 300, 305; purity, 271; rules, 300; vernacular; 16. *See also* Federal; Georgian; Interiors; Moldings; Neoclassicism; Roman; Vitruvius

Claude (Lorrain), 80

Climate, 104, 114, 201, 203, 204, 293, 297

Clocks, 53, 260, 306

Coalbrookdale Bridge (Shropshire, England), 85, 92

Coat of arms, 14, 53, 63, 66, 72, 73, 74, 80, 237, 291

Coffee house, 219

Colleton, Sir John, 273

Collecting, 7, 82, 84, 234. *See also* Painting

Colonnade, 14, 53, 58, 195, 201, 202

Column, 9, 189, 197

Communal structures, 17

Company of Guynney and Binney, 172

Company of Royal Adventurers of England Trading to Africa, 173. *See also* West Africa

Concord, Mass., meetinghouse, 130

East River, S.C., 64
Edenton, N.C., 69
Edict of Nantes, 123, 274
Edinburgh, Scotland, 293
Edgartown, Martha's Vineyard, Mass., 43, 125
Egyaa, Ghana, 174, 175
Elbridge, John, 21, 231, 234–35
Eliot, John, 17, 142–64. *See also* Eliot Tracts; Puritans; Native Americans
Eliot Tracts, 17, 143. *See also* Eliot, John
Elite, 8, 20, 84, 188, 190, 191, 194, 205, 223, 232, 236, 244
Elizabeth City, Va., 38
Elizabeth I, 32, 36
Ell, 297, 302. *See also* Kitchen
Elmina Castle (Ghana), 167
Embrasures, 41
Emigrants, 4, 6, 8, 105. *See also* Immigrants; Migrants
Emigration, 105. *See also* Immigration; Migration
England, 5, 9, 294
English Civil War, 168, 270, 273
English empire, 4, 167
Environment, 146, 205, 293, 304; urban, 148
Etiquette, 265
European civilization, 6; architecture, 6; colonial powers, 8, 9
Evangeline, 293
Evelyn, John, 108, 282
Exchange, 4, 8, 12, 56, 196; artistic, 93; commercial, 212, 217, 223; cultural, 83, 234, 275. *See also* Centre-periphery theory; Networks; Transatlanticism; Trickledown
Experimentation in building, 256

Fairfield, Conn., 121, 127
Falmouth, Jamaica, 19, 188–211, 307. *See also* Jamaica

Family, families, family groups, 120, 198
Faneuil, Peter, 65
Faneuil Hall (Boston, Mass.), 65. *See also* Boston
Farm, 45, 290, 293, 295. *See also* Farmhouse
Farmers and farming families, 4, 5, 6, 292, 293, 295; tenant, 307
Farmhouse, 5, 13, 20, 59, 296, 299, 307. *See also* Farm; Ross Farm
Fashion, 72, 256
Fashionability, 6, 7, 205, 291, 306
Federal, 135; style, 310
Ferme ornée, 84
Fifty New Churches Act, 112
Fillmore, Lavius, 136
Fireplace, 265, 305; surround, 306. *See also* Chimneypiece; Overmantel
Fordwich, Kent, England, town hall, 56
Forests, 17, 86, 290; foresters, 145
Fort George (Halifax, Nova Scotia, Canada), 293
Fort Louisbourg (Cape Breton, Nova Scotia, Canada), 290, 293
Fort Plantation (Barbados), 42, 44
Forts, 5, 9, 13, 14, 18, 149; Bermuda and Caribbean, 31–52; Canada, 293; West Africa, 9, 165–87. *See also forts listed by name*
Fort St. George (Va.), 33, 36
Fort Thornton (Freetown, Sierra Leone), 179–80. *See also* Freetown
Franklin, Benjamin, 242, 243
Fredericksburg Market House (Fredericksburg, Va.), 65
Freetown, Sierra Leone, 180. *See also* Fort Thornton; Sierra Leone
French and Indian War, 80
French Canada, 189. *See also* Acadian; Cajun; Quebec
French empire, 6, 8, 33, 40, 47, 167, 173, 273, 281, 290, 291; exploration of, 273

Furniture, 3, 62, 66, 74, 80, 92, 199, 241, 244, 264, 265, 306; makers, 295. *See also* Tea

Fur trade, 235

Gambia River, 18, 169, 175, 177. *See also* James Fort; James Island; Yamyamacunda

Gaol, 54. *See also* Dungeons

Garden, 15, 78; tour, 79, 83–85, 182, 261

Gender, 5

Gentility, 106, 232, 239, 242, 291. *See also* Politeness

Gentlemen, 4, 9, 113, 233, 234, 237; American, 83; builders, 238; houses, 235–45; justices, 58; planters, 74. *See also* Gentry

Gentry, 21, 61, 65, 84, 233, 235. *See also* Gentlemen

George III, 75; bust of, 70; portrait of, 73, 310

Georgia, 296

Georgian, 310; architecture, 74, 130; churches, 113; cities, 254; style, 83. *See also* Classicism

German migrants, 8, 23

Ghana, 18, 167, 169

Gibbs, James, 280, 281, 282. *See also* Architectural books

Glasgow, 3, 63, 212, 213, 223, 293, 307

Glorious Revolution, 274

Godliness, 6, 18, 21

Gold, 18, 165, 171, 182

Gold Coast, 167, 168, 178; colony, 174

Gothic, style, 287

Government, 13, 21; buildings, 53–77; officials, 4, 58; symbols of, 8, 58, 62, 66. *See also* Public buildings

Grand Tour, 82, 84, 86

Great Lakes, 291

Great Migration, 17, 119. *See also* Puritans

Greek Revival, 136

Guardhouse, 41

Guesthouse, 150, 156

Guildhall, 55

Guilford, Conn., meetinghouse, 132

Gulf of Maine, 291, 295

Gulf of Mexico, 9

Gun platform, 41, 177

Hadley, Mass., meetinghouse, 132

Hagley Hall (West Midlands, England), 78, 84, 85, 90. *See also* Country house

Hakluyt, Richard, 32, 46

Halifax, Nova Scotia, Canada, 3, 290, 295

Hallway, 92, 198, 239

Hamilton, Hon. Charles, 84

Hampton Court (London), 84. *See also* Twickenham

Hanover, Va., courthouse, 61

Harbors, 9, 18, 20, 33, 214, 216. *See also* Ports; Shipping; Wharves

Harpers Ferry, W.Va., 85, 88

Hartford, Conn., 70, 125; meetinghouse, 121

Hawksmoor, Nicholas, 112

Henry VIII, 36

Hereford, Herefordshire, England, 58

Highlanders. *See* Highland Scots

Highland Scots, 290; Gaels, 296, 303

Highlands of Scotland, 10, 295, 302, 307. *See also* Scotland

Hispaniola, 38

Historical geography, influence of, 11

Hobbes, Thomas, 274, 275, 276

Holetown, Barbados, 40; fort, 42

Holy Trinity Church (Wilmington, Del.), 112

Home, 20, 232

Hospitals, 120

Houghton Hall (Norfolk, England), 82, 85, 280. *See also* Country house; Walpole, Robert

House of Assembly (Jamaica), 196

Migration, 4, 7. *See also* Emigration; Immigration

Military architecture, 10, 169. *See also* Castles; Forts

Military personnel, 6. *See also* Militia; Soldiers

Militia, 45. *See also* Military; Soldiers

Milton, John, 276

Missionaries, 17, 142, 143

Mississippi River, 281

Mobility, 6, 7, 8; social, 20, 223, 234

Modernity, 7, 266, 307, 308

Mohawk Valley, N.Y., 10, 296

Moldings, 297, 300, 301. *See also* Classicism

Monticello, Va., 13, 15, 78, 79, 83, 85–99. *See also* Country house; Jefferson, Thomas; Mount Vernon

Montserrat, 39, 47. *See also* Caribbean

Morality, 6, 18, 21, 23, 157, 178, 309

More, Thomas. See *Utopia*

Morris, Robert, 280, 281. *See also* Architectural books

Moulton, Charles, 192

Mount Vernon, Va., 80, 93. *See also* Country house; Monticello; Washington, George

Moxon, Joseph, 261, 302. *See also* Architectural books

Munster, N. Ireland, 47. *See also* Belfast; Ulster

Napoleonic Wars, 296, 298

Natick, Mass., meetinghouse, 132, 142, 143, 147, 148–51

Nation, 12; nationalities, 8

Native Americans, 5, 12, 18, 33, 38, 93, 142–64, 242, 243, 272, 273, 275, 286; ceramics, 286; Indian Hall, 87. *See also* Algonquin; Iroquois; Powhattan people; Praying Indian Towns; Wigwam

Natural Arch, Va., 85

Nature, 37; natural wonders, 85; state of, 274

Neatness, 7, 80, 82. *See also* Classicism; Proportion; Uniformity; Regularity; Symmetry

Neoclassicism, 3, 6, 82, 199. *See also* Adamesque; Classicism

Networks, 4, 232; social, 94; trade, 94, 238. *See also* Exchanges

Nevis, 38, 47, 168. *See also* Caribbean

New Bern, N.C.: market house, 63; statehouse, 70

New Brunswick, Canada, 295

New Castle, Del., market house, 63

New England, 4, 6, 17, 18, 23, 38, 59, 63, 69, 70, 73, 119–65, 180, 236, 272, 291, 293, 295; company, 143

New Englanders, 59, 294, 296, 303

New France. *See* French Canada

New Hampshire, 63, 70, 71, 274

New Haven, Conn.: meetinghouses, 119, 124; statehouse, 71

New Jersey, 69; Quakers, 128

New Orleans, La., 93

Newport, R.I., 70, Brick Market, 65; Colony House, 71

Newport News, Va., 38

New World, 37, 87, 104, 106, 119, 271

New York, 8, 63, 71, 201, 202, 293; City Hall, 54; market, 63; Quakers, 128

Niagara Falls, N.Y., 85, 86

Nicholson, Francis, 72

Nigeria, 168

Nobility, 82, 275

Nonconformists, 16, 110, 127; chapels, 116. *See also* Anabaptists; Baptists; Calvinists; Congregationalists; Dissenters; Methodists; Presbyterians; Protestantism; Puritans; Reformists

Norfolk, Va., 63

Portsmouth, England, 70, 103, 106, 107. *See also* St. George in Portsea

Portuguese empire, 5, 8, 32, 167, 173, 273

Postcolonial theory, 4

Potomac River, Md., 93

Powder house, 120

Powhattan people, 37. *See also* Native Americans

Praying Indian Towns, 17, 142–64. *See also* Eliot, John; Native Americans; Puritans

Presbyterians, 17, 60, 119, 120. *See also* Dissenters; Nonconformists

Price, Francis, 302. *See also* Architectural books

Prince, The (Machiavelli), 44

Prince Edward Island, Canada, 293

Prints, 265, 306. *See also* Painting

Producers, 13

Production, 8; building, 20; spheres of, 20

Proportion, 7, 280, 300. *See also* Neatness; Regularity; Symmetry; Uniformity

Protestantism, 16, 18, 110. *See also* Nonconformism

Providence, R.I., 17, 63, 70, 274. *See also* Rhode Island

Providence Island, 39, 40, 46; company, 40. *See also* Caribbean

Public buildings, 9, 53–77; English, 54, 219, 220, 243. *See also* Government; *buildings also listed by location*

Public space, 58, 189

Pulpit, 124, 125, 128

Puritans, 17, 59, 110, 119, 142. *See also* Eliot, John; Great Migration; Nonconformists; Pilgrims; Praying Indian Towns

Quakers, 120, 127, 231. *See also* Nonconformists

Quebec, 292. *See also* French Canada

Quinnipiac, Conn., 121, 124

Quoin, 73

Raleigh, Sir Walter, 37

Rampart, 41

Rank, 4, 231. *See also* Status

Redoubt, 41

Reformists, 17, 60, 119, 120; Dutch, 17, 119; Scottish, 17, 119. *See also* Nonconformists

Regional building practices, 7, 8, 14, 70, 75; centers of, 5, 7; traditions, 8; variations in, 233. *See also* Craft; Vernacular

Regionalism. *See* Regional building practices

Regularity, 7, 254. *See also* Neatness; Proportion; Symmetry; Uniformity

Republicanism, 9

Respectability, 308. *See also* Politeness

Restoration, The, 110, 168, 173, 273

Revolutionary War. *See* American Revolution

Rhode Island, 69, 70, 120; General Assembly, 71. *See also* Providence

River Avon, England, 214

River Mersey, England, 213

Roads, 147, 149

Roanoke, Va., 34, 36

Roberts, William, 88–89

Roche, John, 124

Roman architecture, 270. *See also* Classicism; Vitruvius

Roof, "English Built," 132; four-square, 119, 120, 124, 130; hipped, 53, 62, 124, 232; walks, 53. *See also* Barn; Bridge-building; Shingles; Timber-framing

Roperies, 222

Ross, William, 296. *See also* Ross Farm

Ross Farm (Lunenberg County, Nova Scotia, Canada), 296. *See also* Farm house

Index

South America, 256

Southampton, England, 3

Southampton Fort (Bermuda), 36, 46

South Carolina, 9, 11, 22, 58, 63, 71, 195, 266, 269, 272; statehouse, 65; trade, 219. *See also* Charleston; Drayton Hall; Lowcountry

Southwark, London, 108, 109

Spanish, Caribbean, 202; empire, 5, 8, 32, 33, 282; exploration, 273; invaders, 40; invasion, 46; sailors, 34

Speightstown, Barbados, fort, 40

Spenser, Edmund, 37

Springfield, Mass., meetinghouse, 125

Square, 20, 73, 214, 220; Bristol, 219; central, 60, 72, 202; London, 219, 222; market, 53. *See also* City; Street; Urban

Stadler, J. C., 89

Stairs, 194, 239, 260, 264, 296, 297

Statehouse, 14, 54, 65–74. *See also statehouses listed by location*

Status, 9, 21, 82, 83, 105, 147, 217, 233–35, 237, 239, 244. *See also* Rank

Stenton (Philadelphia, Pa.), 21, 232, 238–39, 245. *See also* Cote; Country house; Philadelphia

Store, 5, 19, 194, 197. *See also* Shop

Storehouse, 33. *See also* Warehouse

Stowe (Oxfordshire, England), 15, 78, 84. *See also* Country house

Strawberry Hill, 286. *See also* Gothic; Twickenham; Walpole, Horace

Street, 20, 214, 220, 255; shopping, 19, 188, 195, 201, 202, 218. *See also* City; Square; Suburb; Urban

Stucco, 80

Suburb, 20, 112, 234, 254. *See also* City; Street; Urban

Sugar, 19; merchants, 213; plantations, 191, 231; planters, 188, 213; refineries, 218, 222; trade, 217; works, 46

Superior courts, 14

Swedish empire, 173; forts, 174

Sydney, Nova Scotia, Canada, 295

Symmetry, 6, 8, 233, 278, 279, 280, 281. *See also* Neatness; Proportion; Regularity; Uniformity

Taste, 6, 13, 53, 254; architectural, 83; artistic, 79, 82; good, 6, 7, 291; standards of, 233; taste makers, 82

Taverns, 59, 61, 219

Tax, 54, 120, 237

Tea, 107, 265, 199; afternoon tea, 3; room, 88; sets, 291; table, 265. *See also* Furniture; Politeness; Porcelain

Thirteen colonies, 23

Thomson, James, 277

Thornton, Henry, 179

Tidewater, 61. *See also* North Carolina; Virginia

Tierra del Fuego, 273

Timber, 7, 61, 63, 73, 74, 134, 214. *See also* Carpentry; Timber-framing

Timber-framing, 4, houses, 298, 301. *See also* Barn; Bridge-building; Carpentry; Roof

Tobacco, 199; planters, 61, 65; trade, 213, 217; tongs, 242

Town halls, 54, 55; English, 53, 56. *See also town halls listed by location*

Town house, 71, 218. *See also town houses listed by location*

Towns, 18, 58, 136, 147, 148, 157; county, 59; planning, 17, 144–164; small, 295. *See also* Praying Indians; Urban

Trade bodies, 7

Trail blaze, 303. *See also* Pioneers

Transatlantic: approaches, 8; city, 20; culture, 9; emulation, 94

Transatlanticism, concept of, 3, 272. *See also* Exchange

Transnational, 12

Travel, 83

Williamsburg, Va., 63, 71, 293

Window, 300, 301; frames, 260, 297, 299; dormer, 53, 128, 299; shutters, 200, 201

Windsor, Conn., long house, 125

Wither, George, 37

Woburn Abbey (Bedfordshire, England), 78. *See also* Country house

Women, 4, 5, 120, 198, 205

Wood, John the Elder, 219. *See also* Architectural books

Wood, John the Younger, 222. *See also* Architectural books

Woolwich, London, 16, 107

Worcester Guildhall (Worcestershire, England), 58

Wotton House (Surrey, England), 78, 84

Wren, Sir Christopher, 109, 110–11, 120

Yamyamacunda, 18, 169, 175. *See also* Gambia River

Yards, 193, 261

Yarmouth, Nova Scotia, Canada, 295

York River, Va., 37

Yorktown, Va., 61

Zuccarelli, Francesco, 87